# *The Year-Round* FLOWER GARDENER

## *Anne Moyer Halpin*

SUMMIT BOOKS

NEW YORK • LONDON • TORONTO • SYDNEY • TOKYO

SUMMIT BOOKS
Simon & Schuster Building
Rockefeller Center
1230 Avenue of the Americas
New York, NY 10020

10   9   8   7   6   5   4   3   2   1
10   9   8   7   6   5   4   3   2   1 (pbk.)

Library of Congress Cataloging in Publication Data

Halpin, Anne Moyer.
   The year-round flower gardener / Anne Moyer
Halpin; [illustrations by Fran Gallagher].
        p.   cm.
   Includes index
   ISBN 0-671-64950-7
           0-671-67711-X (pbk.)
      1. Flower gardening.  2. Flower gardening—
United States.  3. Flowers.  4. Flowers—United
States. I. Title.
SB405.H35 1989
635.9—dc19                              88-38139
                                              CIP

Photography by Elvin McDonald.
Additional photographs by
Derek Fell (pp. 14, 15, 60, 61, 126, 168, 169, 220,
221, 232, and 233), Peter Loewer (p. 146),
and courtesy of All-America Rose Selections (pp. 78
bottom, 79 top, 94, and 115),
and W. Atlee Burpee Company (pp. 44, 47, 104,
113, 118, and 177 top and bottom left).
Illustrations by Fran Gallagher.

*For Bruce*

# CONTENTS

# ACKNOWLEDGMENTS

This book would not have been possible without the help and support of a number of people to whom I will always be grateful. Special thanks to Elvin McDonald for so generously sharing his extensive photo collection.

Thanks also to the following:

Marie Giasi of the Brooklyn Botanic Garden library for her help when I was researching the book.

Fran Gallagher, for translating my verbal ideas into visual form so gracefully, creatively, and quickly.

All-America Rose Selections and the W. Atlee Burpee Company, for allowing me to reproduce some of their photographs to illustrate the text.

To my editor at Summit, Dominick Anfuso, for his invaluable guidance.

I also want to thank my parents and my brother, Tom, for their constant encouragement and support.

Finally, thanks to my friends Reid Trevaskis and Chris Goger, for their forbearance and good humor during all the months that I worked on the manuscript.

# INTRODUCTION

Flowers have always been a source of great joy and inspiration for people, and for the true flower lover the greatest joy is to grow them for yourself. Spring and summer, when the whole world is in bloom, are the gardener's happiest seasons. The rich colors and sweet scents of flowers surround us in our gardens of perennials, bulbs, and annuals as blossoms spill out of pots and windowboxes, dangle from hanging baskets, twine around trellises, clamber over arbors, and festoon trees and shrubs.

But even better than reveling in the flowers that bloom in spring and summer is being able to enjoy them all year. Nothing is so welcome as a sweetly fragrant jasmine or a vivid magenta cyclamen abloom on a windowsill during the bleak and gray days of January.

To have flowers all year long may seem an impossible dream outside of the Sunbelt, especially for those of us without access to a greenhouse or sizable sums of money. But it's not an impossible dream, and in fact, it's not even difficult. With some advance planning and careful choosing of plants, anyone can enjoy homegrown flowers all year. All you need is enough space for a garden, a sunny window or fluorescent light fixture, and a few hours a week.

The aim of this book is to show you how to grow flowers in every season of the year and how to combine their colors in gardens both outdoors and indoors. No matter where you live or how cold your winters are, you can have flowers blooming all year.

I have organized the book by seasons for two reasons: to avoid tying blooming schedules and growing instructions to specific calendar dates, making the information useful to gardeners in all parts of the country, and to make it possible for you to start growing flowers no matter what time of year you want to start. If you begin in spring, you can plant perennials to bloom in late spring, summer, or autumn, and you can start seeds of annuals that will bloom lavishly in summer. In summer you can buy annuals as young plants at your local garden center and have masses of flowers in your garden in a matter of weeks. Summer is also the time to order and plant bulbs that will bloom in autumn. In fall you can plant bulbs to bloom outdoors in late winter and early spring, as well as spring-blooming perennials. You can also plant bulbs in pots to force into bloom indoors in winter. And you can take cuttings from garden annuals to pot up and grow as winter-flowering houseplants. In winter you can have African violets and other houseplants, and bulbs of paperwhite narcissus and amaryllis that will give you flowers in just a few short weeks.

You can use the information in this book to give you a colorful garden in weeks, but you can also use it to plan for seasons to come. A well-planned garden is far more rewarding than a hastily assembled hodgepodge of plants, and if you take the time to think carefully about what you want from your garden, and the colors and kinds of flowers you like best, your gardening efforts will reap their greatest rewards. You will find that in time your garden will become an expression of your creativity and personal tastes and a source of pride, fulfillment, and great pleasure to you.

This book breaks down each season into three periods—early, middle, and late. In each season, you will learn what blooms and the predominant colors and plant types associated with that time of year. There are also suggestions for combining seasonal flowers in indoor and outdoor gardens.

Each of the book's seasonal sections also includes a chapter on growing some of the season's most beautiful, versatile, and classic plants. These mini-encyclopedias are not exhaustive—there are far too many plants to include them all. Instead, I have chosen what I believe to be some of the best plants for each season, focusing on plants and cultivars that are readily available from suppliers in the United States.

Finally, for each season, you will find a basic rundown of things to be done in the garden during this time and tips on planning ahead for flowers in future seasons. The information in these chapters is organized into early, middle, and late season and is given for both temperate and warm climates.

Basically, temperate climates are regions where winters are cold: the Northeast, mid-Atlantic area, North Central states, and Midwest. Warm climates include the South, Southwest, and West Coast. There are also separate sections on what to do in indoor gardens during each season.

Spring is when the outdoor gardening season begins in most parts of the United States, so it is the first season covered in this book. In addition to seasonal plants and gardening activities, the spring section lists information on basic garden design principles and suggestions for working with colors in the garden. Perennial gardens reach their peak bloom in late spring in many places, and this section of the book will give you tips on planning and caring for perennial beds and borders.

In the section on summer, you will find information on annuals—plants like petunias, marigolds, and wax begonias, which bloom in a single season from seed and highlight summer gardens. You will also learn about special kinds of gardens to be enjoyed in summer, including those for shady places, for growing flowers for cutting, for growing fragrant flowers, and for nighttime enjoyment.

In autumn there is still much color to be found outdoors. Since autumn marks the start of the indoor gardening season, especially for gardeners in places where winters are cold, this part of the book contains information on using plants as a decorative element in your home and suggestions for effective ways to group and display your flowering houseplants.

Except in warm climates, most winter color is indoors and comes from seasonal houseplants and forced bulbs and branches. The focus of the winter section of the book is on these seasonal specialties. But warm-climate gardeners will find information on what they can expect to see and do in their gardens in winter. In addition, there are ways for northerners to get a jump on spring, and as winter draws to a close the earliest outdoor bulbs and shrubs start to bloom. I have also included in this section suggestions for using flowers to decorate your home for the holidays.

The seasons around which this book is organized are not based on the solstices and equinoxes that govern when our calendar seasons begin and end. Instead, they correlate more closely to months and to how the weather typically feels to us. According to the calendar, spring begins around the twenty-first of March. But many spring bulbs are in bloom early in the month, and in warm climates even sooner, so it makes sense to place the start of spring in the garden closer to the beginning of March. I have loosely divided the year so that spring includes the months of March, April, and May; summer takes in June, July, and August; autumn encompasses September, October, and November; and winter includes December, January, and February.

The blooming schedules in the back of the book list and describe plants in bloom, both indoors and outdoors, in each of these seasons. Use them as a general guide. Plants in southern gardens may bloom earlier, and plants farther north may bloom later. The schedules will vary from year to year as well. In gauging when your plants are likely to bloom, you will need to take into account local weather conditions, which are different each year. A cold winter and a late spring will delay flowering times of plants; mild weather will advance them. The microclimate of your garden will also influence flowering times. Plants in a sheltered location will bloom earlier than normal; plants in an exposed site will bloom later than normal.

I have used both botanical and common names for plants throughout the book. Most of us call plants by their common names, but those differ from place to place, and many plants have several. It can be confusing. Botanical names are less ambiguous for the most part, but there are disagreements about them, too. Botanists have reclassified and changed the names of some plants that are still more often sold in seed and nursery catalogs under their old names. In these cases I have either used the old name, since that is how you will find the plant listed when you buy it, or I have given both the old and the new name. If you are confused about the identity of a plant you want to locate, consult the index of plant names in the back of the book.

In the end, my goal in writing this book has been to give you ideas for flowers to enjoy in every season of the year. I hope it will guide and inspire you in your flower gardening efforts.

# SPRING

## ONE

# *Spring Flowers*

The hearts of all gardeners beat faster in spring. Buds swell on trees and shrubs as the days grow longer. And gardeners everywhere rouse themselves from winter lethargy, eager for the first day the garden soil is dry enough to work.

In the flower garden, spring is the season of bulbs and perennials. Starting with Dutch crocuses, daffodils, and narcissus and finishing with peonies and poppies as spring melts into summer, perennial gardens are washed with color that increases and intensifies as the season advances. The perennial garden reaches its peak in late spring and early summer, and it is the focus of most flower gardeners' attention at this time of year. Much of the infor-

mation in this chapter and the two that follow concerns perennial flowers, though the ornamental shrubs that bloom in spring will also be covered.

Although most spring gardening activity goes on outdoors, the indoor garden also needs some care at this time of year. Houseplants that have been dormant over the winter begin to grow actively again and need more water, light, and fertilizer than they did in winter. Some houseplants bloom in spring. There is plenty for flower gardeners to do, both indoors and out, as spring gets under way.

In this chapter we will first look at the colors that predominate in spring flower gardens before turning to some basic parameters for designing your

outdoor flower garden, particularly perennial beds and borders. Then you will find suggestions for some appealing plant combinations you might like to try in your own garden and, finally, some basic guidelines for creating bouquets and arrangements to enjoy indoors.

## SPRING COLORS

The outdoor gardening season really begins in late winter, when the first species crocuses and snowdrops poke their heads above the snow. Those late winter bulbs flower mostly in white, yellow, or purple. Yellow and white are much in evidence in spring, too, and as the season progresses an assortment of soft lavenders, blues, pinks, and roses are added to nature's palette. Spring colors are, for the most part, light and soft, with pastels in abundance. There are some strong reds (tulips, for example) and violets, but on the whole, spring is a time of gentle colors—entirely fitting for a world newly reborn.

The bulbs and shrubs of late winter are joined in the garden by early spring hybrid crocuses, daffodils, and narcissus, then succeeded by tulips. After the glowing rivers of color of the bulbs are gone, herbaceous perennials come into their own. Irises, columbines, peonies, poppies, and other perennials supply the color between bulbs and summer annuals in many gardens.

Of course, to show off spring perennials—and all garden flowers—you have to start with a well-designed garden. Before you can begin gardening, you need first to think about where to put your garden and how to lay it out. The first step in any flower garden is the design, so that's where we'll start.

## DESIGNING YOUR OWN FLOWER GARDEN

It is important to design your flower garden a season or two before you begin planting, as you will need to start preparing the soil ahead of time to allow it the time it needs to mellow and settle before planting. You will also need to know what you will be planting so you can order seeds and plants in advance from mail-order suppliers who offer a much wider selection

*OPPOSITE*
*Hardy bulbs bring the first wave of color to many spring flower gardens. Here early tulips and late crocuses bloom together in contrasting colors of red and purple.*

*The soft pastel shades so abundant in spring are seen in this garden of tulips and primroses.*

than most local garden centers. If you are a new gardener, don't let the lack of a garden plan keep you from planting at least a few flowers this season—you can always grow them in containers and transplant them to the garden later on. But start working out your design for next season or next year and allow yourself time to play with the design and adjust it until it truly satisfies you. If in a fit of spring fever you rush out to the garden center, buy a bunch of plants, and stick them hastily into the ground, you will probably not be happy with the results. So take the time to work out a good plan.

Garden design is a complex process. In addition to knowing which plants bloom in which colors, you have to be aware of when plants bloom, how tall they grow, what kind of soil, moisture, light, and nutrients they need in order to grow well, and other qualities they possess. You will also have to make decisions about which colors and shades of colors you want to see together. Professional garden designers and landscape architects receive extensive training and develop their skills over a lifetime of experience. But there are several basic principles that every flower gardener—beginner to expert—can learn and use in creating a garden that is aesthetically pleasing. There are many good books on garden design that you can study to learn more about the art. But here I'd like to discuss the basic considerations for choosing the best garden site, deciding the garden's size and shape, and planning color schemes.

If you will be starting a new garden, the first decision you face is where to put the new bed or border. The best location for a flower garden is not necessarily the most obvious one. Consider first the property itself. Does your yard have a low, wet area where water tends to stand in puddles after it rains? The poor drainage in such a location would be deadly to most flowering plants—unless, of course, you grow bog plants. Is your property on the side of a hill, where strong winds

*The first step toward a successful garden is understanding the environmental conditions on your property. The second step is choosing flowers that grow well in those conditions. Irises, for example, like plenty of moisture and some kinds, like the Siberian irises in this garden, flourish in wet, even boggy, conditions.*

*In this woodland garden, narcissus have been allowed to naturalize and tulips have been scattered throughout the garden in natural-looking clumps.*

will be a problem, especially in winter? In such a location you will probably need a windbreak. You have to think about your property in terms of the environmental conditions it offers for plants. Here are the major factors for you to consider:

- *Light.* A location that receives full sun—unobstructed sunlight for at least five or six hours a day—will afford you the broadest choice of plants because many flower garden favorites grow and bloom best in full sun. However, there are quite a few flowers that prefer, or at least tolerate, light, dappled shade throughout most of the day. Other plants, particularly crocuses and other spring bulbs, like plenty of sun when they are in bloom but prefer shade when the sun is hotter.

- *Air.* If your location is subject to frequent strong winds, you will probably need to install a windbreak on the side of the garden from which the prevailing winds blow. The windbreak can take the form of plants—a row of evergreen shrubs is one possibility—or it can be a wall or fence. Walls and fences used as windbreaks are most effective when they are of an open construction (like a picket fence, for example) that allows some air to pass through. A solid wall can create strange air-flow patterns that may be nearly as damaging to your plants as the unobstructed winds. Consult a good book on landscape design for more details on siting and installing windbreaks.

- *Soil.* The ideal soil for most plants is porous and crumbly, contains plenty of organic matter, and drains well but

still retains moisture. Very light, sandy soils drain too quickly and do not hold moisture and nutrients long enough for plant roots to absorb them fully. Heavy clay soils have the opposite problem—they are sticky and dense, difficult for plant roots to penetrate, and they drain so slowly that roots can become waterlogged. Few of us are blessed with ideal soil, but any soil can be improved, and you will find information on correcting different types of soil in chapter 3.

One way to gain clues as to the character of your land is to look at what grows wild there. The weeds that come up in your garden can tell you a great deal about the moisture content, pH, texture, and overall fertility of your soil. If you have never had a soil test done, it's a good idea to have your soil analyzed for nutrient content and pH. A number of home soil test kits are available, and the United States Department of Agriculture extension

offices provide a soil-testing service. Look in your phone book under "U.S. Government" to find the listing for your local U.S.D.A. extension office.

- *Moisture.* This is largely determined by climate, but local factors can also be important. If your soil is generally moist, you will do best with plants that prefer wet conditions, such as irises and astilbe. You won't have to water your garden very often—perhaps only during prolonged dry spells. If your soil is very wet, you can either install drainage tiles or a layer of gravel beneath your garden soil to improve drainage, or you can build raised beds by simply mounding up new soil on top of what's already there. Make sure your raised beds are a foot or so high and that the soil is porous and drains well. A mixture of topsoil, compost, and peat moss or builder's sand should serve the purpose. You can keep the beds in place by sloping the sides or edging them with stone, bricks, or wood treated with a preservative that is nontoxic to plants.

• *Temperature.* Are your summers hot and winters cold? What are the average maximum and minimum temperatures in your area? When do you usually get your last frost in spring and your first frost in fall? Do you notice in winter that snow lingers longer or melts away more quickly in your yard than in your neighbor's? Slow melting usually indicates the presence of a "cold pocket." Cold pockets often form at the bottom of slopes, because cold air tends to collect there. If you are new to gardening, or new to the area, your local U.S.D.A. extension office can give you information on the climate in your area and which hardiness zone you live in. But be aware that conditions vary from year to year and that every garden has its own unique environment. The only way to really understand yours is to observe it over a period of years.

Definitions of plant hardiness (how much cold they can stand) and their degree of heat tolerance are approximate. You may find that conditions in your garden allow you to grow some plants that are generally not considered hardy in your area or, conversely, that some plants that should survive in your area just can't survive in your garden. You will come to know the microclimate in your garden, and will learn which kinds of plants grow best for you.

When you have assessed the environmental conditions in your yard, the best spot for your garden will be wherever the best combination of conditions exists. Choose a place that gets the maximum available sunlight throughout the outdoor growing season, where the soil is in the most reasonable condition, and where moisture is adequate or you will be able to

water easily. But always remember that you can have a successful garden almost anywhere by improving the growing conditions and choosing plants that will grow and bloom in the conditions you have to offer.

Other important factors in determining the best place for a flower bed or border are how it will relate to architectural features on the property (the house, garage, sidewalks, fences, walls), the position from which the flowers will most often be viewed (from inside the house, from the yard, from the street), and whether you want to use the garden as a place to entertain or dine, to read or draw on nice days.

Flower gardens should relate in terms of scale and style to the rest of the landscape; they should fit comfortably into the setting. They should also accommodate your life-style and, of course, please your aesthetic sense.

*Island beds add a touch of color to a large or small lawn. This small round bed puts on a springtime display that is meant to be seen from inside the house as well as outdoors. Island beds are planned to be viewed from all sides. This one has tall tulips in the center, surrounded by perennial candytuft and alpine strawberries around the outer edge.*

## OPTIONS FOR LAYING OUT GARDENS

Outdoor flower gardens come in many shapes and sizes. You can grow flowers in borders (long, narrow plantings that serve as edgings or dividers between different areas of a garden, yard, or larger property), in beds of just about any size and a variety of shapes, or in containers grouped on a patio, deck, or rooftop. Except for the cottage gardens and the flowers are planted in flowing drifts instead of straight lines. Island beds are carved out of lawns and usually take a circular, elliptical, or even irregular shape.

One of the best methods to experiment with the shape of a garden-to-be is to lay out a garden hose in the shape you are considering and in the place where the garden will be. Adjust the hose until you find the shape you like

*To find just the right shape for a bed or border before you start to dig, lay out a garden hose and adjust the shape until you find the outline that works best in the place where the garden will be.*

*Flower borders can be large or small, depending on the size of the lawn they edge. For the most natural look, design the border in flowing curves instead of straight lines, and plant the flowers in drifts instead of rows.*

of the English countryside, flower gardens have traditionally been formally laid out, with straight edges and plants lined up in rows, the walkways and planting beds laid out in regular geometric patterns. The enormous, precisely manicured flower borders of the estate gardens in Europe and Great Britain required armies of gardeners to tend them. The amount of work involved in maintaining such classic flower borders put them out of the reach of most people and gave perennials a bad name for years.

But the old, rigidly formal styles have given way to looser, more free-flowing designs, and the grandiose scale has shrunk to proportions more in keeping with today's smaller properties and manageable by one gardener for whom the growing of flowers is a hobby rather than a full-time occupation. Borders today curve gracefully,

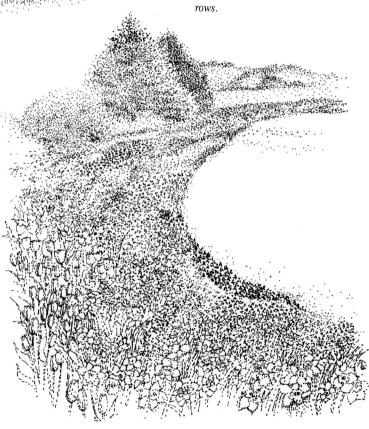

*Deep green hedges and gray stone walls make beautiful backgrounds for flower gardens. Remember to leave enough space between the back of the garden and the hedge or wall so that you can get behind the flowers for regular maintenance chores like weeding and deadheading.*

before you ever touch spade to soil. And take your time—you will be living with your decision for years to come, so don't rush it.

Today's gardens are designed to merge and harmonize with the landscape. Fussy geometric parterres, with their low walls or little hedges of clipped boxwood, are not what most of us want these days. Although informal shapes are the fashion now, don't be a slave to them. Flowing curves are the most natural-looking shape for a garden, but they do not work best in every case. Consider carefully the architectural style of your house and its surroundings. If the other elements of your property are very formal, your garden should echo that feeling.

Size is the next factor to consider in laying out your garden. Gardeners' eyes are usually bigger than our shovels, and we always want to have more flowers than we can realistically take care of. It is only with the severest self-discipline that it is possible to limit the size of the garden so that it can be

reasonably maintained. But nothing is sadder or more frustrating than to find yourself completely overwhelmed sometime in June or July when the garden is overrun with weeds, the spent plants with their dead flowers still clinging to the stems, the plants in bloom all but lost amid the wreckage. So start small. If this is your first garden, pick out just a few different kinds of plants to grow in a modest bed in a simple scheme of one or two colors. It is more effective to have several specimens of a few plants than one or two specimens of a lot of different plants. It is also easier to coordinate colors and blooming schedules when you're working with fewer kinds of plants. Building your garden on an uncomplicated plant grouping that is repeated two or three times will give even a small garden a sense of continuity and a finished, well-planned look. It also makes caring for the garden simpler.

In laying out your garden you also need to take into account such aes-

thetic concerns as viewing angles, as well as the practicalities involved in tending the plants. Remember that you will need easy access to all the plants in the garden in order to weed, fertilize, deadhead, and divide. Unless your garden is very narrow, you will need to be able to reach into it from both front and back in order to get to all the plants. If you are planning on installing your border right next to that charming old stone wall (which *will* set off the flowers handsomely), allow for a little walkway between the back of the garden and the wall so you can reach the tall plants in the rear. The same goes for a garden planted in front of a hedge, although hedges have other drawbacks because the roots of the hedge plants may invade the flower garden and compete with your flowers for water, nutrients, and space.

If the space available for your garden is small, such as a city courtyard or small backyard behind a row home, consider designing the garden in a series of multilevel raised beds. Instead of making one flat garden bed, you can make a raised bed that has two or three different levels and grow flowers on all the levels. This sort of terracing creates an illusion of more space and also allows you to grow more plants than you could in a single flat bed. Terracing is also a good solution to the problems posed by a steep hillside. Even if you have no ground space at all for your garden, and will be growing your flowers in containers on a patio or rooftop, it is still important to plan the layout carefully. Containers can be grouped in various configurations and on different levels to create both height and depth. A well-planned container garden can look every bit as lush and colorful as an in-ground bed or border.

Whether you finally choose a formal or informal design, the garden should have balance and unity. These qualities are obtained primarily by designing the garden around an axis or axes. An axis is an imaginary straight line that passes through the design and around which the different parts of the garden are arranged. The observer's line of vision forms the main axis, and the most important design features of the garden should be positioned along this imaginary line. If the garden is meant to be viewed from the living room, for example, or from right inside the garden gate, the main feature of the garden should be straight ahead when you stand in that spot. If the garden's principal features lie away from the main axis, the garden will appear somehow off balance.

The garden may have a secondary axis perpendicular to the main one.

*A well-planned windowbox contains plants of varying heights, with tall flowers planted in the back, medium-height plants to fill out the middle, and low edging plants to cascade over the front and sides. This summer windowbox is full of colorful annuals— geraniums, petunias, and sweet alyssum.*

The axes in a formal garden are usually paths, and it is important to make them wide enough to serve this visual function. In an informal garden, the axes often cross a lawn and are thus harder to visualize.

A final consideration in designing the layout of your garden is to think about how you will use it, what its purpose is. It can help if you think of your garden as an outdoor room. The borders and beds, pathways, walls or fences, and sculptures and ornaments are the furnishings of this room. The furnishings should match one another in terms of scale and style, just as they do indoors.

## DECIDING WHAT TO GROW

Once you have the site chosen and the shape and dimensions of the garden figured out, it is time to move on to the toughest decision of all—what to grow. There are a number of questions to ask

yourself at that time, and if you want to have a successful garden, by all means take the time to do so. We all have favorites among flowers, but however dearly we love them, they do not work in every location. I learned this lesson the hard way when I started my first garden at my present home in Pennsylvania. My yard is very small and my gardening options limited, particularly so because of a large maple tree that casts shade over much of my yard for part of the day. The first year I planted, among other things, nasturtiums and portulacas because I like them so much. Both of these plants need lots of sun, and they did poorly in my garden. The portulacas hardly bloomed, and the nasturtiums produced little besides leaves, a huge disappointment, to say the least. Over the years I have put in hostas, columbines, and astilbes, and lily-of-the-valley in a particularly troublesome corner. The front of the bed holds impatiens and lobelia during some summers, wax begonias in others, and all are much happier and more productive than the sun lovers I tried first. I've given up nasturtiums and portulacas until I have a sunnier garden somewhere else.

As you can see, there are some important questions to consider when choosing plants for your garden: think about these issues as you start deciding what you will grow. You will find help in answering these questions in the next section and throughout the rest of the book.

When do you want to have flowers in bloom? Do you want some color from spring to fall? Do you have a favorite time of year when a lavish display will be especially gratifying? Do you use the garden during a particular season, such as a summer garden at a weekend home?

Why do you want to have flowers—to beautify the site, to cut, to dry? The greatest variety is possible with a combination of flowering shrubs, bulbs, perennials, and annuals, but such mixed gardens are also the most complicated to plan and to manage. If having cut flowers to bring indoors is most important to you, concentrate on growing the long-stemmed annuals and perennials best suited to the purpose. If you like dried flowers, grow everlastings and other flowers that dry well.

How big is the garden? If your garden is small, rely on just a few different plants with long blooming periods.

How much time will you have to maintain the garden? If your time is limited, concentrate on sturdy, low-maintenance flowers like daylilies, butterfly weed, rudbeckias, impatiens, and salvia.

How definite is your color scheme? If you think you'd like to experiment with different colors for a few seasons, or if you want a lot of color quickly, grow annuals.

## WORKING WITH COLOR

Figuring out your color scheme can be the most challenging and the most fun part of planning a flower garden. Color theory is complex and takes years of study to understand fully. But all of us have our own ideas and feelings about color and about the kinds of colors we like to see together. Although there's no substitute for experience when it comes to combining colors in the garden, your own tastes will always be your best guide. In this section I will give you some basic guidelines for working with color, but don't be afraid to bend the rules. Let yourself play with colors and experiment in your garden.

Here, then, are some issues to consider when you begin to think about color schemes. First of all, do you tend to prefer harmonious, subtle combinations of colors, or do you like contrasting colors? What is the color scheme in your home? You may choose to repeat it in the garden, especially if you will be growing flowers for cutting. Do you want a single color to dominate the garden all season, or would you rather have several colors working together?

One way to achieve a harmonious mix of colors is to grow several varieties of one type of flower—delphiniums, for example, or phlox, or Oriental poppies. The colors among varieties may differ in intensity and in hue, but they will harmonize with one another. Another way to create harmony is to grow different kinds of flowers in the same color. For example, a spring perennial garden might combine the rosy pink of rock cress (*Aubrieta deltoides*) with the brighter, clearer pink of moss pinks (*Phlox subulata*).

There are any number of ways to create contrast in the flower garden as well. Complementary colors, which we will discuss later in this section, create the sharpest contrast. Contrasting color schemes can be unpleasantly jarring. Such schemes are usually most effective when the brightest color is used sparingly as an accent and the less intense color is used over a larger area to balance the brighter color. For example, if you want to plant red tulips with blue forget-me-nots, you will get the best results by planting lots of forget-me-nots among and surrounding the tulips.

Relying on one color to dominate the garden all season is probably the least complicated approach and may be the most successful for beginners. If you choose yellow, for instance, you might have daffodils and basket-of-gold in spring, yellow irises and achillea in late spring and early summer, rudbeckia, gaillardia, or yellow daylilies in summer, and dahlias or chrysanthemums in fall. Against the succession of yellow flowers that form the backbone of the garden, other colors can come and go. The contrasting flowers serve to accentuate—not compete with—the yellow flowers.

Whether you opt for harmonious or contrasting color schemes, remember to consider also the other elements present in the landscape outside the garden. Take into account the colors of trees and shrubs, walls, fences, paving, and outbuildings and the color of your house as well. The colors in the garden should work with these other background colors in order for the garden to look integrated into the site.

Here are some guidelines for working with color:

Use simple colors that relate to the landscape and site.

Plant in generous groups of color for the best effect. Single plants here and there get lost in the design. Even flowers used for accent color should be planted in groups of at least three.

In all but the smallest gardens, col-

Flowers in shades of a single color can produce subtle and quite beautiful harmonies. In this spring garden, pink columbines and hardy geraniums form an exquisitely lovely partnership.

Plants in the same genus usually harmonize well with one another. Here Phlox stolonifera *and* Phlox divaricata *in two shades of blue are tucked into a crack in the stone steps.*

OPPOSITE
*Flowing drifts of yellow daffodils, red tulips, and blue grape hyacinths make a brilliant river of primary colors that might have been taken from a child's box of crayons.*

LEFT
*This spring garden features tulips and grape hyacinths in a bright combination of primary colors.*

BELOW
*Another complementary scheme can be seen in this early spring rock garden. The pastel lavender of the Phlox subulata works beautifully with the clear yellow of basket-of-gold. White perennial candytuft adds sparkle to the scene.*

ors are most effective when the flowers are planted in drifts instead of straight rows like a vegetable garden. Along the edges, drifts should melt into each other, not stop abruptly. Plant a few flowers of each color over the boundary between adjoining drifts.

Avoid bicolors in multicolored gardens, unless you really know what you're doing. Flowers in solid colors will usually produce a more sophisticated look, and they are far easier to work with.

Dark colors are best seen close up. From a distance, or in the shade, they tend to disappear.

Pastels and white flowers can light up shady areas, where they gleam against the dark background. Pastels are also effective in front of stone walls, gray rocks, and hedges. They are especially wonderful in gardens used at night or viewed as the sun goes down. At dusk, light-colored flowers take on a special glow.

Strong, bright colors are especially effective in very sunny gardens. Hot colors are subdued in strong sunlight, but they are not overpowered the way pastels and dark colors are. Brilliantly colored flowers can also be quite striking against dark foliage, a point to keep in mind if you have foundation plantings of evergreens.

Generally speaking, warm colors tend to come forward visually while cool colors recede. I will discuss this in more detail later on.

Contrasting colors modify one another when they are planted together. Blue flowers tend to cast a yellowish shadow on neighboring blossoms; red flowers look orangy when they're next to white. Using white as a contrast color deepens and strengthens the colors next to it.

It is best to avoid combining very pure contrasting colors. Pure blue and clear yellow, for example, look harsh next to each other. But when the blue is deepened toward violet, and the yellow is soft and light, the combination is exquisite.

Viewed as a whole, the garden should create an effect that is either stimulating (warm and contrasting colors) or restful and soothing (cool and harmonious colors).

## SOME BASIC COLOR SCHEMES

There are several approaches you can take in devising color schemes for your garden and many possible color

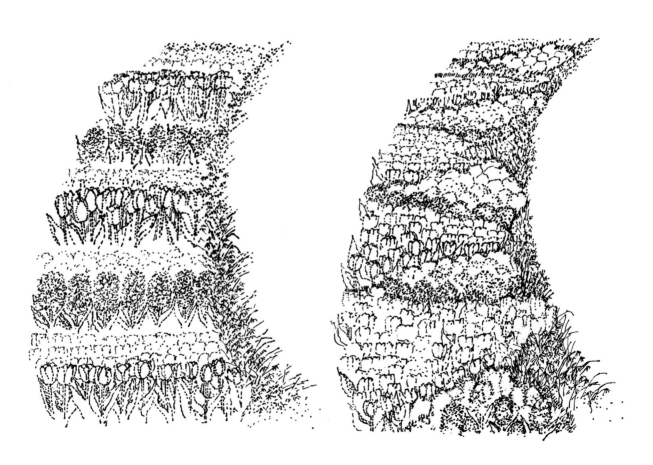

combinations to choose from. In this section we will look at four basic kinds of color schemes—complementary or contrasting, analogous or related, polychromatic or mixed, and monochromatic—and several classic color combinations within those four basic types.

## Monochromatic Color Schemes

The simplest scheme is monochromatic—built around a single color, possibly with a bit of accent color added. Monochromatic schemes generally work best in small gardens and in partial shade where they give a sense of added space, openness, and brightness. Single-color gardens need not be boring, either. You can vary types of flowers, plant heights, shapes, and textures, flower sizes, and tones of color (pale, bright, or dark). Perhaps the best-known single-color garden is the all-white garden designed by Vita Sackville-West at Sissinghurst Castle in England, where she lived with her husband, the publisher Harold Nicolson.

## Analogous Color Schemes

Gardens planted in related, or analogous, colors are quite harmonious, but they can also be surprisingly dramatic. Consider a bed of sunny yellow, yellow-orange, and orange flowers, or an autumn garden of orange, bronze, red, and russet chrysanthemums, perhaps accented with a little purple. A beautifully soft mix of related colors is blue, violet, red, and warm pink. These colors are found in flowers like asters and petunias.

## Contrasting Color Schemes

Complementary colors are opposite one another on a color wheel and contrast more strongly than any other combination of colors. Orange and blue are complementary, as are yellow and violet, red and green. If you want to use one of these intense combinations in your garden, you may need to tone down the contrast by introducing some neutral tones—some white-flowered or silver-leaved plants—into the garden or by planting green foliage plants to absorb some of the color. As a rule, avoid putting very strong colors next to each other if the garden is meant to be viewed at close range rather than from across a lawn. A small garden combining magenta, orange, and purple and located right

*OPPOSITE*

*Lining up flowers like rows of soldiers, as shown with the tulips, hyacinths, and scillas on the left, creates a stiff, awkward-looking garden. Planting the flowers in drifts, as shown on the right, provides a softer, more natural, and more pleasing effect. Although carefully orchestrated, a bed planted in drifts appears closer to the way plants grow in nature.*

*Here's an example of a contrasting color scheme that works. Although orange and blue are complementary colors, the soft shades used in this garden do not fight with each other or with the pink. The neutral brown of the large vase also helps to moderate the colors.*

*Another polychromatic color scheme is evident in this garden of peonies and irises—two classic flowers of late spring and early summer.*

next to a deck or patio would be jarring to the eye.

## Polychromatic Color Schemes

The most common approach taken in flower gardens, it seems, is the polychromatic, or mixed, scheme. English cottage gardens, with their cheerful riot of colors, are a good example of the polychromatic style. In a mixed-color garden the variety of colors included depends entirely on the gardener's taste. Sometimes they work, and sometimes they don't.

## BLENDER COLORS

A useful trick to integrate a garden and harmonize colors that might otherwise be unsettling is to include "blender colors" in the garden. Groups of white or pale yellow flowers are effective

harmonizers for groups of stronger colors. Deep green foliage can be used to harmonize bright colors like red and orange. Gray or silvery white foliage pulls together soft blues, lavenders, and pinks. And distance also blends colors that are quite contrasting when seen close up.

## WARMTH AND COOLNESS OF COLORS

One other aspect of color to consider when designing your garden is the warmth or coolness of the colors. Warm colors (pink, red, orange, yellow) come forward visually—they appear closer. Cool colors (blue, violet, green) recede in space—they look farther away. To create an illusion of depth and space in a small garden, you could plant warm shades in the front and cool shades behind them.

Warm colors are also stimulating and active, even aggressive if they are strong, while cool colors are restful and quiet. For a soothing, peaceful, subtle effect, plant your garden in blues and purples. The cool colors will also create a feeling of distance. For a cheerful but not aggressive feeling, plant warm shades of apricot, salmon, and pink, accented with red and purple. Shades on the borderline between warm and cool, a yellow-green, for instance, or a rosy purple, may have the cheerfulness of the warm colors and the calmness of the cool colors.

Finally, be aware that warm colors harmonize with one another (yellow-orange, orange, red-orange, scarlet), and cool colors harmonize (blue, blue-green, green). This can be important in multicolor gardens because the warmth or coolness of a particular tint can make or break the color scheme. For example, if you are using pink with violet (which can be quite beautiful), make sure you choose a cool shade of pink. On the other hand, a warm shade of pink will be more effective with yellow or red.

It takes time to develop an awareness of the subtleties of flower color and to become familiar with plant varieties that can supply the tints and shades you want. But there's no need to rush. Perennials that don't please you can be moved to a better location next year, and annuals can be chosen afresh. Most good gardens change from year to year—it's part of their charm.

## COMBINING SPRING FLOWERS IN GARDENS AND ARRANGEMENTS

Spring's soft colors can be mixed and matched in many different ways. If you decide on a single-color garden, you might consider a small all-white bed of trilliums and sweet woodruff; if your taste runs more to blues and purples, try deep purple violas with lavender-blue forget-me-nots—a combination that is especially lovely planted beneath the branches of pale purple lilacs or wisterias. Many pink-and-blue partnerships are possible, such as salmon-pink Oriental poppies with purple clustered bellflowers in late spring, or lavender-blue Jacob's ladder with the dainty pink lockets of bleeding heart. You can create a heavenly pink-and-purple garden with Oriental poppies, lupines, and irises. If you like blue-and-yellow schemes, you could plant forget-me-nots, basket-of-gold, and violas, perhaps, or light yellow narcissus behind blue Siberian squills. If red and yellow is your preference, consider mixing the red-and-yellow flowers of American columbines with basket-of-gold or the rich golden yellow of globeflowers.

Looking at other people's gardens is

one of the best ways to get ideas for your own. Visit public gardens, too, and look carefully at the color schemes and plant groupings. Although the plantings in public gardens are usually on a grand scale, you can still find plant pairings to scale down and adapt for your own backyard. Some public gardens have "idea gardens" full of smaller-scale plantings designed specifically to inspire home gardeners to try out the designs and color combinations for themselves.

Spring colors can be combined in innumerable ways in bouquets and arrangements indoors, as well as out in the garden. Classic spring flowers to use in arrangements include daffodils, tulips, irises, Oriental poppies, peonies, and lilacs. Small branches from flowering shrubs and ornamental and fruit trees make nice additions to springtime arrangements. In addition to the popular forsythias and lilacs, try flowering quince, viburnum, apple, cherry, dogwood, apricot, plum, or magnolia blossoms. A beautiful spring bouquet can be as simple as a big bunch of daffodils and narcissus, or violas or sweet peas in assorted colors. Later in the season you can make lavish, sweetly fragrant arrangements with the large flowers of peonies and lilacs. Or try creating charming miniature bouquets of purple and white violets, blue grape hyacinths, sprigs of pink bleeding heart, and creamy white lily-of-the-valley in tiny vases.

The following table, "The Spring Palette," lists spring flowers by color. Use it to get some ideas for plants that bloom in your favorite colors to combine in your spring garden and in bouquets. The table will also show you which kinds of flowers come in more than one color. The seasonal blooming schedules in the appendix will give you more information on when the plants bloom, how tall they grow, and cultivars that are available.

*This beautiful bouquet is made up entirely of flowers from spring bulbs—daffodils, narcissus, and tulips.*

## TIPS FOR GOOD GARDEN DESIGN

- Plant drifts of color, not single plants, and let the colors melt into one another.
- Have a gradation of heights, front to back, but let a few plants drift in and out of their groups for a softer, more integrated look.
- Use a variety of plant forms and flower shapes: round, clustered flowers, flat daisylike flowers, trumpet-shaped flowers, tall spires and spikes, branching flowers.
- Keep the plantings in scale with the site.

- Plan for a succession of bloom.
- Plan the flower garden to have some flowers blooming when trees and shrubs in the surrounding landscape are flowering.
- Start small and simple.
- Don't be afraid to change next year what you don't like this year.
- Follow your instincts.
- Don't forget to include a bench or chairs in your garden so you can sit and enjoy your flowers.

For the most effective display, plant flowers in a gradation of heights. This early summer border has an early-blooming climbing rose trained on the fence. In front of the fence tall Siberian irises blossom amid an underplanting of creeping phlox.

Cut flowers don't have to be large and long-stemmed, but they should be in scale with their container. The violas shown here are just the right size for the tiny vase that holds them.

## RED FLOWERS

Anemone
Azalea
Bougainvillea
Columbine
Coral bells
Crown of thorns
Dianthus
Easter cactus
Epimedium

Episcia
Flowering maple
Fritillaria
Fuchsia
Geranium (regal)
Geum
Hibiscus
Hyacinth
Iceland poppy

Iris
Ixora
Japanese quince
Lychnis
Manettia
Oriental poppy
Pansy
Peony
Primrose

Ranunculus
Rhododendron
Saponaria
Sweet pea
Sweet sultan
Tulip
Turk's cap lily

## PINK FLOWERS

Anemone
Arabis
Armeria
Astrantia
Aubrieta
Azalea
Bachelor's button
Bergenia
Bleeding heart
Bougainvillea
Catharanthus
Clematis

Columbine
Coral bells
Crown of thorns
Dianthus
Easter cactus
Endymion
Epimedium
Erica
Erythronium
Fuchsia
Geranium (cranesbill)
Geranium (pelargonium)

Heucherella
Hibiscus
Honeysuckle
Hyacinth
Incarvillea
Iris
Ixora
Justicia
Peony
Perennial pea
Phlox
Primrose

Ranunculus
Rhododendron
Saponaria
Saxifraga
Sweet pea
Sweet sultan
Thalictrum
Tradescantia
Tulip
Valerian
Veltheimia
Weigela

## ORANGE FLOWERS

Azalea
Chinese lantern
Clivia
Epimedium

Geum
Globeflower
Hibiscus
Iceland poppy

Oriental poppy
Pansy
Ranunculus
Thalictrum

Tulip
Turk's cap lily

## YELLOW FLOWERS

Acacia
Adonis
Arcotheca
Azalea
Basket-of-gold
Buttercup
Coltsfoot
Columbine
Cornelian cherry
Crocus
Crown of thorns
Cytisus

Diosporum
Doronicum
Draba
Epimedium
Erythronium
Euphorbia
Forsythia
Fritillaria
Globeflower
Golden star
Hibiscus
Honeysuckle

Hyacinth
Iceland poppy
Iris
Lachenalia
Lady's mantle
Lemon daylily
Linaria
Lysimachia
Marsh marigold
Meconopsis
Moraea
Narcissus

Nemesia
Pansy
Potentilla
Primrose
Ranunculus
Stylophorum
Sweet pea
Sweet sultan
Thermopsis
Tulip
Uvularia
Winter jasmine

## BLUE FLOWERS

Amsonia
Anemone
Bachelor's button
Baptisia
Bluets
Brunnera
Columbine
Endymion

Forget-me-not
Geranium (cranesbill)
Glory-of-the-snow
Grape hyacinth
Hyacinth
Ipheion
Iris
Jacaranda

Jacob's ladder
Love-in-a-mist
Mountain bluet
Omphalodes
Pansy
Periwinkle
Phlox
Primrose

Pulmonaria
Puschkinia
Rosemary
Scilla
Veronica
Virginia bluebells

## PURPLE FLOWERS

Anemone
Azalea
Campanula
Clematis
Crocus
Daphne
Erica
Erythronium

Fuchsia
Geranium (cranesbill)
Hyacinth
Iris
Lenten rose
Lilac
Nemesia
Pansy

Pasqueflower
Phlox
Primrose
Pulmonaria
Rhododendron
Sweet pea
Sweet sultan
Thalictrum

Tradescantia
Trillium
Tulip
Valerian
Violet
Virginia bluebells
Wisteria

## WHITE FLOWERS

Actaea
Albuca
Allium
Andromeda
Anemone
Arabis
Astrantia
Azalea
Bachelor's button
Baptisia
Bougainvillea
Calla lily
Calochortus
Candytuft
Catharanthus
Cherokee rose
Clematis
Columbine
Crocus
Dianthus
Diosporum

Dodecathon
Dutchman's breeches
Easter cactus
Easter lily
Endymion
Epimedium
Erica
Erythronium
False Solomon's seal
Fothergilla
Fritillaria
Fuchsia
Gardenia
Geranium (pelargonium)
Hepatica
Hesperocallis
Hibiscus
Honeysuckle
Hyacinth
Iceland poppy
Iris

Irish moss
Korean forsythia
Lachenalia
Ledebouria
Lenten rose
Leucojum
Lilac
Lily-of-the-valley
Lloydia
Love-in-a-mist
Mock orange
Narcissus
Nemesia
Oconee bells
Peony
Perennial pea
Phlox
Primrose
Pulmonaria
Pyxidanthera
Rhododendron

Saponaria
Saxifraga
Snow-in-summer
Solomon's seal
Spring beauty
Star magnolia
Star of Bethlehem
Sweet pea
Sweet sultan
Sweet woodruff
Thalictrum
Trillium
Tulip
Valerian
Viburnum
Violet
Weigela
Winter honeysuckle
Wisteria
Zephyranthes

## TWO

# Flowers for Spring Gardens

There are far too many springtime flowers to even attempt to cover all of them in detail in a book of this size. This chapter gives basic cultural directions for some of the stars of the spring garden—and some of my favorites.

### Anemone / Windflower

Anemones belong to the buttercup family, and different species open their bright red, pink, purple, or white flowers in spring or fall. Anemones grow best in partial shade and well-drained soil that contains plenty of organic matter. They do not tolerate drought well, so you must water them during spells of dry weather. You can propa-

gate anemones in spring from seeds or root divisions. In mild parts of the country anemones can be planted in either spring or fall. In temperate zones, you should plant them in spring.

The Greek anemone, *Anemone blanda*, has starlike blue flowers that open in early spring. The tuberous-rooted plants are about 6 to 8 inches high. The Greek anemone is hardy only to − 10° F and will usually not survive winters north of Philadelphia. But lucky gardeners in warmer places can enjoy the abundant flowers in very early spring. Greek anemone can be grown in the front of beds and borders or in rock gardens. Pink- and white-flowered cultivars are available in ad-

dition to the blue-flowered species form.

Poppy or florist's anemone, A. *coronaria*, is often forced indoors for bloom in late winter and early spring. Flowers come in brilliant shades of red, scarlet, rose, pink, blue, purple, and white, with a dark band at the base of the petals. The blossoms are about 2½ inches across, and the plants grow about 18 inches high. Poppy anemones are hardy only in very warm climates, and if grown outdoors in temperate areas, the tubers must be lifted in fall and brought indoors for winter storage like dahlias or gladiolus.

The garden anemone, A. *hortensis*, has flowers similar to those of the poppy anemone, but this plant is hardy in all but the very northernmost parts of the United States. The 10-inch plants bear large flowers in red, purple, or white in late spring.

The Japanese anemone blooms in autumn and is discussed in chapter 8.

## *Aquilegia* / *Columbine*

Columbines are native to the mountainous regions of the world. These gracefully spurred flowers are a highlight of many spring flower gardens. A number of species are native to North America, and a host of hybrid cultivars in a lovely range of colors is available. Columbines will grow all over the United States and bloom for a month to six weeks in late spring and early summer. The flowers are borne atop slender stalks arising from a low mound of distinctively scalloped leaves.

You should grow columbines in either full sun or partial shade in the middle of the perennial bed or border. The smaller species are well suited to rock gardens. Columbines thrive in soil that is moist but well drained. The plants tend to be short-lived and need to be replaced after a few years. If you grow the species forms, you may find that they reseed themselves. A clump of purple columbines in my garden has come back each year for at least five years, with new plants popping up all over, happily colonizing an entire area.

The Colorado columbine, *Aquilegia caerulea*, has blue blossoms with white centers and grows about 2 feet high.

*Daisies and ranunculus fill this charming May basket. The informal arrangement is well-suited to the natural look of the basket.*

The American columbine, A. *canadensis*, is a lovely native wildflower in the eastern part of the country. The dainty flowers have yellow sepals and red spurs and dance on top of 1- to 2-foot stems. The plants self-sow readily and tend to spread.

Hybrids are available in many shades of purple, blue, pink, rose, red, and deep yellow. They include the Biedermeier Strain, Dragonfly Hybrids, Langdon's Rainbow Hybrids, McKana Hybrids, and Spring Song Strain.

## *Arabis*

This genus of low-growing plants includes several species that are standards in spring rock gardens. Their small, dainty flowers brighten up the front of beds and borders, where they make excellent edging plants.

Arabis is easy to grow and hardy all over the United States. Give it full sun and well-drained soil and it will reward you with masses of flowers. The plants get weedy-looking after they finish blooming, so cut them back in early

summer. If you want to start new plants, take cuttings from the old ones instead of simply shearing them back. Overgrown plants can be divided in early autumn.

Double wall rock cress, *Arabis albida*, produces lots of little white double flowers throughout spring. The plants grow about 10 inches high. A single-flowered cultivar, Snow Cap, has sweet-scented blossoms and grows about a foot tall. It can tolerate some shade.

The hybrid Rosabella grows only 5 inches high and bears rosy pink flowers in mid- to late spring. This plant is a charming companion for spring bulbs.

Wall rock cress, *A. caucasica*, grows 6 to 10 inches tall and produces fragrant white flowers in early spring. The soft foliage is also attractive, making the plant doubly valuable. The best cultivar is the double-flowered Flore-Pleno. There is also a pink form and another with variegated leaves.

*A. procurrens* is the other familiar member of this genus. Reaching a height of about a foot, this species thrives in sun or light shade, in practically any kind of soil. It has a mat-forming habit and spreads rapidly, filling empty spaces with its shiny green leaves. The racemes of white flowers appear in mid- to late spring.

## Aubrieta / Rock Cress

Another classic plant for the spring rock garden or front of the border is purple rock cress, *Aubrieta deltoides*. A perennial member of the mustard family, this low-growing, mat-forming plant resembles arabis but is not as easy to grow. It is, however, pretty and floriferous, producing small blossoms of pinkish violet to light purple from mid-spring to early summer.

Purple rock cress grows to 6 inches in height and is hardy everywhere in the United States. It needs well-drained soil and lots of sun. If you shear back the plants when they finish blooming, they may reward you with a second flush of flowers in fall. Propagate new plants by layering in summer.

Another rock cress is A. *hybrida*, 'Cascade Strain', which cascades its softly shaded pink, lavender, to deep purple flowers gently over rocks or walls or sends them tumbling down slopes.

## Aurinia / Basket-of-Gold

*Aurinia saxatilis*, basket-of-gold, is better known to most gardeners by the botanic name of *Alyssum saxatile*. Although botanists have reclassified the plant into the genus *Aurinia*, many plantsmen still sell it as *Alyssum*. Whatever you call it, it remains a delightful and widely grown perennial, a standard of the spring rock garden and a lovely edging plant for beds and borders. Basket-of-gold is also handsome when grown in containers.

Basket-of-gold is a low, creeping plant about 6 to 12 inches high, with gray-green foliage and bright yellow flowers in early spring. It is hardy throughout the United States and grows best in full sun, in well-drained soil of average fertility with a slightly acid pH.

Several cultivars are available, including Citrinum, which has pale lemon yellow flowers, and Compactum, a smaller plant that has bright yellow flowers.

## Brunnera / Siberian Bugloss

Siberian bugloss (*Brunnera macrophylla*) is a tough, undemanding perennial that produces sprays of heavenly little sky-blue flowers that resemble forget-me-nots. The flowers bloom in mid- to late spring but leave behind them the plant's interesting mounds of large, deep green, heart-shaped leaves. The stems are covered with bristly hairs (not surprising, since the plant belongs to the borage family), so you might want to wear gloves when working around these plants.

Siberian bugloss reaches about 1 to 1½ feet in height, and the plants spread rapidly. In fact, the plant can be invasive. I pull up lots of unwelcome volunteers in my garden in summer and fall. The plants are quite hardy.

Plant brunnera 1 to 1½ feet apart in full or partial shade or in full sun, in deep, moist, well-drained soil containing lots of organic matter. Propagate new plants in spring or fall by division, root cuttings, or from seed.

Siberian bugloss is also sold under the name of *Anchusa*, and you will find it listed different ways in different nursery catalogs. But *Brunnera* is the name most widely accepted by botanists and gardeners.

## Convallaria
## Lily-of-the-Valley

Lily-of-the-valley, *Convallaria majalis*, is a carefree perennial with sweet-scented white flowers. The waxy bell-shaped flowers dance along slender little stems in late spring, perfuming the air with an unmistakable, and equally indescribable, fruity-sweet fragrance.

Lily-of-the-valley is hardy and quite easy to grow, spreading rapidly once established. Some gardeners find it invasive, but I can never have too much of it in my garden. The best way to grow lily-of-the-valley is as a ground cover, especially in shady areas. The large, elliptical leaves, about 8 inches tall, remain after the flowers are gone and hold up until late in summer, when they begin to turn brown and die back.

Lily-of-the-valley thrives in woodsy conditions—moist (but well-drained) humusy soil in partial shade or filtered sunlight. Plant the pips (they are not true bulbs) horizontally, 2 inches deep and about 4 inches apart. Unlike most spring-blooming bulbs, these are best planted in spring, when nurseries ship them.

Several cultivars are on the market. Giant Bells is larger than the species, growing to 10 inches tall, with larger flowers. Rosea has pink flowers.

## Crocus

Dutch hybrid crocuses bloom in early spring, a bit later than the earliest spring-blooming species crocuses. Their chalice-shaped flowers are larger than those of the species, but the color range is typical of all crocuses: deep purple, lavender, lilac, golden yellow, yellow-orange, white, and white striped with purple. The plants grow 4 to 6 inches tall.

Crocuses should be planted at the front of beds or borders, beneath the branches of spring-flowering trees and shrubs, indoors for winter flowers. The corms spread quickly if the grassy leaves are left in place until they die back naturally.

Crocuses need lots of sun, and if you place them in a spot that is sunny and protected, they will bloom a couple of weeks earlier than normal.

Plant crocuses in early fall in any average garden soil. Set the corms 4 inches deep, in groups of six or more. When the plants become crowded after several years and produce fewer flowers, lift and divide the corms in early fall or late spring when the foliage has died back.

## Dianthus / Garden Pinks

The clove-scented flowers of the genus *Dianthus* are versatile and delightful in the garden. Various species are annual, biennial, or perennial. Collectively they are known as garden pinks, and most of them bloom in late spring or early summer. American gardeners can't grow as many different kinds as can gardeners in the British Isles—our climate is too severe. But there are a number of species that thrive under American conditions, several of which are discussed below.

Allwood pinks, *Dianthus ×allwoodii*, are hybrids between one of the grass pinks (low-growing types), *D. plumarius*, and the carnation. The easy-to-grow plant is perennial, between 4 and 20 inches high, with a tufted growth habit. Allwood pinks propagate readily by layering. They are hardy throughout the United States.

Maiden pinks, *D. deltoides*, are also perennials and tolerate some shade. The maiden pinks grow in mats close to the ground, seldom growing a foot

A *cultivar of grass pinks*, Dianthus plumarius.

high, and work well in rock gardens or on slopes. They are easy to grow as long as the soil is well drained, and they often self-sow.

A third perennial species is the cheddar pink, *D. gratianopolitanus*. These small, vigorous plants produce a thick carpet of blue-green foliage and send out their fragrant pink flowers in late spring and early summer. Cheddar pinks make good ground covers, filling empty spaces quickly and staying just 4 to 6 inches high.

An enchanting old-fashioned member of the tribe is sweet william, *D. barbatus*. The plant is grown as a biennial but can be brought into bloom from seed the first year if seeds are started indoors in early spring and moved outdoors after frost danger is past. The plants grow about 2 feet high and bear clusters of flowers, many of them with rings of a color lighter or darker than the main petal color. The range includes shades of pink, rose, red-violet, purple, and white.

All the garden pinks make fine cut flowers with their spicy-sweet scents and cheerful combinations of colors. Generally speaking, the plants need well-drained soil with a slightly alkaline pH and full sun. If you live where winters are severe, protect your pinks with a covering of evergreen boughs or other loose mulch. The perennials are relatively short-lived and should be propagated every few years by dividing the clumps in spring, by layering, or from cuttings taken in mid-summer. Shearing or cutting off dead flowers sometimes coaxes the plants into blooming a second time.

## *Dicentra* / *Bleeding Heart*

This genus contains both the lovely bleeding heart and the wildflower known as Dutchman's breeches. Bleeding heart produces distinctive heart-shaped flowers that dangle from their slender stems like a string of lockets. If you turn the locket upside down, the flower resembles a lady in full skirts or pantaloons. Dutchman's breeches is a smaller plant with white flowers that resemble pairs of little white pantaloons hung out on the line to dry.

Grow bleeding heart or Dutchman's breeches in partial shade, in rich, moist, humusy soil. The plants appreciate a topdressing of compost or manure in fall. They sometimes self-sow but are better propagated by division in early spring or from root cuttings taken in early summer.

A couple of different species of bleeding heart are worthy of a place in the garden. The familiar, old-fashioned species that our grandmothers grew is *D. spectabilis*. It needs well-drained soil and blooms from late spring into early summer. Plants grow 2 to 2½ feet tall and should be planted 2 feet apart. A white-flowered cultivar, Alba, is also available.

Fringed bleeding heart, *D. eximia*, is favored by many gardeners because the lacy foliage grows in a neat clump. The plants bloom in summer, and the flowers are a deeper shade of pink than those of *D. spectabilis*. Fringed bleeding heart grows to about 1½ feet high and does best in moist, partially shaded places.

Dutchman's breeches, *D. cucullaria*, puts out its white flowers in early spring. The plant grows only a foot high, and its leaves die back after flowering is over.

## *Episcia* / *Flame Violet*

Like its better-known relative, the African violet, the flame violet is a member of the Gesneriad family. Gesneriads are arguably the most popular family of flowering houseplants among gardeners in the United States. In addition to African violets and episcias, the group includes gloxinias, cape primroses, and numerous other flowering species. With their decorative foliage episcias are handsome houseplants all year, but in spring they burst into bloom, producing lots of tube-shaped flowers with five flared petals on the end. The flower form is common to gesneriads, and the long tubular necks hold the petals above the foliage where they can be seen. The plants have a semitrailing habit and look nice in either hanging baskets or standard flowerpots.

Flame violets thrive under the same conditions as most other gesneriads— bright light but not direct sun, plenty of humidity, and warm temperatures. During the day, episcias like temperatures around 70° to 75° F; at night they appreciate a five-degree drop. The growing medium for episcias needs to contain plenty of humus, must hold moisture and still drain well, but it does not necessarily have to contain any soil. A classic potting mixture for gesneriads is one developed years ago at Cornell University; it consists of equal parts of vermiculite, perlite, and milled sphagnum peat moss. Keep the soil mix evenly moist but not soggy, and mist flame violets lightly every day to help keep the humidity level high around the plants. When the plants are growing actively in spring and summer, feed them every two weeks with a dilute all-purpose houseplant fertilizer.

There are a number of *Episcia* species and cultivars available. The best known is *E. cupreata*. This plant has large, rough-textured deep bronzy green leaves with contrasting light green veins. The leaves sometimes have a slightly metallic sheen. The brilliant scarlet-red flowers appear in mid- to late spring and may continue into summer. Sometimes the plant blooms again, though not as heavily, in fall.

Another species, *E. dianthiflora*, has small green leaves and frilly-edged white flowers.

*E. punctata* has velvety green leaves and white flowers with purple spots.

## Gardenia / Cape Jasmine

A classic florist flower that is a popular gift plant on Mother's Day, the gardenia (*Gardenia jasminoides*) is grown outdoors in the South and indoors in cooler climates. The plant is a woody shrub growing 2 to 5 feet high. Its glossy dark green leaves beautifully set off the large, creamy white, intensely fragrant flowers. Outdoors, gardenias bloom all spring and summer; indoors they may bloom in either season, but most often in spring.

Outdoors, plant gardenias 4 to 5 feet apart in rich, moist soil with an acid pH. Feed the plants every other month during the growing season with the same kind of fertilizer used for azaleas and camellias. They are good foundation plants in warm climates.

Growing gardenias indoors can be tricky, but it is richly rewarding when the flowers waft their sweet perfume all through the house. Indoor gardenias like cool temperatures (60° to 65° F), bright light without direct sun, even moisture, and ample humidity when the plants are setting buds. They cannot tolerate drafts or sudden sharp changes in temperature, both of which cause the buds to drop before they open. The plants tend to bloom better when they are potbound.

A good potting mix for gardenias is one part potting soil, two parts compost or peat moss, and one part perlite. Add about a teaspoon of bonemeal to the soil in each pot and feed with an all-purpose fertilizer every two weeks during spring and summer when they are in active growth.

After the plant finishes blooming, you should prune it back and allow it to rest over winter. Stop fertilizing, and gradually cut back on watering to let the soil become dry to the touch between waterings.

## Geranium / Cranesbill

Hardy geraniums, also called cranesbills, are perennial flowers not to be confused with the tender geranium so popular in the summer garden and as a houseplant, which actually belongs to the genus *Pelargonium*. If you want to read about that kind of geranium, look in chapter 5. Here we are considering the hardy outdoor inhabitants of the perennial garden.

Cranesbills are hardy, adaptable plants, most of them relatively low-growing. Many of them make good ground covers or additions to the rock garden. They are also attractive in the front of beds and borders. Hardy geraniums are widely grown in Europe and are starting to become better known in North America. Their durability and ease of culture make them worthy of consideration for a place in your flower garden.

Geranium species are hardy throughout the United States and are tolerant of hot weather as well as cold. They are not fussy about soil—they thrive in any well-drained soil of average fertility. Most will bloom in either full sun or partial shade. Cranesbills can generally withstand dry spells, so long as the drought is not too prolonged or severe. Most of them start blooming in early to mid-spring and continue through most of the summer. A range of pretty colors is available, and they harmonize beautifully with many other spring and summer flowers. You can propagate them by division in early spring or in autumn. Plant them 8 to 12 inches apart.

There are over two hundred geranium species. Several of the best ones for home gardeners are described here.

*Geranium cinereum* is a low, almost prostrate plant that grows just 6 to 8 inches high. The pink, 1-inch-wide flowers bloom among bluish green leaves.

*G. endressii* grows taller than the other cranesbills, reaching a height of 1 to 1½ feet. The best-known cultivar, Wargrave Pink, has rosy pink flowers that keep blooming until fall. The leaves are bright green. The plants grow vigorously, smothering any weeds in the vicinity. Wargrave Pink harmonizes beautifully with purple flowers like irises.

*G.* 'Johnson's Blue' produces striking bright blue flowers from late spring into fall. The 1½-foot plants have a compact growth habit and handsome, finely divided foliage. Johnson's Blue is among the most heat-tolerant, easiest to grow of all hardy geraniums.

*G. sanguineum* is called the bloody or blood-red cranesbill, but its flowers are actually a rich magenta color. They bloom from late spring into fall. They form neat mounds and grow 10 to 12 inches tall. This species does best in full sun and is a good one for southern gardens. The plants will self-sow and spread if you let them go to seed. The cultivar Lancastriense has pink flowers.

## Heuchera / Coral Bells

The airy, graceful plants in this genus are most often called coral bells or alum root. They come into bloom in very late spring, and most of them keep flowering until midsummer or even later. The species are American natives, many of them from the Rocky Mountains, but some of the nicest cultivars were bred in Europe and introduced here by seed and nursery companies. The plants are characterized by the tall, slender stems of tiny bell-shaped flowers, usually red, arising from low mounds of rounded, ivy-shaped leaves. Plant them in beds and borders, rock gardens, or massed as a ground cover. The red-flowered varieties are attractive to butterflies.

Coral bells grow in either full sun or partial shade, but most of them prefer a bit of shade. They make themselves at home in a variety of soils, though they prefer a slightly acid pH and good drainage. Propagate them by division every four years or so, in autumn or early spring. Plant coral bells a foot apart, and be sure to cover the whole rootstock, leaving only the crown exposed. The plants appreciate a top-dressing of compost once a year and a mulch in winter to prevent heaving.

The Bressingham Hybrids is a strain developed in England, blooming in assorted shades of pink, red, and deep crimson. The plants grow a foot high and bloom in late spring and early summer.

*H. micrantha* is a white-flowered species native to the western part of the country. It reaches a height of about 2 feet. It is not reliably hardy in the East. A cultivar, Palace Purple, has bronzy purple leaves and flowers that carry a faint blush of pink. The plant blooms in midsummer to late summer and is hardier than the species form. Palace Purple grows about 15 inches tall.

*H. sanguinea* is the classic garden species and the easiest one to grow. The red blossoms appear from late spring all through summer and make lovely cut flowers. The plants reach a height of 1 to 2 feet.

## Hyacinthus / Hyacinth

Most of the hyacinths found in American gardens are hybrid bulbs grown in Holland and bred from the common garden species, *Hyacinthus orientalis*. The color range for hyacinths has expanded beyond the traditional pink, white, and blue to include red, yellow, deep purple, and even apricot. The intense, sweet fragrance of the flowers provokes decided reactions—you either love the scent or detest it, but it's hard to ignore.

Hyacinths are easy to force indoors, and they can be grown for mid-spring flowers in the outdoor garden in most

areas except northern New England. In northern regions the bulbs should be lifted and stored indoors during the winter, then replanted in early spring. Gardeners elsewhere can plant the bulbs in mid-autumn, about 9 inches apart and 4 to 6 inches deep. They will grow in any well-drained soil of average fertility. Dutch hyacinths reach slightly less than a foot in height. Plant them in beds and borders, or naturalize them in the lawn.

## Iberis / Candytuft

The charming candytuft comes in both annual and perennial forms, both of which are versatile, easy-to-grow plants with a variety of uses in the garden. The low-growing candytufts bear flat-topped or rounded clusters of dainty flowers in white or shades of pink and lavender. Use them in the front of a bed or border, in the rock garden, to edge sidewalks and paths, or next to driveways. They bloom lustily from spring right through summer.

The generic name, *Iberis*, is derived from Iberia, which was the name once given to Spain, the homeland of some of them. As their Mediterranean origin would suggest, candytufts prosper in full sun and rich, well-drained soil. Although they can tolerate some dryness, they bloom better with plenty of moisture. Water them during dry spells to maintain the best display. Shearing back the plants after the first flush of flowers fades (there are too many to pick off individually) will prompt them to bloom again.

The perennial species, *Iberis sempervirens*, is evergreen in moderate to warm climates. Farther north, you can trim off dead leaf tips at the end of winter to encourage new green growth. Propagate new plants by division or from cuttings taken in late summer.

*I. umbellatus*, the annual species of candytuft, is sometimes called globe

candytuft. The plants grow 8 to 15 inches high, and the flower clusters are held well above the foliage. The color range includes red, pink, lavender, and purple. The plants self-sow readily in my Pennsylvania garden when I don't pick off the spent blossoms. A cultivar, Dwarf Fairy, offers flowers in shades of pink, rose, carmine, crimson, lavender, purple, and white on 8-inch-high plants.

## Iris

The stately, elegant iris has been a favorite among both gardeners and artists for centuries, having played important roles in both worlds. Most of them grow from rhizomes, some from bulbs, but all are distinguished by their straight, tall, swordlike or grassy leaves. Most irises bloom in spring and early summer, and they are a feature of many late spring gardens. Irises have varying degrees of hardiness. Many of them grow best in the North, some only in the South, and a few others, such as the flamboyant Pacific Coast iris, are generally grown only along the West Coast where they are native.

The parts of the iris flower are called by special names, which are helpful to know when you read catalog descriptions. The innermost petallike structures, which are very narrow, are called "style branches." The upright petals are called "standards." The three outer parts of the flower, the sepals, are called "falls," which usually droop or curve downward.

Irises are divided into a number of classes. For gardeners the easiest way to categorize them is as bearded, beardless, intermediate, Dutch, dwarf, Spuria, Siberian, or Japanese types. The tall bearded irises are the best known and most widely grown kinds; Spuria and Siberian irises are the hardiest.

Individual varieties have a short blooming period—one to three weeks—so you should plant several types to extend the season. With careful planning (and enough different species) you can have irises in your garden from early spring until high summer. There are irises for the back of the bed or border, for rock gardens, for bog and water gardens, cutting gardens, and naturalized wild gardens. There are even varieties to force indoors for winter flowers. Plant irises in their own beds, along walks or driveways, in front of a hedge or wall, or in clumps in mixed flower gardens. The shapes of the flowers are bold, so use them carefully. Many gardeners like to grow irises with other perennials like blue flax, columbines, painted daisies, meadow rue, and gas plant.

The earliest irises to bloom outdoors are the bulbous types: *I. histrioides*, *I. danfordiae*, and *I. reticulata*. Next come the small dwarf bearded species, *I. pumila* and its hybrids. Larger dwarf types bloom next, just as the daffodils are finishing up. The intermediate irises follow, blooming along with tulips, and are succeeded by the tall bearded varieties. Next come the Spurias, then Siberians, and finally the Japanese types. Japanese irises are lovely next to a pool or pond and in warm climates can be grown with the Louisiana iris. Irises to grow in pools or water gardens include blue-and-white *I. laevigata*, yellow *I. pseudacorus*, and rose or red-violet *I. versicolor*.

All irises are heavy feeders and like well-drained soil that is rich in organic matter. They need full sun for at least six hours a day. Bearded irises are the most widely grown types and have been extensively bred. The bearded hybrids we know today are genetically quite complex and vary in their cultural needs. They are easy to grow in zones 5 and 6, where the coldest winter temperatures are −20° F or above. Farther north, the bearded varieties may not be entirely hardy; far-

ther south, they may not get enough of a dormant period in winter and may suffer stress from the intense summer heat.

Most bearded irises are not particular about the soil in which they grow, although they do need good drainage. Some will bloom in spring and again in summer if conditions are to their liking. In the open garden, shorter bearded types are easiest to work with. The tall bearded varieties, which may grow 4 feet or taller, need to be grown next to a wall or other windbreak or their stems may snap in high wind. Border and intermediate types are perfect for small gardens.

The American Iris Society classifies bearded irises as follows: miniature bearded are 4 to 8 inches high or less; standard dwarf bearded are 8 to 15 inches; intermediate bearded grow 16 to 27 inches high; miniature tall bearded (border and table irises) are the same size as intermediate but bloom slightly later; and tall bearded irises are 28 inches tall or more. Most tall bearded irises are about 3 feet tall, but some grow as high as 4 or 5 feet.

The newer bearded irises are striking presences in the garden, though they are not as durable as older forms. Bearded irises come in a stunning range of colors, including white, pale ivory to deep yellow and gold, apricot, orange, pink, magenta, maroon, brownish red, lavender, orchid, blue, blue-violet, purple, and deep purple-black.

Plant bearded irises when the blooming season is over in midsummer in the North; in the South, wait until the hottest part of the summer has passed. This is also the time to divide and replant crowded clumps. To plant, dig a deep hole and make a mound of soil in the center. The top of the mound should be level with the surrounding soil. Set the rhizome horizontally on top of the mound and

spread the roots down over the mound. Fill the hole with soil, firm it around the roots, and water thoroughly. After planting, the only time you will have to water is during prolonged dry spells. Plant tall bearded irises 2 to 2½ feet apart, standard dwarfs 1 foot apart, and miniature dwarfs 8 inches apart.

Tall bearded irises need to be moved after three or four years. To divide old clumps, discard the old central parts of the rhizomes and replant the younger outer parts.

Border and table irises are grown in the same way as the tall bearded types. and harmonize nicely with tulips. They come in the same range of colors as the tall bearded types. Dwarfs, which bloom earlier still, are vigorous, reliable flowers that are handsome additions to mixed flower gardens. The dwarfs are very hardy, but their root systems are shallow and may be damaged by soil heaving in winter. If you grow them, mulch the plantings in winter to prevent heaving.

Siberians are late-blooming beardless irises in shades of blue, violet, purple, rose, and white. They are hardy and easy to grow and don't need to be divided very often. Siberian irises thrive in soil enriched with plenty of organic matter and some low-nitrogen fertilizer. The plants have vigorous root systems, so plant them in deep holes with some compost and bonemeal in the bottom. Firm the soil well around the rhizomes when planting, and keep the bed watered until the plants establish themselves. Pick off spent flowers to prevent the formation of seed pods, which are a favorite residence of various insect pests. Siberian irises combine beautifully in the garden with peonies, Oriental poppies (especially in shades of pink and salmon), campanulas, foxgloves, and early-blooming daylilies in yellow or apricot shades. The plants grow 2 to 3 feet high.

Japanese irises are also beardless, with large, wide-petaled flowers somewhat resembling orchids or peonies. They bloom in late spring and early summer, and most of them grow 2½ to 3 feet tall. Japanese irises like rich, slightly acid soil that is moist but well drained. Where summers are hot they will need to be watered. Plant them so the crowns are 2 inches below the soil surface. The plants may need winter protection in the North. Japanese irises need to be divided every three or four years. When dividing them, keep three or four fans of leaves in each division.

The color range for Japanese irises is limited to blues, purples, and white, but the flowers are beautifully patterned with contrasting veins, spots, splashes, or flushes of color.

Dutch irises grow from bulbs, and their graceful, narrow-petaled blossoms have become widely popular cut flowers. They are a staple in many florist shops in winter, when they are forced in greenhouses. Dutch irises are not hardy in the far North and are not reliable wherever temperatures routinely drop below zero in winter. In cold climates, mulch the beds well in winter, or lift the bulbs in fall and store them indoors over winter as you do gladiolus and dahlias.

Plant Dutch iris bulbs in spring in the North and autumn in the South. They should be set 5 inches deep.

In the outdoor garden, Dutch irises bloom late in the iris season, usually in early summer. If you want cut flowers, cut the stems when the buds are plump and let them unfurl indoors. Cut flowers last up to two weeks. Dutch irises grow about 1½ feet high.

The other most often grown bulbous irises are the diminutive reticulata types ("reticulata" means netted and refers to the pattern on the bulbs), *I. reticulata*, *I. danfordiae*, and *I. histrioides*. These little irises bloom with the crocuses and are easy to force indoors

for winter flowers. They are discussed in chapter 11.

## *Lupinus* / *Lupine*

Lupines belong to the pea family; if you are a vegetable gardener, the shape of the lupine flower will look familiar to you. Unlike peas, though, lupines gather their flowers into dense upright

*Hybrid lupines.*

spikes and produce them in an assortment of pretty shades of pink and lavender in late spring to early summer.

Lupines are practically synonymous with English cottage gardens, but they grow just fine in North America, too. Hybrid strains offered in nursery catalogs are hardy to −20° or −30° F. Give them full sun, plenty of moisture, and well-drained soil that is reasonably rich in nutrients and organic matter. They tend *not* to like lime or manure. If you live in an area buffeted by hot winds during the summer, shield your lupines from their drying effects with a good windbreak, and stake the tall stems.

There are numerous species of lupines, but the best ones to grow are the hybrids developed by an English gardener, George Russell, for whom the cultivation of lupines was a hobby. Russell Hybrid or Russell Strain lupines produce their gorgeous flower spikes on 2½- to 4-foot stems. Colors include pink, rose, red, lavender, purple, blue, yellow, white, and bicolors. Many plantsmen offer them in various combinations of colors—red shades, for example, or blue shades, or rose and white.

## Myosotis / Forget-Me-Nots

The true forget-me-nots, which belong to the genus *Myosotis*, are the source of one of the most beautiful blues in the plant world. Most of the flowers classified as blue are actually closer to violet, deep blues with a hint of red in their color. But forget-me-nots are true blue, and all the more welcome because their dainty spring flowers combine handsomely with daffodils, tulips, azaleas, and other favorites of the season. There are both annual and perennial species of forget-me-nots and several cultivars in different colors.

Forget-me-nots like lots of moisture, and in some parts of the eastern United States and Canada, escapees from flower gardens have colonized along streams and in wet meadows and bottomlands. In the garden you can grow them in full sun or in partial shade, wherever the soil is damp. Forget-me-nots start blooming in mid- to late spring and continue into summer; in fact, some of them bloom all summer long.

The best-known species is *Myosotis scorpioides* (sometimes known as *M. palustris*). This perennial has a prostrate growth habit, spreading itself around and among larger companions with which it is planted. The plants grow from 12 to 20 inches high and bloom from late spring until late summer. The plants may self-seed, or you can propagate new ones from cuttings. The variety *semperflorens* grows just 8 inches high and blooms in mid- to late summer. The variety *rosea* bears pink flowers.

The alpine forget-me-not, *M. alpestris*, is a small, tufted plant growing 6 inches high. If you want to grow it, be certain of your sources to be sure you are getting the right plant. Some catalogs incorrectly list as *M. alpestris* seeds or plants that are actually those of the annual forget-me-not, *M. sylvatica*. The cultivar Victoria grows in neat mounds rather than sprawling along the ground.

*M. sylvatica*, sometimes called the woodland forget-me-not, is a popular annual native to Asia and Europe. The plant grows anywhere from 9 to 24 inches tall and prefers some shade. Plant seeds indoors in early spring or, in milder climates, sow directly in the garden in late summer for flowers the following year. When the plants become established they readily self-sow. In addition to the blue-flowered species, cultivars are available with pink or white flowers.

## Narcissus
### Daffodil, Narcissus, Jonquil

There are many kinds of narcissus. For our purposes the plants can be divided into two groups—the small-growing species and their derivatives, which are grown in rock gardens and in the front of the garden, and the vast group of larger cultivars and hybrids.

The species group includes *Narcissus minor*, a small yellow trumpet; a group of small white trumpets derived mainly from N. *moschatus*; N. *cyclamineus*, a trumpet flower with reflexed (backward-curving) petals; the hoop petticoat daffodils, N. *bulbocodium*; N. *triandrus* and its cultivars; and the true jonquils. All these plants are small and their flowers dainty.

The other group of narcissus contains the many hybrids and cultivars grown in flower gardens. They have been bred from the common trumpet narcissus, which most of us call daffodils, and the poet's narcissus, N. *poeticus*, which has a smaller central cup surrounded by six broad, flat petals. In warm climates a tender type of narcissus that bears its flowers in bunches instead of one to a stem, N. *tazetta*, is more often grown.

Narcissus and daffodils are divided into several categories according to their flower type. Trumpet narcissus have flowers in which the central trumpet is as long as, or longer than, the length of the outer petals (called the "perianth"). The flowers may be all yellow, all white, bicolored, or may have a yellow trumpet and a white perianth. Large-cupped narcissus have central cups that are large, but not as long as trumpets. The flowers may have a yellow perianth and a colored (often orange) cup, a white perianth and a colored cup, a white perianth and cup, or a white or yellow perianth with a salmon or pink cup. In small-cupped narcissus flowers the cup is smaller and substantially shorter than the length of the petals. There are also double-flowered narcissus varieties.

Triandrus narcissus have their own category, as do cyclamineus kinds, which are distinguished by their backward-curving petals. Jonquilla narcissus, the jonquils, are also placed in their own category, although some of them resemble the small-cupped types. The Tazetta group includes the paperwhite narcissus that is so popular for indoor forcing, along with its relatives, and a group of hybrids that used to be called "poetaz."

Poeticus narcissus include both species and hybrids, all of them recognizable by their large white petals and contrasting small, flat central cup.

Daffodils and narcissus can be grown in most climates, but different types do better in different places. In the far North, small-cupped, poeticus, and jonquilla types work best. In the South, try small-cupped, jonquilla, triandrus, and tazetta types. Stay away from late-blooming varieties if you live in a warm climate, because the weather will be too hot for them when they bloom.

Plant narcissus one and one-half times as deep as the height of the bulb. When in doubt, plant deeper rather than shallower. If you want the plants to naturalize without dividing the bulbs often, plant them deeper than normal—the plants will not spread as fast and will be maintenance-free for a longer time. Plant narcissus bulbs in fall, at least a month before you expect the first frost, in soil with good drainage. Feed the plants once a year with compost or an all-purpose fertilizer.

In beds and borders, narcissus need to be lifted and divided every four years or so. Dig the bulbs after the foliage dies back in late spring or early summer. Let them dry in the shade and don't divide them until the offsets break off easily. Otherwise you risk damaging the bulb's basal plate. You can replant the divided bulbs right away or store them until autumn in a cool, dry, well-ventilated place.

## Paeonia / Peony

Peonies come in two forms—the familiar herbaceous kind, which dies back to the ground each winter, and the less well known tree peony, which has woody stems. Herbaceous peonies are among the most beloved garden flowers in temperate climates. Their huge single or double blossoms are showy and sweetly fragrant. The plants are easy to grow, dependable bloomers that live long and ask little of the gardener. The flowers come in many shades of red, rose, and pink, as well as cream and white, and they make marvelous cut flowers. Because of their hardiness, peonies are good choices for northern gardeners; because of their tenacity, they're good choices for lazy gardeners.

Peonies grow well in just about any reasonable soil. The one thing they can't tolerate is wet feet; the soil must be well drained. They prefer a pH that is slightly—but not strongly—acid. Enriching the planting bed with compost, manure, and other sorts of organic matter will help to insure good texture, drainage capacity, and nutritional value. Give your peonies full sun if you can, although they will perform reasonably well in partial shade. The flowers can be damaged by high winds, so put the plants in a sheltered spot.

To plant new peony plants, first dig the soil to a depth of 1½ feet and dig in some organic matter. Add two or three handfuls of bonemeal or superphosphate for each plant and position them so that the crown is 1 to 2 inches below the soil surface. It is important not to plant peonies too deep or they will not bloom, regardless of how much you fertilize them. Peonies resent being moved, so plant them where you will want them for the long term. All they will need in terms of care is an annual feeding in early spring with a balanced, all-purpose fertilizer and perhaps staking to keep the heavy blossoms from bending their stems toward the ground. In autumn cut back the stems to ground level.

When you cut peonies for the vase, take the buds that are just beginning to open. If you notice ants crawling on the buds, don't be alarmed. They are there to eat a sweet syrup carried on the buds. Shake them off any flowers you cut to bring indoors.

Propagate new bushes in autumn by digging and dividing established plants. Dig the large, fleshy roots with a garden fork and cut them into pieces with three or more eyes. Then replant the pieces and you can enjoy more peonies next spring.

In northern gardens a loose winter mulch is a good idea, particularly during the plants' first winter in the garden.

Herbaceous peonies come in a number of flower forms. Single-flowered types have five or more petals with colorful stamens in the center. Japanese peonies are similar, being distinguished by their single layer of large petals. Anemone forms are similar to the Japanese but have larger, petallike stamens. Double-flowered peonies are the most familiar, with their big, full, creamy-textured, sweet-scented flowers.

Tree peonies are not nearly so well known as the herbaceous kinds, but their exquisite flowers make devotees of gardeners who grow them. The plants are not trees, but they do have permanent, woody stems of 4 feet or more in height.

The flowers are enormous—as much as 10 inches across—and delicately textured; fluted and ruffled and translucent, they have a soft, diaphanous quality. The color range is heavenly, encompassing yellow, apricot, salmon, peach, pink, rose, red, and white. Both pastels and bright shades are available. The flowers bloom in late spring.

Tree peonies are not difficult to grow, but they grow slowly and like their herbaceous cousins do not like to be moved. Keep this in mind when selecting a spot for them. They need several hours of sun a day but appreciate some shade in midafternoon, when the intense late spring sun can bleach their flowers. A spot sheltered from wind is beneficial, too. But the final consideration in choosing a location for tree peonies is to make sure they are in plain view of the house and parts of the yard where you spend time. The flowers are so spectacular that you will want to enjoy them fully and show them off to visitors, too.

Plant tree peonies in early to midautumn, in well-drained, humusy soil with a slightly alkaline pH. Put some bonemeal or superphosphate in the bottom of each planting hole. Position each plant so the graft union (recognizable as a bump on the stem) is 4 inches below the soil surface. Fill in around the roots with soil and firm it down to eliminate air pockets. Leave a depression around the truck to hold water, then water thoroughly. Apply a loose mulch if your weather is very hot.

Next prune away any dead or damaged branches. Be careful not to cut tips that will bloom next spring. Established tree peonies will need a bit of pruning each year to help them maintain an attractive shape.

Tree peony flowers are classified into three groups: Japanese, which have wide, satiny petals; Chinese or European, which have double flowers similar to those of herbaceous peonies; and lutea, which have larger flowers than the others in shades of yellow.

## Papaver / Poppy

There are both annual and perennial kinds of poppies, and all of them are useful in the flower garden. The perennials, Iceland and Oriental poppies, are classic late spring flowers, blooming in a wide range of lovely colors. The annual, the Shirley poppy, blooms a bit later in an assortment of bright colors.

Poppies are generally easy to grow.

*Iceland poppies; the cultivar is Burpee's Champagne Bubbles.*

They need light sandy or loamy soil with plenty of organic matter and a spot in full sun or some light shade. The plants do not like to be crowded. Poppies make lovely, long-stemmed cut flowers, their silky, ruffled petals resembling tissue paper.

The Iceland poppy, *Papaver nudicaule*, is a hardy perennial growing 12 to 15 inches high. Its pleasantly scented flowers are 1 to 2 inches in diameter and bloom in shades of yellow, orange, pink, red, and white. Many pretty pastel pinks and salmons are available. Iceland poppies need light soil with excellent drainage (they are prone to rot in heavy, soggy soil). They may bloom the first year from seed, and they often self-sow. Plant them in early spring in most climates and in autumn in the South and Pacific Southwest. Cultivars include Champagne Bubbles (a mixture of soft colors) and Sparkling Bubbles (mixed colors in brighter shades of yellow, orange, scarlet, rose, and red, along with cream and pastels).

The Oriental poppy, *P. orientale*, is a vigorous perennial 3 to 4 feet high and hardy to −30° F. It blooms in bright colors of scarlet, red, orange, and burgundy, as well as pastel shades of apricot, salmon, and pink. There are also white-flowered forms. The large flowers are distinguished by their contrasting dark centers. Oriental poppies are grown much like Iceland poppies, but they prefer a somewhat richer soil. The tall plants may need staking, too. Don't move or divide the plants for several years after planting to allow them a chance to establish themselves and develop their full beauty. Mulch the plants in fall with compost or well-rotted manure; in spring dig the old mulch into the soil to nourish the plants. To propagate new plants, dig up the large taproot when the plant is dormant in late summer, cut it into pieces, and root the divisions in light,

sandy soil. Plant them 12 to 14 inches apart in the garden.

The Shirley or corn poppy, *P. rhoeas*, is a hardy annual that grows 1½ to 2 feet high. The flowers are about 2 inches across and come in shades of apricot, salmon, red, scarlet, purple, and white. The plants can withstand frost, and seeds need only a good mulch to survive all but the coldest winters.

Sow the seeds shallowly in autumn, except in the far North (sow them there in early spring). Shirley poppies don't take well to transplanting, so plant them directly in the garden where they are to grow. The plants will grow in poor soil, but they do beautifully in good soil.

## Phlox

The tall-growing *Phlox paniculata* is a mainstay of many summer perennial gardens. But there are beautiful spring-blooming phloxes, too, and they should not be overlooked.

Spring phlox is generally fairly easy to grow. Most kinds will grow and bloom in any reasonably fertile garden soil, but for the strongest plants and best flowers, give them rich soil and plenty of water during dry spells. Perennial phlox needs to be lifted and divided every three years or so, after the plants finish blooming. You can propagate new plants from cuttings taken in mid- to late summer.

The best-known spring phlox is *Phlox subulata*, more often called moss pinks. These low-growing ground covers spread their cheerful pink flowers over rock gardens and slopes in gardens all over the United States. In the East they seem to be everywhere in mid- to late spring. The plants are evergreen and creeping in habit, seldom growing more than 6 inches high. The dainty flowers come in shades of pink, red, lavender-blue, and white, but pink is the most popular color.

They are lovely planted along the edge of a wall or on a gently sloping bank, where they form a luxuriant carpet of soft color. Trim back the plants after they finish blooming to maintain a neat shape. Cultivars include Emerald Blue (pale to medium blue), Pink Surprise (soft pink), Red Wings (vivid crimson), and White Delight (white).

Blue phlox or wild sweet william (*P. divaricata*) blooms earlier than moss pinks—in early to mid-spring. It is a wildflower native to the eastern part of the country. Blue phlox grows 15 to 18 inches high and in addition to flowers produces creeping stems that root and cause the plants to spread quickly. This species likes a little shade and needs little or no attention. Cultivars include Laphamii (rich blue), Alba (white), and Fuller's White (white).

Creeping phlox (*P. stolonifera*) is another native of eastern American forests. As its name implies, the plant has a creeping habit and spreads rapidly. The flowering stems are about a foot high, and flowers appear in mid- to late spring. Given a fairly rich, humusy soil that is moist but not soggy, creeping phlox will bloom vigorously. It is a good companion for spring bulbs and a handsome ground cover under trees and shrubs. Cultivars include Blue Ridge (sky blue), Bruce's White (white), Osborne's White (white), Pink Ridge (soft pink), and Sherwood Purple (blue-violet).

A spring-blooming hybrid, *P.* 'Chatahoochee', bears lavender-blue flowers with red eyes in the middle and latter weeks of the season. The plants grow 1 to 1½ feet tall and thrive in partly shaded, well-drained soil. Cut back the plants after they bloom to keep them shapely and vigorous.

## Primula / Primrose

Botanists have given primroses a family all their own, and it is a large one—

there are over three hundred kinds of primroses. Some are difficult to grow, but there are many hardy and delightful perennial cultivars for gardeners to choose among.

The key to growing primroses successfully is to remember that they are native to woodland areas. As such, they like partial shade and rich, moist soil with an acid pH. Give them plenty of humus (peat and leaf mold are good sources). Primroses are lovely planted under trees, alongside a stream or pool, and in the rock garden. In temperate climates they bloom in early to mid-spring; in warm climates they are wonderful in winter gardens.

Lift and divide the plants every few years as soon as they finish blooming. You can also propagate new plants from seeds in early to mid-autumn or in early spring. Sow the seeds indoors or in a cold frame, and move transplants to their permanent garden location when the danger of frost is past in spring. There are numerous beautiful primroses beloved of rock gardeners and collectors, but those described below are among the most useful and adaptable for flower gardens.

*Primula denticulata* grows 10 to 15 inches high and produces clusters of lilac to purple flowers in early spring. This species is the earliest primrose to flower.

*P. japonica* is a vigorous, hardy plant that reaches a height of about 2 feet. Sometimes called the candelabra primrose, its clustered purple, pink, or white flowers are borne atop the tall stems in late spring.

Juliana hybrid primroses have one flower to each stem, but established plants send up lots of them, blooming for several weeks in mid- to late spring.

Polyanthus primroses (*P.* × *polyantha*) are the most widely grown of all. Their distinctive clustered flowers bloom in a spectrum of rich colors—golden yellow, pink, rose,

red, magenta, blue-violet, and white—and most have a bright yellow eye. The broad-leaved plants are small, growing just 6 to 8 inches high, and the flowers are large and held nicely above the foliage. They bloom with the bulbs in early spring. Space the plants 6 to 8 inches apart in the garden. Polyanthus primroses are generally sold in mixtures. You will find catalog listings by color, such as Blue Shades, Gold Shades, and Pink Shades, and also cultivars that bloom in the entire color range. Polyanthus primroses can also be grown indoors in cool, bright rooms for winter flowers.

## *Rhipsalidopsis* / *Easter Cactus*

One houseplant you can always count on to bloom in spring is the Easter cactus, *Rhipsalidopsis gaertneri*. The plant closely resembles the Christmas cactus, *Schlumbergera bridgesii*, and the Thanksgiving cactus, *S. truncata*, and in fact it used to be classified in the same genus. The Easter cactus has jointed stems made up of flat, oval segments joined together. The stems form many branches, growing upright when young and then drooping over as the stems grow longer. The plant as a whole has a gracefully arching form. The species has bright red blossoms, and cultivars are available with flowers in various shades of pink, rose, and red.

Like its fall and winter holiday cousins, Easter cactus is an epiphyte, meaning that in its native habitat the plant grows on other plants (trees, usually) instead of in the ground. Many orchids and bromeliads are also epiphytes. Grow Easter cactus in a potting mix that is one part potting soil, two parts peat moss, and one part perlite or builder's sand. Add a tablespoon of bonemeal to each quart of potting mix. The plant does well in an east or west window, with a tempera-

ture around 70° F. When the plant is growing actively it needs abundant moisture and high humidity. Feed with a balanced all-purpose fertilizer once a month except when the plant is dormant. When flower buds form, fertilize with a high-potassium plant food throughout the blooming period.

After Easter cactus has finished blooming it enters a brief dormant period for about a month. During this time stop fertilizing, and water only enough to keep the plant from shriveling. Repot the plant in fresh potting mix when it begins to grow again.

## *Tulipa* / *Tulip*

There are thousands of tulip cultivars available to gardeners today. Tulips were introduced into Europe centuries ago by the Turks. In more recent times, the Dutch have become the foremost breeders; the bulb fields of the Netherlands are spectacular in bloom. Most of our garden bulbs come from Holland. Gardeners can choose among species tulips, which come true from seed, and hybrid garden tulips, which generally do not and must be propagated from bulbs. There are many lovely species tulips, and some of them are included in the blooming schedules at the back of the book. Here I'll concentrate on the various types of garden tulips, which are more widely grown.

A tremendous selection of heights, colors, and blooming times is available, and there are several different flower forms. Most nursery catalogs divide tulips into groups according to their blooming time and flower form.

Early-flowered tulips, the first group, bloom early (along with hyacinths), are usually short-stemmed, and come in a range of colors.

Kaufmanniana hybrids, sometimes called waterlily tulips, bloom closer to mid-spring.

Fosteriana tulips bloom in mid-spring. The plants grow 12 to 16 inches high, and the flowers are quite large.

Greigii hybrids are low-growing and have foliage that is streaked and mottled with purple. They bloom in mid-spring, after Kaufmanniana hybrids.

Darwin hybrids are large-flowered, tall-growing plants that bloom in mid-spring in a range of bright colors.

Triumph hybrids bloom right in the middle of the tulip season, in mid-spring. The color range is mostly red, white, and shades of pink, and many of the flowers have a second color flamed onto the petals.

Lily-flowered tulips have pointed petals and a gracefully curving shape. They come in colors representing the entire tulip range, except for dark purples and maroons. The plants are tall and bloom late.

Parrot tulips are distinguished by their fringed petals. Many of the flowers are streaked with a contrasting color. The flowers are large and sometimes droop on the stems.

Single late-flowering tulips used to be called cottage tulips. This group also includes what used to be called Darwin tulips, which are not the same as the newer Darwin hybrids. Cottage tulips have pointed petals and long stems.

Other hybrids are also available. There are fringed tulips, and viridiflora types, which have green markings on the petals. There are also double late-flowering hybrids. Check nursery catalogs to learn more about the many kinds of tulips that are available.

Plant tulip bulbs in mid-fall (October in most places) in deep, rich, well-drained soil with a neutral to slightly alkaline pH. Give them lots of sun. Planting depth varies with the type and size of bulb. Follow the directions sent by the nursery.

## Viola / Violet, Pansy

This genus includes annuals, biennials, and perennials and numbers among its members some garden favorites: pansies, johnny jump-ups, sweet violets, violas, and horned violets (also called tufted pansies). Johnny jump-ups and horned violets bloom in summer. Pansies and sweet violets, though, grace the spring garden.

The sweet violet (*Viola odorata*) is a diminutive plant with small, fragrant flowers in various shades of purple or white, carried on slender stems above mounds of heart-shaped leaves. The species form of the plant is an American native and can be found growing in woodlands and meadows. Violets grow about 6 inches tall; they prefer rich, moist soil and some shade. Dig lots of organic matter into the soil where violets will grow. The plants spread rapidly and can become a bit invasive, but they are so charming it's worth it to plant them where they will have room to ramble. Try them as a ground cover, to edge a bed or border,

*Pansies in a host of colors.*

*Violets bloom in a basket.*

or in the rock garden. Violets make wonderful miniature arrangements in mid- to late spring when you put them in a tiny vase along with lilies-of-the-valley and forget-me-nots. Cultivars include Royal Robe (deep violet), Red Charm (rose-red), and White Czar (white).

Pansies (V. × *wittrockiana*) are either annual or biennial. Their distinctive flowers with the clown-face dark markings are available in an extensive range of colors as a result of breeding. Pansies are found in practically every garden center where bedding plants are sold. What you may not know about them is how cold-tolerant they are. Pansies bloom best in cool weather and can be planted in the bulb bed. A combination of bright yellow daffodils and blue and violet pansies is a show-

stopper. Pansies are also fine plants for containers and windowboxes.

Like violets, pansies do best in rich, moist soil. They like full sun but will bloom nicely in partial shade. Keeping faded flowers picked off and pinching back the plants will encourage continued bloom. Most pansies grow 6 to 10 inches high.

Northern gardeners can plant pansy seeds indoors in early winter and set out transplants in early spring, as soon as the threat of heavy frost is gone. Pansies can tolerate light frost. To get flowers even earlier, sow the seed in midsummer and get the plants through winter in a cold frame or under a good layer of mulch. Warm-climate gardeners can plant pansies in fall for late winter flowers.

There are many pansy varieties on

the market. Some have the characteristic facelike markings, and others bloom in solid colors. The color range includes red, rose, maroon, pink, lavender, true blue, deep blue, purple, orange, gold, yellow, and creamy white.

Two particularly good cultivars deserve mention. Super Swiss Giants is quite popular, with good reason. The plants are compact but very vigorous, and the large flowers come in shades of blue, wine red, crimson, red, rose, pink, and yellow, with dark faces. They bloom a little later than some of the other varieties. Universal Hybrid Mixture blooms early and long on compact plants, in a range of shades including purple, red-orange, orange, and two-toned purple and white. This variety tolerates both heat and cold.

## THREE
# *Spring Gardening Activities*

Spring marks the start of the outdoor growing season—the time to work the soil, prepare new planting beds, and rejuvenate old ones. It's a time to plant, setting out transplants of hardy annuals and perennials and sowing seeds of summer annuals, outdoors or indoors. As we have seen, spring is also a time to enjoy outdoor flowers, especially in the perennial garden. Most perennial gardens reach their peak bloom in late spring and early summer. More color is available in May and June than at any other time of the

gardening year, but when that wonderful symphony of bloom has reached its crescendo and the colors start to fade, there is work to be done. Dying flowers need to be deadheaded, early-blooming plants may need to be pruned or trimmed and reshaped. Dried foliage must be removed from spring bulbs. Lilies and tender bulbs like dahlias and cannas need to be planted out for flowers in summer and early fall.

Here is a rundown of basic garden maintenance chores for spring, fol-

lowed by more detailed information on soil preparation and planting techniques.

If you live where winters are cold—the Northeast, mid-Atlantic area, North Central states, or Midwest—use the sections on temperate climates as your basic guide. If you live in the South, Southwest, or a mild region along the West Coast, you will find the information given for warm climates to be the most useful.

## TEMPERATE CLIMATES

For gardeners in temperate and northern climates, one of the first springtime chores is to remove the mulch that covered perennial beds and rose plantings over the winter. Depending on weather conditions in your area, the mulch can start coming off perennial beds around the end of March. You can start pulling mulch away from roses whenever nighttime temperatures routinely stay above 25° F. After you have removed the mulch, cut any blackened, winter-killed canes back to healthy tissue. As the weather grows warmer and the ground thaws, gradually remove the soil mound you built around the crowns last fall. Cut back the healthy canes by about one-third while they are still dormant.

Rake up all the leaves that have blown into your hedges and shrubs over the winter, and use them to start a new compost pile. Shredding the leaves will make them break down faster. If you don't have a shredder, spread the leaves in a layer on the lawn and run over them a few times with a power lawn mower to shred them.

Fertilize established perennials, bulbs, and shrubs with compost, bonemeal, rock powders, and other natural materials if you garden organically, or with 5-10-5 or another balanced type of fertilizer if you use synthetic fertilizers. Powdered and granular fertilizers need to be scratched into the soil around plant crowns. You should be careful not to damage young perennial shoots when you apply fertilizers.

Another early spring task is dividing perennials that bloom later in spring and in summer. Daylilies, lilies, and early chrysanthemums fall into this category. Daylilies don't need dividing often, but if yours didn't bloom very heavily last year, it probably means they are crowded and ready to be divided. Chrysanthemums, on the other hand, need to be divided every couple of years in order to remain vigorous. Dig up the root clumps, throw away the old, woody central part, and replant the healthy younger roots from the outside of the clump. You should plant new divisions from whatever perennials you are propagating in loose, fertile soil that has been enriched with compost or well-rotted manure, along with some bonemeal, rock phosphate, superphosphate, or other high-phosphorus fertilizer.

Prune spring-blooming shrubs early in the season just to remove weak and damaged branches and to shape the bushes. They will get their real pruning after they finish flowering later in spring.

Early spring is also a good time to check arbors, trellises, and other structures to see if they need repairs or repainting. If you did not get your pruning shears and other tools sharpened over the winter, do it now, before you need to use them often for deadheading and other maintenance chores.

You can start to sow seeds of hardy annuals and perennials directly in the garden as soon as the soil can be worked. Good candidates for early planting include calendulas, candytuft, columbines, dianthus, larkspur, lupines, poppies, snapdragons, and sweet peas. An old gardener's rule says that sweet peas should be planted on St. Patrick's Day, along with the garden peas.

Pansies are also cool-weather flowers. If you started seeds indoors in late winter, you can plant out the seedlings when the soil is workable.

Gardeners everywhere should start to order new summer bulbs to plant outdoors after the last frost.

## WARM CLIMATES

In early spring, gardeners in warm climates can begin preparing the soil in beds and borders for summer flowers. Dig in plenty of compost or manure and, if you like, a balanced, slow-release fertilizer. Established plants can be fed, too. Fertilize perennials, shrubs, and vines, such as clematis and jasmine, and begin to feed roses once a month as they move into their blooming season. Spring bulbs should be fertilized when they finish blooming.

Early spring is the time to divide crowded plantings of summer- and fall-blooming perennials, too. Likely candidates include chrysanthemums, shasta daisies, daylilies, hostas, marguerites, and summer phlox. In anticipation of the hot weather ahead, put down fresh mulch around your roses and perennials. Spring is also the time to put in stakes for delphiniums and other long-stemmed late spring and summer bloomers that need them.

If you have started late spring and summer annuals and perennials from seed indoors, you can start moving the seedlings out to the cold frame to harden off before planting them in the outdoor garden.

West Coast gardeners should prune any summer-flowering shrubs that bloom on new growth, such as crape myrtle and hibiscus. You can also clip or pinch back azaleas, camellias, and rhododendrons to shape them after they finish blooming. Feed them afterward with an all-purpose fertilizer for acid-loving plants.

For warm climate gardeners, too, this is the season to check arbors, trellises, and other garden structures to see if they need repairs or repainting. Make sure all your tools are cleaned and sharpened as you head into the busiest season in the garden.

Fast-growing cold-tolerant flowers can be sown directly in the garden. You can also plant out hardened-off seedlings of asters, baby's breath, columbines, dianthus, larkspur, oxalis, and phlox for summer flowers. If you did not plant pansies in the garden last fall, you can set them out in early spring.

Gardeners in very mild areas can set out ageratum, balsam, celosia, geraniums, portulacas, salvia, zinnias, and other bedding plants. All these plants like lots of sun. In shady beds plant coleus, impatiens, and torenia.

## INDOOR GARDENS

Many houseplants resume active growth in spring as the lengthening days bring the end of a winter dormant period. Watch for signs that your indoor plants are breaking dormancy. When they do, you can begin to water them more often and feed them with an all-purpose houseplant fertilizer. If you garden organically, feed houseplants with fish emulsion or seaweed extract. Plants in active growth can be fertilized once a month. As flowering time approaches you can feed plants every two weeks with a diluted liquid fertilizer that is high in phosphorus. If you moved any plants to western or northern windowsills to reduce light levels during the winter, move them back to bright eastern or southern windows when they start to put forth new growth.

If you started annuals or perennials from seed indoors in late winter, fertilize the young plants lightly every two weeks from now until it is time to plant them out in the garden. Use a more dilute fertilizer solution than you are using to feed mature houseplants. Overfeeding seedlings makes them grow too fast, and they may become weak and spindly. Compact, sturdy seedlings survive the stress of transplanting much better; they will make the transition to the outdoors more quickly and will suffer less transplant shock than weak, overstimulated seedlings. If your indoor seedlings start to look straggly, they may be getting too much fertilizer, too high temperatures, not enough light, or all of the above. Most seedlings do best when the temperature is between 50° and 65° F, and they need as much light as you can give them. Keep seedlings in a bright south window, or if you are raising them under fluorescent lights, keep the tops of the plants only a few inches below the lamps.

Early spring is the time to start summer annuals from seed indoors in temperate regions. Sow ageratum, asters, bachelor's buttons, calendulas, celosia, cosmos, dusty miller, gazania, hollyhocks, impatiens, lisianthus, marigolds, nasturtiums, nicotiana, nierembergia, petunias, phlox, portulacas, salvia, snapdragons, strawflowers, and verbena. As soon as the seeds germinate, move the seedlings to a bright, cool windowsill, to a place under fluorescent lights, or outdoors into the cold frame.

Warm-climate gardeners who started sowing annual seeds in late winter should finish the planting early in spring, so plants will be big enough to move outdoors before the weather gets too hot.

Early spring is also the time to propagate some summer bloomers by means other than seed. You can take stem cuttings from begonias, coleus, geraniums, and impatiens you have been growing indoors and root them in pots or flats of vermiculite or a mixture of peat moss and soil. Pot up tubers of caladiums, dahlias, and tuberous begonias so you will have plants ready to set outdoors in late spring when the weather is warm. If the tubers were stored in their pots over winter, remove the top 2 inches of soil from each pot, replace it with fresh potting mix, and water to start the sprouting process.

African violets that have developed long "necks" can be divided now and repotted in fresh soil mix. A good growing medium for African violets is one part each of builder's sand, peat moss, and potting soil with one-half part of perlite or vermiculite. See the section on African violets in chapter 11 for information on how to rejuvenate plants that have developed necks.

## MID-SPRING

### TEMPERATE CLIMATES

Gardeners in the far North should finish removing winter mulches from perennials and roses in mid-spring. You can lightly fertilize perennials as their new shoots appear aboveground. Feed the plants with well-rotted manure and rock powders if you garden organically, or with an all-purpose fertilizer such as 5-10-5. As early spring bulbs finish blooming, feed them with bonemeal or a little bit of superphosphate. And don't forget about spring bulbs that are still in bloom; clip off flowers when they die, but leave the foliage to mature. This is a good time to take note of empty spots in your bulb beds and decide what to order to plant in fall and fill the gaps. Now that spring is well under way, you can begin to fertilize roses once a month as their flowering season approaches.

As spring progresses, you can also continue to dig and divide summer- and fall-blooming perennials that have become crowded or spread beyond their allotted area in the garden.

As the weather grows warmer, it's time to begin moving annual and perennial seedlings you started indoors out to the cold frame to begin hardening off before transplanting. Ventilate the cold frame whenever the outdoor temperature rises above 45° F. On very sunny days you may need to ventilate the cold frame even when outdoor temperatures are below 45° F to avoid cooking your seedlings.

As soon as the soil can be worked, you can sow seeds of hardy annuals and perennials (such as columbines, dianthus, larkspur, lupines, poppies, and sweet peas) directly in the garden. Plant less hardy alyssum, baby's breath, morning glories, nicotiana, salvia, snapdragons, and verbena in the cold frame.

If you purchased bare-root roses and shrubs from the nursery, you should plant them in spring, when the soil can be worked and while the plants are still dormant. Now is also the time to plant out lily-of-the-valley, daylilies, hybrid lilies, hardy waterlilies, and new perennial plants, when the danger of heavy frost is past. You can set out pansy seedlings, too.

As you work on spring maintenance chores, it's a good idea to think ahead to summer and decide what you'd like to grow in containers on the patio or in other places this year. For the best results, plan container groupings just as you plan beds and borders, taking into consideration plant forms and growth habits, heights and textures, flower color and fragrance, and blooming time. To start preparing your container garden, clean out the pots you will use and get them ready for planting. By the middle of spring you can plant container flowers that can tolerate some cold weather.

## WARM CLIMATES

As spring progresses, gardeners in warm climates should continue to fertilize emerging perennials (lightly), bulbs (as they finish blooming), and roses (monthly). If you started summer annuals from seed indoors, you can continue moving the seedlings to the cold frame for hardening off. To ensure vigorous, well-nourished plants, fertilize the seedlings with a diluted, balanced water-soluble fertilizer. Now that the sun is growing stronger, it's important to remember to ventilate the cold frame on sunny days and anytime the outside temperature rises above 45° F.

As spring bulbs finish blooming, you should remove the dead flowers, but leave the foliage to mature. Don't remove the leaves until they have turned brown and dried out.

If you grow asters and chrysanthe-mums for fall bloom, after the plants are 6 inches high you can begin to pinch the tops once a month to promote bushier plants with more flowers.

Outdoor planting is in full swing in the middle of spring in warm climates. This is the time to plant and transplant out annuals, summer-blooming perennials, summer bulbs, tropical waterlilies, and container plants. To get double duty from beds of spring bulbs, you can plant annuals among and around the bulbs and have flowers throughout the summer.

## INDOOR GARDENS

Gardeners in temperate zones should finish sowing indoors any annual seeds still not planted. In warm climates mid-spring is too late to start annuals indoors.

No matter where you live, continue to watch your houseplants for signs that dormancy is over. Repot in fresh potting medium houseplants that have outgrown their pots. Move them to larger pots or prune back the roots and top growth by about one-third to maintain the plant in the same-size pot. To prune roots, remove the plant from its pot, carefully untangle as much of the root ball as you can, and trim off the outer roots along the bottom and sides of the root ball. To remove a plant from its pot, don't just tug on the stem. First, loosen the root ball by sliding a dull knife around the inside of the pot to separate the soil from the sides of the pot. Then, supporting the stem near the soil line with one hand, overturn the pot with your other hand and shake it gently. The plant should slide easily out of the pot.

### TEMPERATE CLIMATES

When early perennials finish blooming in late spring, you can divide and replant those that need it. You should also prune forsythias, lilacs, and other spring shrubs when they finish blooming; if you wait until later in the season to prune these shrubs, you may cut off next year's flower buds. Continue to deadhead tulips and other late spring bulbs, too. Gardeners in temperate climates can now start to pinch back fall-blooming asters and mums once a month after they are 6 inches high. You can pinch back summer phlox, too, to make it bushier.

If your summers are hot, late spring is a good time to give azaleas and rhododendrons a thick mulch of acid plant matter (pine needles or oak leaves, for instance) to conserve moisture. It is also a good idea to fertilize summer-blooming perennials, annuals, and container plants with a fertilizer rich in phosphorus and potassium. If you grow roses, continue to feed them monthly as they enter their blooming season.

New plants need tender loving care as they settle into the garden. It's important to water all new plantings regularly until the plants become established.

Another reminder for late spring is to divide chrysanthemums and other autumn-blooming perennials that need it, if you have not already done so.

Now is the time to put in place stakes for delphiniums, lilies, and other summer bloomers that need the support. And as you go about your garden chores, clip off dead flowers from pansies, violets, and other early plants to prolong blooming.

There's still plenty of planting to do in late spring, too. Northern gardeners can set out perennials newly arrived from the nursery, such as bleeding heart, columbines, delphiniums, irises, lupines, peonies, and primroses. If the plants are very dry when they arrive from the nursery, soak them in water before you plant them. When the danger of frost is past, you can plant tropical waterlilies, outdoor containers, and windowboxes. It is now too late to plant bare-root roses, except in the northernmost gardens.

Tender summer annuals can be seeded directly in the garden if you did not start seeds indoors earlier. Candidates for direct-sowing include African daisies, asters, bachelor's buttons, balsam, clarkias, impatiens, marigolds, mignonette, salpiglossis, stocks, sunflowers, and zinnias. Keep an eye on the weather, though, and cover the plants if frost threatens. To get more flowers from a limited space, you can overplant spring bulbs with annuals and have color all summer.

Temperate-zone gardeners can also plant out seedlings of asters, calendulas, nasturtiums, petunias, snapdragons, and other flowers started indoors a couple of months ago. Harden off the seedlings before you plant them in the garden. Around the middle of May you can start to harden off seedlings of tender annuals that will go into the garden in early summer.

Northern gardeners can plant out tuberous begonias, cannas, dahlias, gladiolus, and other tender bulbs in late spring. Put a little compost in the bottom of each planting hole.

### WARM CLIMATES

It's now time to thin the annuals that you seeded directly in the garden last month. You should also continue to deadhead perennials and annuals as the flowers fade. Deadhead spring shrubs, too, and prune them when the plants have finished blooming. When impatiens and other plants with long blooming seasons start to flower, you can pinch them back to encourage bushier growth and more blossoms.

It is a good idea to fertilize annuals and perennials for continued healthy growth and prolific flowering. Organic gardeners can side-dress with compost or apply a liquid solution of fish emulsion or seaweed extract to the soil above roots or as a foliar spray. Or, if you prefer, you can scratch some all-purpose fertilizer into the soil in a ring around plant stems. Be careful not to let the fertilizer come in contact with plant stems, though, or it could burn them.

It is important to mulch perennials and ornamental shrubs to help them withstand summer's hot, dry weather. If you wait to mulch until the plants show signs of water stress, it may be too late. The best time to mulch is before the summer heat sets in in earnest.

You should continue to dig, divide, and replant early-blooming perennials after they finish flowering. As early annuals finish blooming, pull them up and replace them with summer flowers.

Before the weather gets too hot, finish planting container-grown roses, perennials, annuals, and containers. When you set out annuals, pinch back the main stem by about one-third so the plants produce more flowers over a longer time. It is also time to plant tropical waterlilies and summer bulbs like dahlias, tuberous begonias, gladiolus, and tuberoses. Staggering your bulb plantings ten days to two weeks apart will give you a succession of bloom in summer.

## INDOOR GARDENS

When nighttime temperatures stay above 65° F, you can start moving houseplants to a shady spot outdoors for a summer vacation. Put out cool-loving plants first: azaleas, camellias, Christmas cactus, cyclamen, garde-

nias, and others. Tender tropical plants should stay indoors until summer.

Gardeners in the North can plant trailing plants in hanging baskets indoors in late spring, so the plants can establish themselves and begin to fill the baskets before they are moved outdoors in summer.

## CULTIVATION

Digging new beds and borders is the hardest work involved in gardening. The classic method for preparing a new garden bed is double digging. Double digging involves removing the top layer of soil from the garden about a spade deep, loosening the subsoil below with a garden fork, then replacing the topsoil with new topsoil that has been enriched with compost, manure, or another form of organic matter.

Double digging produces a beautifully porous, fine-textured planting area. But it is an enormous amount of work, and unless your soil is severely compacted it is probably not necessary. When pressed, many of the experts who regularly recommend double digging admit that they've never followed their own advice. I have never double-dug any of my gardens, and the plants have always managed to grow anyway.

That's not to say cultivation is not important; it is. If you want to double-dig your garden, you will get good results. But if your tolerance for back-breaking labor is limited, try the following simpler procedure instead.

If you are making a new garden in an area that is now a lawn, you need to remove the sod first. Push the spade into the ground and slide the blade horizontally under the grass roots, then lift up the sod in chunks. Pile the turves outside the garden. (If you pile

them in an undisturbed place, layering them with like sides together—grass to grass and root to root—they will break down into a nicely textured compost.) After the sod (if you have it) is removed, dig the soil to a depth of 1 to 1½ feet, turning it over and breaking up any clods. Spread a 2-inch layer of compost, well-rotted manure, peat moss, or leaf mold over the entire garden, then dig it in. You can also lighten the soil with perlite or vermiculite, as you do potting soil for houseplants, but these materials are very expensive to use over such a large area, and they supply no organic matter or nutrients to the soil.

I cannot overemphasize the importance of organic matter to a healthy garden soil. Organic matter corrects both sandy and clay soils, improving drainage in clay soils and increasing

the water-holding capacity of sandy soils. If you have never had your soil tested, it is a good idea to have a test done to find out the pH and nutrient content of the garden. Then you will be able to correct any deficiencies with the appropriate fertilizers.

The procedures described above are fine for new gardens or gardens of annuals that come out of the ground every autumn. But cultivation is trickier in beds of established perennials or bulbs. You have to be careful not to disturb plant roots, crowns, or bulbs. Use a hand cultivator to loosen the soil between and around plants. Established gardens benefit from the addition of a 1-inch layer of compost each year. When working compost and fertilizers into these beds, scratch them in lightly around plant roots and crowns. Do not disturb the roots themselves,

## HOW TO TELL WHEN SOIL IS WORKABLE

• All gardeners are anxious to get out into the garden in spring, but digging too early is not good for the soil. In fact, soil structure can break down and compact if you dig while the ground is still half-frozen or wet. There is a simple old trick you can use to tell if your soil is ready to work in spring.

• Scoop up a handful of dirt and squeeze it into a ball inside your fist. Then open your fingers. If the soil ball sticks together, the ground is still too wet to work. But if the ball crumbles when you release your fingers, it's okay to start digging.

and be careful not to get chemical fertilizers on crowns, where the concentrated materials could injure delicate plant tissues.

# STARTING PLANTS FROM SEED

Growing your own seedlings affords you a much greater choice of plants and varieties for your garden than purchasing plants from the local garden center. And seeds are much cheaper than started plants sold by mail-order nurseries. It requires some effort and some patience, but starting plants from seed vastly increases your versatility as a gardener. Seeds for hardy plants can be sown directly out in the garden. But tender plants and slow-growing ones can be started indoors to produce flowers earlier than they would if sown outdoors.

Before you plant any seeds, be sure the containers and tools you plan to use are clean. Seedlings are easy prey for disease-causing organisms. It's best to start seeds in a growing medium that is sterile and less rich in nutrients than regular potting mixes. A number of commercial seed-starting mixes are available, or you can make your own mix from one part peat moss, one part perlite or vermiculite, and one part sterilized or pasteurized soil. Some gardeners prefer to start their seeds in a soilless medium and supply the nutrients in the form of mild liquid fertilizer solutions. A simple soilless mix combines equal parts of peat moss and vermiculite or perlite.

## HOW TO PLANT SEEDS

Most seed packets carry instructions on planting depth and spacing for the seeds. A general rule of thumb is to plant seeds at a depth that is two to three times their diameter. Tiny seeds (like those of begonias or African violets) can be mixed with sand to make them easier to handle, then sprinkled on top of the potting mix. The seeds will become covered when you mist the soil surface to water them. Plant larger seeds in individual holes, or make furrows like you do in the outdoor garden.

Some gardeners cover their seeds with a 1-inch layer of fine sphagnum moss to protect the seedlings from damping-off (a fungus disease). Sphagnum moss has fungicidal properties. If you use it in your seed flats, make sure it stays moist at all times; when the moss dries out it becomes hard and stiff, and tender seedlings have difficulty penetrating it. It is also a good idea to wear gloves when you work with sphagnum moss, because it can cause skin irritations if it gets into cuts or scratches.

## TEMPERATURE, LIGHT, AND WATER

The best temperature for germination varies from plant to plant. Generally speaking, flowering houseplants usually sprout best in warm temperatures of 70° to 75° F. A five- to ten-degree drop at night is very beneficial. Cool-season flowers germinate better in cooler temperatures around 60° to 65° F, also with a drop at night. Shrubs and perennials often need even cooler temperatures—55° or so—to sprout.

Seedlings need plenty of light after they break through the soil surface. The best place to grow them is in a south window that's covered by sheer curtains (to keep the heat from becoming too intense) or a bright, unshaded east or west window. Turn the flats of seedlings every day so the stems grow straight.

Fluorescent fixtures are a better way to supply light for indoor seedlings. The light is very even, and the plants don't need to be turned in order to grow straight. You can use special "grow light" tubes, full-spectrum daylight tubes, or a combination of warm white and cool white lights. The tops of the seedlings should be 6 to 12 inches below the lights. Start out with the seedling flats elevated on some sort of stand that can be gradually lowered as the plants grow taller (a pile of books works nicely). Or you can suspend the light fixture on chains that allow it to be raised as the plants grow.

Seeds and young seedlings need to be watered carefully so seeds are not washed out of the ground and delicate new roots are not disturbed. The best approach is to water from below, setting the flats or pots in lukewarm water in a sink or bathtub. Another technique is to mist the soil surface with a plant mister until the soil is thoroughly moistened. It is important not to allow your seedlings to dry out; water stress can set them back permanently at this stage, when plant tissues are young. But don't overwater, either. Constantly soggy soil encourages root rot, damping-off, and other problems. Water your seedlings when the soil is somewhat dry.

## THINNING AND TRANSPLANTING

When the seedlings develop their first true leaves (the first leaves that have the shape characteristic of that plant, usually the second set of leaves to actually appear on the plant), it is time to thin them. You can thin by pulling up unwanted seedlings individually, snipping off the stems at soil level with a nail scissors, or carefully lifting and transplanting the young plants to other containers.

Spacing for seedlings depends on the size of their leaves. The leaves should not touch, so that air can circulate freely around the plants (good air circulation helps to prevent disease problems). Three inches is considered a good average spacing distance for many seedlings at this stage. Crowding seedlings together increases root competition, encourages the spread of damping-off and other diseases, and causes plants to shade each other, which in turn makes them spindly.

If you are using a soilless planting medium, fertilize the seedlings after transplanting them. When the leaves touch again, the plants are probably big enough to go into individual pots or outdoors into the garden (if weather conditions are right). Using a spoon or a wooden plant label, dig the seedlings gently out of the ground. Be sure to take as much of each plant's root system as you can and lift carefully to leave soil clinging around the roots. Then plant the seedlings at the same depth they were growing before.

If you grew your seedlings in peat pots, tear the sides of the pot when putting the plants out in the garden, so the roots can easily grow through the pot walls as they are supposed to. Sometimes peat pots are too stiff and roots have difficulty breaking through them. This leads to confined roots and slow growth. When planting, make sure the rims of the peat pots are below the soil surface. If the pot rims dry out, they act as wicks, drawing moisture out of the soil and evaporating it into the air. On a sunny, breezy day this wicking action could seriously water-stress young plants.

## HARDENING OFF

Seedlings started indoors need to adjust gradually to the harsher environment outdoors. Before you move your seed-

## ANNUALS TO START IN SPRING

The annuals listed here grow quickly and should bloom outdoors in summer if you start seeds indoors in March.

| | |
|---|---|
| Ageratum | Lobelia |
| Balsam | Marigold |
| Blue lace flower | Moonflower |
| Browallia | Nemesia |
| Candytuft | Nicotiana |
| Celosia | Petunia |
| China aster | Phlox (annual type) |
| Clarkia | Sweet alyssum |
| Forget-me-not (annual) | Thunbergia |
| Ice plant | Tithonia |
| Impatiens | |

lings from indoors out to the garden, it is important, especially in spring, to harden the plants over a two-week period by exposing them to increasingly colder temperatures and by halting fertilization. Plants can be hardened off in a cold frame if you open the lid a bit farther each day, removing it entirely for the last two or three days. Or you can harden plants by moving them outside for a longer time each day, eventually leaving them out overnight. By the end of the second week the plants should be ready to move into the garden.

## PLANTING OUTDOORS

Outdoor planting is largely governed by weather conditions. Still, some advance planning is needed to prepare the seedlings for transplanting. Seedlings in unsegmented flats need to be blocked to separate their roots a few days before transplanting. Use a sharp knife and cut down into the soil, cutting it into blocks in which the plants are centered. The severed roots will heal in a few days, and the plants will not suffer shock at transplanting time.

The best day for transplanting is a cloudy, calm one. Bright sun and wind can dry out transplants and newly arrived nursery plants.

Even on a cloudy, humid day it is important to dig the planting hole *before* you remove a plant from its pot or flat. The hole should be big enough to comfortably accommodate all the roots and deep enough to allow the plant to sit at the same depth as it did growing in its container. If the garden soil is dry, pour some water into the hole before planting. Set the plant in the hole and fill in around its roots with soil. Firm the soil gently; do not pack it down hard. Then water the plant thoroughly to help it settle in.

# SUMMER

## FOUR

# *Summer Flowers*

Summer is the season of annuals, of roses, lilies and daylilies, phlox, clematis, and wisteria. It is the time when annuals combine with perennials to provide a nonstop show of color—instantly, if you buy annuals as plants from the nursery or garden center. In the wild, our fields and meadows are full of Queen Anne's lace and black-eyed Susans.

This is the season of outdoor living—picnicking on the lawn, lounging by the pool, catching the soft summer breeze on the patio. And everywhere we are surrounded by flowers. Pots, planters, and windowboxes spill over with the glorious hues of easy-to-grow geraniums, marigolds, begonias, and other annuals. This is the season when flower gardeners are

most richly rewarded, and the cutting garden is at its height.

In this chapter we will first take a look at summer colors and the palette available to gardeners for outdoor plantings and indoor arrangements. Summer is also the season for special kinds of gardens—gardens in containers, for fragrance, for nighttime enjoyment, for shade. Annuals play a special role in the summer garden, and the many possibilities they offer to gardeners will be described here, too.

## SUMMER COLORS

Summer offers a whole palette of brilliant colors for the garden and for fresh bouquets. In contrast with the softer

colors of spring, summer brings rosy reds and the blazing colors of annuals—yellow and orange marigolds, scarlet salvia, hot magenta, gold celosia, geraniums in a whole range of warm tones, and petunias in just about every shade of pink, red, and purple along with white and pale yellow. Deep blues are also in evidence: purply blue mealycup sage is a wonderful companion for some of the golden, white, and melon-colored flowers. Bachelor's buttons in their classic shade of clear cornflower blue are delightful in bouquets, where they seem to bring a bit of the summer sky indoors.

The bright colors of summer flowers seem to reflect the warmth and intensity of the season. Many gardeners like

*The rich colors so much in evidence in summer are seen in these red geraniums and purple petunias.*

*For many gardeners summer just wouldn't be summer without roses. Climbing roses trained over an arbor create an inviting entrance for this home.*

to tone down the brilliance of summer colors by mixing white flowers and silver-leaved plants into beds and borders, but all in all, the richness and abundance of summer flowers are good for the gardener's soul.

## COMBINING SUMMER FLOWERS

I always find myself wanting to have loads and loads of flowers in summer, but with my small yard I have to limit my choices. A combination of annuals and perennials usually works best for me, along with a few herbs in the flower garden. An accidental partnership was formed in my garden when some Siberian bugloss volunteers came up next to a clump of chives. I've grown to like the purplish pink chive flowers next to the little sky blue blossoms of the bugloss, so I've left the combination in place. This kind of serendipity makes gardening fun, if you let it.

I've always been partial to pink-and-blue or pink-and-purple color combinations in the garden, and many are possible in summertime. If you like pink and blue, you might decide to grow pink perennial phlox (*Phlox paniculata*) with one of the blue salvias, or you could plant tall, steel-blue globe thistles (*Echinops* 'Taplow Blue') behind a rosy beebalm cultivar called Granite Pink or the softer pink cultivar Croftway Pink. If pink and purple is

your fancy, you can mix pink-and-purple petunias with pink phlox, purple salvia, and pink sedums. Early in the season you could pair purple columbines with pink and mauve foxgloves. Another pretty combination is blue delphiniums or violet larkspur with purple loosestrife, perhaps some lavender, and a pink cultivar of coral bells (*Heuchera sanguinea*). You can

brighten the scheme with some golden marguerites or a pale yellow coreopsis cultivar called Moonbeam.

A wide range of blue-and-yellow color schemes is also possible in summer. Consider, for example, blue-violet larkspur or blue delphiniums with pale yellow *Achillea* 'Moonshine' and low-growing golden marguerites. Or try Moonshine with the rich yellow of another achillea, Coronation Gold, and a violet-blue salvia.

A combination that I find especially beautiful is blue mealycup sage with zinnias, early dahlias, or daylilies in soft shades of melon, salmon, and peach. Shasta daisies or other white flowers add sparkle to this color scheme.

If you like warm colors, you might plant yellow marigolds, scarlet salvia, orange dahlias, and golden rudbeckias or yellow-and-red gaillardias. Or you could grow tall annual snapdragons (the Rocket hybrids are especially good) in shades of yellow, apricot, bronze, and pink with early mums or dahlias in gold and bronze tones.

If, on the other hand, you're looking for a cool oasis to beat the heat, the sight of a clean, crisp, all-white garden can be refreshing. As you can see in the table "The Summer Palette," there are lots of white flowers to choose from for summer gardens. Here's just one possibility for an all-white (or silver-and-white) garden: the cotton-ball flowers of *Achillea ptarmica* 'The Pearl' with white valerian and feathery wormwood (*Artemisia absinthium*) or Silver Mound artemisia, backed by tall white delphiniums. A white annual garden might have cleomes, zinnias, sweet alyssum, a white salvia cultivar, and silver-leaved dusty miller. To introduce a little color, you could add some pink or melon-colored zinnias.

If you have always wanted a cottage garden with a riot of richly colored flowers, you could grow a combination of campanulas, columbines, delphiniums, foxgloves, hollyhocks, and garden pinks. A cottage-style garden consisting entirely of annuals might include bachelor's buttons, cosmos, larkspur, nicotiana, scabiosa, and Shirley poppies. For another pleasing mixture of several colors, try red and pink snapdragons with orange and yellow calendulas, yellow irises, and blue marguerites (*Felicia amelloides*).

*Nasturtiums produce masses of flowers in hot summer colors if they get plenty of sun and soil that is not too rich in nitrogen.*

*This lovely pink and blue garden of summer annuals combines pink petunias, lavender-blue alyssum, pale blue tradescantia, and deep blue salvia.*

*Here's a pink and blue combination for a summer container: annual phlox and blue lobelia.*

*Purple salvia and red geraniums make an eye-popping duo.*

*Two popular annuals—tall cleomes, or spider flowers, and bright rose petunias—join in this simple pink and purple bed.*

### RED FLOWERS

| | | | |
|---|---|---|---|
| Astilbe | Clematis | Kniphofia | Rose |
| Beebalm | Crape myrtle | Lily | Salvia |
| Begonia | Dahlia | Lobelia | Scabiosa |
| Bougainvillea | Daylily | Lupine | Snapdragon |
| California fuchsia | Fuchsia | Lychnis | Tritonia |
| Campsis | Geranium (pelargonium) | Marigold | Verbena |
| Carnation | Gladiolus | Nasturtium | Waterlily |
| Celosia | Helenium | Penstemon | Zinnia |
| China aster | Hibiscus | Petunia | |
| Chrysanthemum | Hollyhock | Pyrethrum | |

### PINK FLOWERS

| | | | |
|---|---|---|---|
| Abelia | Chelone | Gladiolus | Pyrethrum |
| Acanthus | China aster | Hibiscus | Rose |
| Achillea | Chrysanthemum | Hollyhock | Sanguisorba |
| Allium | Clematis | Hydrangea | Saponaria |
| Armeria | Cleome | Larkspur | Scabiosa |
| Astilbe | Coreopsis | Lisianthus | Sedum |
| Azalea | Crape myrtle | Lupine | Sidalcea |
| Baby's breath | Dahlia | Lychnis | Snapdragon |
| Beebalm | Delphinium | Lythrum | Statice |
| Begonia | Erigeron | Malva | Stokesia |
| Bougainvillea | Filipendulina | Nasturtium | Tradescantia |
| California rhododendron | Foxglove | Oenothera | Tunica |
| Candytuft | Fuchsia | Petunia | Verbena |
| Carnation | Galega | Phlox | Veronica |
| Celosia | Geranium (cranesbill) | Physostegia | Waterlily |
| Centaurea | Geranium (pelargonium) | Potentilla | Zinnia |

### ORANGE FLOWERS

| | | | |
|---|---|---|---|
| Asclepias | Chrysanthemum | Hollyhock | Petunia |
| Azalea | Dahlia | Kniphofia | Rose |
| Belamcanda | Daylily | Ligularia | Snapdragon |
| Bougainvillea | Erigeron | Lily | Zinnia |
| Calendula | Gladiolus | Marigold | |
| Celosia | Helenium | Nasturtium | |

### YELLOW FLOWERS

| | | | |
|---|---|---|---|
| Achillea | Cassia | Eremurus | Helianthus |
| Anthemis | Celosia | Evening primrose | Heliopsis |
| Artemisia | China aster | Gaillardia | Hypericum |
| Azalea | Chrysanthemum | Gladiolus | Inula |
| Black-eyed Susan | Coreopsis | Globe centaurea | Kniphofia |
| Calendula | Dahlia | Helenium | Lily |

## YELLOW FLOWERS

| | | | |
|---|---|---|---|
| Linum | Opuntia | Rudbeckia | Verbena |
| Lupine | Petunia | Snapdragon | Waterlily |
| Marigold | Potentilla | Statice | Zinnia |
| Nasturtium | Rose | Verbascum | |

## BLUE AND VIOLET FLOWERS

| | | | |
|---|---|---|---|
| Adenophora | Erigeron | Larkspur | Scabiosa |
| Agapanthus | Eryngium | Linum | Stachys |
| Ageratum | Gentian | Lisianthus | Statice |
| Amorpha | Geranium (cranesbill) | Lobelia | Stokesia |
| Baptisia | Globe thistle | Lupine | Tradescantia |
| Campanula | Hollyhock | Monkshood | Veronica |
| China aster | Hydrangea | Mountain bluet | |
| Clematis | Hyssop | Petunia | |
| Delphinium | Iris | Salvia | |

## PURPLE FLOWERS

| | | | |
|---|---|---|---|
| Acanthus | Clematis | Hesperis | Physostegia |
| Allium | Cleome | Honeysuckle | Pyrethrum |
| Armeria | Dahlia | Hosta | Salvia |
| Aster | Delphinium | Iris | Scabiosa |
| Balloon flower | Echinacea | Larkspur | Statice |
| Bougainvillea | Erigeron | Lavender | Thalictrum |
| Buddleia | Foxglove | Liatris | Tunica |
| California rhododendron | Fuchsia | Lupine | Waterlily |
| Candytuft | Galega | Lythrum | Zinnia |
| Centaurea | Geranium (cranesbill) | Petunia | |
| Chrysanthemum | Gladiolus | Phlox | |

## WHITE FLOWERS

| | | | |
|---|---|---|---|
| Abelia | Chelone | Gladiolus | Polygonum |
| Acanthus | China aster | Hibiscus | Pyrethrum |
| Achillea | Chrysanthemum | Hollyhock | Rose |
| Agapanthus | Cimicifuga | Honeysuckle | Sanguisorba |
| Ageratum | Clematis | Hydrangea | Saponaria |
| Anthericum | Cleome | Lamium | Scabiosa |
| Armeria | Clethra | Larkspur | Shasta daisy |
| Artemisia | Crape myrtle | Liatris | Sidalcea |
| Aruncus | Dahlia | Lily | Snapdragon |
| Astilbe | Delphinium | Lisianthus | Statice |
| Azalea | Erodium | Lupine | Stokesia |
| Baby's breath | Euphorbia | Lysimachia | Verbascum |
| Balloon flower | Feverfew | Macleya | Verbena |
| Begonia | Filipendulina | Malva | Veronica |
| Bougainvillea | Foxglove | Marigold | Waterlily |
| Campanula | Fuchsia | Nasturtium | Yucca |
| Candytuft | Galega | Pearly everlasting | Zinnia |
| Carnation | Gas plant | Petunia | |
| Centaurea | Geranium (pelargonium) | Phlox | |

This garden provides a good example of how gray and silver-leaved plants can brighten and soften strong colors. Without the silvery artemisia this red and purple garden would look dark and somber.

In this effective monochromatic summer garden, golden achillea is played against a rich green background of lawn and shrubs.

The pink hibiscus in this garden is lovely in front of the gray stone wall. Note how the pink flowers peeking over the top of the wall pick up the pink of the hibiscus and pull the garden together.

Roses are time-consuming and demanding to grow, but they are spectacular and versatile. A classic red climbing rose covers this white trellis with fragrant blossoms.

*This cottage garden combines flowers in many colors. The faded whitewash on the brick wall softens the colors and keeps them from becoming discordant.*

## GARDENING IN CONTAINERS

Plants in pots are great ways to dress up a window, provide a welcome by the front door, or create the perfect setting for relaxing on a deck or city rooftop. You can place large tubs of bright flowers next to the front door or set smaller pots with just one or two plants on all or some of the steps leading up to your front porch.

Porches are another good place to put containers of flowers, if you place them where they will get some light. Hanging baskets can be suspended from the underside of the porch roof at varying heights to create a pleasant effect. You can also train climbing plants in pots on trellises or let long trailers dangle from hanging baskets to create a living privacy screen or to shade the porch.

Out in the yard or on a patio or rooftop, tubs of trellised climbing plants can be used to screen off unsightly areas, divide space, create privacy, or provide some shade.

Other good places for plants include balconies and fire escapes, on the paving next to a swimming pool, and along a driveway or short path. If you have several plants in small individual pots, group them in a fernery, windowbox, or tub to create a massed effect. Cover the tops of the pots with sphagnum moss to hide them.

Finally, don't overlook windowboxes, which can be colorful and charming, especially if they can be seen from the street.

When you are ready to plan which plants to grow in containers, there are many possibilities to consider.

Good plants for pots, tubs, and windowboxes in sunny places include sweet alyssum, wax begonias, candytuft, cleomes, dianthus, fuchsias, geraniums, lobelia, browallia, nastur-

*Flowers in containers can turn a rooftop, deck, or patio into a garden.*

*Containers of annuals offer a warm and colorful welcome at the front door. This informal grouping has annuals blooming in a windowbox, tall terra-cotta tubs, and a low iron kettle. A climbing rose planted in the ground adds height.*

*Agapanthus, a tender bulb, can be grown in containers in cool climates and taken indoors for the winter.*

*Geraniums make wonderful pot plants for sunny locations. Conventional bedding geraniums have large flower clusters and an upright growth habit, while ivy-leaved geraniums have smaller flowers and a semi-trailing habit that makes them good plants to grow in hanging baskets.*

tiums, marigolds, pansies, portulacas, impatiens, salvia, verbena, and zinnias. Miniature roses and compact varieties of hybrid roses also take well to containers.

If you want to brighten up a shady spot, consider these container candidates: wax begonias, tuberous begonias, browallia, impatiens, lobelia, nicotiana, coleus, and vinca (periwinkle).

Some good plants to grow in hanging baskets are African daisies, annual phlox, cup and saucer vine, cascading varieties of geraniums and petunias, ivy-leaved geraniums, dwarf morning glory, dwarf nasturtiums, Ligurian bellflower, portulacas, black-eyed Susan vine, lantana, and vinca.

Planning a container garden is just like planning a garden bed or border, but on a smaller scale. A well-planned container garden, whether it consists of many different containers of plants or several plants in a large tub or windowbox, still takes into account variation of plant heights and compatibility of forms, textures, and colors. The most successful color schemes for container gardens are generally those built on just a few colors. Polychromatic schemes are usually too chaotic in the confines of a container garden.

A container garden can be as simple as pots of all-red geraniums or petunias in mixed colors fastened to an outdoor balcony or fire escape. Or you could group individual pots of smaller plants like impatiens and browallia in a Victorian fernery (a rectangular plant stand made of wicker). One lovely combination for a large planter is blue-violet salvia and white sweet alyssum surrounded by cascading varieties of petunias in shades of pink, red, and purple. Another handsome grouping is red geraniums, white snapdragons, and white petunias, with red ivy-leaved geraniums cascading over the edge of the tub. An all-white combination for a patio used at night might include

white varieties of zonal geraniums, salvia, and daisies, with ivy-leaved geraniums or sweet alyssum spilling over the edge of the container.

If you live where summers tend to be cool, a blue-and-yellow container garden of yellow snapdragons surrounded by blue and yellow pansies, with blue lobelia spilling over the front of the container, should work beautifully for you. A good container combination for a hot climate is ornamental peppers with portulacas in brilliant rose, orange, and yellow.

Windowboxes require plants with shallow root systems, since space is limited. But because windowboxes are only viewed from one side, they are easier to plan than freestanding container gardens. One pretty grouping for a pink-and-purple windowbox consists

*Containers can be placed to mimic the masses and drifts of flowers found in beds and borders. The formal evergreen topiaries by this front door are softened by pots of white impatiens massed along the sidewalk leading to the door, in front of some low-growing shrubs. The pots are so close together that the containers practically disappear under the clouds of flowers.*

of geraniums in soft pink and deep rose planted in the back of the box, lavender petunias in the middle, and a mixture of purple lobelia and white sweet alyssum planted in the front and cascading over the edge of the box. A successful combination of warm colors might include tall yellow marigolds at the rear, dwarf zinnias in shades of salmon, orange, and gold in the center of the windowbox, and sanvitalia and sweet alyssum spilling over the front. For a charming windowbox in a shady spot, plant begonias, impatiens, and vinca to trail over the front and sides. Above all, don't be afraid to use your imagination when planning container and windowbox gardens.

## PLANTING AND CARING FOR CONTAINER GARDENS

Once you've decided which plants to grow, the first step in creating a container garden, indoors or outdoors, is to select the containers to hold the plants. There are, of course, many kinds of pots, tubs, barrels, and windowboxes available, and your choice will be based on the sizes and kinds of plants you will grow, your climate and growing conditions, and your aesthetic sense.

The most important difference between growing flowers in pots and growing them in the ground is that you have a greater degree of control over the environment in which container plants grow. In fact, plants in pots are lots more dependent on you to supply certain of their needs than plants in the ground. For one thing, the soil in containers dries out more quickly than garden soil because there is less of it and because moisture evaporates through the sides and bottom of the pot, as well as from the soil surface. That means you need to water a container garden more often than a garden in the ground. But it is far easier to achieve an ideal soil for container growing than in garden beds and borders. In fact, you can create your own soil mix for potted plants—you don't have to work with the soil nature has provided on your property. I'll discuss soil mixes for contained plants in more detail a bit later. First let's consider the merits of different kinds of containers.

*Impatiens are ideal for containers in partly shaded locations, although they will bloom nicely in full sun if you give them enough water.*

The traditional type of container, and still the favorite of many gardeners, is an unglazed clay pot that is generally higher than it is wide and wider at the top than the bottom. Standard clay pots have a number of advantages. For one thing, they come in a broad range of sizes, from 2½ to 15 inches in diameter at the top. The drainage hole in the bottom allows excess water to drain off, decreasing

*Well-placed containers of flowers can make sitting on your patio feel like sitting in the middle of the garden. This well-planned patio combines portable pots and tubs of flowers with windowboxes to supply lots of color. The brick wall contains open space in the top to hold more flowers. A raised bed built around a nearby shade tree holds shade-tolerant impatiens.*

This container garden features impatiens, petunias, snapdragons, and small dahlias. The fence in the background is lined with gaillardias and coleus, with more impatiens in half-pots attached to the fence.

Containers stacked vertically create an unusual tower of geraniums.

the chance that plant roots could become waterlogged and develop rot. The rim around the top of a clay pot makes it easy to pick up, and the tapered sides allow you to easily remove a plant from the pot when its growing season ends or when it needs repotting.

Clay pots are porous, allowing air and moisture to pass through their walls. This is in most cases a very valuable characteristic because a well-drained, well-aerated soil promotes healthy roots. The porosity of a clay pot can be a drawback, though, in very hot, dry climates where you need to conserve soil moisture to keep plants from drying out and soil temperatures from rising too high.

There are a couple of drawbacks to consider with clay pots, too. They are heavy, especially when they are full of damp soil, and they are also breakable. They cannot withstand freezing temperatures, and if you leave your clay pots outdoors during a cold winter, you will probably find them cracked by spring.

On the whole, though, clay pots are versatile and dependable. I rely on them both indoors and outdoors. In addition to the familiar tapered shapes, there are wider, shallower clay pots designed for forcing bulbs and growing orchids.

The other most popular material for containers is plastic. Plastic pots are also available in a wide assortment of sizes and are cheaper than clay, lighter in weight, and difficult to break. Unlike clay pots, they come in many different colors. One recent trend is to coordinate the colors of plastic pots with the colors of the flowers planted in them and with the color scheme of the surroundings.

It is important to remember that because plastic is not porous, these

Simple pots of orange marigolds and yellow coreopsis dress up this California terrace with its magnificent view of the sea.

Petunias in window boxes soften the severe facade of a city apartment building.

containers retain water longer than clay pots. A light, well-drained soil mix and multiple drainage holes in the bottom of the pot are essential for healthy plants in plastic containers in most climates.

If you grow your plants in standard clay or plastic pots indoors or in an outdoor area where you need to protect furniture or surroundings from runoff water, you will need to place saucers under the pots. Plastic saucers are waterproof, but those made of unglazed clay are not. If you want to use clay saucers, you can waterproof them by giving the bottoms a coat of shellac.

*Many houseplants enjoy spending summer outdoors. This group includes, clockwise from right, fuchsias, columnea (a relative of the African violet), a bougainvillea with variegated leaves, and an orange-flowered begonia.*

A third material widely used for containers is wood. Windowboxes are often made of wood, and large wooden barrels and tubs are ideal for holding big plants or several smaller ones planted together. Unfortunately, wooden containers are heavy, and moist soil will eventually cause them to rot. Redwood planters are the most durable and also the most expensive. Oak barrels and half barrels also make perfectly serviceable containers for plants. Other kinds of wood can be treated with a wood preservative that is nontoxic to plants.

In addition to standard flowerpots and wooden tubs and boxes, all sorts of fancy containers are available, too, with various patterns and designs painted on them. I prefer plain pots in my garden because they don't detract attention from the plants. But if you like more decorative containers, I'd suggest choosing colors and designs that harmonize with the colors of the flowers growing in them as well as with the surroundings. Indoors especially, it's a good idea to make sure the design on the pot is not too bold or too busy for the room in which you will use it. Also, it's important to make sure the container has adequate drainage holes. If it doesn't, put your plant in a clay pot and set that on a layer of gravel or sphagnum moss inside the fancy cachepot.

Containers do need a certain amount of maintenance. They should be cleaned every couple of years, when fertilizer salts and, in areas with hard water, lime deposits start to build up around the rim of the pot. These deposits can harm plants if you don't remove them periodically. Cleaning containers is not difficult. Just scrub the empty pots in soapy water and rinse them thoroughly. If you want to reuse a pot that has held a diseased plant, soak it for several hours after cleaning in a solution of one part liquid chlorine

bleach to nine parts water, then rinse it thoroughly. Clay pots can also be disinfected by soaking them in boiling water for about twenty minutes.

## SOIL MIXES FOR CONTAINERS

The best growing medium for plants in containers—indoors or outdoors—is one that is loose-textured, well aerated, and well drained. The relationship between plants and soil is complex, but a basic understanding of it will help you to better understand what plants need to grow well. Plant roots don't really grow *in* soil; they grow in the spaces between soil particles. Air and water also travel through these spaces. Water is the medium that carries the nutrients plants need to grow, and air is important to the survival of the soil microorganisms that assist in the transfer of moisture and nutrients from soil to plant roots. When soil is watered from rain or from a gardener's hose, the air between the soil particles is replaced by the water. If excess water cannot drain away, new air cannot enter, and eventually roots will suffocate. Root rot is caused more by the presence of too little air than by too much water. In heavy, dense soil, the particles are so close together that there is little room for air, water, and roots. That is why a light soil mix is so important for plants in pots.

A good potting mix should contain soil (except in certain cases, which I'll discuss in a minute), a lightening agent (usually vermiculite, perlite, or builder's sand), organic matter (peat moss, leaf mold, or compost), and additional nutrients from fertilizers of either natural or man-made origin. You can use a packaged potting soil or garden soil in your potting mixes. If you use commercial potting soil, I recommend that you choose a brand that does not contain any fertilizers. The fertilizers that some manufacturers add to potting soil are sometimes too strong for young seedlings and delicate plants. If you use garden soil in your containers, you should first pasteurize it by baking it in a low (200° F) oven for half an hour to kill disease organisms and other pathogens that may be present.

Soilless potting mixes are useful in certain situations. A soilless mix is generally sterile, and because it contains no nutrients you can rely exclusively on fertilizers to control the amount and kinds of nutrients your plants receive. A sterile growing medium is usually recommended for starting seeds, since young seedlings are easy prey for disease organisms. Soilless mixes are also used for special kinds of plants that respond well to them. African violets and other gesneriads, for example, are often grown in soilless mixes.

Here are a few recipes for making your own potting mixes. One good all-purpose mix consists of one part soil, one part builder's sand, and one part peat moss, with one tablespoon of bonemeal added for each quart of mix. Another all-purpose mix contains two parts soil, one part compost, one part sand, perlite, or vermiculite, and a tablespoon of bonemeal per quart. A richer mix for humus-loving plants combines one part soil, two parts compost, and one part sand, perlite, or vermiculite. Finally, you can concoct a soilless potting mix from three parts peat moss and one part sand, perlite, or vermiculite. Unless you are growing acid-loving plants, add three-fourths cup of horticultural lime to each bushel of the mix to neutralize the acidity of the peat.

When planting in containers, some gardeners like to put a layer of gravel or filter charcoal in the bottom of each pot to promote drainage. Others say it's unnecessary. I've potted plants both

ways and have never really noticed a difference in performance either way. One thing gravel will do is keep soil from leaking out the drainage hole in the bottom of the pot. I've found that a small piece of paper towel placed over the drainage hole serves the same function—it allows runoff water to drain out but keeps the soil from escaping with it.

# SUMMER BEDS AND BORDERS

The perennial garden slows down as summer progresses, but annuals can fill in empty spots in perennial beds and borders. Most gardeners mix annuals and perennials—a tradition that goes back to the English cottage garden style. Some people find the mixture of plant forms, heights, colors, and growing habits that characterizes the cottage garden to be unsettling, busy, and chaotic. Others find the style exuberant and charming. In any case, more American gardeners have been trying their hand at cottage gardens in recent years.

If you decide to combine annuals and perennials, pay attention to plant forms and colors. Look for annuals with growing habits that are hard to find in perennials. For example, summer perennials tend to be round in form—daisylike rayed flowers abound (asters, chrysanthemums, coreopsis, helianthus, and rudbeckia are some good examples). Spiky shapes are harder to find, and some of these, like delphiniums, can be notoriously difficult to grow. You might choose instead spiky annuals such as salvia and gladiolus.

Another way to create a lush flower border in summer is to mass annual flowers in drifts the way you would in a perennial border. You can create a similar effect, even in high summer,

with masses of annuals in harmonious colors. For the most natural look, plant your drifts of colors with soft edges, allowing plants of adjoining drifts to intermingle along their border.

## ANNUAL BORDERS

If you want to create an annual border with the rich look of the spring perennial garden, choose plants according to their height, color, form, and growing conditions.

Tall annuals for the back of the border include tall-growing zinnias, African marigolds, tall snapdragons (especially the Rocket series), nicotiana, dahlias, and cosmos.

Middle-of-the-border plants include petunias, impatiens, salvias, geraniums, anemones, calendulas, daisies, coreopsis, gaillardia, rudbeckia, helianthus, begonias, and coleus.

Low-growing plants for the front of the border include sweet alyssum, lobelia, portulaca, dwarf zinnias, sanvitalia, verbena, and ornamental peppers.

It is important to match plants to growing conditions, too. If your summers are cool, you will have better luck with snapdragons, penstemon, vinca, and lobelia. Where summers are very hot, you can rely on portulacas and ornamental peppers.

Annuals in the border let you change your garden every year. If you don't like aspects of this year's plant combinations, next year you can change them without digging and moving established plants. You can change your color scheme, too, especially if you have an all-annuals garden: you might want a yellow-and-orange garden one year, a pink-and-blue theme next, or a red, green, and white combination.

In addition to choosing plants for their color and shape, you can plan

*This summer dooryard garden of perennials contains pinkish purple echinacea, rosy lavender liatris, tall yellow sunflowers, golden-flowered senna, and to the right, globe thistles.*

*Beds of roses line a suburban driveway.*

In this country rose garden, the weathered barn makes a perfect background against which to view the flowers.

This spectacular rose garden is meant to be enjoyed—the gazebo offers a comfortable place to sit down and take in the colors and scents of the flowers.

*Low-growing plants allowed to sprawl along the top of a stone wall can soften the sharp lines of the wall.*

*Pink and white petunias and fragrant greenish white nicotiana fill a container.*

gardens for special purposes, such as for fragrance or nighttime viewing; to fit particular environmental conditions, such as hot, dry weather or shade; or to produce flowers for cutting or drying.

## FRAGRANT GARDENS

Flowers that are deliciously scented as well as colorful are a special pleasure in the garden. Scents are often strongest in flowers with waxy petals or those with a lot of petals. In many flowers, especially those that bloom at night, the fragrance serves to attract the insects that pollinate them. Many of our showiest, most brilliantly colored flowers have hardly any scent, but they don't need it. Their pollinators are attracted by sight instead of by smell.

There are many different kinds of floral fragrance. Flowers can smell fruity and sweet, like orange blossoms; honey-scented, like wax plant or mignonette; or spicy and clove-scented, like carnations and pinks. Some flowers have an aroma similar to vanilla—sweet peas are a good example. Other flowers smell like violets—some tulips have this kind of scent. There is, of

course, the incredible, unmistakable fragrance of damask roses. And still other flowers, many of them tropical or from warm, temperate climates, possess a heady perfume that is strong, sweet, and almost overpowering. Jasmine and gardenias fit into this category.

Good plants for a fragrance garden include sweet alyssum, balsam, carnations and clove pinks, nasturtiums, nicotiana, petunias, sweet peas, sweet sultan, heliotrope, mignonette, lavender, a species of gladiolus that releases its perfume at night (*G. tristis*), scented geraniums, stocks, verbena, and, of course, roses. All these flowers bloom in summer, when the hot, heavy air intensifies their scents. Vines such as honeysuckle and wisteria can perfume a trellised gazebo or arbor with their heavenly sweet aromas.

Warm-climate gardeners can grow Carolina jessamine (*Gelsemium sempervirens*) and Madagascar jasmine (*Stephanotis floribunda*).

Earlier in the season, you will find fragrance in shrubs like lilac, mock orange, peonies, and Russian olive in the North or frangipani and jasmine in the South. Scented spring-blooming bulbs and corms include hyacinths, irises, and lily-of-the-valley.

If you want fragrance indoors, you could add gardenia, Persian violet (*Exacum affine*), wax plant (*Hoya carnosa*), or various kinds of jasmine to your houseplant collection.

## NIGHT GARDENS

Summer evenings are a beautiful time to enjoy your garden. In fact, for many of us, it's the only time during the week when we *can* get out in the garden. If you will be spending time outdoors at night, why not plan your garden to put on a good show when the sun goes down? Whether you garden in the ground or in containers, there are two ways to approach the night garden.

One is to plant flowers that are visible at night—white and pastel colors. If you sit outdoors in the evening when the sun goes down, you will notice that as the twilight deepens, the vivid reds, blues, oranges, and purples that stand up so well to strong sunlight start to fade and disappear. But flowers of white, pale pink, cream, and pale yellow begin to glow in the fading light.

The other way to choose plants for night gardens is to include flowers that don't open until sunset and those whose fragrance intensifies after dark. Most night-blooming flowers are white, and many are sweetly scented to attract the night-flying moths that pollinate them. Be sure to include some of the night-blooming flowers listed below in your after-dark garden.

You will also want to consider lighting. There are numerous kinds of outdoor lighting fixtures available. The type you choose will depend upon the effect you want to achieve. For example, floodlights mounted in trees cast a soft light on paths or garden beds on the ground and at the same time cast interesting shadow patterns from tree limbs and foliage. This kind of lighting can create a mysterious quality as well as being functional. Lamps can be mounted on posts or poles of various heights to light different areas of the garden from above. These fixtures can illuminate a patio or other area used at night for dining or entertaining or perhaps a part of the yard where you want to sit and enjoy the night air or even play evening games of volleyball or badminton.

*A sweet-scented potpourri can be made from the petals of common garden flowers. This one contains roses, lilacs, and violets.*

Along pathways you might consider downlights in short, fat posts known as bollards, which have the lamps built into them. There are also low-voltage lighting systems available for this purpose.

To highlight night-blooming gardens or particular plants, you can install swivel-mounted fixtures at ground level to cast light upward or lamps recessed into the ground, which also provide uplighting. Spotlights trained on plants create very dramatic effects, and you can also light plants from behind to silhouette them. For a soft light on a patio or deck, you might try bouncing light off the back wall of the house for an indirect, gentle effect.

## SOME NIGHT-BLOOMING FLOWERS

Here are some night-blooming flowers you might want to consider growing in your garden to enjoy when the sun goes down.

DATURA (*Datura meteloides* or *D. fastuosa*). A vining plant that produces huge, white, trumpet-shaped flowers with an intense, sweet scent. This plant is not recommended for households with children and pets because it is extremely poisonous.

NICOTIANA (*Nicotiana alata*). These fragrant annuals intensify their scents at night, and there is a white-flowered type that blooms at night.

MOONFLOWER. This vining relative of the morning glory, known botanically as *Ipomoea alba*, produces fragrant white 4- to 6-inch flowers that look like morning glories.

EVENING PRIMROSE. A weedy-looking wildflower, the evening primrose (*Oenothera biennis*) looks good in gardens when its yellow, scented flowers are massed together. A relative, the gumbo lily (*O. caespitosa*), grows in low rosettes and produces 4-inch-wide white flowers. It thrives in dense, clay soil.

NIGHT-BLOOMING CEREUS. Also called the queen of the night, this houseplant (*Hylocereus undatus*), a cactus, is big and ungainly-looking

most of the year. But in summer it produces enormous white flowers sometimes almost a foot across. The flowers open after dark, occasionally late at night, unfolding so quickly that you can watch the process. They release a rich, heady perfume and are one of the most glorious of all flowers. But they last for only a single night; before dawn the flowers have wilted and dropped from the plant.

EVENING-SCENTED STOCK. This rather small plant (*Matthiola bicornis*) is unremarkable during the day. At night, however, it opens its purple flowers to release their heavenly scent. The plant will bloom all summer long.

## PLANTS FOR DRY GARDENS

Gardeners in climates where summers are dry (or those in other areas who are looking for low-maintenance plants) can still have plenty of flowers. Choosing the right location for the garden will help. One tactic for conserving moisture is to site the garden where it will get some shade during the hottest part of the afternoon. You should avoid planting your flowers on sloping ground that drains quickly or in exposed, windy locations. Trees with shallow root systems, such as maples, steal moisture and nutrients from the surrounding soil, making conditions difficult at best for flowering plants growing nearby. Plant as far away from these trees as you can. In any dry garden, mulching will help conserve moisture and moderate soil temperatures.

Some plants that ordinarily grow best in full sun when the soil is rich and moist will manage in drier soil if they receive some shade during the day. Some perennials that behave this way are lady's mantle, Japanese anem-

one, bergenia, columbine, purple coneflower, peach-leaved bellflower, snakeroot, bleeding heart, cranesbills, daylilies, coral bells, loosestrife, perennial phlox, and meadow rue.

Perennials especially good for dry, sunny gardens include achillea, butterfly weed, coreopsis, echinops, amethyst sea holly, gaillardia or blanket flower, Oriental poppy, balloon flower, black-eyed Susan, and *Sedum* 'Autumn Joy'. Hollyhocks, golden marguerite, artemisia, baby's breath, candytuft, rose campion, sundrops, evening primroses, lamb's ears, and yucca also resist drought.

Annuals that can withstand hot, dry conditions include coreopsis (*C. tinctorea*), bachelor's buttons, morning glories, portulacas, snow-on-the-mountain, sunflowers (*Helianthus*), and zinnias.

## GARDENS FOR SHADE

Most gardeners, especially those of us with small backyards, tree-filled suburban lawns, and city courtyards or rooftops surrounded by tall buildings, have to contend with some sort of shade, at least part of the year. But shade is not without its benefits. For one thing, a shady environment is more comfortable for gardeners in summer than bright, hot sun. And shady gardens generally need less care than sunny gardens. There are fewer weeds, fewer pests, and the plants need less frequent watering.

Shade gardens are hardly the colorless, boring places some gardeners think them to be. There are many colorful flowers that need or can tolerate varying degrees of shade. Because the plants are not seen in the blinding glare of full summer sun, their colors appear richer, and subtleties of plant texture and form are more obvious. In

a shade garden you are more likely to notice the many tones of green foliage, yellow-green to bright green to blue-green to deep green; the subtle interplay of textures, feathery against bold, fuzzy against glossy; the ever-changing patterns of sunlight and shadow that dance over leaves and ground when the breeze blows. If you have shade on your property, think of it as an opportunity rather than a liability.

The first step in planning a shade garden is to evaluate the kind of shade you have to work with. Shade is not a simple concept. Shade cast by buildings is different from shade cast by trees. The shade beneath a tall, open tree like an elm is brighter than the shade under a lower, denser tree like a maple. There is deep shade, partial shade, or light shade. Morning sun is different from afternoon sun. When assessing the shade in your garden spot, you will need to think about its quality and duration—how dense is the shade, at what time of day does it strike your garden, and for how long? Consider how it changes from season to season (shadows fall in a different place in August from where they lay in April). Consider reflected light, too: is there a white wall near your garden that will bounce additional light onto the plants or, conversely, a black paved driveway that will absorb whatever light hits it?

Unless your garden is in full shade—that is, it receives no direct light all day (which is unlikely unless you live in the middle of a forest)—there are flowers you can grow. In fact, you may be surprised at how many flowers will bloom happily in the shade. When planning your shade garden, choose white or pastel flowers for the areas of deepest shadow; dark-colored flowers will get lost in the dim light. Here is a list of some flowers for shady gardens, with their season of bloom and the degree of shade they can take.

Annuals for shade include:
Ageratum
Annual forget-me-not
Balsam (*Impatiens balsamina*)
Begonias, wax and tuberous
Browallia
Coleus (grown for foliage)
Impatiens
Lobelia
Madagascar periwinkle (*Catharanthus roseus*)
Monkey flower (*Mimulus*)
Nicotiana
Pansy
Sweet alyssum
Wishbone flower (*Torenia*)

Some shade-loving annuals planted in containers will survive a few days in light shade for special occasions. Likely candidates include petunias, snapdragons, and verbena.

Perennials for shade include:
Astilbe
Bergenia
Bleeding heart
Bluets (*Houstonia caerulea*)
Brunnera
Columbines
Cranesbills
Creeping phlox (*Phlox divaricata*)
Daylilies
Epimedium
False Solomon's seal (*Smilacina racemosa*)
Foamflower (*Tiarella cordifolia*)
Forget-me-not (*Myosotis*)
Foxgloves
Golden star
Globeflower
Hardy ageratum
Hosta
Jacob's ladder (*Polemonium caeruleum*)
Japanese anemone
Lady's mantle (*Alchemilla vulgaris*)
Leopard's bane (*Doronicum*)
Lungwort (*Pulmonaria angustifolia*)

*Astilbe thrives in a moist, partially shaded spot.*

Monkshood (*Aconitum*)
Periwinkle (*Vinca minor*)
Primroses
Purple rock cress (*Aubrieta deltoides*)
Silver lace vine (*Polygonum aubertii*)

Solomon's seal (*Polygonatum multiflorum*)
Sweet rocket (*Hesperis matronalis*)
Sweet woodruff
Violets

*Impatiens and ivy make nice container companions for a shady location.*

Remember, too, that you can plant sun-loving crocuses and other spring bulbs in places that are shaded in summer by deciduous trees, which don't get their leaves until after the bulbs have bloomed. Some summer lilies, such as the turk's cap lilies, don't mind a bit of shade, either. Autumn-blooming colchicums, lycoris, and hardy cyclamen will also grow well in light shade.

## ANNUALS IN THE FLOWER GARDEN

Annuals are wonderfully versatile plants. Some gardeners don't consider annuals to be "serious" garden plants,

while others consider them indispensable. When used intelligently annuals can serve a host of functions. They can be planted in beds and borders, either by themselves or mixed with perennials. They burst into lavish bloom at the time of year when color in the perennial garden is declining. They can be planted with spring bulbs, and their leaves and flowers will hide the yellowing foliage of bulb plants. They can be used to fill gaps between shrubs and foundation plantings or planted around the base of trees, where their colors brighten the shade. Annuals are classic container and windowbox plants; they bring instant color to patios, decks, and rooftops and can intermingle with vegetables and herbs to dress up the food garden. They can line a sidewalk or driveway, softening the harsh look of pavement and extending a welcome to visitors to your home. (Keep in mind that plants near driveways, streets, and sidewalks are subject to stress from dust, fumes, and traffic. Use tough plants like marigolds, geraniums, and petunias in these locations.)

Many annuals make excellent cut flowers, providing armloads of blossoms for lavish and inexpensive bouquets. Some of them can be potted up in autumn and brought indoors to continue flowering well into winter. Annuals are convenient and easy to grow and offer a whole spectrum of colors.

What, exactly, is an annual? To botanists, an annual is a plant that completes its entire life cycle in a single growing season. But to gardeners, the category also includes biennial plants that will bloom from seed in one season if given an early start indoors and tender perennials that are killed by frost and thus treated as annuals in all but warm climates (examples include snapdragons, salvia, and zonal geraniums).

*An assortment of annuals at the garden center.*

Annuals do require some study so you can determine the best colors for your needs, the suitability of plants to your climate, and their adaptability to the place you want to plant them. The hardiness of annuals varies. Plants classified as hardy annuals (such as bachelor's buttons, calendula, and larkspur) can withstand cool temperatures and even some light frost. They are usually started from seed directly outdoors in spring. Tender annuals (impatiens, marigolds, and zinnias, for example) are sensitive to cold and are not planted outdoors until frost danger is past and the soil is warm. In most parts of the country, tender annuals are started indoors in early spring and transplanted out when the weather has warmed. An indoor start is particularly important in the northern states, where the frost-free growing season is short. A third category of annual plants—half-hardy—is accepted by some horticulturists and not by others. Half-hardy annuals are in between the other two types in terms of hardiness. They can tolerate some cool weather, but they are usually damaged by frost. They are generally started indoors in all but the warmer climates.

## THE CUTTING GARDEN

One of the greatest rewards of flower gardening is having lots of blossoms to cut for bouquets and arrangements. If you enjoy bringing fresh flowers indoors, you might like to establish a cutting garden. Growing your own cutting flowers is easy to do and provides you with fresher flowers than those you buy at the florist—and for a fraction of the cost. A cutting garden

*In this red, white, and green garden, petunias in half-pots cascade down the fence in luxuriant flower "falls," blending into a "pool" of blossoms below.*

need not be large to be productive. Even a garden as small as 10 feet by 20 feet, if it's thoughtfully designed, will give you plenty of flowers from spring until frost.

A cutting garden is most useful when its primary function is production rather than display. Of course, you can cut bouquets from a display garden, but you must be very careful not to cut so many flowers that the garden becomes unbalanced or too empty. It's all too easy to strip a display garden of its looks when cutting flowers for indoors. A better approach is to leave your display gardens alone and establish a separate garden just for growing cut flowers.

The best location is in an out-of-the-way corner of your property, out of sight from visitors. Most people put their cutting gardens along the border of their property or out behind the gardens meant for viewing. Of course, the farther away from the house you locate the garden, the less convenient will be its upkeep. It will be harder to water, for example, and you may be more likely to forget to weed, water, and fertilize.

You could, instead, plant a small cutting garden close to the house—perhaps right outside the back door—so upkeep will be easier. Vegetable gardeners often plant a few rows of cutting flowers in the food garden where their color is a welcome addition; herb gardeners sometimes mix flowers and herbs in the same plot.

Because so many good cutting flowers are sun lovers, siting the cutting garden in full sun will give you the greatest selection of plants. If your garden site gets less than four hours of sun a day, concentrate on growing shade-tolerant flowers. Even shade gardeners may have a wider range of choices than they realize.

*Scarlet geraniums and coleus in mixed colors are an intense combination.*

## PLANNING
## THE CUTTING GARDEN

There are several factors to consider in planning the cutting garden. Remember, above all, to plan the layout with the plants' growing conditions and maintenance needs—rather than the garden's appearance—in mind. Put plants with similar cultural needs together, and be sure to leave enough space between rows or blocks of plants to allow room for you to get in to cut flowers, pull weeds, and do other maintenance chores.

Put the tallest plants at the back, which is, ideally, the north side of the garden, with medium-size ones next and shorter ones in front. In between the rows or beds, plant grass or cover pathways with a good layer of mulch. Some gardeners lay out their cutting gardens by flower color, planting in blocks or rows of red, purple, yellow, and so forth.

If the garden includes perennials, try to plan for bloom in different seasons. Where annuals are concerned, you can stagger your plantings two weeks apart to provide a succession of flowers to cut through the season.

In selecting flowers to grow, you will of course want to include the colors you like best. But take some time also to consider colors that will go with your decorating scheme indoors. Also think about the forms of the flowers and the sorts of shapes you will need in composing bouquets and arrangements

*Annuals can serve many functions. In this California garden, ivy geraniums are massed in pots atop a wall to create a hedgelike effect.*

for your home. Traditional arrangements call for three basic plant forms: tall, spiky flowers; rounded shapes; and small, airy "filler" blooms. Most cutting flowers are long-stemmed, but you can use diminutive blossoms in charming miniature arrangements. One characteristic that all good cutting flowers share is the ability to retain their freshness for at least several days indoors.

Perennials and bulbs to consider growing in a cutting garden include anemones, asters, astilbe, baby's breath, liatris, penstemons, coral bells,

coneflowers, coreopsis, daffodils, dahlias, gladiolus, globe thistles, hollyhocks, Jacob's ladder, lilies, lavender, lupines, peonies, phlox, dianthus, poppies, tulips, yarrow, and, of course, roses.

Annuals that make good cut flowers include bachelor's buttons, blanket flowers, calendulas, California poppies, China asters, candytuft, celosia, globe amaranth, gloriosa daisies, love-in-a-mist, nicotiana, salpiglossis, Shirley poppies, salvias, snapdragons, spider flowers, statice, stocks, sweet peas, verbena, and zinnias.

## A Baker's Dozen Summer Bouquets

Here are some especially lovely combinations of summer flowers for bouquets and arrangements:
• Shasta daisies, white Japanese irises, and dainty sprays of white baby's breath.
• An all-annuals blend of white and cream-colored zinnias, cream snapdragons, and white spider flowers.
• Marigolds and zinnias in yellow, deep gold, cream, and white.
• Pink zinnias, white phlox, and white nicotiana.
• Bright yellow calendulas, yellow and white roses, and baby's breath, with trailing stems of morning glories, periwinkle, or ivy.
• A blue-and-lavender mixture of agapanthus, ornamental alliums, and scabiosa.
• Yellow calendulas with red-and-yellow gloriosa daisies.

• Pink lilies, light purple scabiosa, blue delphiniums, white daisies, and spikes of blue salvia or lavender.
• Salmon-pink roses, white snapdragons, and blue hydrangeas.
• White hybrid lilies, lavender-blue agapanthus or spider flowers, mauve scabiosa, and baby's breath.
• White phlox, blue veronicas, dahlias in bright red and deep carmine, tea roses in pink and red-orange, and pink rambler roses.
• A fan-shaped arrangement of spiky flowers, including blue and white delphiniums, blue-violet larkspur, and pink and white snapdragons.
• Finally, roses or tuberous begonias floated in bowls of water along with some floating candles make wonderful centerpieces for summertime dinner parties.

## HOW TO HARVEST AND CARE FOR CUT FLOWERS

Cutting flowers from your own garden is one of the gardener's greatest summer pleasures. Flowers respond differently to cutting, and knowing how to handle them will prolong their lives in vases and arrangements indoors.

Above all, it is essential to understand that cut flowers are alive and continue to grow even after they are separated from the plant. Your efforts in caring for cut flowers will be directed toward allowing them to continue absorbing water and nutrients.

But first, let's think about cutting the flowers. The best time to cut flowers is early in the morning before the dew has dried. That's when plants contain the most water, and stems, leaves, and flowers are full and turgid. If you can't get out to the garden early to harvest your flowers, wait until evening. Although the blossoms will contain less water after spending the day in the sunshine, the plants will have been manufacturing food for themselves throughout the daylight hours, and the blossoms will be well supplied with nutrients when you cut them, which will help them survive in the vase.

Take a pail of lukewarm (110° F) water out to the garden with you and plunge the flowers into it as you cut

A *red pyrethrum cultivar and rosy pink thrift* (Armeria maritima) *make a handsome garden duo, and both are good flowers for cutting.*

OPPOSITE
*Silver perks up this annual border of red geraniums and blue salvia. Spider flowers and ornamental grasses add soft colors to the background. All these plants are grown as annuals in most parts of the United States, and all of them are good for cutting.*

them. You should be sure your cutting tools are sharp—dull tools can crush the capillaries in stems, making it difficult for the flowers to draw up water. Use a sharp knife to cut soft-stemmed flowers. Woody-stemmed plants such as chrysanthemums, and branches of trees and shrubs, are best severed with pruning shears.

As a general rule, don't cut tightly closed buds or mature flowers. Most flowers are best cut when the buds are about half-open and showing color. Some exceptions to the rule are asters, mums, marigolds, and zinnias, which should be cut when they're fully open. In all cases, take only flowers that are in perfect condition: those damaged by disease or insects probably won't last long. It is best for the plant if you cut the stem right above a node; that way, the plant will be able to send out a new shoot from the node.

Flowers have to be handled carefully when you cut them. More particular care is needed for double flowers. They tend to shatter easily and will have to be discarded, or their petals painstakingly refastened with melted wax, if they are manhandled.

When you get your flowers into the house, some of them will benefit from having their stems recut underwater. African violets, carnations, sweet williams, pinks and other *Dianthus* species, China asters, marguerites, marigolds, snapdragons, and sweet peas in particular will do better if their stems are recut underwater. When flowers are out of water for even a few seconds, their stems seal off. Recutting the stems allows your delicate flowers to again draw up water. If you don't cut the stems underwater (in a bowl or under a running tap), they will take in air. A bubble of air inside the stem can prevent the flower from getting water, and you will soon see the flower heads drooping over and wilting even though the stems are firm and straight.

Cut the stems on a slant, to increase surface area and to keep the water-conducting cells in contact with water even when the ends of the stems are resting on the bottom of the container.

Some flowers bleed a milky sap or clear fluid when they are cut. Nutrients flow out of the stem along with the sap, and in a vase those nutrients provide a perfect growing medium for bacteria. To extend the life of these flowers after cutting, seal the stem ends by dipping them quickly in boiling water or searing them slightly over a lighted candle. You will have stopped the flow of sap, but the water-conducting cells will still be able to function. Flowers that need to be sealed include campanulas, hardy chrysanthemums, daffodils, dahlias, forget-me-nots, heliotrope, hollyhocks, hydrangeas, lantana, lobelia, poinsettias, poppies, and stephanotis.

The ends of woody stems, such as those of lilacs, mock orange, rhododendrons, and other shrubs, should be split (not mashed) with a hammer or slit with a sharp knife.

*When cutting roses for arrangements, cut them from the plant just above an outward-facing node, from which a new shoot will grow. Remove any leaves that will be below the waterline before you put the flowers in the vase.*

*Many cut flowers last longer in the vase if you recut the stems underwater when you are ready to arrange the flowers.*

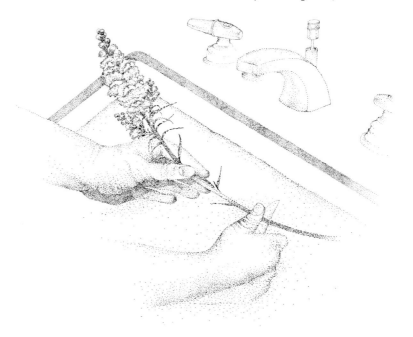

The abundance of the summer garden is captured in this big bouquet of white shasta daisies, yellow and pale orange lilies, roses in red, pink, and white, and Queen Anne's lace from a nearby field. The spiky purple flowers at top are liatris, and the bell-shaped rose-purple flower heads on the right belong to Phlox paniculata.

# CONDITIONING YOUR FLOWERS

For a longer-lasting arrangement, condition (or harden) your cut flowers before you put them on display. Conditioning is a simple process: just stand the flowers *loosely* in a big container of water so that air can circulate around the stems. Most flowers can be conditioned in lukewarm water, but some—daffodils, dahlias, forget-me-nots, hydrangeas, poinsettias, and poppies, among them—should be conditioned in cold water. If you like, you can add a flower preservative to the conditioning water. Preservatives can prolong the life of some cut flowers by as much as 200 percent, but this varies from flower to flower. Leave the flowers in the dark at room temperature for a couple of hours or overnight. Then move them to a cool location.

Flowers are conditioned in the dark so that their stomata (tiny openings in

*The stems of some flowers, such as hardy chrysanthemums, bleed when cut and can foul the water in a vase. To prolong their life, seal the stem ends by holding them briefly over a candle flame or dipping them quickly in boiling water.*

the leaves and stems) will close, reducing the amount of water that would be lost by transpiration. Very delicate flowers or those with limp stems, such as tulips, can be wrapped in paper before you put them into the conditioning water. Florist's tissue is the best paper to use—it is lightly waxed and will not fall apart underwater. But you can also use newspaper or plain tissue paper. Wrap flowers for hardening the same way a florist would wrap a bouquet: lay the flowers diagonally across a sheet of paper and roll the paper around them. Be sure to leave the ends of the stems exposed.

# ARRANGING THE FLOWERS

When you are ready to arrange your flowers, make sure you are starting with a clean vase. Wash it first in a mild solution of ammonia or white vinegar in water to eliminate any bacteria that might have collected in the vase from previous bouquets. To minimize the growth of new bacteria—which would shorten the life of your flowers—remove all leaves and thorns that would be underwater in the vase.

*A galvanized flower bucket like the one shown here is a perfect container for conditioning cut flowers. The buckets are widely used in France and are available in the United States from some mail-order garden supply companies.*

*Wrap tulips and other weak-stemmed flowers in florist's tissue or newspaper for conditioning.*

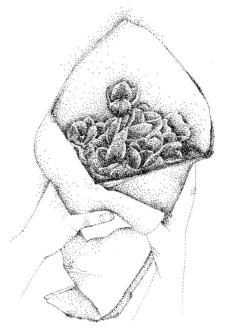

You can leave some foliage above the water level for most flowers, but for lilacs, mock orange, and zinnias, strip off *all* the leaves. If your flowers look a little stark with so much of their foliage removed, you can fill some space with a few leaves from long-stemmed houseplants.

Most flowers aren't too fussy about the pH of the water and like it to be about the same as their soil pH. Acid-loving plants include azaleas, carnations, delphiniums, hydrangeas, larkspur, rhododendrons, and stocks. If your tapwater is alkaline, acidify it for these flowers by adding a teaspoon or two of white vinegar to the vase. Flowers that definitely prefer alkaline water include hollyhocks, irises, lilacs, mock orange, and peonies. In most parts of the United States tapwater is alkaline, but if yours is not, you can add some baking soda to it.

Fill the vase with lukewarm water (very hot or very cold water can shock your flowers). You can extend the life of the arrangement by adding a flower preservative to the water. The preservative will help the water-intake cells in the stems to stay open, will help slow the growth of bacteria, and will provide nutrients for the flowers (remember, they are still growing). Some preservatives also contain an ingredient that causes harmful substances such as fluorine to precipitate out of the water. Several good commercial preservatives are available, or you can make your own by adding three tablespoons of sugar and one tablespoon of alum to a gallon of warm water (the two items are available at good pharmacies). You can also add a bit of charcoal to the water to keep it fresh. Use the kind of charcoal sold for filtering water; do *not* use barbecue briquettes, which contain chemicals harmful to plants. If you will be arranging your flowers in a metal vase that is not lined with glass, plastic, or ceramic, skip the preserva-

*An informal bouquet of summer flowers is charmingly complemented by a wicker basket. To use a basket to hold cut flowers, line the inside with plastic and arrange the flowers in a block of florist's foam. If you keep the foam saturated with water, the flowers will get all the moisture they need for a special occasion or short-term display.*

tive. It may react with the metal and lose its effectiveness.

If you are anchoring flowers in a block of florists' foam, soak the foam in water to which preservative has been added before you put the foam in the vase.

## CARING FOR FRESH FLOWERS

When the arrangement is finished, put it in a cool, airy, but draft-free place. Keep the flowers away from fireplaces, lamps, sunny windows, and other heat sources because heat will draw moisture out of the petals. Short-lived flowers like primroses, violets, and forget-me-nots will appreciate a daily misting. Violets, which are especially fragile, will last longer if the whole arrangement is wrapped in damp tissue paper and kept in the refrigerator at night.

Add fresh water to your flowers every day, but don't add more preservative until you change the water in the vase. Some flowers, including asters, calendulas, dahlias, marigolds, snapdragons, and stocks, tend to foul water very quickly. A complete daily change of water with new preservative added will keep these flowers fresher longer.

When the flowers do begin to fade, removing spent blossoms from the vase will let you get more mileage out of your arrangement. Dead or fading flowers (and some fresh flowers, including narcissus and peonies) give off ethylene gas, which causes many cut flowers to wilt. Roses, carnations, and tulips are especially susceptible. Ripening fruit gives off ethylene, too, so keep your fresh flowers away from fruit bowls.

## HOW TO CUT AND CONDITION FAVORITE FLOWERS

Here are specific directions for cutting many popular flowers.

AFRICAN VIOLET. Cut stems with newly opened flowers. Condition overnight in warm water. The flowers should last up to a week.

AGERATUM. Cut when the buds show color and when half the flowers in each head are open. If cut too early, buds will not open. Condition overnight in warm water. The flowers should last a week.

ANEMONE. Cut when the buds show color, but before they open. Condition annual anemones in warm water to the base of the buds. Condition perennial anemones in cold water.

ASTER (Michaelmas daisy). Cut when half of the buds are open; strip off excess leaves; split the stems and recut them underwater. Condition in warm water up to the base of the leaves.

*Pink roses and white baby's breath gleam in a copper bowl.*

CHINA ASTER. Cut when the buds are three-quarters to fully open. Recut stems underwater before conditioning, then condition overnight. Remove the leaves before arranging—they wilt quickly. The flowers should last up to two weeks.

ASTILBE. Cut when half the flowers in the feathery head are open. Split the stems and condition overnight. The flowers will last about a week.

BABY'S BREATH. Cut sprays when half the flowers are open. Condition overnight in cold water to the base of the lowest flowers. The flowers will last about a week.

BACHELOR'S BUTTON. Cut when the flowers are fully or nearly open; buds will not open in water. Condition overnight. The flower colors will fade slightly indoors, but the blossoms will last up to a week.

BALSAM. Cut as soon as the blossom at the tip of the stem is fully open. Split stems and remove excess foliage. Condition the flowers overnight.

BASKET FLOWER. Cut at any stage from tight buds to fully open flowers. Fully open flowers are fragile, so handle them carefully. Flowers half- or more open last about a week; tight buds last longer. Split the stems and then condition the flowers overnight in warm water.

TUBEROUS BEGONIA. Cut well-developed buds or fully open flowers. Split the stems. Condition in cold water to which you have added one tablespoon of salt per quart.

BELLS OF IRELAND. These flowers can be cut at any stage. Strip off all the leaves. Submerge the flowers and stems completely in cold water for an hour or so. Shake off the excess water and arrange the blossoms in cold water. They will last a week or two.

BLANKET FLOWER. Cut when the petals are open but the centers are still tight. The flowers should last a week or more.

BLEEDING HEART. Cut stems carefully when half the flowers are open. Be careful—the stems bruise easily. Condition overnight in cold water. The flowers will last about five days.

BLUE LACE FLOWER. Cut when half the flowers in the cluster are open. Condition overnight in cold water almost to the base of the flowers. They should last up to a week.

BUTTERFLY BUSH. Cut spikes when half the flowers are open. Strip off excess leaves, and split the stems. Condition in warm water to the base of the remaining leaves. Limp flower spikes can be revived by placing the stems in hot water before conditioning.

CALENDULA. Cut when the flowers are three-quarters to fully open. Remove excess leaves, then condition the flowers in warm water to the base of the remaining leaves. Recut the stems underwater before conditioning to make the flowers last longer.

CALLA LILY. Cut at any stage from bud to full bloom. Submerge most of the stem and leaves in cold water for an hour or two. Then shake off the excess water and arrange the flowers. Open flowers last up to a week; buds last longer.

CAMELLIA. Cut when the flowers are partially open and the outer petals are just separating from the bud. Handle camellias with care; the delicate flowers bruise easily. Mist the flowers with cold water once a day and keep them out of direct light. If the flowers wilt, submerge them completely in cold water until they revive. Camellias last only a few days as cut flowers.

CANDYTUFT. Cut when half the flowers in the cluster are open. Condition overnight in cold water.

CANTERBURY BELLS. Cut when the flowers are one-quarter to half open. Split the stems and sear the ends over a candle flame to prevent bleeding. Condition overnight in warm water. The flowers usually last up to two weeks. If they wilt too soon, recut and sear the stems, and condition the flowers in hot water.

CARDINAL FLOWER. Cut when one-quarter of the flowers on the stem are open. Split the stems and sear the ends over a candle flame or dip them in boiling water. Condition overnight in warm water. The flowers last about a week.

CARNATION. Cut when the flowers are half-open. Strip off excess leaves, then condition in warm water to the base of the remaining leaves. Recutting the stems every day will make the flowers last longer.

CELOSIA. Cut flowers when they are fully developed; cool weather intensifies their colors. Strip off excess leaves. Condition overnight or until both stems and flowers are firm.

FLORIST'S CHRYSANTHEMUMS (pompon and spider mums). Cut when the first flowers are open. Strip off excess leaves and split the stems. Condition in warm water to the base of the remaining leaves.

HARDY CHRYSANTHEMUMS. Split the stems 2 to 3 inches and dip the split ends in boiling water. Condition the flowers in warm water to which you have added a floral preservative. Leave foliage on stems above the water level to help the flowers last longer.

CLARKIA. Cut stems when three or four of the lower blossoms are open and the rest of the buds are just ready to open. Split the stems and condition overnight before arranging.

CLEOME. Cut when the flower clusters are half-open. Split the stems and condition overnight in warm water. Spider flowers wilt when cut, but they usually revive quickly during conditioning and last for several days.

COLUMBINE. Cut when half the flowers on the stem are open. Dipping the stems in salt water immediately after cutting may prolong the life of the flowers. Condition overnight in cool water to the base of the flowers.

CONEFLOWER. Cut when the flowers are open but the centers are still tight. Condition overnight in cold water. Remove leaves as they wilt; the flowers should last a week or two.

CORAL BELLS. Cut when half the flowers on the spray are open; buds will not open in water. Condition the flowers overnight in cold water.

COREOPSIS. Cut when the flowers are completely open but the centers are still tight. Condition the flowers overnight in cold water with one tablespoon of salt added per quart. The conditioning water should reach to the base of the flowers.

COSMOS. Cut when the flowers are open but the heads are still tight. Condition overnight in cold water to the base of the flowers. Flowers last about a week, but may drop pollen as they mature.

CROCUS. Cut when the buds show color. Condition overnight in cold water. Before arranging drop a bit of melted candle wax inside the base of the flowers to hold the petals. Cut crocuses usually last several days.

DAFFODIL, NARCISSUS. Cut when buds are beginning to open. Split the stems and dip the ends in hot water to seal them. Condition the flowers overnight in cold water.

DAHLIA. Cut when the flowers are just fully open. Strip off all the leaves that will be below the water level in the vase, and seal the stem ends over a candle or in hot water. Condition in cold water. You can revive prematurely wilted flowers by recutting the stems and placing them in warm water.

DAYLILY. Cut stems with several well-developed buds; they will open in water. Condition overnight in cold water. Remove flowers from the stem as they fade.

DELPHINIUM. Cut the large spikes when the first flowers open, and strip off excess leaves. Turn the flowers upside down, fill the hollow stems with water, and plug the ends with wax. Change the water daily after arranging the flowers.

EUPHORBIA. Cut when half the flowers on the stem are open. Dip the end of the stem in hot water to seal before arranging.

FALSE DRAGONHEAD. Cut when the flowers are half-open.

FEVERFEW. Cut when half the flowers are open. Split the stems and condition overnight in warm water.

FILIPENDULA. Cut when half the flowers on the branch are open. Split the stems and condition overnight in warm water.

FLEECE FLOWER. Cut branches when they are half in flower. Split the stems and remove some leaves to make the flowers last longer. Condition overnight in warm water.

FORGET-ME-NOT. Cut when half the flowers on the stem are open. Strip off all the excess leaves, and seal the stems over a candle or in boiling water. Condition in warm water; if the flowers are wilted, completely submerge them when conditioning.

FOXGLOVE. Cut the stems when the first flowers are open. Split the stem ends an inch or more. Condition in warm water to the base of the flowers.

FREESIA. Cut when several flowers on the stem have opened. Submerge stems and flowers entirely in cold water overnight. The flowers should last several days.

GARDENIA. Cut when the flowers are nearly open. Split the woody stems and condition the flowers overnight in cold water. Handle with care; gardenia petals bruise easily. The flowers should last almost a week.

GERBERA. Cut when the flowers are open but the centers are still tight. Submerge both stems and flowers completely in cold water overnight. Gerberas usually last about a week.

GEUM. Cut when the flowers are half- to three-quarters open. Scald or sear the stem ends to seal them, and remove excess leaves. Condition in warm water to the base of the flowers. They should last almost a week.

GLADIOLUS. Cut the flower spikes when in bud. Split the stems and condition overnight in warm water to the base of the leaves.

GLOBE AMARANTH. Cut when the

*A bouquet with late orange tulips, daisies, and yellow lilies.*

flowers are at least three-quarters open. Remove excess foliage and split the stems. Condition overnight in warm water. The flowers should last a week.

GLOBE THISTLE. Cut when a quarter of the little flowers on the globe are open. Condition overnight in cold water. The flowers should last about a week.

HELIOTROPE. Cut when half to three-quarters of the flowers in the cluster are open; include part of the woody stem if possible. Split the stems and seal them in boiling water. Condition overnight in warm water. Be sure to keep all the foliage above the water level.

HOLLYHOCK. Cut in late afternoon or early morning, when three or four flowers on the stem are open. Split the

stem ends 4 to 6 inches, and sear the ends over a candle. Condition in warm water to the base of the buds. Double-flowered varieties generally last longer in the vase than single-flowered types.

HOSTA. Cut when two or three lower flowers on the stem are open. Split the stems and condition overnight in cold water to the base of the flowers.

HYACINTH. Cut when the first flowers open. Dip the stem ends in hot water for a minute. Condition overnight in cold water to retain the most fragrance, and wrap the flowers loosely in tissue while conditioning.

HYDRANGEA. Cut the big flower heads when in full bloom. Strip off excess leaves and split the stems an inch or more. Seal the stem ends in boiling water or over a candle. Condi-

tion in warm water to the base of the remaining leaves.

IMPATIENS. Cut as soon as the flower at the tip of the stem is open. Split the stems and remove excess foliage. Condition overnight.

IRIS. Cut English, Dutch, and Spanish irises as the first flower on the stem opens. Cut German, Japanese, and Siberian irises when the first bud begins to unfold. Condition all irises in room temperature water to the base of the flowers. The cut flowers last only a few days.

JUPITER'S BEARD. Cut when the flower clusters are no more than half-open. Split the stems and condition overnight in cold water. The flowers should last about a week.

LANTANA. Cut when three or four of

the outer flowers in the cluster are open. Include part of the woody stem when cutting. Split the stem ends and seal them. Condition in warm water. The flowers last almost a week.

LARKSPUR. Cut when the first flowers on the spike are open. Condition for two or more hours in cold water with one-half teaspoon of denatured alcohol or two tablespoons of white vinegar added per quart. Larkspurs usually last a week or more.

LAVENDER. Cut when the buds are fully colored but before they open. Strip off excess foliage and split the stem. Condition in warm water to the base of the flowers. They should last a week or more.

LILAC. Cut when the first flowers in the head are open. Remove all the foliage and make several splits in the stem. Condition in cool water to the base of the flowers.

LILIES. Cut when the first flowers on the stem open. Split the stem an inch or so and condition overnight in warm water to the base of the buds. Remove the anthers if you want to keep pollen from dropping onto nearby furniture.

LILY-OF-THE-VALLEY. Cut stems when the first flowers open. Dip the stem ends in hot water, then condition in cool water to the base of the flowers.

LOBELIA. Cut when the first two flowers are open. Strip off excess foliage and seal stem ends over a candle or in boiling water. Condition in warm water to the base of the remaining leaves.

LOVE-IN-A-MIST. Cut when the central flower and one or two more on the stem are open. Condition overnight in warm water.

LUPINE. Cut spikes when the first flowers open; leave as much foliage as possible. Condition in warm water to the base of the remaining leaves. The flowers will last about a week. If the buds start to shrivel, mist them with water.

LYCORIS (hardy amaryllis). Cut when the first bud opens. Wrap the base of the stem with a rubber band to keep the stem from splitting. Condition in warm water to the base of the buds.

MARIGOLD. Cut when the flowers are just fully open. Strip off excess leaves, then condition overnight in cool water to the base of the remaining leaves. The flowers last a week or two.

MIGNONETTE. Cut when a quarter to half the flowers in the spike are open. Condition overnight in warm water.

MONKSHOOD. Cut when half the flowers on the spike are open. Condition them overnight. They should last about a week.

MORNING GLORY. Cut stems with lots of developed buds and a few open flowers. Split the stems and condition overnight. Wrap large buds in tissue to keep them from opening; unwrap before arranging. Flowers last only a day or two, but the buds will continue to open.

NASTURTIUM. Cut as soon as the flowers are fully open, with large buds ready to unfold. Split the stems. Condition overnight in cold water. Nasturtium leaves are also nice in arrangements; condition them for twenty-four hours in warm water.

NICOTIANA. Cut when one or two flowers in the cluster are fully open. Condition overnight in warm water to the base of the flowers. The flowers last only a few days, but the buds will continue to open for as long as a week.

PANSY. Cut flowers when they are fully open. Leave foliage attached to make the flowers last longer. Condition in cool water to the base of the flowers. Pansies will last about five days.

PEONY. Cut when the buds show color. Remove excess leaves and split the stems. Condition in warm water to the base of the remaining leaves.

PETUNIA. Cut when the flowers are nearly open. Flowers and leaves may wilt when cut but revive with condi-

*A bouquet of roses.*

tioning. Strip the leaves below the water level and condition overnight in water with a flower preservative added. Petunias last up to a week.

PHLOX. Cut when half the flowers in the cluster are open. Split the stems and condition overnight in cold water. Flowers cut at this stage should last ten days to two weeks.

PERENNIAL PINKS (*Dianthus*). Cut flowers when they are three-quarters open. Recut the stems under cold water and condition overnight in water up to the base of the flowers. Remove foliage only below the water line. Pinks last a week or more.

CALIFORNIA POPPY. Cut buds when they are fully elongated but not yet open. Condition overnight. The buds will open in the vase, and the flowers should last several days.

ICELAND POPPY. Cut when the buds are still tight. Seal the stem ends over a candle or in boiling water, then condition for forty-eight hours in cool water in a cool, dark place. The flowers open quickly in warm water.

ORIENTAL POPPY. Cut when the buds are still tight. Sear the base of the stem over a candle. Condition in cool water up to the base of the bud. Before arranging, carefully drip a bit of candle wax inside the flowers at the base of the petals to keep them from shattering.

PRIMROSE. Cut when the flower clusters are half- to three-quarters open. Condition overnight in cool water. Primroses generally last about a week.

PURPLE CONEFLOWER. Cut flowers when they are fully open but the centers are still tight.

PYRETHRUM. Cut when the first flowers open. Split the stems and condition in warm water.

RANUNCULUS. Cut when the flowers are opening but the centers are still tight. The flowers wilt when cut but revive when conditioned. Condition them overnight in warm water.

ROSE. Cut roses when in bud. It's best to cut them in late afternoon. Recut the stems before conditioning, just below a leaf node. Split the stems. Strip the leaves from the bottom of the stem, but leave as many as possible. Submerge most of the stem in cold water overnight; wrap the buds in tissue before conditioning. Roses last about a week.

SALPIGLOSSIS. Cut flowers as soon as they are fully open. Condition overnight in cold water to the base of the flowers. The flowers should last about a week.

SALVIA. Cut blue salvia when the flowers on the lower half of the spike are open. Cut scarlet salvia when half to three-quarters of the flowers on the spike are open. Split the stems. Condition both types of salvia overnight in warm water.

SCABIOSA. Cut when the flowers are almost fully open. Split the stems and condition overnight in cool water to the base of the flowers. Scabiosa buds won't open in water unless they are fully developed.

SHASTA DAISY. Cut when the flowers are just fully open. Split the stems and condition in warm water with flower preservative added.

SNAPDRAGON. Cut spikes when the first flowers open. Strip off excess leaves. Condition to the base of the remaining leaves.

STATICE. Cut flower clusters when they are half-open. Condition overnight in cold water. The flowers will last a week or more.

STEPHANOTIS. Cut flowers when they are nearly open. If you cut them with short stems, sear the ends. If you cut longer stems, split the ends before searing. Condition overnight in cold water. The flowers should last about a week.

STOCK. Cut when the first flowers open, before the lower flowers start to fade. Strip excess leaves and split the

stems. Condition to the base of the remaining leaves in cold water containing a flower preservative.

SUNFLOWER. Cut when the flowers are fully open. Strip off excess leaves and split the stems. Condition for twenty-four to forty-eight hours in warm water to the base of the remaining leaves. The giant sunflower needs heavy wire inserted in its stem to support the weight of the flower.

SWEET ALYSSUM. Cut stems when half the flowers are open. Condition overnight. Buds will open in water, and the flowers will last about a week.

SWEET PEA. Break off stems of annual types when they are almost completely in bloom. Cut perennials when the clusters are half-open. Condition overnight at room temperature in water with a flower preservative added. Sweet peas will last about a week.

TULIP. Cut when the buds show color. Wrap stems and flowers in florist's tissue, then condition overnight in cold water to the base of the buds. When the flowers open, drip melted candle wax inside at the base of the petals to hold them longer.

VERBENA. Cut when two or three outside rows of flowers are open and the rest of the buds show their true color. Split the stems and condition overnight in warm water with flower preservative added.

VERONICA (SPEEDWELL). Cut when the flower spikes are half-open. Condition overnight in warm water. The flowers will last for several days.

VIOLET. Cut when the flowers are open. Submerge the entire flower and stem in cool water to condition. The flowers will last longest in a cool room.

VIRGINIA BLUEBELL. Cut when three or four flowers on the stem are open. Split the stems and condition overnight in warm water.

YARROW. Cut when half the flowers in the cluster are open. Condition overnight in cold water with two table-

*Flowers can be dried in three ways: tied in bunches and hung upside down to air-dry, placed in a desiccant such as silica gel, or simply stood upright in a vase.*

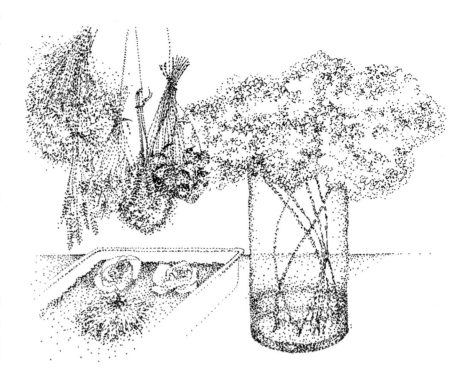

spoons of salt added per quart. The flowers should last a week or two.

ZINNIA. Cut when the flowers are fully open but the centers are still tight. Strip off excess leaves. Dip the end of the stem quickly in boiling water, then in cold water. Condition the flowers in cool water. They should last up to two weeks.

## FLOWERS FOR DRYING

Dried flowers remind us of the glories of the summer garden long after the winds have turned biting and cold and the garden lies buried under snow. Dried flowers have become tremendously popular in recent years—wreaths and arrangements seem ubiquitous in gift and florist's shops. Although it is nice to have the immediate satisfaction of purchasing dried flowers rather than going to the bother of growing your own, there is something infinitely more rewarding about a basket of dried flowers that came from your garden.

Dried flowers are not the focus of this book; there are a number of good books available on the subject if you want to learn more about it. But because drying your own flowers adds so much to the enjoyment of having a summer flower garden, here are some basic directions for getting started.

Although most of the classic everlastings (flowers that air-dry very easily) are annuals, there are also quite a few perennials that dry well. The list below focuses on flowers that can be dried easily and successfully. Many more flowers besides these can be dried, but you will find in the list some good

candidates in a range of forms and colors.

### HOW TO DRY FLOWERS

Harvest the flowers you want to dry on a sunny, warm day when the plants are dry. It is best to pick most flowers for drying just as they mature. To air-dry flowers, strip off the leaves and tie the stems in small bunches with twine or rubber bands. Hang the bunches upside down in a dark, dry, airy place.

To dry flowers in silica gel (a desiccant sold in garden centers and craft shops), begin by standing the cut flowers in water for several hours to let the petals become firm. Do not, however, get the flowers wet. Then cut off the stems to leave only an inch or so.

Dry the flowers in airtight plastic or metal containers. Put a ½-inch-deep layer of silica gel in the bottom of the container if the flowers are to be dried facedown; use more silica gel if the flowers are to be dried faceup.

Dry flat, daisylike flowers facedown in a single layer; the flowers should not touch one another. Most other flowers dry best faceup. Insert a piece of heavy-gauge green florist's wire into the stem and bend a sharp angle in it so the other end of the wire protrudes from the silica gel (this is to make it easier to remove the dried flowers from the container). Long sprays and spikes of flowers can be laid horizontally to dry.

Lay the flowers carefully on top of the silica gel, then sprinkle more desiccant around and over them until they are completely covered. Put the lid on the container, label with the type of flower and the date, and set the container in a warm, dry place.

Flowers in silica gel take anywhere from a couple of days to a week to dry. Check one flower to see if the batch is dried; if it is, carefully pour off the desiccant and remove the flowers.

Silica gel is not cheap, but it is clean and effective, and it can be reused. When the crystals turn pink they cannot absorb any more moisture. Spread them in a shallow layer in a baking pan and place in a low oven (250° F) until the crystals turn blue again—it will take half an hour or longer. Then remove the pans from the oven and put the crystals in an airtight container while they are still hot. Don't use them until they are cool.

Flowers can also be dried in a mixture of borax and cornmeal, but it tends to stick to the petals and is messier to work with, at least in my experience.

## HOW TO CARE FOR DRIED FLOWERS

In humid weather dried flowers absorb moisture from the surrounding air. This hurts the quality of the flowers, and if they become too damp, they may even become moldy. Flowers dried in a desiccant should be stored in airtight containers to protect them from humidity. Put some desiccant in the storage containers, too. Check the stored flowers periodically to make sure the silica gel is still blue. If it has turned pink, remove and dry it as described above.

Professionals often dip dried flowers in a satin-finish lacquer to preserve their shape and keep them from shattering. Dilute the lacquer with thinner to get a lighter, less viscous consistency.

One problem with dried flowers is that thin stems are brittle and tend to break easily. To avoid the aggravation of broken stems, cut the stems short when you prepare the fresh flowers for drying, and insert a piece of heavy-gauge green wire through each stem and into the head of the flower. If the wire tends to slip out, you can bend a tiny hook into the end that goes into the flower. Insert one end of the un-

bent wire through the stem and into the flower until it comes out the center, then make the hook and gently pull the wire back through until the hook catches in the center of the flower. The hook will be hidden inside the flower.

Bugs sometimes get into dried flower arrangements and chew small holes in them. This kind of insect damage ruins the look of the flowers and may also cause them to shatter. The simplest preventive measure is to put the arrangement in your freezer for a day or two a few times a year. The cold won't hurt the flowers, and it will kill any beetle larvae or other bugs that may be hiding in the flowers. If some of your dried flowers do shatter, you can save any undamaged petals to add color to potpourris.

Finally, it is important to realize that dried flowers will not last forever. After several months or a year the flowers start to look dusty (they're pretty impossible to clean), and the colors begin to fade. Enjoy them as winter reminders of summer's bounty, but replace them when their quality starts to decline.

## FLOWERS TO DRY

ACHILLEA. Perennial; air-dry.
*Achillea* 'Coronation Gold'. Golden yellow.
A. *ptarmica* 'The Pearl'. White.
A. *millefolium*, wild yarrow. White.
AGERATUM (*Ageratum houstonianum*). Annual; blue-violet, purple; dry in silica gel.
ORNAMENTAL ALLIUM (*Allium aflatunense*, A. *giganteum*). Perennial; purple; dry the seed heads, not the flowers; air-dry.
AMMOBIUM (*Ammobium alatum*). Annual; small, white, daisylike flowers; air-dry.
ARTEMISIA (*Artemisia* 'Silver

Mound'). Perennial; dry the foliage.
ASTILBE (*Astilbe* species and cultivars). Perennial; white, pink, red; the feathery flower plumes turn beige when dried; air-dry.
BABY'S BREATH (*Gypsophila* species). Annual or perennial; sprays of tiny white flowers; air-dry.
CELOSIA, crested types (*Celosia cristata*). Annual; red, crimson, magenta, pink; air-dry.
CELOSIA, plume types (*C. plumosa*). Annual; red, orange, apricot, gold; air-dry.
DUSTY MILLER (*Cineraria maritima*). Annual; air-dry the foliage.
ECHINOPS (*Echinops* 'Taplow Blue'). Perennial; steel-blue globe-shaped flower heads; air-dry.
ERYNGIUM (*Eryngium amethystinum*). Perennial; metallic blue flowers, unusually shaped but somewhat like thistles; air-dry.
GLOBE AMARANTH (*Gomphrena globosa*). Annual; small, round, purple, magenta, pink, white, orange flowers; air-dry.
GOLDENROD (*Solidago canadensis*). Perennial; bright to deep yellow plumes; air-dry garden varieties or wild species.
HYDRANGEA (*Hydrangea* species). Perennial; the big flower heads fade eventually to beige as they dry. To dry them, stand stems upright in a vase with a little water in the bottom and let the flowers dry in this position.
LARKSPUR (*Delphinium ajacis*). Annual; purple, blue-violet, pink; air-dry or use silica gel.
LAVENDER (*Lavandula angustifolia*). Perennial; light to deep purple; air-dry.
LIATRIS (*Liatris* species). Perennial; tall, rosy purple flower spikes; air-dry.
LOVE-IN-A-MIST (*Nigella damascena*). Annual; the unusual seed pods resemble birds' nests; air-dry.
MARIGOLD (*Tagetes* species). Annual; yellow, gold, orange, mahogany, bicolors; dry in silica gel.

Rose (*Rosa* hybrids). Perennial; shades of red, pink, yellow, orange, white; dry buds in silica gel; individual petals can be air-dried.

Sedum (*Sedum sieboldii, S.* 'Autumn Joy'). Perennial; flower heads turn beige, rust, or brown when dried; air-dry.

Statice (*Statice sinuata*). Annual; purple, pink, yellow, white; air-dry.

Strawflowers (*Helichrysum bracteatum*). Annual; red, crimson, rose, pink, salmon, bronze, yellow, gold, white; pick before fully open; air-dry.

Xeranthemum (*Xeranthemum annuum*). Annual; pink, lavender, purple, white; air-dry or use silica gel.

Zinnia (*Zinnia elegans*). Annual; many shades of red, orange, yellow, salmon, pink, rose, cream; dry in silica gel.

Creeping zinnia (*Sanvitalia procumbens*). Annual; small yellow flowers with dark centers; air-dry or use silica gel.

# FIVE

# Flowers for Summer Gardens

Summer's palette is rich and varied. There are so many colors to choose among, so many kinds of plants, so many places to grow them. This chapter offers basic cultural directions for some of summer's classic flower garden plants.

### Achillea / Yarrow

These perennials are grown for their flat-topped clusters of white, pink, or yellow flowers. Most of these plants grow tall, and their foliage is fernlike: toothed or divided and in some species more finely divided and feathery-looking. Often the leaves are aromatic

when crushed, and some yarrows are grown in the herb garden for their healing applications. The genus was named for Achilles, the hero of Greek mythology who used yarrow leaves to heal his battle wounds. Yarrow flowers can be cut for fresh arrangements or dried.

Achillea is generally easy to grow, and the taller species are handsome in the perennial garden. There are lower-growing species also, which are usually grown in rock gardens, but we will focus here on the species and cultivars that are best for beds and borders.

Yarrow is tolerant of hot, dry conditions and does well in dry, exposed places. The plants are not particular

about soil, but they will grow best in a well-drained, loamy soil of average fertility. Most yarrows are hardy throughout the United States. You should plant them 1½ feet apart and divide the plants every three years or so, in either spring or fall.

*Achillea filipendulina* is a tall border plant that can reach 3 to 4 feet in height. The leaves are finely divided and are about 6 inches long. The flowers are yellow. The most popular cultivar is Coronation Gold, which blooms all summer in the middle of the border. Its large, deep yellow flower heads are excellent for cutting or for drying.

*A. millefolium*, also called milfoil,

is a shorter plant, growing about 2 feet tall. Its flowers in the species form are white—this is the wild yarrow seen in herb gardens and growing near beaches and other dry waste places. There are garden cultivars that bear red or pink flowers. The best known of these is Red Beauty, whose flowers are a bright rosy red when they open, then fade gradually through various shades of pink. The plant blooms from midsummer into fall and is excellent in the middle of the border and for cutting. Its leaves are finely dissected and silvery green in color.

Sneezewort, A. *ptarmica*, is seldom grown in its species form, but it is the parent of some favorite flower garden cultivars. The most popular is The Pearl, a medium-size middle-of-the-border plant that grows 1½ to 3 feet tall. Its leaves are bright green and undivided, and the pure white double flowers look like little powder puffs. The Pearl blooms enthusiastically all summer and into fall. The plants tend to spread vigorously and need dividing more often than other yarrows.

A. *taygetea* grows about 1½ feet high, with beautiful silvery leaves and golden yellow flowers. The plants bloom all summer and into fall. A wonderfully versatile cultivar is Moonshine, whose light yellow flowers are striking in combination with flowers in shades of blue and violet. Moonshine grows 1½ to 2 feet tall and has silvery gray leaves. Like the other yarrows, it is excellent for cutting and for drying.

## Ageratum / Flossflower

These popular and easy-to-grow annuals belong to the daisy family. The common garden species is a low-growing favorite for edging flower beds and windowboxes. Ageratum blooms in compact mounds from early summer until frost. Plants will also bloom indoors in winter from seed sown in September if you can give them lots of sun. The most familiar color for ageratum is a purplish blue, but there are also pink- and white-flowered forms. The flowers are useful for both cutting and drying.

Plants grow from 6 to 12 inches tall, depending on the variety, and have dark green leaves that are almost hidden by the fluffy flowers. Ageratum flourishes in average soil in either full sun or light shade. The plants cannot tolerate frost, so do not plant them out until all danger of frost is past in spring.

The following cultivars are all derived from the common garden species, *Ageratum houstonianum*.

Blue Danube Hybrid grows 6 inches tall, with lavender-blue flowers.

Blue Mink is taller, growing to a height of 10 inches, and has large flower heads of rich lavender-blue. The plant is a vigorous grower, and in England it received a royal Horticultural Society Award of Merit in 1981.

Pink Powderpuffs bears flowers of soft rose-pink. The plants are a compact 5 inches high and bloom freely all summer.

Summer Snow Hybrid blooms early with pure white flowers.

## Althaea / Hollyhock

The charming, old-fashioned hollyhock has been a favorite of flower gardeners for generations. The biennial plants grow in tall, slender spikes with showy flowers in a range of warm colors that can be had today in either single- or double-petaled forms. Since they've been grown here since colonial days, many people think hollyhocks are native Americans. But the plants have been cultivated in Europe since the sixteenth century and were grown in China for a thousand years before that.

Although hollyhocks are biennials, they may persist for a few years under favorable conditions. Because of their size, it's best to give hollyhocks a place of their own in the garden, rather than trying to fit them into a mixed border. A row of hollyhocks can look just right next to a white picket fence or a stone wall, or you can plant them in clumps next to the house.

The plants will thrive in almost any garden soil, as long as they get plenty of sun and moisture. To establish new plants, sow seeds in spring, mulch the plants to winter them over, and transplant the young plants the following spring to their permanent location. Hollyhocks self-sow readily, so you need not start new plants every year. Because of their height, the plants need to be staked or grown in a spot protected from wind.

The common garden species is *Althaea rosea*, and numerous single- and double-flowered cultivars are available.

## Antirrhinum / Snapdragon

The colorful spikes of snapdragons are splendid both in the garden and as cut flowers. The genus name is derived from the Greek word for nose, which refers to the shape of the flowers on the spike. Snapdragons can be either annual or perennial, but both kinds are grown as annuals. In most parts of the country snapdragons bloom in early summer, but in mild climates they bloom in winter and spring.

The plants are easy to grow and are available in such a broad range of warm colors that they make wonderfully versatile additions to beds and borders. Snapdragons are divided into three groups according to size. Tall varieties can reach 4 feet in height and are often grown for the florist trade. Intermediate varieties grow about 20 inches tall, and dwarf varieties average 9 inches in height.

Snapdragons will grow in either full sun or partial shade, and they do best in cool weather. They like a moderately rich soil. In northern areas, start seeds indoors eight to twelve weeks before the last expected spring frost and set out seedlings as soon as the soil can be worked. The blooming period can be extended by sowing seeds in batches several weeks apart and by keeping faded flowers picked off. If you cut off entire spikes when the flowers fade, the plants may bloom again in fall.

Most of the varieties sold by seed companies have been bred from the species *Antirrhinum majus*. All the plants have narrow, bright green leaves.

## *Artemisia*
## *Wormwood, Dusty Miller*

Artemisias are a large genus of aromatic plants grown primarily for their foliage, and they are extremely useful in flower gardens. The genus includes the wormwood from which absinthe is made (*Artemisia absinthium*), as well as the culinary herb tarragon (*A. dracunculus*). In the flower garden, the silvery white foliage of artemisias is an excellent modifier for very bright color combinations that might otherwise be hard on the eyes.

Artemisias are easy to grow and do best in well-drained, sandy soils of no more than average fertility. They need full sun. Plants may start to look straggly in hot, humid weather; if this happens, cut back the plants to stimulate new growth. Most artemisias are hardy to −10° or −20°F; in gardens where winter temperatures drop lower, grow them as annuals.

A. *abrotanum*, called southernwood, old man, or lad's love, can grow as tall as 4 feet and sheds its leaves in winter. The grayish green leaves make southernwood very useful as a back-of-the-border plant. The aromatic foliage, when dried, is said to repel insects. Yellowish flowers bloom in summer.

*A. schmidtiana* var. *nana* is a low, cushiony plant best grown at the front of the border or in the rock garden. Plants grow about 6 inches high. The finely divided foliage is delicate in appearance and silky in texture.

*A. stelleriana*, also called dusty miller or old woman, is extremely well suited to seaside gardens. It grows about 2 feet tall, and its dense, toothed leaves look woolly and white.

Silver Mound is a hybrid often grown as an edging plant. Its ferny, silver-gray foliage forms a compact mound about 6 inches high.

## Astilbe

This lovely, feathery perennial garden favorite, sometimes (incorrectly) called spiraea, is native to China and Japan. Tall, airy panicles of tiny fluffy flowers arise from a mass of glossy green, toothed foliage in early to midsummer. Astilbes make good cut flowers, too, and they can also be dried.

Astilbe grows well in any good garden soil, as long as it is moist and contains plenty of organic matter. The plants do best in partial shade; full sun may burn the foliage and bleach out the flowers. Use astilbes in the perennial border or massed by themselves in damp, shady spots. The durable plants can be propagated by division in spring or fall. Astilbes are hardy throughout the United States.

The most widely grown species is *Astilbe* × *arendsii*, which is available in several varieties, with flowers of white, carmine red, or various shades of pink and rose.

Another species, *A. chinensis*, is more compact. The hybrid cultivar Finale blooms in mid-summer, after the *arendsii* hybrids, and extends the astilbe season. It has compact panicles of light pink flowers on drought-tolerant, 15- to 18-inch plants. A dwarf cultivar, Pumila, grows a foot high and produces raspberry-pink flower spikes from mid- to late summer.

*A. taquetii* produces flower panicles that are more conical and upright, less airy than those of other species. The cultivar Superba blooms late, with bright rosy pink flowers on 3- to 4-foot stems.

## Begonia

This large and universally popular group of plants is widely grown as houseplants and as outdoor bedding and container flowers. None of the begonias can tolerate frost, so they can only be grown outdoors year-round in subtropical gardens where frost does not occur.

Hundreds of species and varieties are available—the selection is so vast that some aficionados become collectors and specialize in growing nothing but begonias. Some begonias are grown for their decorative foliage, but the best-known garden types are favored for their flowers. The two most widely grown types of begonias are wax begonias (*Begonia* × *semperflorens-cultorum*) and tuberous begonias (*B.* × *tuberhybrida*).

### Wax Begonias

The wax begonia is a fibrous-rooted plant native to Brazil. It has glossy, rounded leaves 2 to 4 inches long in varying shades of green and bronze. The inch-wide flowers can be either single or double (depending on the variety) and come in shades of pink and red as well as white. As a rule, green-leaved varieties can tolerate more shade than bronze-leaved types.

Wax begonias bloom continuously all summer. They are excellent bedding plants and work beautifully in containers and windowboxes. Wax begonias make good houseplants, too. In autumn, before the first frost, you can dig up plants or take cuttings to root and pot up for bloom indoors over the winter.

To start wax begonias from seed, sow seeds indoors in mid-winter—January or February—to plant outdoors in spring. The seed is very fine; mixing it with sand will make it a bit easier to sow. Scatter seeds evenly over the surface of a fine potting medium and press them in gently. Keep the soil moist, with lots of light and temperatures above 50°F. Transplant the seedlings to individual pots when they are big enough to handle, and plant them out after all danger of frost is past. Wax begonias grow in either sun or shade but do best in light shade. If you locate them where the sun is intense, try to provide some shade during the afternoon. Plants grown in medium to deep shade will not produce as many flowers as those in brighter light, but they will bloom. Many varieties of wax begonias are available.

### Tuberous Begonias

Arguably the most spectacular flower for shade, tuberous begonias produce their big, splashy blossoms in brilliant warm colors and show them off against contrasting dark green leaves. The flowers of some varieties resemble camellias, roses, or carnations in form. Tuberous begonias grow and bloom beautifully in shady or partly shady gardens or in pots, tubs, windowboxes, or hanging baskets on shady porches or patios.

The plants grow from tender bulbs that must be dug up and stored in fall (even in the South) and replanted the following spring. The plants need a long growing season; if you live in the North, start the tubers indoors in February or March. Plant only tubers that are firm and free of disease. Start them in pots of a good, balanced potting mixture, making sure the rounded side of the tuber is down and the concave, depressed side is facing upward. Barely cover the tubers with potting mixture. Keep the soil moist but not sopping wet. The temperature should be about 75°F during the day, with a small drop at night. When the sprouts push their way through the soil, make sure the plants get strong light or even direct sun for part of the day. Less light will give you weak, gangly plants.

Keep the plants in good, strong light until it's time to plant them outdoors, when all danger of frost has passed. They will need a rich, moist but well-drained, deeply dug soil and shade for at least part of the day. Fertilize them once a month with an all-purpose fertilizer until blooming begins and a low-nitrogen fertilizer after that.

Because the flowers are large and heavy, tuberous begonias usually need staking. But it's worth the trouble—the dazzling display begins in mid-summer and continues until the frost.

Northern gardeners should dig their begonia tubers after the first frost; southern gardeners can wait until the leaves yellow and start to turn brown at the end of the season. Spread out newly dug tubers and let them dry in the sun for a few days. Then cut off the tops an inch above the tops of the tubers. Shake off the soil, lay the tubers in a shallow box or tray, and cover them with peat moss or dry sand. It is a good idea to keep tubers of the same color flower together and label the boxes so you know what you're planting in spring. The best storage temperature is 40° to 50°F.

Seed and nursery companies sell many tuberous begonia varieties in the form of seeds and tubers.

## Callistephus / China Aster

Most garden asters are of two basic types: perennial species, which belong to the genus *Aster* and are popularly known as Michaelmas daisies, and annual China asters, which are members of the genus *Callistephus*. Both kinds make excellent garden flowers and cut flowers. Although both types of asters come into bloom in summer, the perennials are most valuable in autumn gardens, and their culture is discussed in chapter 8. Here we will concentrate on China asters for summer gardens.

The annual China aster, *Callistephus chinensis*, is a dependable garden flower that is terrific for cutting as well. Native to China and Japan, the China aster is available in a range of cultivars growing from 9 inches to 2 feet high. Flowers come in white, purple, blue-violet, and various shades of pink and rosy red.

China asters can be classified into several groups according to their flower structure. There are flat, single, daisy-like flowers; incurved types that have more rays (petals) than single flowers, with the rays curved toward the center of the flower; reflexed blossoms, in which the tips curve outward; and quilled flowers, in which the rays are tubular. From these four primary types, hundreds of varieties have been developed, with varying plant heights, growing habits, seasons of bloom, and flower colors.

The dwarf varieties are perfect for edgings, for the front of the border, and for growing in containers on a sunny porch or patio.

Treat China asters as tender annuals, starting seeds indoors about six weeks before your last expected spring frost or direct-seeding outdoors after frost danger has passed. China asters thrive in rich, well-drained soil in full sun. They need to be watered during dry spells. The only caution is to not plant them where other asters grew last year, to prevent the development of diseases to which asters are prone.

## Campanula / Bellflower

Known for their bell-shaped flowers, campanulas come in a large assortment of annual and perennial forms. There are tall, upright species for beds and borders, diminutive forms best suited to rock gardens, and trailing species perfect for hanging baskets. Campanulas bloom in summer, with flowers in various shades of violet-blue or white. They are generally easy to grow in ordinary garden soil; most of them like full sun. Many species are known and loved by gardeners, and several of them are described below.

Carpathian harebell, *Campanula carpatica*, grows in tufts 6 to 10 inches high and produces loads of violet-blue flowers beginning in midsummer. It is a good edging plant for perennial borders and rock gardens and is hardy throughout the United States. Both blue- and white-flowered varieties are available, including Alba (white), Jingle Bells (white, light blue, lilac, and deep blue), Wedgewood Blue, and Wedgewood White.

Clustered bellflower, *C. glomerata*, is a 2-foot-tall, upright species with rich violet-blue flowers in clusters atop the stems. Its major flush of bloom occurs in mid-summer, but it will continue to produce flowers into late summer. This is a useful plant for the perennial border, and both blue- and white-flowered varieties are available. The species is hardy throughout the country.

Italian bellflower, *C. isophylla*, is a trailer that is lovely in hanging baskets indoors or on a sunny porch or patio. The plant is perennial in warm climates but tender in the northern half of the country, where winter temperatures go below 10°F. Both pale blue-

and white-flowered forms are available. One cultivar, Kristal Mixed, is supposed to bloom in summer from seed sown indoors the preceding February.

The milky bellflower, *C. lactiflora*, is a sturdy 3 to 4 feet tall, with large panicles of medium blue or pale white flowers from mid- to late summer. The plant is easy to grow and will tolerate partial shade, although it prefers full sun. This species usually needs staking.

Canterbury bells, *C. medium*, is a very popular biennial that is grown as a hardy annual. Plants are 2 to 4 feet high, with loose spikes of cup-shaped flowers in early summer. Flowers are typically blue, but white, mauve, and pink forms have also been developed.

Canterbury bells does best in cool weather and can be sown outdoors in fall and protected with mulch over the winter for bloom the following year. One variety, *calycanthema*, is called cup-and-saucer because its unusually shaped flowers resemble a cup with a saucer attached.

The peach-leaved bellflower or peach bells, *C. persicifolia*, is another widely grown campanula well suited to the middle of beds and borders. It is a perennial, hardy throughout the United States, and grows 2 to 3 feet tall. The plants form upright leafy clumps, with one or a few flowers on each stalk. Picking off faded flowers will prolong the blooming season. A number of cultivars are available, including Alba and Grandiflora Alba, with white flowers, and Telham Beauty, with large blossoms of lavender-blue.

## Coreopsis / Tickseed

The yellow daisylike flowers of coreopsis are a mainstay of the summer flower garden. The plants are easy to grow and bloom abundantly all summer long. There are both perennial species and annuals, which are sometimes called calliopsis. The perennials are more widely grown and are hardy throughout the United States. Perennials and annuals alike hold up well in hot weather.

Coreopsis grows in practically any garden soil. All it asks is full sun. The plants are seldom bothered by pests and diseases, and the flowers are excellent for cutting, lasting a long time in the vase. Various kinds grow from 1 to 3 feet tall and make attractive additions to the front or middle of the flower garden. Picking off spent flowers will keep the plants producing plenty of new ones.

Plant coreopsis in spring, 15 to 18 inches apart. You can propagate new plants by dividing established clumps in spring or fall.

*Coreopsis grandiflora* is a perennial growing 2 feet high. The flowers are about 2½ inches across, and the petals are often notched. This species is native to the southern part of the country and is a good plant for warm-climate gardens.

*C. lanceolata* is an eastern native growing up to 2 feet high, with long-stemmed yellow flowers.

Golden coreopsis, *C. tinctoria*, is an annual growing 2 to 3 feet tall. The yellow-petaled flowers have reddish brown centers and appear from midsummer until the middle of autumn. This species blooms best when the plants are crowded.

Thread-leaf coreopsis, *C. verticillata*, has finely divided, threadlike leaves and masses of yellow flowers. The plants grow up to 3 feet high. Several fine cultivars are available. Grandiflora grows 2 feet high and bears golden yellow flowers. With its fine-textured foliage, this variety makes a good companion for bolder-leaved plants such as gaillardia and summer phlox. Moonbeam is probably the most versatile of all coreopsis cultivars in mixed flower gardens. Its unusual pale yellow flowers harmonize beautifully with many different colors, especially blues, violets, and purples. The plants grow 2 feet tall.

## Dahlia

Members of this genus of tender tuberous plants native to Mexico and Central America have been extensively bred into thousands of flamboyant, large-flowered varieties. The flowers resemble chrysanthemums, and they come in a wide range of warm colors, flower forms, and sizes. Flower forms are classified as single, mignon, anemone, collarette, duplex, peony, incurved cactus, recurved and straight cactus, semicactus, formal decorative, informal decorative, ball, miniature, and pompon. Some of these are grown primarily by specialists and collectors, but there are many fine dahlias for general gardeners, and some of them are described below.

Dahlias flourish in loose, rich, loamy soil with excellent drainage. They like lots of moisture after they flower, but the plants do not like soggy soil. They need at least six hours of sun a day to produce the best flowers. Prepare the bed for dahlias by digging in a 1-inch layer of compost or manure the autumn before planting. In spring till the soil again and incorporate some bonemeal, superphosphate and wood ashes, or an all-purpose fertilizer such as 5-10-5. Scratch a handful of fertilizer into the soil around each plant about the middle of August to give the flowers a boost.

In the far North, plant out dahlia tubers as soon as the danger of frost is past, or start them indoors in pots to get earlier flowers. In warm climates dahlias can be planted out in early spring. Elsewhere, set them out in late spring, around the end of May or beginning of June. Space the tubers 2 to 3 feet apart. All but the dwarf varieties will need staking, and it is best to set the stakes in place before planting, to avoid damaging the tuberous roots.

Plant the tubers 4 to 6 inches deep, depending on the eventual size of the plants. Lay the root horizontally in the hole, with the eye, or growing point, facing upward and toward the stake. Cover the tuber with 2 to 3 inches of soil at planting, leaving a depression in the soil. As the shoots grow, gradually fill in around them with more soil, until just a very shallow depression is left (it will hold water for the plant).

Allow only the one or two strongest shoots to develop on each plant—cut back the rest at ground level. Cultivate lightly once a week to keep the soil well aerated until the end of summer. By that time the plants will have developed a lot of shallow feeder roots that will be damaged if you continue to cultivate. A late summer mulch of compost will help to hold moisture for the plants as they bloom. While the plants are flowering, give them a good soaking once a week.

Dahlias bloom in temperate climates in late summer and well into autumn. In many gardens they put on their finest show in September.

In autumn when a heavy frost has blackened the plants, cut back the stems to 4 inches above ground level. Dig up the clumps of tubers and store them indoors over winter as described in chapter 9.

Divide the clumps before replanting in spring. Cut apart the tubers with a sharp knife, making sure each division has one healthy-looking eye. You will find the eyes, or buds, near the crown of the plant, where the stem joins the roots. Medium-size tubers are usually best for replanting. Cut off the lower half of large tubers and just plant the upper portion. Cut back any long sprouts to about one-quarter inch before planting.

Here is a listing of some of the many dahlia cultivars:

Anemone-flowered dahlias have a single row of rayed petals surrounding a large pincushionlike center that is actually made up of tubular petals. They grow from 2½ to 3½ feet high, with flowers 3 to 8 inches across.

Cactus dahlias have large single or double flowers with rolled petals. The petals may be straight, incurved (turning upward and in toward the center of the flower), or recurved. Most grow 2 to 3½ feet high, with flowers up to 6 inches across.

Decorative dahlias have fully double flowers with broad, flat petals either curved back in a regular arrangement or long and twisted or pointed in an irregular pattern. They grow 2 to 3½ feet in height, with flowers up to 6 inches across.

Miniatures have flowers no more than 4 inches across. Pompons have ball-like little flowers only 2 inches across.

## Delphinium

Delphiniums, also called larkspurs, are highlights of the summer flower garden for two reasons: the glorious shades of blue in which their flowers bloom and the sheer size of their flower spikes—at 6 or 7 feet they tower over most other perennials. Almost every gardener who sees delphiniums in their full glory wants to grow them, but there's a catch: they are hard to grow, and you have to be able to meet their demands in order to succeed. But the rewards justify the effort—delphiniums are truly splendid.

The first thing you need to know is that delphiniums do not take kindly to hot climates. They are native to cool, temperate parts of Europe and Asia, and they do not generally grow well in hot soils. On the other hand, where it's too cold the plants are not reliably

hardy. If you live in the North, you may have to treat them as hardy annuals. The second important factor to recognize if you want to succeed with delphiniums is that they must have extremely rich soil that is loose to a depth of at least 2 feet. If your soil is of average fertility, and especially if it is very sandy and light, you will have better luck if you build up the soil with organic matter for a year or two before attempting these finicky plants.

To prepare the garden for delphiniums, put down a 2-inch layer of compost or well-rotted manure two seasons before you expect to plant (autumn if you will plant the following spring; spring if you want to plant in fall), and dig it into the soil. A month or two before planting, spread an all-purpose fertilizer over the bed (5-10-5 can be applied at a rate of one pound per one hundred square feet of bed), then put another 2 inches of compost or manure on top of that and till it into the soil. Some gardeners prefer to incorporate all the organic matter and fertilizer two seasons before planting and let the prepared bed mellow before planting time so it has a chance to break down and begin releasing its nutrients into the soil. If you do not have access to compost or manure, you can substitute peat moss, but be very careful to see that it is thoroughly moist before you plant. Moisture is another requirement of delphiniums. When the plants are established, topdress the bed with organic matter every year, and fertilize the plants generously.

Choose a site in full sun and protected from wind. The tall, heavy flower spikes are likely to break in strong wind or heavy rain. Stake the plants to avoid trouble. Pick a place that is far away from tree roots— delphiniums will succumb to their competition.

Space the plants 2 to 2½ feet apart when planting. Putting a handful of compost in the bottom of each planting hole is not a bad idea. Position the plants with the crowns 2 inches below the soil surface. After setting the plants, firm the soil around them. If your soil is heavy, dig the planting holes deeper and put a layer of gravel in the very bottom to improve drainage.

When the plants begin to grow, scratch an additional handful of fertilizer into the soil around each one. Water them regularly, irrigating the soil rather than sprinkling from overhead because the crowns are prone to rot. Stake the plants when the spikes grow tall, before the buds open. As the season progresses, keep an eye out for black spot on the leaves, another delphinium nemesis. At the first sign of black spot, spray the plants immediately with a fungicide.

After the first year you will need to thin the flower stems. Each plant will send up lots of them, but it can only support four or five. Wait until the shoots are several inches tall, then save only the strongest, sturdiest ones. Cut off the others at ground level.

Given this kind of painstaking care, your delphiniums should reward you with stately spires of the showiest flowers imaginable.

Most delphiniums available today are hybrids, but there are also cultivars of an annuals species on the market.

Chinese delphinium (sometimes sold as *Delphinium chinense*) is the shortest of the perennial types, growing just 1½ to 2 feet high. The flowers are generally a rich deep blue, similar to that of gentians. The Chinese delphinium blooms in early to mid-summer. Although it is a perennial, it is better treated as a biennial in most places. It makes a long-lasting cut flower.

The Blackmore and Langdon strain is a series of hybrids developed in England. Colors range from deep violet and blue to pale blue and pure white. The plants are vigorous, and

they are reliably hardy to zone 5, where winter temperatures do not drop below −20°F. There are also dwarf forms available.

Giant Pacific Hybrids, also known as the Round Table series, are the most popular among American gardeners. The flowers are large, and so are the plants—giants indeed, they grow to 7 feet tall. If you cut off the flowers as soon as they fade, the plants usually bloom again (although the spikes are only half as big) in fall.

Connecticut Yankee is a dwarf strain, growing about 2½ feet high. It blooms in a range of blue shades and has a bushy habit.

The garland larkspur, *D. belladonna*, is less imposing than the hybrids, but it is sturdier and easier to grow. It reaches a height of 3 to 4 feet and will produce more flowers if you keep the spent ones cut. The species has light blue flowers. The cultivar Bellamosa has deep blue flowers, and Casa Blanca has white ones.

The annual or rocket larkspur, *D. ajacis*, is a lovely cut flower and can be dried as well. It grows about 4 feet tall and produces flowers in shades of blue, pink, and white in mid- to late summer. The plant is a hardy annual and grows best in cool weather.

## Gladiolus

The gladiolus has been with us for a long time—as far back as A.D. 200. Dioscorides described the flowers, which were known then as corn lilies. Today there are so many hybrids that it's difficult, if not impossible, to trace the parentage of many of our contemporary varieties. The bold, brightly colored flower spikes are a familiar summertime sight in backyards, flower stands, and farmer's markets.

Gladiolus is a fairly demanding plant. It needs deep, loose, rich soil to grow well. To ensure high fertility,

incorporate plenty of organic matter into the bed and put some bonemeal and all-purpose fertilizer in the bottom of the planting holes or trenches (dig a couple of inches deeper than the necessary planting depth to allow for this).

The plants grow from tender corms that are planted in spring, dug up in fall, and stored indoors over winter. For a succession of bloom, plant your gladiolus in batches two weeks apart from early spring after the last frost until midsummer. The plants will flower from midsummer until early fall. Planting depth depends on the size of the corms: plant corms larger than 1 inch across 6 to 8 inches deep; medium-size corms (½ to 1 inch) 4 to 5 inches deep; and smaller corms 3 inches deep. Set the corms about 6 inches apart.

Gladiolus spikes grow quite tall and often need staking. There are also some smaller-growing miniature varieties on the market.

As the plants grow, it is important to keep the bed watered. When the flower spike appears make sure the plants get plenty of water. During dry weather you will need to water deeply every two or three days.

When you cut glads to bring indoors, cut the spikes when the first flower opens. Condition the flowers for twenty-four hours before arranging them, as described in chapter 4. When you cut the flowers, remember to leave at least five leaves on the plant to nourish the corm.

At the end of the growing season, you can start lifting the corms a month to six weeks after the plants have finished blooming. Unlike spring bulbs, gladiolus corms can be dug before the leaves die. Although the corms are frost-tender, warm-climate gardeners must lift them, too, to allow them a dormant rest period in winter. As soon as you dig the corms, cut off the leaves to the top of the corm. Destroy the old foliage—it can harbor pests and diseases to which glads are prone. Spread the corms in an open container to dry, and separate the smaller offsets when you can pull them off easily. Store them over winter in a cool, dry, well-ventilated place. If you live in a warm climate, place the corms in cold storage to make sure they enter dormancy.

The color range of today's gladiolus hybrids includes practically every warm color imaginable, plus various shades of lavender, an unusual lime green, and white.

Burpee offers the Summer Days series, a group of large, showy-flowered varieties.

Standard-size and miniature hybrids are also available in mixed colors.

## Hemerocallis / Daylily

Daylilies are one of the best garden flowers around because they are incredibly easy to grow, come in a huge (and ever-expanding) range of colors, and require practically no care. How could any gardener go wrong with such a plant?

The tawny daylily (*Hemerocallis fulva*) is a familiar wildflower in the eastern United States. Its rusty orange flowers can be seen along roadsides all over this part of the country in summer. The garden daylilies are just as undemanding in their cultural needs. Daylilies grow vigorously in any soil that's damper than a desert and drier than a swamp. They'll make themselves at home in any ordinary garden soil. Daylilies bloom in either full sun or partial shade, although they will bend toward the light if you put them in a shady spot. Flowers in pastel shades hold their color better in partial shade, though; full sun tends to bleach them. Daylilies are seldom bothered by pests and diseases and don't even need to be watered except during a severe drought.

Plant your daylilies in clumps in the flower garden or at the back of the border. They are particularly handsome massed in front of a fence or beside a driveway.

Daylilies are tuberous plants that spread rapidly and are easily propagated by division. The plants don't need dividing very often, but when after several years you notice that the plants are very crowded and not producing as many flowers as they used to, division is in order. Dig up the clumps with a spading fork in late summer or early fall, when the plants are finished blooming. Shake off the loose soil and cut apart the clumps. Replant the outer portions, leaving about three tubers in each division, and throw out the old central parts. Replant the divisions in loose soil to which you have added some compost, leaf mold, or aged manure.

A bonus with daylilies is that their long, narrow leaves are attractive all season. As plantings become established over a couple of years, the leaves grow so thick that they shade the ground, eliminating most weeds.

There are far too many daylilies to even attempt a comprehensive listing here. Individual plants bloom for a few weeks, but if you plant early, midseason, and late varieties, you can have daylilies blooming in your garden through most of the summer.

## Impatiens

The colorful, free-blooming impatiens is currently the most widely grown flower in American gardens. Its mounds of pink, red, and white flowers light up shady beds and borders all across the country. The plant is grown as an annual and is easy to start from seeds or cuttings. Garden centers also sell started plants in a wide selection of colors. Breeding has given us impatiens in practically every imaginable

shade of pink, along with reds, oranges, violets, and whites.

The hybrids we grow today come in two basic forms: the low-growing bedding type, which bears individual flowers, and the balsam type, which grows taller and carries its flowers in clusters in the axils of the leaves. A third type, the New Guinea impatiens, has orange flowers and variegated leaves, but it is not as popular as the other two forms.

The versatility of impatiens, along with its ease of culture, is probably the reason for its popularity. You can grow impatiens in the front of shady gardens, around the base of a tree, along a sidewalk or driveway, next to a fence—the options are practically unlimited. In addition, impatiens is wonderful in pots, hanging baskets, and windowboxes, by itself or combined with other plants. Cuttings taken late in summer and rooted indoors will provide you with winter flowers in the house.

Although best known as a shade-loving plant, impatiens also grows well in sunny places, as long as you give it plenty of water. The plants are not particular about soil and do just fine in any average garden soil that is moist but well drained. The balsam types do best with more sun and richer soil than the more common bedding types. Both kinds of impatiens are tender, but if planted out after the danger of frost is past in spring, they will bloom until the first fall frost wipes them out. Pick off as many of the spent blossoms as you can throughout the season to keep the plants flowering. If blooming slows down markedly in midsummer, shearing back the plants will encourage a new flush of flowers.

If you plan to grow impatiens from seed for summer flowers, start the seeds four to six weeks before you expect your last spring frost.

The bedding types of impatiens, which have been bred primarily from

*Impatiens.*

the species *Impatiens sultani*, grow from 4 to 12 inches high, depending on the variety and cultural conditions.

## *Lilium* / *Lily*

Lilies have traditionally been considered hard to grow, but today's hybrids are sturdier than their predecessors and bloom beautifully if you give them the growing conditions they prefer. Chief among their needs is light, loamy soil with absolutely perfect drainage. Lilies cannot tolerate moisture standing around the bulbs. They also do not like hot soil; either mulch them or overplant them with annuals or ground covers to shade the roots and help keep the soil cool. Most lilies grow best in not-quite-full sun. A spot where the plants get filtered sun for most of the day is ideal. Full sun bleaches out the colors of some lily flowers.

Most lily bulbs are planted in fall, but some of the late-blooming types can be planted in spring. Plant the bulbs three times as deep as the bulbs are tall. Planting depth is usually from 4 to 8 inches. The plants are heavy feeders and benefit from one to two applications of an all-purpose fertilizer in spring. During dry weather, water the plants once a week until they bloom. After they finish flowering, the plants like drier conditions. Many lilies grow tall—6 feet or even taller—and need to be staked. In fact, it is a good idea to stake all cultivars that get taller than 3 feet. The stakes need to be far enough away from the plants that they don't touch the bulbs and should be put in place just before the first flowers open. Tie the plants loosely to the stakes so the stems will not be damaged.

Every few years, when the plants become crowded, you will need to lift and divide the bulbs. After the plants have finished blooming and the foliage has died back in fall, carefully dig up the clumps, leaving as many of the roots intact as you can. Very gently separate the bulbs, and replant them immediately. Keep the bulbs out of the soil for only the briefest-possible time so they do not dry out.

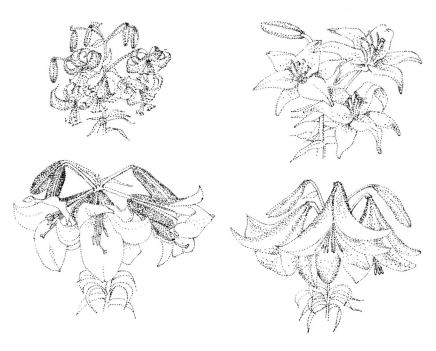

The classification of lilies is extremely complicated. Both species and hybrids are available for home gardeners. There are Asiatic Hybrids, Aurelian Hybrids, martagons, trumpets, and many more. Instead of attempting to group lilies by their respective flower types, it is easier for gardeners to consider them in terms of their flowering time—early, mid-, or late summer. Many nursery catalogs list them this way, too. There are far too many hybrid lilies to attempt a listing here—consult the catalogs of some reliable suppliers to see what's available.

Species lilies for early summer include the coral lily, *Lilium pumilum* (reflexed flowers of coral red, 18 to 20 inches tall), and the turk's cap lily, *L. martagon* (reflexed flowers of wine red or pinkish purple, 3 to 4 feet tall).

Midsummer species lilies include the gold band lily, *L. auratum* (white flowers with a central yellow stripe and spotted with gold, red, and maroon), several cultivars of *L. henryi* (reflexed flowers, light orange, 6 feet high), the Madonna lily, *L. candidum* (pure white fragrant flowers), and *L. superbum*, or swamp lily (reflexed flowers in yellow-orange to red-orange, varying in height from 3 to 7 feet).

Species blooming late in the season include *L. speciosum* cultivars such as Album Novum (white with a green stripe), Cinderella (blush pink shading to white, 4 to 5 feet tall), Everest (white, fragrant, 5 feet high), Magnificum (deep ruby red with white edges), and Rubrum (recurved crimson-and-white flowers, 5 feet high). Tiger lilies, *L. tigrinum*, also bloom in late summer. The familiar spotted orange flowers have been joined by cultivars in red, salmon-pink, and white, as a result of breeding work.

## Pelargonium / Geranium

Our common garden geraniums—zonal geraniums, ivy geraniums, and Martha Washington (or regal) geraniums—belong to the genus *Pelargonium* (which is the name English gardeners use). They are tender perennials native to South Africa, and we grow the plants as annuals. Geraniums are handsome in summer gardens, especially in containers, and cuttings taken late in the season will give you flowers indoors in winter if you grow them on a sunny but cool windowsill or under fluorescent lights.

Zonal geraniums (*Pelargonium ×hortorum*) are the most widely grown, although they are no longer as popular as they were a generation ago. The plants have round, medium green leaves with scalloped and slightly fluted edges, sometimes marked with a dark band. They are excellent plants for tubs or pots on patios and rooftops and for the back of a windowbox. Zonal geraniums bloom in assorted shades of red, pink, orange, and white from early summer well into autumn. They thrive in any ordinary garden soil, as long as it is not too rich in nitrogen, which causes the plants to produce too many leaves and too few flowers. Geraniums like lots of sun, although they can tolerate a little shade. They do not like wet feet.

Temperate-climate gardeners can start plants from seed indoors or in a cold frame ten to twelve weeks before the last heavy frost is likely in spring. Transplant them outdoors after the danger of heavy frost is past, spacing the plants a foot apart.

Gardeners in warm climates can grow zonal geraniums outdoors all year and can sow seeds in either spring or fall. The rest of us should take cuttings in late summer to root for indoor flowers later on. Take cuttings 3 to 5 inches long from young, sturdy shoots. Root them in a mixture of two parts potting soil, one part sand, and one part vermiculite. Transplant to individual pots when new leaves start to appear, a sign that roots have formed. Although the plants are tender, they grow best indoors in winter, where temperatures are cool—50° to 60°F. Give them as much light as you can and plenty of air circulation. Water them sparingly, though, or the stems may rot.

Martha Washington, or regal, geraniums (P. ×domesticum) have dark green leaves that are slightly toothed instead of scalloped. Their flowers are the largest of all geraniums, in pink, red, or white. Most of the flowers have interesting dark blotches on the upper petals. Martha Washington geraniums are not as tough as the zonals, and they are most often grown indoors on sunny windowsills or in cool greenhouses. They do make lovely container plants for partly shaded patios or porches.

The ivy geranium (P. peltatum) has trailing stems that make it perfect for growing in hanging baskets and windowboxes. As its name suggests, this plant's leaves resemble those of English ivy. The flower clusters are looser than those of other geraniums, and the overall plant has an airy, gracefully cascading look. The flowers come in shades of burgundy, red, rose, pink, lavender, and white.

## Petunia

Another tremendously popular summer annual, petunias are seen everywhere in flower beds, pots, and windowboxes. The color range is concentrated in reds, purples, pinks, and whites, but there are many shades of these colors, along with some unusual colors, such as yellow. There are also many bicolored petunias, striped or edged or ruffled with white, but be aware that they are harder to work into color schemes in mixed gardens than single-colored flowers. The basic petunia flower is funnel-shaped, but breed-

ers have given us frilled, ruffled, wavy, and doubled flowers in larger and larger sizes. There are upright petunias and cascading varieties bred for hanging baskets and windowboxes.

Petunias are widely available in garden centers and are also fairly easy to grow from seeds. In either case, do not put the plants out in the garden until all danger of frost is past and the weather is warm. Petunias cannot tolerate the cold.

Start seeds indoors six to ten weeks before you expect the last spring frost. Keep the growing medium moist and give the seedlings plenty of light on a sunny windowsill or under fluorescent fixtures.

In the garden, petunias bloom happily all summer in any average garden soil, as long as they get full sun. Pick off faded flowers to keep the plants flowering lavishly. Petunias may self-sow, but the new generation of plants will not look like its hybrid parent. Pull up any volunteer seedlings and start

with new seeds or plants each year.

Petunias come in three basic forms: grandiflora types have the biggest flowers, 3 or more inches across, in a number of forms; multifloras have smaller flowers, usually single, and bloom their hearts out all season; cascading petunias have tumbling stems that spill over the edges of windowboxes and hanging baskets. Most petunias (except for the cascading types) grow 10 to 15 inches tall.

## Phlox

Summer-blooming phlox plays a starring role in flower gardens all over the country, although it does not grow well for everyone. There are both annual and perennial species, although the perennial garden phlox, *Phlox paniculata*, with its big, showy flower heads, is the favorite.

Summer phloxes need full sun, rich, loamy soil, and lots of moisture. They bloom lavishly and for a long

*Red Flair petunias.*

time, and many cultivars are available in shades of pink, purple, and white. The plants are hardy to −20° or −30°F. Their weakness is that they are prone to attack by mold and mildew in hot, humid weather. To help prevent this, space plants far enough apart to allow air to circulate between them, and water the plants at ground level rather than sprinkling the leaves from overhead. Another helpful measure is to thin the plants. Perennial phloxes send up numerous shoots; allowing just three or four to remain on each plant will promote good air circulation, strong growth, and large, abundant flowers. You can propagate new plants from cuttings taken from the tips of new shoots in late summer.

Lift and divide perennial phlox about every three years, when the plants finish blooming, to maintain the vigor of the plants. Cut off the flower clusters as the blossoms fade to keep the plants blooming longer. The plants are heavy feeders and appreciate an annual topdressing of compost or well-rotted manure. Scratch some all-purpose fertilizer into the soil around the plants when they start growing in spring.

Perennial garden phlox grows from 2 to 4 feet high, depending on the variety. Use taller cultivars in the back of the garden and shorter ones in the middle. The flowers are fragrant and good for cutting. Space the plants 1½ to 3 feet apart.

Cultivars bloom from midsummer to early fall. One perennial species, Carolina phlox (*P. carolina*), grows 3 feet high and blooms in early to midsummer in shades of purple, rose, and white. These plants are less prone to mildew than the garden phlox varieties. The best-known cultivar is the white-flowered Miss Lingard.

Annual phlox, *P. drummondii*, grows up to 1½ feet tall and blooms all summer, sometimes starting in late spring. It mixes nicely with other annuals in summer gardens, especially sweet alyssum, ageratum, and petunias in harmonious shades. The dwarf cultivars make good container or window-box plants. Annual phlox blooms in shades of red, rose, pink, lavender-blue, and white.

## *Rosa* / *Rose*

Roses have always symbolized romance, and their beautifully colored, enchantingly fragrant flowers have been grown for more than two thousand years. Today the rose is our national flower and a favorite with gardeners everywhere. Few yards are without at least one rosebush, and many gardeners grow entire beds and gardens of them, despite the meticulous care they require in order to grow well.

There are many ways to use roses in the landscape. You can plant them in formal beds by themselves, in borders along property lines, fences, sidewalks, and driveways, in mixed informal gardens with shrubs or perennials and annuals, in doorstep or foundation plantings in front of the house, on a trellis by the back door, trained over an arbor or gazebo, or in pots on the patio.

There are thousands of rose varieties in existence today, with new ones being introduced all the time. They can be classified into four broad categories: bush roses, climbers, shrub roses, and tree roses.

Bush roses include hybrid teas, floribundas, grandifloras, polyanthas, miniatures, and old-fashioned or heirloom varieties. Bush roses can be anywhere from 6 inches to 6 feet tall, and they produce most of their flowers on the tops of the plants. Hybrid tea roses, the most widely grown kind, grow 3 or more feet tall and have long, slender buds that open into large, long-stemmed flowers. Floribundas grow 2 to 3 feet high and bear their flowers in

Phlox drummondii, *annual phlox.*

clusters throughout the summer. Grandifloras are a cross between hybrid teas and floribundas and combine the features of both. They grow tall—5 or 6 feet—and produce clusters of large flowers all summer. Miniatures bear small flowers on small plants that seldom grow taller than 2 feet. They are nice in very small gardens and in containers. Heirloom, or heritage, roses are all varieties that were developed before the first hybrid tea rose was introduced in 1867. They encompass a wide range of flower and plant forms and include most of the highly fragrant roses beloved of perfumers—damask and musk roses, for example.

Climbing roses have long canes that are fastened to trellises, arbors, fences, and other supports. Large-flowered climbing roses bloom repeatedly or continuously through summer and even into early fall. Rambler roses have longer, thinner canes and smaller flowers and bloom only once in late spring or early summer.

Shrub roses have an upright growth habit, and their canes arch gracefully. They can be trained as hedges or massed in groups. Shrub roses grow between 4 and 12 feet tall and bear flowers in a variety of forms and colors. Some of them bloom all season, and others bloom only once in spring.

Tree roses have been grafted onto straight woody stems of varying heights and are grown as standards. They are the most demanding and least hardy of all roses.

Nurseries sell roses either in dormant and bare-rooted form or in containers. Bare-root roses are usually packaged in special plastic bags with their roots wrapped to keep them moist or in cardboard boxes that are theoretically (but not always actually) biodegradable and meant to be planted right along with the plants.

Bare-root roses are planted while the plants are still dormant. Temperate-climate gardeners plant them in early spring, when the soil can be worked and no more heavy freezes are expected. Warm-climate gardeners plant bare-root roses in fall.

Container-grown roses can be planted anytime during the growing season. They are more convenient, but they are also more expensive, and not as broad a selection is available as with bare-root roses.

Whatever types of roses you buy, inspect them carefully when they arrive from the mail-order nursery or before you take them home from the garden center. The canes should be firm, smooth, and green or reddish in color. The best-quality plants have at least three sturdy canes that are about 3/8 inch in diameter.

Plant roses where they will get at least four hours of sun a day, preferably in the morning. Good air circulation is essential, for roses are subject to fungus diseases. They need deep, well-drained, loamy soil that contains substantial amounts of organic matter. Keep roses away from vigorous-rooted

*A hybrid tea rose, Touch of Class.*

*A popular shrub rose, Bonica.*

trees and shrubs that would compete with them for water and nutrients.

Dig the planting holes 15 to 18 inches deep and just as wide, and put a few shovelfuls of compost, peat moss, or leaf mold in the bottom and mix it into the soil. The soil in the bottom of the planting hole should be nice and loose. Form the soil into a mound in the bottom of the hole.

Soak bare-root roses in a bucket of muddy water for four hours or so before you plant them. Cut any damaged or broken canes, or canes smaller than the thickness of a pencil, from the bush. Set the plant on top of the soil mound and position it so the graft union (recognizable as a swelling near the base of the stem) will be at the correct height. In temperate climates, the graft union should be a couple of inches below the soil surface; in warm climates, the graft union should be just above the soil surface. Set the plant on the soil mound and spread the roots down over the sides of the mound.

Fill in around the roots with soil until the hole is half-filled. Firm the soil around the roots with your hands, then fill the hole with water. This will help eliminate air pockets and ensure that the roots make good contact with the soil. When the water drains off, fill the hole the rest of the way with soil and tamp it down.

Cut back all the canes to 8 inches, just above an outward-facing bud, at a 45-degree angle. Then mound up soil around the plant about 6 inches high, to help the plant adjust to its new conditions. When the plant begins to send out new growth in a week or so, gradually remove the soil mound.

In subsequent years you should feed the plants right after you prune them in early spring, spreading a handful of 5-10-5 or other all-purpose fertilizer in a ring around the plant. Feed the plants again when they have set buds and a third time a couple of months before the first fall frost. Use an all-purpose fertilizer for the first two feedings and a low-nitrogen formula for the third.

Whether or not to mulch roses over the summer is a somewhat debatable issue. In hot climates, mulch is probably necessary to hold moisture and shade the roots. In the North, mulch may serve as a hiding place for pests and may actually do more harm than good. At any rate, roses need regular watering. Unless you have gotten an inch of rain during the week, water your roses thoroughly once a week.

Roses are subject to aphids, spider mites, Japanese beetles, and several fungal diseases. If you notice any of these problems, treat them at once with natural controls or chemical sprays as you prefer.

Roses need to be pruned severely in early spring just as the buds begin to swell. During the growing season, prune off any diseased foliage or damaged canes, and cut off faded flowers just above the uppermost five-part leaf. If you discover any suckers growing from the rootstock, cut them off at ground level.

Climbers, old-fashioned roses, and other kinds that bloom on wood formed from the previous year's growth should receive their major pruning as soon as the plants are finished blooming.

Winter protection for roses in cold climates is described in chapter 9.

## Salvia / Sage

There are annual, biennial, and perennial sages grown for their flowers. Members of the mint family, salvias have aromatic leaves; one of them is the sage familiar to herb gardeners and cooks. They are easy to grow, and their spikes of flowers enliven the garden in summer and early fall, in strong colors of the most flaming scarlet and shades of deep blue and violet. Plant them in beds and borders, in pots on the patio, and dwarf types in windowboxes.

Salvias all need lots of sun and light, and well-drained soil. Most of them tolerate some dryness.

Annual salvias grow quickly from seeds sown indoors about eight weeks before the last expected spring frost. Set the plants out in the garden after all danger of frost is past. Salvias grow best in warm soil.

Perennials thrive in any good garden soil, and their spikes of blue-and-purple flowers are welcome additions to summer flower gardens and cut flower arrangements. New plants are easily propagated from cuttings or divisions. Take cuttings in early fall or early spring. Crowded plants can be dug and divided in early fall or early to mid-spring. Water perennial salvias during dry weather. Plant them 1 to 2 feet apart.

Several of the best salvias for flower gardens are described below.

Azure sage, *Salvia azurea*, is a perennial that grows about 4 feet high and has azure-blue flowers. It is hardy to about −10°F.

Mealycup sage, *S. farinacea*, is another blue-flowered perennial, with flowers of deep violet-blue. This species is not frost-hardy, and in all but the warmest climates it is grown as an annual. The plants grow to a height of 3 feet. The cultivar Victoria has flowers of intense violet-blue on compact plants. It makes an excellent cut flower and dries well, too.

*S. haematodes* is a biennial growing 2 to 3 feet high with violet-blue flowers carried above a basal rosette of leaves. It blooms all summer. The cultivar Indigo has vibrant blue flowers in early summer; if you cut them off when they fade, the plants will bloom again in fall.

Violet sage, *S. nemorosa* or *S. superba*, is a vigorous 3-foot-tall perennial with long spikes of violet-purple flowers. The plants are hardy to −10°F, will bloom in partial shade and need little care. Cultivars include May Night (indigo-blue flowers with purple bracts on 1½-foot plants), East Friesland (a classic, with intense violet-blue flowers on 1½-foot plants, good for cutting), and Blue Queen (short spikes of deep violet-blue flowers on 1½- to 2-foot plants in late spring and early summer; the plants will keep blooming until late summer if you keep faded flowers cut off).

Scarlet sage, *S. splendens*, has become almost ubiquitous in annual flower beds in backyards and public parks all across the country. The brilliant scarlet flowers are of an intensity of hue that can be difficult to combine with other colors in the garden. It is very flashy. Still, this kind of sage is extremely popular, and some new colors have been introduced. The plants flower all summer long until cut down by frost.

## *Tagetes* / *Marigold*

This genus includes the very popular African and French marigolds, but they are from neither Africa nor France. The plants are native to Mexico and South America. Marigolds are tender annuals, appreciated for their cheerful yellow, orange, and mahogany flowers.

Marigolds are easy to grow, asking only full sun and well-drained soil of average fertility. You can start plants from seed indoors in late winter or buy plants at a garden center in spring. Marigolds thrive in hot weather; don't plant them out in the garden until all danger of frost is past.

The two types of marigolds are easy to tell apart by their size: African marigolds grow taller and have larger flowers than French marigolds.

African marigolds (*Tagetes erecta*) grow 1½ to 2 feet high and have yellow or orange flowers 2 to 4 inches across. The hybrids and cultivars on the market today are usually called American marigolds.

French marigolds are ideal for windowboxes, the front of the garden, in beds, or in edgings along sidewalks and driveways.

## *Veronica* / *Speedwell*

Veronicas are handsome, easy-to-grow, hardy perennials with a multiplicity of uses in flower gardens. The taller-growing kinds, with their spikes of little blue, purple, pink, red, or white flowers, are excellent in the middle of flower beds and borders, and the low-growing types work well in the front of the garden, in rock gardens, and as edging plants.

If you grow several different cultivars, you can have veronicas in bloom all summer long. But even when the plants are not flowering, their compact mounds of emerald green leaves are attractive in the garden.

Veronicas need full sun and appreciate a decently fertile, moist, but well-drained soil, although they will grow in most average soils. The plants tolerate both heat and drought, but they are not always entirely hardy in very cold winters. If you live in the far North, you might want to dig up the plants in fall and put them in a cold frame over winter, just to be safe.

The plants are not grown from seed; order plants from a nursery for spring planting. You can propagate new plants by lifting and dividing established plants in spring or by taking cuttings in summer. Warm-climate gardeners can divide the plants in early fall, after they finish blooming.

*Veronica alpina* is a low, mat-forming plant for rock gardens and edgings. It covers the ground with 6- to 9-inch spikes of flowers in early sum-mer and will bloom again and again all summer if you clip off the flowers as they fade. The cultivar Alba is a fine white-flowered form. Space the plants a foot apart in the garden.

*V. latifolia* is a favorite with many gardeners. It grows 1 to 1½ feet tall and produces its blue flower spikes in early summer. The plants tend to sprawl and may look a little unruly, but you won't care when you see the masses of flowers—they practically cover the plants. The best-loved cultivar is Crater Lake Blue, which has flowers of true gentian blue. Set the plants 14 to 18 inches apart.

*V. longifolia* grows 2 to 3 feet tall and blooms in midsummer. Its flowers are purplish blue and are gathered in dense spikes. The variety *subsessilis* has flowers of beautiful deep royal blue.

*V. prostrata*, another low, mat-forming species, grows 5 inches high and flowers in early summer, sometimes beginning in late spring. The glossy, dark green leaves add to the beauty of the plant. The cultivar Heavenly Blue has deep blue flowers; Rosea bears pink semidouble flowers. The plants will bloom in either full sun or partial shade. Space them 8 to 10 inches apart.

The spikes of V. *spicata* make good cut flowers, and growing several different cultivars can give you flowers from June to August. The cultivar Barcarolle has rosy pink flowers starting in early summer and grows 10 inches high. Blue Peter has dark blue flowers on 1½- to 2-foot plants in mid- to late summer. Icicle bears white flowers in mid- and late summer, on plants that also grow 1½ to 2 feet tall. Minuet has rosy flowers and silvery leaves; the plants grow 2 feet tall and bloom in mid- to late summer. Red Fox is a fairly new cultivar, with midsummer flowers of deep rose-pink on 15-inch-high plants.

## Zinnia

Gardeners who grow zinnias consider them among the most rewarding of all flowers. They are easy to grow, bloom like crazy, and come in a wide range of sizes and colors. There are tall, large-flowered zinnias for the back of the garden, dwarf sizes for the front of the garden and for edging, and medium-size plants to use in between. The palette contains many shades of red, orange, pink, and yellow, along with creamy whites and an unusual light green. They make wonderful, long-lasting cut flowers.

Zinnias thrive in hot weather and can tolerate dryness and intense sun.

*Cut and Come Again zinnias.*

They'll grow in just about any soil and bloom quickly from seeds. In fact, they are good plants to include in a child's first garden. Zinnias were one of the first plants my parents helped me grow when I was little.

The plants are seldom troubled by pests and diseases except in cool, humid climates, where they sometimes get mildew. Sow the seeds directly in the garden after all danger of frost is past in spring, or, if you want earlier flowers, start seeds indoors several weeks earlier.

Our garden zinnias have been bred from the species *Zinnia elegans*, an annual plant native to Mexico.

# Summer Gardening Activities

In most parts of the United States, summer brings basic garden maintenance chores—weeding, watering, fertilizing, mulching. Throughout the summer gardeners everywhere are busy cutting flowers for bouquets and arrangements and, later in the season, for drying. At the same time there are cleanup chores to be done—picking off faded blossoms is important in both the perennial garden, where some plants may be stimulated to bloom a second time, and in the annual garden, where removing dead flowers keeps the plants producing more. Houseplants can be treated to an outdoor vacation in summer, on a shady deck or patio, sunk in their pots in a protected corner of the garden, or placed in an arbor, gazebo, or lath house.

As summer draws to a close, it's time to think about ordering bulbs for fall planting and making notes for changes in next year's beds and borders. In fact, make it a point to take some time out in the midst of summer's activity to look carefully at your garden and assess which plants are really thriving and which aren't doing as well; which combinations of flower color and plant form please you and which seem less successful; and whether your color scheme is working. Then make your plans for next year accordingly. It's important as you make your observations to jot down some notes. You may think you will remember to order a second daylily variety to fill in that sparse area along the fence, but it's all too easy to forget later on. When inspiration strikes, write down your ideas right away, lest you lose them in the summer haze.

Following is a rundown of basic summer garden activities. You can use it as a general guideline for maintaining your summer garden and planning ahead for fall and winter and for next year. Adjust the schedule according to your climate and microclimate, your site, and the kind of weather you are experiencing this summer.

## TEMPERATE CLIMATES

Summer means maintenance in gardens everywhere. It's time to deadhead peonies and other spring perennials as their flowers fade. Don't forget to pick off the dead flowers from lilacs and other spring-blooming shrubs, too. Pinching the faded flowers from early-blooming annuals encourages them to keep blooming. Remove the foliage from spring bulbs, too, as it yellows and dries, except for the leaves of fritillaries and crown imperials—leave their foliage intact.

It is time to weed your perennial beds and mulch them if your summers tend to be hot and dry. It's also time to fertilize, mulch, and if necessary weed early-blooming annuals such as sweet alyssum, asters, candytuft, and nasturtiums. Fertilize and mulch lilacs and other spring shrubs when they are finished blooming.

After floribunda and hybrid tea roses complete their first blooming, you will need to fertilize and mulch the plants. Cut back the flower stems when the blossoms start to fade in order to prolong bloom. Cut blooming canes of rambler roses back to the ground when they finish flowering. And keep an eye out for aphids and black spot on your roses. Take appropriate measures at the first sign of trouble.

If you are growing sweet peas, which are touchy in most climates, mulch them in early summer to keep their roots moist. Be sure to water them during periods of dry weather.

Pinch back bushy annuals and other plants that need it to produce compact growth and lots of flowers. Pinching tall chrysanthemum varieties will promote bushier plants. It's a good idea to fertilize them in early summer as well.

As summer gets under way, check delphiniums and other tall-growing, summer-blooming perennials to make sure they are staked.

In addition to garden maintenance chores, there are flowers to be planted, propagated, and ordered during summer for future seasons. Gardeners in temperate climates should plant gladiolus, dahlias, cannas, and tuberous begonias if they have not already been planted. You can sow seeds of fast-growing annuals such as sweet alyssum, morning glories, moonflowers, marigolds, nasturtiums, and zinnias directly in the garden for late summer flowers. You can also make a second sowing of cosmos, annual larkspur, and salpiglossis for late season bloom.

Early summer is also the time to set out annual bedding plants—begonias, impatiens, lobelia, and other annuals. Feed the transplants with a balanced fertilizer and water them well after planting.

If you want to grow spring and summer perennials from seeds to have flowers next year, now is the time to sow the seeds. Columbines, delphiniums, and primroses are some candidates for early summer sowing.

If you like to propagate your own plants from established specimens, this is a good time to take root cuttings from lavender, perennial phlox, and chrysanthemums and to layer azaleas, forsythias, and roses.

*Pinching chrysanthemums (top) produces bushier plants with more flowers. Disbudding, or removing all but one bud from each stem (bottom), produces fewer but larger flowers.*

*There are a number of ways to stake tall-growing plants. Plants that produce several stems can be surrounded with stakes with string wrapped around them at intervals as shown on the left. Plants that produce single stems can be staked individually as shown on the right.*

## WARM CLIMATES

In the South, Southwest, and along the West Coast, gardeners should pinch off the dead flowers of annuals in early summer to keep the plants blooming. Pruning or shearing back the plants will promote bushier, more compact growth. It is also important to remove the dead foliage from spring bulbs. Early summer is the time to give spring-blooming shrubs such as azaleas and forsythias a light pruning. Later-blooming spring shrubs such as lilacs need to have their spent flowers picked off regularly.

If you grow delphiniums, cut them back halfway when they finish blooming to encourage a second flush of flowers later in the season. If you grow chrysanthemums, pinch back the plants for the first time in early summer to make them bushy and produce more flowers.

If your gladiolus is in bloom, you can start to cut flowers for indoor arrangements. When cutting, remove the least possible amount of foliage with each flower spike. See chapter 4 for information on handling cut gladiolus blossoms.

Mulch all your flower gardens to help hold moisture around the plants' roots during the stressful hot weather ahead. Annuals, perennials, roses, and shrubs, especially broad-leaved evergreens like azaleas, rhododendrons, and camellias, should all be mulched for summer in warm-climate gardens.

Water is especially essential, too, at this time of year. You should water established perennials, annuals, and shrubs regularly and deeply during dry weather to prevent heat stress. It is essential to water newly planted roses and other plants to help them get established. Late-blooming shrubs such as hydrangeas and crape myrtles also need plenty of water as their buds develop. Finally, don't forget about plants in containers and windowboxes. They will need to be watered every day—sometimes twice a day—during very hot weather. Check soil moisture by sticking a finger into the pot—don't wait to water until the plants go limp, for by that time they will already be suffering from water stress. One exception to the watering rule is geraniums—they bloom best if kept a bit dry.

Shade-loving plants such as fuchsias and tuberous begonias are at their peak of bloom now in many southern gardens. Keep the plants in light shade and give them plenty of water. Don't forget to fertilize them.

Roses should be fertilized after their first blooming is over. Check to make sure stakes are in place for lilies and other tall plants that will be coming into bloom soon.

Another early summer chore for warm-climate gardeners is digging up spring bulbs and storing them over summer to replant in fall or, in climates that permit bulbs to stay outdoors all year, digging and dividing offsets from mature bulbs. Transplant the divisions as soon as you make them. Most irises, too, are finished blooming by now in warm areas and can be dug, divided, and transplanted.

In the Southwest, replace early plantings of annuals and spring bulbs with heat-tolerant flowers such as cosmos, marigolds, gaillardia, portulacas, tithonia, and zinnias. In all warm climates, it is also time to set out bedding plants in shady places. Set out caladiums, coleus, and impatiens if you haven't already done so. There is still time to plant the last of your dahlias and gladiolus if planting is not yet finished. And you can also plant tropical waterlilies in ponds or tubs.

Continue to direct-seed ageratum, celosias, marigolds, nasturtiums, globe amaranth, sunflowers, and zinnias for late summer and autumn flowers. Plant seeds or transplants of annuals in, among, or over tulips, narcissus, and other early-blooming bulbs to hide the dying foliage. You can also sow seeds of perennials and biennials to have flowers next spring. Sow the seeds outdoors in protected areas where they will get some shade.

## INDOOR GARDENS

Although the focus is definitely on the outdoor garden in summer, don't neglect your houseplants. Now that the weather is quite warm you can move tender and tropical houseplants outdoors for the season. Prune back any plants that need it when you take them outdoors. Sink the pots into the garden, or transplant the plants directly into the soil outdoors. If you have problems with slugs and other pests, slip an old nylon stocking over pots to keep pests from crawling in through the drainage holes. Houseplants summering outdoors should be kept in the shade—they will not be able to tolerate the intense, direct summer sun.

If you are growing poinsettias for Christmas display, keep the plants pinched back to encourage branching, and fertilize them regularly.

Early summer is the time to plant chrysanthemum cuttings to bloom indoors in autumn and to sow seeds of fairy primroses and cinerarias to have flowers in winter.

## MIDSUMMER

### TEMPERATE CLIMATES

Basic maintenance chores continue to be the focus of activity for flower gardeners in midsummer. But it is such a pleasure to be outdoors in the garden surrounded by all the flowers in bloom that the work doesn't seem so bad. In fact, I think most of us find that weeding, watering, and deadheading are enjoyable, soothing activities.

Deadheading spent flowers continues to be a primary activity in midsummer. It is important to cut off dying blossoms both to keep many plants producing more flowers and to keep them healthy. Dead flowers are often the first place diseases and pests attack, and keeping the plants free of them goes a long way toward preventing problems in the garden. It's easier to prevent pests and diseases than to fight them when they establish a foothold among your plants.

As summer progresses, you will need to keep on removing faded flowers from perennials and roses. Remember that cutting off rose blossoms is also pruning the plants, so do it carefully. Cut back to an outward-facing bud above a shoot that has five leaves. Deadhead your annuals, too; plants that produce too many flowers to pick off individually, such as sweet alyssum and, if you have a lot of plants, impatiens, can simply be sheared back and shaped, and a new flush of blossoms will follow. Bachelor's buttons tend to look straggly in midsummer; if you cut back the plants by 6 inches after the first flowering is over, it will encourage them to bloom again.

If you are growing chrysanthemums, stop pinching them back by the middle of July or flowering will be delayed in fall.

Remember to prune climbing and rambler roses when they finish blooming. Climbers will usually bloom again in fall, but ramblers will not.

Watering is another important summertime task, especially now that the hot weather has really arrived in your area. Be especially vigilant with plants in pots, tubs, and windowboxes. Containers dry out far more quickly than garden soil, and in hot, dry weather you will probably have to water them at least once every day. Remember, too, that unglazed clay pots allow water to evaporate through their walls and dry out faster than plastic containers. In the garden, roses and delphiniums are especially sensitive to drought, so be sure to keep them well watered.

Lightly fertilize container plants in midsummer to ensure that the plants have plenty of nutrients. Don't overfeed them, though; too much fertilizer causes weak, too rapid growth that is easy prey for pests and diseases. Midsummer is also the time to fertilize poinsettias, if you have planted cuttings outdoors for the summer in preparation for winter color.

Weeding is the other big summer maintenance activity. Handweed or lightly cultivate unmulched beds of annuals and perennials to keep weeds down. Rake fallen leaves and other debris out of the garden, too. Pests and diseases are likely to take up residence there and go on to attack your plants. Keeping the garden clean is the best preventive measure you can take.

Tall summer perennials should be staked before they come into full bloom. Check to see that stakes are in place for delphiniums, lilies, tall dahlias, and garden phlox.

If you have sunken potted houseplants into the garden for the summer, give the pots a twist to break off any roots that may have grown through the drainage holes.

Check your rosebushes for suckers

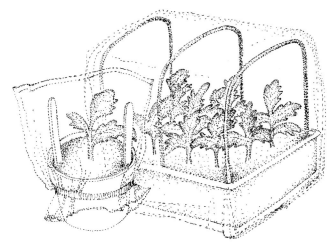

*Take cuttings of outdoor plants—especially summer annuals—and root them in pots for new plants that will bloom indoors in winter. For tip cuttings, cut the stem below the youngest set of leaves. Cut right above the next lowest leaves, as shown in the detail.*

*To make sure cuttings get plenty of humidity while they are forming roots, enclose individual pots or entire flats in plastic bags. The plastic should not come in contact with plant leaves, so support it underneath with Popsicle sticks or wire hoops made from bent coat hangers. Keep plastic-covered pots out of direct sunlight.*

growing from the rootstock. Suckers can be recognized as leafy shoots growing next to the main part of the plant. Sometimes they appear as seven-part leaves on plants that have five-part leaves. Cut off any suckers you find.

In the midst of maintaining the plants you already have, you can also be thinking ahead to starting new ones. If you still have ten weeks remaining before you are likely to get your first fall frost, you can sow seeds of short-season annuals for late-season flowers. California poppies, marigolds, nasturtiums, petunias, portulacas, Shirley poppies, and sweet alyssum are some good candidates.

Midsummer is also the time to plant seeds of such perennials and biennials as coreopsis, delphiniums, foxgloves, gaillardias, lupines, campanulas, hollyhocks, shasta daisies, pansies, sweet williams, and dianthus for flowers next summer.

You can sow seeds now of browallia, calendulas, cinerarias, primroses, snapdragons, schizanthus, stocks, and sweet peas for indoor flowers in late winter and early spring.

Other plants can be propagated from cuttings at this time of year. You can take cuttings from begonias, geraniums, gloxinias, jasmine, and perennial morning glories to start new plants.

Finally, in midsummer you can order new daylilies from nursery catalogs, to fill in gaps in your plantings or add some new colors for next year.

## WARM CLIMATES

Maintenance is the name of the game in midsummer for gardeners in warm climates, too. If you still have some spring bulbs remaining in your garden, dig them up when the foliage has died and store them to replant in fall. Narcissus bulbs can be left undisturbed for a few years, but tulips perform better in the South when they are dug and replanted every year.

It's important to deadhead perennials and deadhead or shear back annuals to keep them blooming and to keep the garden clean. Dahlias, marigolds, petunias, salvia, and verbena are a few plants that will rebloom if you keep picking off faded blossoms. If you are growing wisteria, prune it when it finishes blooming.

You can pinch back chrysanthemums and poinsettias one last time in early July. It is also time to disbud dahlias and late-blooming roses if you want to have fewer but larger flowers.

Watering is of course critical in warm climates during the hottest part of the year. Water annuals and perennials deeply and regularly. Deep-rooted perennials should be watered more deeply and less often than annuals. And don't forget about your shrubs: azaleas, rhododendrons, camellias, and hydrangeas all need lots of water to keep their shallow roots from drying out. Depending on your rainfall, you will probably need to water your shrubs every week to ten days. As temperatures soar, keep a close watch on all plants growing in pots, tubs, windowboxes, and hanging baskets. You will need to water them once or even twice a day in midsummer.

Mulch plays an important role in many warm-climate gardens, because it helps hold moisture around plant roots and keeps the soil cooler. If you live in the South, Southwest, or along the West Coast, make sure your perennials and roses, in particular, are well mulched to help get them through the summer.

Midsummer is a good time to fertilize heavy-feeding perennials such as delphiniums, shasta daisies, and chrysanthemums. You can fertilize all your container plants, too, but be careful not to overfeed them. Annuals also appreciate a midsummer feeding, especially those that you have cut back to encourage a new flush of flowers.

Fertilizing roses now will encourage them to bloom again in late summer and autumn. Although suckering is less likely in warm climates where roses are planted with the graft union aboveground, it still sometimes occurs. Check your roses for suckers, and if you find any, cut them off.

As summer progresses, check to make sure stakes are in place for tall-growing lilies, gladiolus, dahlias, hardy asters, and chrysanthemums before the plants come into bloom.

If you have sunk potted houseplants into the garden for the summer, give the pots a twist to break off any roots that may have grown through the drainage holes.

Another midsummer activity for warm-climate gardeners is to dig, divide, and replant crowded irises, Easter lilies, daylilies, primroses, and violas when they have finished blooming.

It is very important to keep your garden beds free of weeds, dead foliage, and plant debris to help prevent pest and disease problems.

Gardeners in warm climates have plenty of planting to do in midsummer to have flowers in seasons to come. Plant seeds of cosmos, marigolds, salvia, spider lilies, verbena, zinnias, and other fast-growing annuals for fall flowers. In addition, this is the time to plant autumn crocuses. You can also plant seeds of Iceland poppies, pansies, and snapdragons for flowers in late winter and early spring. And sow biennials and perennials like columbines, dianthus, hollyhocks, and primroses to bloom next year.

Some plants can be propagated by means other than seeds. You can take cuttings from shade lovers such as impatiens and begonias and root them to have new plants that will bloom in fall. You can also take cuttings from azaleas, bougainvillea, camellias, gardenias, hydrangeas, jasmine, lilacs, and mock orange.

You can continue to plant dahlias, gladiolus, and mums until the middle of August for autumn flowers.

## INDOOR GARDENS

During summer, don't forget to regularly water and fertilize your houseplants, both those spending the season outdoors and the ones still indoors. In warm climates, put heat-sensitive houseplants in a lath house or in the shade. Begonias, fuchsias, and primroses are especially prone to heat damage.

Potted cyclamens, freesias, oxalis, and tritoma that have been resting can be started growing again to bloom indoors in autumn and winter.

Midsummer is the time to start seeds of snapdragons for indoor flowers in late autumn; wax begonias and sweet peas to bloom in winter; kalanchoes to bloom in late winter; and calceolaria for flowers next spring. You can also plant chrysanthemum cuttings for flowers in late fall.

## LATE SUMMER

### TEMPERATE CLIMATES

As summer winds down, it is time to harvest everlastings, baby's breath, celosia, globe amaranth, statice, strawflowers, and other flowers to dry for winter arrangements.

You should continue to deadhead perennials and annuals and pinch back begonias, impatiens, and other shade plants that have gotten leggy. Don't let biennials like foxgloves and sweet williams go to seed unless you want them to self-sow. When hollyhocks finish blooming, cut them back to the ground and dispose of all tops and leaves, which are very sensitive to disease.

This late in the season, you no longer have to worry about staking summer perennials. But it is time to stake late-blooming dahlias, glads, and mums that need it.

Cleanup continues in flower gardens, too. Rake up and get rid of any fallen leaves and other plant debris. Keep the garden weeded; especially do not allow any weeds to go to seed, or you'll have many more to contend with next year.

Late summer weather is hot all over the country. Now that the dog days have arrived, keep your flowers well watered. By all means continue to monitor plants in containers closely, and water them as often as they need it.

You can fertilize poinsettias again in late summer if you are growing them, but stop feeding perennials, roses, and shrubs so they will have time to harden for winter.

Sometime in August you should finish sowing seeds of biennials and perennials for spring bloom: campanulas, delphiniums, English daisies, forget-me-nots, foxgloves, hollyhocks, sweet williams, and others should all be sown before the end of summer so the seedlings have a chance to establish themselves before the ground freezes in late fall.

As the end of summer approaches, you can order spring-blooming perennial plants and bulbs for autumn planting and winter forcing.

## WARM CLIMATES

Continue to remove dead flowers in late summer from annuals and perennials and from summer-blooming shrubs like hydrangeas. Prune summer shrubs when they have finished blooming and dahlias and roses, too, to promote new growth.

During the intense heat of late summer, it's essential to keep all your flower beds and borders well watered and mulched. Be sure to water container plants as often as they need it. You should continue to fertilize, too. In particular, fertilize and stake tall lilies that have not yet bloomed. Be careful when working around areas where spider lilies and magic lilies (hardy amaryllis) are planted—their foliage has died back, but the flower stems will come up soon.

If you live where late summer brings heavy, humid air, watch out for fungus in beds and borders, especially on mums, roses, crape myrtle, verbena, and zinnias. Get rid of any affected leaves as soon as you spot signs of fungus or mildew. If necessary, spray with a fungicide.

In early August, feed roses and dahlias to encourage them to bloom in fall. You can feed chrysanthemums one last time as they get ready to flower. In late summer, too, you can divide and replant crowded daylilies, Madonna lilies, spider lilies, irises, poppies, primroses, marguerites, and shasta daisies when they finish blooming.

This is also a good time to think ahead to flowers you will want to have in seasons to come. Start by renewing the soil in beds where you will plant in fall. Dig in compost or leaf mold and some rock phosphate or bonemeal. There's still time in early August to sow seeds or set out transplants of ageratum, sweet alyssum, calendulas, cosmos, marigolds, nemesias, sunflowers, snapdragons, zinnias, and other annuals to bloom in fall. You can plant pansies in partly shaded areas or sow seeds for winter bloom.

If you want to grow annual larkspur, refrigerate the seeds until outdoor temperatures dip to 40° or 45°F, then plant them outdoors where they will bloom in spring. The seeds need cold weather to germinate.

Gardeners in the Southwest can sow calendulas, forget-me-nots, snapdragons, stocks, violas, and sweet peas for winter bloom. You can also set out Madonna lily bulbs and iris rhizomes. And you can sow columbine and gaillardia seeds for flowers next spring. In late August plant campanulas, dianthus, foxgloves, hollyhocks, poppies, sweet peas, and spider lilies for flowers next year. In mild areas of the South, late summer is a good time to plant calla lilies, magic lilies, Dutch irises, freesias, Madonna lilies, oxalis, tritonias, and other bulbs. You can also still plant colchicums and autumn crocuses for fall flowers.

In addition, this is the best time to take cuttings from azaleas, rhododendrons, camellias, and other shrubs to start new plants. Finally, as summer draws to a close, remember to order spring-blooming bulbs and perennials for fall planting and winter forcing.

## INDOOR GARDENS

In late summer it's time to start preparing your houseplants for winter. Pinch back plants that are spending summer outdoors so they will be bushy and well shaped when you bring them back indoors in fall.

If you are growing chrysanthemums to use as indoor plants in fall and winter, pinch them back for the last time in late summer.

Finally, you can, if you wish, take cuttings from geraniums, lantana, poinsettias, and other plants that can be grown to bloom indoors in winter.

# AUTUMN

## SEVEN

# *Autumn Flowers*

In the East, where I live, autumn is a season of many moods: some days are clear and crisp; on other days summer lingers, soft and mellow, hazy and warm; then there are gray and blustery days, harbingers of the coming winter. Gardeners in the North become wistful in autumn, finding themselves wishing the warm days of summer would go on forever, wanting to make the most of the warm weather that remains but also starting to think about cleaning up the garden and putting it to rest for the winter. Gardeners in the South, on the other hand, breathe a sigh of relief in fall, when the intense heat of summer starts to abate and it becomes more enjoyable to spend time outdoors in the garden.

Gardeners everywhere in the United States notice as September begins that the quality of the light outdoors has changed. The sun is lower in the sky and less intense; afternoons are suffused with a rich golden light.

For most gardeners, autumn means the fiery colors of fall leaves—glowing gold, rich red, flaming orange, tawny rust, mellow bronzes and browns. These colors, along with the vibrant purple that also typifies fall, are echoed in the colors of the most classic of autumn flowers—chrysanthemums. Autumn is a far richer season than you may realize. In early fall, dahlias reach their peak, and roses often send up a second flush of bloom. Then the chrysanthemums and asters burst

forth, continuing into mid- and late fall, up until the first frost. In addition, there are bulbs that come into bloom in autumn, and Japanese anemones, along with a whole host of annuals still flowering from summer. From fields, meadows, and roadsides, long-stemmed grasses, pods, and berries add softness and interest to bouquets and arrangements. The tans, beiges, and browns of dried grasses harmonize beautifully with the warm tones of autumn flowers. Add some deep purple asters and you have a concert of color that captures the very essence of the season. There is plenty of color to be had outdoors right up until frost.

Autumn also marks the start of the indoor gardening season. Cuttings

### RED FLOWERS

| | | | |
|---|---|---|---|
| Camellia | Globe amaranth | Michaelmas daisy | Thanksgiving cactus |
| Chrysanthemum | Japanese anemone | New England aster | |
| Dahlia | Jupiter's beard | Schizostylis | |

### PINK FLOWERS

| | | | |
|---|---|---|---|
| Camellia | Hardy cyclamen | Nerine | Phalaenopsis |
| Chrysanthemum | Japanese anemone | New England aster | Sedum |
| Colchicum | Lycoris | Oxalis | Thanksgiving cactus |
| Dahlia | Michaelmas daisy | Pentas | |

### ORANGE FLOWERS

| | | |
|---|---|---|
| Chrysanthemum | Dahlia | Tiger lily |

### YELLOW FLOWERS

| | | |
|---|---|---|
| Chrysanthemum | Gloriosa daisy | Helianthus |
| Dahlia | Helenium | Sternbergia |

### BLUE AND VIOLET FLOWERS

| | | |
|---|---|---|
| Aster | Exacum | Michaelmas daisy |
| Caryopteris | Gentian | Monkshood |
| Ceratostigma | Globe thistle | Salvia |

### PURPLE FLOWERS

| | | | |
|---|---|---|---|
| Autumn crocus | Eupatorium | Michaelmas daisy | Veronica |
| Chrysanthemum | Globe amaranth | New England aster | |
| Colchicum | Lespedeza | Oxalis | |
| Dahlia | Liatris | Pentas | |

### WHITE FLOWERS

| | | | |
|---|---|---|---|
| Abelia | Clematis | Michaelmas daisy | Silver fleece vine |
| Aster | Crocus | Myrtus | Thanksgiving cactus |
| Autumn snowflake | Dahlia | Osmanthus | Tuberose |
| Boltonia | Garlic chives | Pentas | Yucca |
| Camellia | Great burnet | Phalaenopsis | |
| Chrysanthemum | Japanese anemone | Salvia | |
| Cimicifuga | Jewel orchid | Saxifraga | |

*Miniature dahlias bloom in a pot.*

dormancy when they will need less care. Some classic houseplants begin their own show in fall: Thanksgiving cactus, for example, and Jerusalem cherry with its bright red fruit. Sweet olive (*Osmanthus fragrans*) will bloom indoors from September to May in a cool, bright spot, perfuming an entire room. A number of orchids suited for indoor growing bloom in autumn, too.

## COMBINING AUTUMN FLOWERS IN GARDENS AND ARRANGEMENTS

Lots of summer annuals, and some perennials, too, continue to fill flower gardens with color in early fall. Annuals still blooming include sweet alyssum, impatiens, marigolds, nasturtiums, petunias, stocks, lobelia, and geraniums. Gardeners in warm climates have a much bigger selection than gardeners in colder areas. Dahlias, gladiolus, and early chrysanthemums that started blooming in summer continue into autumn, with dahlias putting on their finest show in many gardens in September. The list of summer perennials still blooming in fall includes Michaelmas daisies (especially the New England asters, many of which come into bloom in September), sunflowers, salvias, veronicas, yarrows, turtlehead, coneflowers, coreopsis, gaillardia, hardy ageratum, daylilies, goldenrod, tiger lilies, sedums, statice, garden phlox, and shasta daisies.

But autumn has its stars in the garden as well. In addition to the bright, hot colors of dahlias, the warm

taken from garden annuals late in summer can be potted and brought indoors for bloom later on. Some plants can be lifted entirely and planted in pots to keep blooming on a sunny windowsill. Spring bulbs are potted and the forcing process begun to provide color in the gloomiest depths of winter. Houseplants that have spent the summer outdoors are brought back inside, and those that bloomed in spring and summer enter a period of

OPPOSITE
*Two shades of purple—false dragonhead (Physostegia) and asters—against a blue autumn sky.*

*Asters in pink, rose, and purple.*

earth tones of mums, the blues and violets of monkshoods, and the soft roses, pinks, and whites of Japanese anemones can all serve as the basis on which to build autumn color schemes. Autumn crocuses can be combined with other fall bulbs in gardens of their own or planted in front of autumn perennials.

Many classic autumn color schemes can be created with chrysanthemums of different sizes and types. You can plant cultivars in shades of rich scarlet, red-orange, bright yellow, russet, and deep gold or combine deep crimson, coppery bronze, and yellow shades. Another yellow-based color combination for mums mixes orange, gold, yellow, and bronze. Or you could grow bronze and yellow mums with a rich purple cultivar such as Tinkerbell. You can create similar color schemes with dahlias in early fall.

Orange dahlias also work well with yellow rudbeckias and plume-type celosias in deep gold and yellow-orange, which will still be in bloom in early autumn. A planting of yellow gloriosa daisies and orange-and-yellow red-hot poker will also flower into autumn. If you like pink-and-blue color schemes, there are numerous possibilities for autumn gardens. For example, the lavender-blue flowers of *Aster* ×*frikartii* combine beautifully with the rosy pink New England aster cultivar Alma Potschke and the clear pink flowers of another cultivar, Harrington's Pink. You can also grow blue-violet monkshood with Japanese anemones in shades of rosy pink and silvery pink. Or grow monkshood with *Sedum* 'Autumn Joy'. The flowers of Autumn Joy are pink when they first open in late summer and deepen gradually to an unusual salmony bronze color. Another duo that blooms from summer into early fall is garden phlox in deep rose-red and rosy pink with steely blue globe thistle.

*Chrysanthemums in shades of scarlet, terra cotta, crimson, and rose.*

Yellow can be introduced into pink-and-blue fall gardens if you want more brightness. Yellow helianthus will still be blooming in fall and marries well with the purply blue New England aster Professor Kippenburg and a late-blooming bright pink cultivar of false dragonhead, Vivid. An autumn bulb garden might combine autumn crocuses in lilac-blue and violet with lavender and mauve-pink colchicums and golden yellow sternbergias.

Red-and-pink color schemes are also possible in fall. You can mix chrysanthemums or dahlias in these shades and add some purple or yellow, too, if you like. Try mixing deep carmine red, rose-pink, and clear pink cultivars or rose-pink, lavender, and purple. The deep red flowers of Jupiter's beard are still blooming in early fall and make a lovely combination with clear pink asters or mums. You can also

combine New England asters such as the deep crimson September Ruby and the pure pink Harrington's Pink with Japanese anemones in rose and soft pink. Plant some white ones, too, to lend a note of freshness to the composition.

Another classic autumn color combination is yellow with purple or blue. One way to achieve this kind of grouping is with chrysanthemums or to grow goldenrod with purple asters or steel-blue globe thistles.

The other direction to go with autumn colors is to mix white flowers with a second color. The white flowers of boltonia, for example, resemble asters and bloom at the same time. You might want to try growing boltonia with asters in shades of rose-red and rose-pink, with perhaps a lavender-blue cultivar as well. Japanese anemones are lovely in their soft shades of

rose, rosy pink, light pink, and white, and make a lovely planting all by themselves. The lacy white flower heads of garlic chives (*Allium tuberosum*) look lovely in the fall border in front of deep red chrysanthemums. Or try growing them near *Sedum* 'Autumn Joy' or asters in shades of deep crimson or rose-pink. The tall white flower spikes of great burnet (*Sanguisorba canadensis*) nicely set off the flat flower heads of Autumn Joy sedums, too. Globe amaranth is still blooming in many fall gardens, and it makes a handsome display in mixed shades of red, red-violet, and creamy white.

In southern gardens, fragrant white tuberoses combine well in autumn gardens with a white cultivar of mealy-cup sage (actually a slightly grayish shade) and red-violet globe amaranth. Finally, camellias are a late autumn and winter highlight in many warm-climate gardens, with their large flowers in shades of red, rose, pink, and white.

As the transitional time between outdoor and indoor gardening seasons, autumn offers opportunities for displaying the products of both environments. Varied bouquets and arrangements can still be created from the outdoor garden, and fall-blooming houseplants can be shown off on windowsills or used as centerpieces for special dinners. Fall arrangements can combine fresh garden flowers, wildflowers, and roadside grasses and dried everlastings.

Some flower arrangers like to include lots of green in autumn displays to tone down the brilliance of the predominant colors and provide some visual relief. Greenish flowers can serve this purpose (mignonette and lime-colored varieties of nicotiana and zinnia are still blooming in many gardens in early fall), as can foliage clipped from ferns, wild grasses, and herbs. You can even steal a stem or two from some of your leafy houseplants: coleus is one possibility, and trailing plants like ivy, grape ivy, peperomias, and philodendrons offer other alternatives.

One tempting autumn element that is better *not* to include in arrangements is leaves from deciduous trees. Although their fiery colors are beautiful, they will not last indoors: the leaves will simply continue the process they have begun and turn brown.

# THE INDOOR GARDEN: DISPLAYING AND DECORATING WITH HOUSEPLANTS

As the indoor gardening season gets under way, it is time to give some thought to displaying your houseplants. Plants in bloom deserve a prominent place in your home, adding interest and brightness to a room, enlivening a dull area like a foyer or entrance hall, and bringing a welcome note of colorful contrast to a neutral color scheme.

To use plants effectively as part of indoor decor, it is important to consider both the characteristics of the plants themselves and the qualities of the rooms in which you want to place them. Plants should be considered in terms of their color, texture, and form; for flowering plants, color is the most important factor. Rooms should be judged in terms of their size, style of furnishings, color scheme, and environment for plants—light, humidity, and temperature.

## FLOWER COLORS AND ROOM COLORS

The spots of color provided by flowers, whether they are blooming on living plants or in a vase, can be used to harmonize with or complement the overall color scheme of the decor, to pick up an accent color that occurs in upholstery or wallpaper, or to provide a dash of dramatic contrast in a neutral room.

If the room is decorated in a monochromatic scheme, flowers should probably be a shade of the same color. If the room is neutral, decorated in grays or browns or whites, flowers in a bright, clear color will add life to the space. Except in neutral rooms, it is generally best to avoid introducing a color not already present. Unless your color sense is finely developed, bringing in flowers of a color that is not already part of the decor could create chaos and discord instead of harmony.

In choosing flowers to blend comfortably with walls and furnishings, consider not only the colors themselves, but the warmth or coolness of the colors, and stay within the same temperature range for harmony. For example, pink can be either warm, tending toward a salmon or peach tone, or it can be cool, with a bluish or purplish cast. In selecting a red geranium to match the pink in a drapery pattern, if the pink is warm, an orangy red geranium would harmonize nicely, while a cherry red or magenta flower would clash. With a purply pink the opposite would be true.

Remember, too, that warm colors are active and tend to come forward visually. Cool colors are calming and restful and tend to recede in space. In a blue room, red, yellow, or orange flowers would create contrast and action. Purple or blue flowers would offer serenity and quiet; they would be less distracting and be a better choice for a bedroom, where the overall effect should be soothing and pleasant.

Finally, it helps to remember that the texture of flowers also affects how we perceive their colors. Fuzzy flowers like petunias or gloxinias appear softer in color than smooth-petaled impatiens or tulips.

Whatever the colors of the flowers you are working with, they will undoubtedly look better when viewed against a background of foliage. Like the green leaves of trees and shrubs in the outdoor landscape, the foliage of indoor plants sets off the flowers. Many indoor gardeners like to display flowering houseplants in a verdant setting of large foliage plants—palms, dracaenas, ficus, and dieffenbachias are some favorites.

Indoor foliage has other benefits, too. It softens the sharp lines of architecture and furnishings. In front of a window the leaves filter the sunlight streaming into the room, creating a pleasantly dappled effect.

*Purple coneflowers and rudbeckias bloom into autumn in many gardens.*

## TEXTURE, FORM, AND SCALE

To fully integrate flowering plants into interior decor, you would do well to think about a few other design qualities in addition to color. Since you will most likely be displaying your plants in groups for greater impact, be aware of the texture of each one. Texture is a twofold quality; there is the texture of individual leaves—glossy, fuzzy, smooth, waxy, wavy, toothed—which we notice at close range and the texture of the plant as a whole—delicate and lacy, bold and angular—which becomes apparent from across a room. If you have difficulty "seeing" the texture of the plant as a whole, try looking at the shadow it casts on a wall when a light shines on it. When you plan plant groupings, try to place similarly textured plants together. A delicate Tahitian bridal veil would look silly next to a starkly angular yucca or a bold-leaved bromeliad. If your plant group docs include a range of textures, at least arrange them with the boldest on one extreme and the most delicate on the other, with plants of moderate textures in between.

The shapes and growing habits of plants also play an important part in indoor displays. You can use plant shape like an architectural element, to create or alleviate tension in the design or to direct a viewer's eye toward a prominent feature in the room. Plants have three primary styles of growth: upright (which includes both spiky and mounded or ball-shaped plants), horizontal or spreading, and trailing or climbing. Upright plants appear static when they are about as wide as they are high, or dynamic when they have a strong vertical line. A dramatically vertical plant can direct the eye upward. Horizontal plants are static, but they can draw the viewer's eye to the

right or left. Trailers and climbers are the most active plants of all. Their stems cascade downward in graceful curves, taking our gaze with them, or they push upward, often twining around their support and again drawing our attention in the direction of their growth. Making use of the effects of plant shapes on the way our eyes travel around a room makes it possible to create either bold, dramatic, or subtly integrated effects with plant displays.

Along with texture and growth habit, it is also important to consider scale and to match plant size to room size. In a small room with a subdued color scheme, finely textured, soft-colored plants work better than boldly textured, bright-colored ones. A collection of African violets would look better in a small office than would a big, shrubby gardenia or hibiscus. On the other hand, those same violets would disappear in an open-plan loft space, where the larger shrubs would

be far more appropriate. Think about using large plants in large open rooms, alcoves, or hallways, or to divide rooms or screen off parts of rooms. Use smaller plants on windowsills, shelves, bookcases, end tables, desks, or dining tables. Combine them with candles for centerpieces and elevate them on pedestals or plant stands to view at eye level.

Plants should also work with the style in which the room is furnished. A boldly shaped succulent or bromeliad that has a contemporary look would seem out of place in a Victorian-style parlor with lace curtains and chintz-covered sofas.

## THE INDOOR ENVIRONMENT

Most homes offer an assortment of growing conditions that suit flowering plants in varying degrees. You don't

*OPPOSITE*
*For the best visual effect, group houseplants of similar texture. The trio on this windowsill—a bold aechmea on the left, a fuzzy-leaved African violet in the middle, and a fine-textured dwarf pomegranate on the right—does not cohere well visually and does not make a very effective display.*

*BELOW*
*Consider the growing habits of indoor plants when planning an attractive display. The yucca standing on the floor has a strongly upright line. The campanula in the hanging basket has a horizontal line. Vining plants like the passionflower trained around the window provide graceful ascending and descending curves, according to the way they are trained and supported.*

*BELOW RIGHT*
*This diagram of the plants in the preceding illustration shows how different growing habits direct the eye of the viewer.*

necessarily have to show off your flowering favorites in the same place where you grow them. Most plants can stand a dim spot for a few days and can take center stage for a dinner party or family gathering. Just return it to a brightly lit place as soon as it finishes blooming or, if you notice any signs of distress, for some R and R. You can also use well-placed room lighting to supplement natural light and create a more hospitable environment for plants. You can buy plant lights that fit into standard track-mounted fixtures and full-spectrum fluorescent tubes that fit into compact, inconspicuous fixtures to attach above dark shelves and in dim corners. If you do not have decent window exposures at all, you can set up a light garden in the basement or a back room and rotate plants in and out

of it for display during their peak blooming periods.

If you do not have bright windowsills and are terminally lazy, or if you just want to augment the supply of flowers from your indoor garden, you can rely on certain seasonal bloomers from the florist. Florist plants like cinerarias and calceolarias are often forced by commercial growers and are very difficult to rebloom under home conditions, as are paperwhite narcissus and some other bulbs. These plants are generally discarded after they finish blooming, freeing you from any further responsibility for their upkeep.

Other environmental factors to keep in mind besides light are room temperature during the day and at night, the locations of heat sources and entrances where drafts may be a problem, air

circulation in general, and humidity. All these factors are discussed in more detail elsewhere in this book.

## GROUPING PLANTS FOR DISPLAY

There are limitless ways to group flowering plants to show them off indoors. One obvious and effective approach is to group several plants of the same type: indoor favorites like begonias and African violets come in many sizes, growing habits, and colors, and you may find yourself becoming a collector of a type of plant that does particularly well for you. My own indoor garden contains several varieties of Thanksgiving and Christmas cactus, which bloom in varying shades of pink and red, from October or November into February and some years even into spring. Each plant seems to have its own particular schedule. As you learn what grows best under your particular set of conditions, you, too, will find your favorites.

If you want to design a really effective and interesting plant grouping, try thinking about your indoor garden as if it were an outdoor border. Think three-dimensionally, arranging the plants with shorter ones in front and taller ones in back, with a background of tall foliage plants taking the place of trees and shrubs that form the backbone of the outdoor garden. Create depth with tiered plant stands or low stands placed in front of a windowsill. If your space is too limited to provide for much depth, at least position the plants on different levels, using shelves, stands, and hanging baskets to gain height.

If you have a big picture window or sliding glass doors onto a deck, patio, or lawn, you can achieve wonderful effects by relating your indoor plants to the outdoor landscape, creating a vi-

*Flowering plants can help to divide space in open-plan homes or lofts. Here, pots of flowers are grouped atop a storage unit, with hanging plants suspended from the ceiling above, to separate the kitchen from the dining room. Using plants as a room divider breaks up the space without closing it off and making it feel smaller.*

sual transition from outdoors to indoors. Choose houseplants that echo the landscape plants in your area: cacti and succulents in a desert climate; bromeliads, hibiscus, gardenias, and tropicals in the South; bulbs and azaleas in a wooded setting.

You can even try a few decorator's tricks to create added impact if you are so inclined. Spotlighting plants creates drama and interesting shadow patterns on a nearby wall. Plants set in front of a mirror are multiplied—an effect that can be fun.

*To create interest and depth in your indoor garden, group plants on different levels with plant stands and hanging baskets. A gradation of heights makes the most attractive display indoors, just as it does in the outdoor garden.*

# EIGHT

# Flowers for Autumn Gardens

Although the growing season winds down in autumn for most of us, autumn gardens can still be full of color, even in the North. Some of the plants discussed in this chapter actually begin blooming in summer, but all of them make their most important contribution to the garden in fall. In addition to the outdoor plants, a few autumn-blooming houseplants are covered in these pages.

## *Aconitum* / Monkshood

The aconites are members of the buttercup family. The species of most interest to flower gardeners is *Aconitum napellus*, monkshood, which is available in several cultivar forms.

Monkshood is the source of the drug aconite, and the plant is poisonous. However, it is a lovely addition to perennial beds and borders, sporting attractive, glossy deep green leaves that are lobed and divided like fingers on a hand. The helmet-shaped flowers are borne in spikes beginning in mid- to late summer and continuing into fall, and they are very useful in early autumn for bridging the gap between summer annuals and perennials and autumn chrysanthemums.

Monkshood needs a deeply dug, fertile soil that retains moisture but does not become waterlogged. The plants grow best in sun or partial shade and are hardy throughout the United States.

A. *napellus* 'Album' bears white flowers on 3- to 4-foot stems in midsummer to late summer.

Another cultivar, Spark's Variety, produces flowers of rich violet-blue from late summer into fall. Its branching stems can reach 4 feet in height.

Bressingham Spire is a hybrid cultivar introduced to the market by the venerable British plantsman Alan Bloom. Its sturdy 3-foot spikes of deep violet-blue flowers need no staking and appear from midsummer into fall.

A. × *bicolor* is a hybrid species with unusual two-toned flowers of blue and white. The blossoms are produced in loose spikes about 4 feet tall, from midsummer into fall.

## Anemone / *Japanese Anemone*

Japanese anemones are marvelous in fall gardens, and not enough gardeners grow them. They bloom abundantly in September and October, filling the garden with their pastel flowers until heavy frost brings down the curtain on their show.

There is a certain amount of confusion over the botanical name assigned to the plants. You may find them listed as *Anemone japonica*, *A. hupehensis*, or *A.* × *hybrida*. But whatever you call them, Japanese anemones are well worth considering for your garden. They make a nice change from chrysanthemums and are less trouble to grow. The flowers are good for cutting, too.

Most Japanese anemones grow about 2 to 2½ feet high with sturdy stems that form many branches. The flowers come in various shades of pink, rose, and white. They grow well in any average garden soil, as long as it is well drained. You can plant them in either full sun or partial shade. The plants do need generous amounts of moisture, so remember to water them regularly and deeply during hot, dry summer weather. Japanese anemones are hardy to about −20°F. In colder climates, give the plants a good covering of loose mulch (such as salt hay or shredded leaves) over the winter.

Temperate-zone gardeners should plant Japanese anemones in spring; warm-climate gardeners can plant in either spring or fall. Space the plants 8 to 12 inches apart in the garden.

New plants can be propagated from root cuttings taken from established specimens. When the plants finish blooming in fall, dig up a plant, cut off the roots, and cut the roots into pieces 2 inches long. Spread the pieces on top of a light, loose soil mix in a flat indoors or in a cold frame, and cover them with another inch of soil. Keep the soil moist but not wet. When shoots pop through the soil, plant each root with its shoot in an individual pot. Let the new plants spend the winter in the cold frame, and transplant them out to the garden in spring.

## Aster / *Michaelmas Daisy*

The best perennial asters for gardens belong to three different species. All three are loosely grouped under the common name Michaelmas daisy. They bloom from late summer into fall and are at their best in autumn gardens.

Michaelmas daisies are very undemanding in terms of their culture; they will grow in just about any soil, as long as they get lots of sun and plenty of water. To maintain top blooming quality, dig up your aster crowns every few years in very early spring, cut off the vigorous outside growth and replant it, and throw away the old center part of the crown. As the asters grow, either stake them to support the stems or pinch back the plants to keep them more compact. Although the cultivated forms of Michaelmas daisies have been bred from wild asters native to North America, they are far more widely grown by English gardeners than gardeners here. Certainly they deserve to be better known in the United States.

*Aster* × *frikartii* grows 2 to 3 feet high, with fragrant, single-petaled flowers 2 to 3 inches across. This reliable species blooms from midsummer until frost, and plants can survive winter temperatures down to −10°F. Cultivars include Monch, which produces flowers of a rich, clear, lavender-blue, and Wonder of Staffa, with large, airy clusters of pale lavender-blue blossoms.

*A. novae-angliae*, the New England aster, grows 3 to 5 feet high and starts blooming in late summer. The plants are hardy to −20°F. New England asters are seldom troubled by the mildew that can plague asters. Many cultivars have been developed; the following are some of the best.

Alma Potschke, a recent introduction, gets to be 3 feet tall and has flowers of an unusual warm shade of pink. The plants bloom from late summer into fall.

Harrington's Pink grows to 4 feet tall and produces its clear pink blossoms from late summer until frost. In northern gardens, this plant should not be pinched back or its flowers may bloom too late and be lost to an early freeze.

Professor Kippenburg grows just a foot high and covers itself with masses of light blue flowers in late summer and early fall.

September Ruby blooms for several weeks in September and October, its deep crimson flowers appearing on 3½-foot plants.

*A. novi-belgii*, the New York aster, is native to eastern North America. It blooms in late summer and fall, and is hardy to −20°F. Of all the Michaelmas daisies, this species produces the best cut flowers. Extensive breeding work has given us cultivars with a range of flower colors and plant heights.

Ada Ballard grows about 3 feet tall and has semidouble lavender-blue flowers.

Audrey, a dwarf cultivar, forms a compact 15-inch-high mound of foliage that is covered with lavender-blue flowers in late summer and fall.

Boningale White grows to 3½ feet and has double white flowers. The sturdy stems may not need staking.

Crimson Brocade grows 3 feet high, with semidouble crimson-red flowers.

Patricia Ballard bears masses of pink flowers on 2-foot plants.

## Boltonia

Sometimes known as the thousand-flowered aster, boltonia deserves to be better known among gardeners. It is very easy to grow, and its masses of starry white flowers make an excellent companion for asters and mums in the autumn garden.

The species form of the plant, *Boltonia asteroides*, bears purple flowers and is seldom grown in gardens, little wonder since it grows an ungainly 6 or 7 feet high. The white-flowered cultivar Snowbank is the plant you will find offered in nursery catalogs, and it is the one whose culture is described here.

Boltonia grows best in full sun, but it is not at all fussy about soil. It thrives in practically any soil of average fertility, in either a moist or a dry place, so long as it is not too extreme in either direction. The plants branch freely and practically cover themselves with flowers from September until October or November, depending on the climate. The flowers can withstand several light frosts and hold up well in hot, humid summer weather, too. Plants are hardy to −30°F.

Boltonia is best grown in beds and borders, although you can also grow it as a hedge if you set the plants close together. The plant's blue-green leaves are attractive all season, and the 3- to 4-foot flower stems are sturdy and do not need staking. Boltonia is virtually maintenance-free.

You can propagate new plants by division in early spring. Plants ordered from the nursery are also planted in spring.

## Chrysanthemum

The chrysanthemum is the undisputed queen of the fall garden and a staple of the cut-flower and gift plant market as well. Commercial greenhouses force mums into bloom year-round, but for gardeners, chrysanthemums and autumn are pretty much synonymous.

Despite their popularity, chrysanthemums are not the easiest plants to

*Chrysanthemums in yellow and orange.*

grow. They need pinching to keep the plants bushy, they need to be divided often, and they are subject to a number of diseases. Still, their rich, earthy colors are unbeatable in fall, and it's worth the trouble to grow at least a few

of them. Individual plants bloom for three or four weeks, but choosing cultivars with different blooming periods can give you flowers from late summer well into fall, through several frosts.

There are thousands of cultivars on

*The types of chrysanthemum flowers include, clockwise from top left, single or daisy-flowered, pompon, spider, spoon, reflexed, anemone-flowered, and incurved.*

the U.S. market alone, with new ones being developed all the time, and a large assortment of plant heights, flower forms, and flower sizes is available.

Pompon chrysanthemums, the smallest kind, have ball-shaped flowers. When the flowers are less than an inch in diameter, they are called button mums. The plants are low growers, most being less than a foot tall, and are good for the front of the garden.

Cushion mums are low growing, too, usually 10 to 15 inches tall and just as wide. The plants are very compact and dense and bear their flowers at the tips of the stems.

Single or daisy mums have flat, daisylike flowers with an open, disk-shaped center. Semidoubles are similar in shape but have more rows of rays (petals). Another related type, anemone mums, have larger centers.

Decorative chrysanthemums grow taller and have larger flowers with many rays. They need staking and pinching to produce the best flowers and work best in the back of the garden.

Spoon chrysanthemums have an unusual form. The rays are rolled in the center and flattened at the outer edge, giving them a spatulate shape.

Spider mums have long, tubular rays that often curve and twist gracefully in different directions.

Incurved chrysanthemums have smooth rays that curve up and inward toward the center of the flowers. The big flowers we know as football mums are usually the incurved type.

Reflexed mums have rays that curve outward and down.

There are other, more unusual kinds of chrysanthemums, too, including quill forms, brush types, and thistle types. The chrysanthemum clan is extremely large and varied.

To get off to a good start with chrysanthemums, it is essential to plan ahead. When scouting around for a good spot in the garden, pick a place where you will be able to see and really appreciate the color in fall. Full sun is crucial—even a little bit of shade will interfere with chrysanthemum performance.

Rich, well-drained soil is another requirement. Start preparing the soil for mums a couple of months or even a season before you intend to plant them. Dig plenty of compost, leaf mold, or well-rotted manure into the bed. It is vital that the soil be light, loose, and very well drained, for chrysanthemums are subject to root rot in wet soils. If your soil is heavy, you might want to make raised beds for

your mums to give them better drainage.

A few weeks before planting time in spring, fertilize the planting area with an all-purpose fertilizer and some superphosphate. If you garden organically, incorporate rock phosphate and granite dust into the soil when you dig in the compost or manure.

It's best to start your chrysanthemum bed with plants or rooted cuttings from a nursery. Hybrid varieties will not come true from seed, and plants from the florist do not often survive in the garden. Spacing distance will vary according to the sizes of the cultivars you are growing.

During the growing season, feed the plants weekly with fish emulsion or less often with a commercial time-release fertilizer. Make sure the plants get plenty of moisture, especially during hot summer weather. Many gardeners like to keep their plants mulched as they grow.

Most chrysanthemums (except for the cushion types) need to be pinched back as well. When the plant is at least 5 inches tall, pinch out the growing tip to force the plant to branch. Pinch the plant at least once more as it grows, and pinch the tips evenly all over the plant to give it a symmetrical shape. If you live in the North, stop pinching in midsummer so that the plants will bloom before cold weather sets in.

In northern gardens a good winter mulch is important, because the plants are not always entirely hardy. As an alternative to mulching you can dig up the plants after they bloom and put them in a cold frame for the winter.

Divide your mums every year to maintain vigorous plants with the best flowers. Dig up the plants in spring, discard the woody central parts of the root clump, and replant the fleshy outer parts.

Even though you grow your own plants for fall flowers, it's awfully tempting to buy a plant or two from the florist at other times during the year to enjoy the flowers indoors. Commercial growers have become so adept at forcing mums that they are available year-round. Here are some tips on how to get the most mileage out of the plants you buy from a florist.

First, choose carefully. Buy a plant that is full of buds instead of open flowers to enjoy the longest possible bloom. A plant in bud will last up to a month indoors if you keep it on a sunny but cool windowsill. Look for a

Colchicum *Waterlily is a heavenly color that's a blend of pink and pale gold.*

plant that is compact, bushy, and symmetrically shaped, with healthy green leaves. Inspect the plant carefully for signs of aphids and other pests before you buy it. Bringing home an infested plant will spread the problem to your other houseplants.

When you get the plant home, put it in a cool place where it will get sun at least half the day. Keep the soil evenly moist at all times.

When the plant is finished blooming, throw it away. Although it may seem wasteful, chrysanthemum plants forced into bloom outside their normal outdoor season do not usually survive the transition to the outdoor garden. Just enjoy them while they last.

## Colchicum

Colchicums bloom with autumn crocuses and have similar chalice-shaped flowers, although colchicum flowers are larger. They are not widely grown by American gardeners, but they should be—they are reliable and easy to grow, and their beautiful flowers are a welcome addition to fall gardens. Colchicums bloom in shades of pink, rose, lilac, and white, and they are lovely naturalized in a lawn. You can also plant them in beds and borders or in rock gardens.

Colchicums are the source of colchicine, a chemical that was introduced as a drug in the 1920s but has found its greatest use among plant breeders. Colchicine affects the number of chromosomes in plant cells, and breeders have used it for years to produce bigger, hardier plants with larger flowers.

Colchicum plants grow from corms that are planted in late summer and burst into bloom just a few weeks later. Most species send up their autumn flowers on leafless stems, and the foli-

age does not appear until the following spring. The leaves grow about a foot high and die back in late spring or early summer along with the foliage of spring bulbs.

Colchicum bulbs are shipped from mail-order nurseries in July or August when they are dormant. You should plant them as soon as you receive them. Any well-drained soil of average fertility will suit them. When planting, set the corms so their tops are 3 to 4 inches below the soil surface.

A number of available colchicum species and cultivars are described below.

*Colchicum autumnale* var. *album* grows just 3 inches high and produces white flowers. Its diminutive stature makes it an excellent choice for rock gardens.

*C. autumnale* var. *plenum* has double lilac flowers that look like peonies. The flowers bloom in late fall and last for several weeks. The plants are about 4 inches high.

*C. bornmuelleri* is considered one of the best species. Its large flowers are carried on 6-inch stalks, continuing to bloom until late fall. The blossoms are pale mauve-pink when they open, and the color gradually deepens as the flowers mature.

*C. byzantium* bears a succession of large 4-inch flowers of a beautiful rosy lilac color. The plants bloom in September and flower freely for several weeks. The stems are about 6 inches high. Unlike most other colchicums, this species produces leaves as soon as its flowers fade.

*C. speciosum* is a wonderful raspberry-red color and fragrant, too. The plants grow 5 inches high. This species is a strong grower and spreads more quickly than most other colchicums. That means it needs to be divided more frequently—as often as every three years.

Perhaps the most stunning of all the

colchicums is the hybrid called Water-lily. Its large double flowers have pointed petals that, when fully open on a sunny day, look incredibly like waterlilies. The color is a hard-to-describe shade of soft, warm rosy pink, with a sort of golden glow to it. The flowers are quite beautiful. The plants grow 6 inches high.

## Crocus

Like their spring-blooming relatives, autumn crocuses are good flowers for rock gardens, for the front of beds and borders, and for naturalizing in a lawn. They bloom in shades of lavender, lilac, and purple—colors that lend a welcome contrast to the more typical golds, oranges, and russets that are so much a part of most autumn gardens. Wherever you plant autumn crocuses, plant lots of them. The carpet of blue or purple their flowers create when planted in masses is a stunning sight against the warm earth colors, the soft beiges and deep browns of the autumn landscape, a reminder of springs past and a harbinger of springs to come.

Autumn crocuses are grown like colchicums. The corms are shipped from suppliers in August. Plant them right away, and the flowers will bloom in September, October, and November. For the best flowers, plant your crocuses in full sun, in any average, well-drained soil. Plant the corms 3 to 4 inches deep. Autumn crocuses spread like the spring ones do, so give them room to expand.

Several autumn-blooming crocus species and cultivars are available, including those described below.

Crocus goulimyi blooms in early fall. Its round, cup-shaped flowers come in shades of pale to deep purple with long, slender white necks. They grow 4 inches high. This species is hardy only in the South, and its corms actually thrive in hot, sun-baked soil

while they are dormant in summer.

C. kotschyanus is a good choice for northern gardens, for it does well in cool, damp conditions. But the plants will perform satisfactorily in most parts of the country, and they are easy to grow. The flowers are pale lilac veined with darker purple and have a soft yellow throat. The flowers are followed immediately by leaves, and the plants grow about 4 inches tall. The vigorous corms spread freely. These plants also grow 4 inches tall.

C. laevigatus var. fontenayi is a winter-blooming species that is not hardy in the North where temperatures drop below −10°F. Gardeners in the more northern parts of the country will not find them hardy, but most of the rest of us will. These plants bloom from December to February, producing rosy lilac flowers with a fragrance similar to that of freesias. The plants grow only 2½ inches tall.

C. medius is one of the best of the autumn crocuses. Its deep lavender-purple flowers are feathered with darker purple near the center. Its brilliant red styles offer a striking contrast to the petal color. Hardy only to −10°F, the plants grow 4 inches high and bloom in mid-autumn.

The saffron crocus (C. sativus) also blooms in fall. This is the flower whose long styles are dried and used as the costly flavoring ingredient that imparts an unmistakable flavor to paella and other dishes. The rich purple flowers bloom on 4-inch stems. This species is hardy only to around 0°F. A white-flowered variety, cartwright-ianus albus, is also available.

C. speciosus flowers earlier than the other fall-blooming species, starting in September, and is a good choice for northern gardens where winter comes early and later flowers would be buried under snow. The flowers are lilac-purple, and plants grow 4 inches high. This crocus spreads quickly and is

perfect for naturalizing. The variety albus has white flowers with a yellow throat. One cultivar, Cassiope, has blue flowers with a yellow base and blooms later in the season.

## Leucojum
### Autumn Snowflake

This genus of white-flowered bulbs is better known as snowflakes. The most commonly available species and cultivars bloom in spring and summer, but there is also an autumn-flowering species, Leucojum autumnale. Its little bell-shaped blossoms dangle from slender stems singly or in groups of two or three. The base of the flowers is sometimes tinged with pink. You can plant snowflakes in clumps in the rock garden, under and between shrubs, or in beds and borders, or you can naturalize them in a lawn.

Snowflakes are hardy everywhere. They grow best in rich, light, somewhat sandy soil, and bloom in either full sun or partial shade. Plant the bulbs 4 to 5 inches deep and about 4 inches apart. After that they need little care. You won't have to divide them for quite a few years unless you want to move them or propagate new plants from offsets.

Autumn snowflake grows about 8 inches high, and the flowering stems are followed by slender, shorter, grass-like leaves.

## Lycoris

These relatives of the amaryllis are sometimes called spider lilies or magic lilies, and magical their flowers certainly are. The funnel-shaped flowers closely resemble those of amaryllis, but they are more delicate in their size, shape, and colors. Their petals are long and narrow, and many of the flowers have long, spidery stamens that curve and twist out into space from the center of the flower. Best of all, spider

lilies bloom from late summer into autumn, when their fanciful, exotic forms lend a touch of grace to gardens or patios.

Only one species is hardy in the North, but the tender kinds can be grown in pots and moved indoors for the winter in areas where they are not hardy. You can plant lycoris in beds and borders or grow them in pots on patios and terraces.

The bulbs are planted during their summer dormant period. They appreciate a sunny spot and well-drained soil that tends to be dry in summer. Set the bulbs a foot apart, with the tops of the necks just below the soil surface. Magic lilies are treated differently from most other plants in one important respect: do not water them in summer—they need a dry dormant period rather than a cold one.

The straplike leaves appear in spring, and the plants do need to be watered regularly during this active growing period. In summer the leaves die back and the plant vanishes for its dormancy. But in late summer the flower stalks burst through the soil, springing up as if by magic. The stems grow 1 1/2 to 2 feet tall and are topped by clusters of the most exquisite, fragrant flowers, mostly in shades of pink and lilac-pink. The plants seldom need to be dug and divided unless you want to move them or propagate new plants.

The golden spider lily, *Lycoris aurea*, is a tender species with orange-yellow flowers that resemble those of nerine lilies. The plants grow 14 to 20 inches tall.

*L. radiata*, often called spider lily, has crimson blossoms with long, spidery anthers that give the flowers a mysterious, other-worldly look. Actually the plant is native to Japan and China, and it has been in cultivation since the 1700s. Spider lily plants grow

*Lycoris blooming with some late achillea.*

to 1 1/2 feet high, and they cannot tolerate frost.

The plant that is most often called magic lily is *L. squamigera*, the best-known hardy member of the clan. Its flowers look very much like those of the hardy amaryllis, and this plant is a better choice in cold climates where hardy amaryllis will not grow. Its flowers are a heavenly rose-pink, tinged with a soft purplish blue, and are carried on 1 1/2- to 2-foot stems that pop out of the ground in late August and September. Magic lilies grow happily in just about any average garden soil. A very similar species, also hardy, is *L. sprengeri*. Its purplish pink flowers are a bit smaller than those of *L. squamigera*, and the plants grow just 15 inches high.

## *Polianthes* / *Tuberose*

Tuberoses (*Polianthes tuberosa*) are among the most fragrant flowers on earth and have been an important ingredient in perfume formulas for generations. Today they are grown primarily in France for the perfume industry. But tuberoses are not difficult to grow, and if you love fragrant flowers, the intoxicating scent of this one belongs in your garden. The plants bloom from late summer into autumn, when most other fragrant flowers are long gone.

Tuberoses grow from rhizomes that are not hardy, but they can be grown in cold climates if you store them indoors over the winter along with your dahlias and tuberous begonias. Warm-climate gardeners can grow tuberoses in beds and borders; northerners may prefer to plant them in pots. In fact, containers is where tuberoses belong, because they can perfume a patio or terrace close by the house where you can enjoy them most.

The flowers themselves are not terribly striking, although they are attractive. They are waxy, white, and borne

in clusters near the tops of the 3-foot stems. The leaves are long and grassy and appear before the flowers. The flowers bloom in late summer and autumn, and the plants need a long, warm growing season in order to produce them. In the North, you will need to start the rhizomes growing indoors in spring.

Tuberoses grow best in rich, well-drained soil that contains plenty of organic matter. Set the rhizomes 2 inches deep and 4 to 6 inches apart. The plants need full sun and plenty of moisture. It is important to water regularly when the leaves appear. Tuberoses grow best in soil with an acid pH. If your soil is alkaline, you should feed the plants as they grow with a fertilizer intended for other acid-loving plants like camellias and azaleas.

When the leaves start to turn yellow in fall, stop watering the plants and let the soil dry out. When the leaves are dead, dig up the plants or remove them from their pots. Cut off the dead leaves and let the rhizomes dry for two weeks in a dry, airy place. Then store them as you do other tender bulbs.

Both single- and double-flowered tuberoses are available, as well as a cultivar with variegated leaves.

## *Schlumbergera*
### *Thanksgiving Cactus*

Thanksgiving cactus (*Schlumbergera truncata*) is an easy-to-grow houseplant that blooms dependably and lavishly every fall. My eight-year-old plant likes to vary its schedule from year to year, sometimes starting to bloom in summer and sometimes waiting until December. In fact, it has only once reached its peak bloom at Thanksgiving. But bloom it does, usually continuing for about a month and sometimes sending out a few surprise flowers in spring.

My plant has flowers of rich scarlet-

*Thanksgiving cactus.*

red, but there are numerous other shades of red, pink, and white available, too. Newer cultivars with flowers in unusual shades like salmon and pale pink flushed with gold are being introduced as well.

The plants have stems made up of a series of jointed flat, basically oval segments. The edges of each segment are notched, and the notches provide the easiest way to distinguish Thanksgiving cactus from Christmas cactus, which has scalloped edges. The stems grow upright at first, then nod over as they elongate. Eventually the plant will develop a gracefully arching shape. The stems also branch as they become longer. The plants grow slowly, and it takes a few years for them to branch and droop.

Like its other holiday-blooming relatives, the Thanksgiving cactus is an epiphyte. Its roots are wiry and thin and grow best in a light, well-drained potting mix. A blend of one part potting soil, two parts peat moss, and one part perlite or builder's sand will serve nicely.

The cactus likes a warm room (around 70°F is good) and thrives in either eastern or western windows (mine has grown well in both). I've heard a lot of dismal warnings over the years about how the plants need cool temperatures or exactly the right day length in order to set buds, but mine has had no such special treatment and has bloomed without fail every year. I keep it close by the window, where it gets whatever light comes through the glass, but other lights in the room are often turned on at night and have never disturbed the plant's bud setting or blooming.

Individual flowers last only a few days, but the plant sets many buds and continues to set more after the first flowers wilt. Picking off wilted flowers appears to extend the blooming period. After blooming is finished (usually sometime in December), the plant produces new leaves. Throughout this time it appreciates a weekly or biweekly watering and an occasional dose of all-purpose plant food. Sometime in spring, growth stops and the plant rests. During this time, water it only every three or four weeks, when the leaves start to look a little shriveled.

In late summer or early autumn, you can start to water more often and fertilize the cactus as it begins to set buds.

## *Solanum* / *Jerusalem Cherry*

Jerusalem cherries (sometimes called Christmas cherries, although they usually begin producing their colorful fruits in fall) are popular gift plants that offer an easy source of indoor color in fall and winter. They belong to the same genus as eggplant and potatoes, but unlike them, the Jerusalem cherry *Solanum pseudocapsicum*) is not edible. In fact, its fruits are poisonous.

The shrubby plants grow 1 to 3 feet high, with glossy, dark green leaves. In summer they produce small white flowers that are followed by round, cherrylike fruits in fall. The ripe fruits turn bright scarlet-orange and usually stay on the plants for most of the winter. You can generally get the plants to rebloom a second year, but after that it's best to throw them out and buy new plants.

Jerusalem cherries grow well in a potting mix of one part potting soil, one part peat moss, and one part builder's sand or perlite, or any other all-purpose potting mix with good drainage.

Indoors the plants like good light. Give them a southern exposure during the winter and an eastern window in other seasons. Warm temperatures around 70°F are best during the day, and the plants appreciate a ten-degree drop at night. Keep the soil evenly moist, and increase the humidity around the plants by misting the foliage every day or setting the plants on top of pebbles in a shallow tray of water. Feed the plants with a mild all-purpose fertilizer every couple of weeks while they're growing actively.

If you want to keep your Jerusalem cherry plant for a second year, let it rest for a month or so toward the end of winter. Put the plant in a cool (60°F) place during this time, stop fertilizing, and water just enough to keep the soil from drying out.

When the weather becomes warm in spring, you can repot the plant in fresh soil mix and move it outdoors for the summer. Remember to bring the plant back indoors before the first fall frost.

## Sternbergia / Winter Daffodil

This golden-flowered bulb blooms with colchicums and autumn crocuses, and makes a good companion for their lavender and blue flowers. Its nickname is a bit misleading because it is the plant's leaves, not its flowers, that are usually in evidence during the winter.

Winter daffodils are most valuable for their color, since most other fall bulbs bloom in purples, blues, or lavender-pinks. Another virtue of these plants is their toughness—both flowers and leaves are able to withstand weather conditions that would ruin the more delicate colchicums and crocuses. The bulbs are hardy to −20°F.

The bulbs are shipped from mail-order nurseries in midsummer and should be planted right away for flowers beginning around the middle of September and continuing into October. Plant the bulbs 4 inches deep and about 6 inches apart in well-drained soil in a sunny location. Sternbergia bulbs like a good baking in summer, so temperate-climate gardeners would do well to plant them next to a south-facing wall or in a similarly sheltered spot with plenty of sun.

The plants need lots of moisture as they grow and bloom; you may need to water them if your weather is dry. In northern gardens, winter daffodils need a good mulch to protect them from the cold winter weather.

Sternbergias come into bloom in early fall. Each plant sends up several flowering stems about 8 inches high. The deep yellow flowers are chalice-shaped when they first open, but in bright sunlight they spread their pointed petals wide into a star.

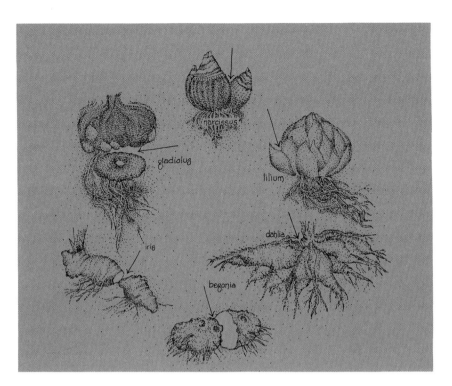

## NINE

# *Autumn Gardening Activities*

For gardeners everywhere, fall is cleanup time. Fallen leaves, spent flowers, and garden trash should be removed from the garden and added to the compost pile. Crowded clumps of spring perennials are ready to be dug up and transplanted. It's time to plant spring bulbs and sow hardy annuals for early bloom next year.

Autumn is a great time to be out in the garden. The days are pleasantly warm (in the South) or cool (in the North), and we can work surrounded by the many beauties of the autumn landscape and of garden flowers still in bloom. In this season of harvest and completion, gardeners enjoy a sense of satisfaction for the successes of this year's plantings and begin to look ahead to what to do differently next year. As you go about your garden chores in fall, it's helpful to keep a little notebook in your pocket to jot down ideas and sudden inspirations about new colors to try next year and what plant might look just right in that empty spot next to the garage. You can also start thinking about revising your garden plans in preparation for making your seed and nursery orders in winter.

Autumn is the time to plan for winter flowers indoors and for early spring flowers outdoors. Now is the time to pot up or take cuttings of garden annuals to bring indoors. It's the time to prepare daffodils, hya-cinths, crocuses, and other hardy bulbs for forcing into bloom indoors during the winter. It is also the time to plant these bulbs in the outdoor garden to produce early spring flowers according to their natural schedules.

Besides the classic hardy bulbs, a whole host of other bulbs can be brought into bloom indoors over winter if you start the process now. Your indoor bulb garden can reward you with surprisingly diverse and lavish displays of color and, in some cases, fragrance. Your choices include the big, trumpet-shaped flowers of amaryllis, brilliant red, pink, or blue-violet poppy anemones, elegant calla lilies, exquisitely fragrant freesias, clivias, agapanthus, tuberous begonias, irises, and even lilies. The key is to plant the bulbs in autumn, following the directions given later.

This chapter begins with a rundown of basic gardening activities for autumn. I will discuss several of the more complicated tasks—like lifting tender bulbs, winterizing roses, and forcing bulbs indoors—in more detail following this section.

## EARLY AUTUMN

### TEMPERATE CLIMATES

Maintenance chores continue as the outdoor gardening season nears its end. As the days grow shorter and the temperatures turn cooler, remember to keep spent flowers picked off mums, dahlias, late-blooming roses, and other fall flowers. Look over your chrysanthemums as they come into bloom, and label or note on your garden plan the ones that will need to be divided next spring.

Early fall is the time to begin the fall garden cleanup, particularly in beds where spring and summer flowers are finished blooming and no autumn flowers are planted. You should edge and mulch existing beds of perennials and bulbs. Early in the season you should also prepare garden beds for autumn planting of perennials, roses, and bulbs. Dig the soil deeply, work compost or other organic matter into the soil, and rake the beds smooth. In other parts of the garden, pull up and dispose of annuals as they finish blooming or are killed by frost.

If your first frost is still several weeks away, you should continue to fertilize outdoor annuals and container plants that are still in bloom. But stop fertilizing perennials and shrubs so they will have a chance to harden before the ground freezes. One exception to the rule, though, is peonies. You can fertilize peonies that do not need dividing with bonemeal or all-purpose fertilizer. If your garden includes roses, keep watering late roses as they finish blooming, but stop fertilizing them.

It's time to start dividing and transplanting early-blooming perennials. Dig and divide crowded clumps of daylilies, peonies, and other spring and summer flowers. After the first light frost, dig dahlias, gladiolus, and other tender bulbs for winter storage.

Early fall is also the time to dig and transplant into pots marigolds, nasturtiums, petunias, and other annuals that will continue to bloom indoors during fall and winter. You can take cuttings from begonias, geraniums, and impatiens before the first frost to start new plants indoors.

If you are growing perennials from seed, seedlings of early bloomers can be transplanted (if they're big enough) to their permanent locations in the garden. Smaller seedlings can be kept in a cold frame over the winter and moved to the garden in spring.

In the North, it's time to plant bulbs that bloom in late winter and spring, such as winter aconite, crocuses, daffodils, scillas, and snowdrops.

Plant peonies, Oriental poppies, and other perennials as soon as they arrive from the nursery. Pansies and lily bulbs can be planted now, too.

Except in the far North, you can sow seeds of early-blooming hardy annuals, such as larkspurs and poppies, for bloom next spring.

Gardeners in the North should start moving their houseplants back indoors. You can leave out for a few more weeks plants that need cool weather to set buds (such as Christmas cactus and some orchids) and those that bloom in cool weather (camellias and azaleas, for instance).

After frost strikes, cut back all the perennials in your garden that are finished blooming. As you go about your autumn chores, take time to evaluate the results of this year's garden. You can make notes on successes and failures, low points in blooming schedules, colors to add next year. Then later in the season you can use the notes to make alterations in your garden plans for next year.

### WARM CLIMATES

Plenty of plants are still blooming in warm parts of the country. Southern gardeners are busy deadheading annuals and perennials as their flowers fade. If you are growing camellias, you will need to disbud them when the flower buds are big enough to distinguish from leaf buds. Thin each flower cluster to one bud, or at least thin them so the buds are not touching. Disbud dahlias, roses, and mums to get bigger flowers, if you want them.

Early autumn weather is still quite warm in the South and Southwest, and you will need to keep the garden watered during hot dry spells.

If you are growing chrysanthemums, fertilize them for the last time when they have set flower buds. You can also continue to feed annuals and container plants that are still in bloom.

As time permits, you can start preparing garden beds where you will be planting later in fall. Dig in some compost or other organic matter, and rake the soil smooth.

Fall cleanup can begin, too. Weeds and annuals that have finished blooming can be pulled up and tossed on the compost pile. You can edge and mulch existing beds of perennials and bulbs where you will not be dividing plants or planting new ones this season. Put leaves and plant debris (as long as the plants are not diseased or infested with pests) on the compost pile.

You can begin to dig and divide perennials that bloom in spring and early summer. It's also time to start digging dahlias, gladiolus, and other summer bulbs for winter storage. If you started any biennials and perennials from seed over the summer, they should be ready to transplant to their permanent locations in the garden in early fall.

Put new hyacinth and tulip bulbs in the refrigerator when they arrive from the nursery until it's time to plant them in late November. If you live in southern California or other very mild climates, you should refrigerate daffodil bulbs as well. Mail-order nurseries begin shipping spring-blooming perennials in early fall. If you have ordered new plants, plant them when they arrive from the nursery. Be sure to note on your garden plan where you put them if you haven't already done so. You can plant pansies for winter color, too. Gardeners in very mild regions can sow seeds of sweet peas and other annuals for winter flowers.

Finally, you can start to take cuttings from garden annuals to pot up for indoor flowers in winter.

## INDOOR GARDENS

Although there's plenty to do in outdoor gardens in fall, it's also time to give some thought to your indoor garden and to plan what you will want to have blooming indoors in winter. You can start to pot up any plants from the garden that you want to bring indoors over winter. The plants can stay outdoors until the weather turns cool, but don't forget to water them.

If you want to start new poinsettias for Christmas flowers, you will need to take cuttings from existing plants by the middle of September.

Some indoor plants are ready for a dormant period about now. Vines such as bougainvillea and golden trumpet vine (*Allamanda*) usually stop blooming sometime in autumn. When they do, cut back on water, stop fertilizing, and prune back the bougainvillea to prepare the plants for a winter rest. Amaryllis, depending on when you started it growing, may also begin its dormant period now. Remove the leaves as they fade and die back. Then let the bulb rest for at least a month before repotting and starting to water and feed it again.

In early fall you can sow seeds of sweet peas to bloom indoors after Christmas; calendulas and blue lace flowers to bloom in February; calceolarias and cinerarias to bloom in February and March; and larkspurs and lupines to bloom in April. If you have a sunny but cool (50°F) spot, you can plant snapdragons and stocks to bloom in March.

## MID-AUTUMN

### TEMPERATE CLIMATES

Fall garden cleanup continues as the season progresses. Weed and cultivate garden beds and borders where tender plants have been killed by frost. Cultivation helps to get rid of perennial weeds and also aerates the soil. But you must be careful not to disturb the roots of perennials and bulbs in these beds. Hardy bulbs will not be visible above the soil surface now, but your garden plans should remind you where they are planted. Rake up fallen leaves and put them on the compost pile or shred them to use as mulch. Pull up annuals as they are killed by frost. This is also a good time to collect stakes from the garden and tie them in bundles to store them for next year.

If you have not yet had your first frost, watch for it and lift most of your tender bulbs as soon as it occurs and put them in winter storage. Tuberous begonias and tuberoses should be dug *before* the first frost strikes. Move to the cold frame any tender perennials that you want to winter over.

In established gardens it is time to dig and divide bulb plantings that are crowded: lilies, crocuses, daffodils, and others. In addition, you should dig and divide late spring perennials and any others still remaining to be divided this season.

If you are growing roses, it is essential to winterize them before the ground freezes. Lightly prune them, mound up soil around the base of the plants, and mulch the plants to protect the canes from winter damage. More details on protecting roses for winter are given later in this chapter.

As the weather turns cooler, bring the rest of your houseplants that spent the summer outside back indoors.

In October you can continue planting early spring bulbs and start planting tulips. If you live where winters are very cold and without much snow cover, mulch beds of newly planted bulbs to minimize soil heaving.

It's smart to think ahead, too. Although most seed and nursery orders won't be made until the new spring catalogs arrive in winter, it's a good idea to order special rose varieties now for shipment early next year. If you wait until January, nurseries may be sold out of rare or popular varieties.

## WARM CLIMATES

In warm climates, too, garden cleanup continues in fall. Gardeners are busy pulling perennial weeds from garden beds and raking and composting leaves. As annuals finish blooming you can pull up the plants and put them on the compost pile, too. The autumn garden is in full bloom now in warm climates. To keep plants healthy, continue to fertilize heavy feeders like chrysanthemums and roses. Stake tall-growing mums to prevent wind damage.

Bulb gardens need attention, too. You can dig and divide crowded plantings of bulbs such as crocuses, daffodils, and lilies. You can also continue to lift tender bulbs for winter storage. If you live in an area where frost occurs, dig tuberous begonias and tuberoses before the first frost and dahlias, glad-

iolus and other tender bulbs after the first frost.

In established perennial gardens, division and transplanting continue for late-blooming perennials and any other perennials that still need to be divided this season.

If you planted new perennials this season, you can mulch them in mid-autumn. You can start mulching your roses, too, but wait until mid- or late winter to prune them.

It's a good idea to check on any seedlings you set out in the garden last month. Water them if the weather is dry.

If the weather is still mild, you can continue to plant new perennials from the nursery. You can also plant spring bulbs except for tulips and hyacinths, which should stay in the refrigerator for six to eight weeks. Plant them out later in the season when the weather stays cool.

Warm-climate gardeners can begin to sow seeds of cool-weather annuals and biennials like ageratum, sweet alyssum, bachelor's buttons, calendulas, larkspurs, nasturtiums, phlox,

poppies, snapdragons, sweet peas, and sweet williams for flowers in winter and spring.

If you grow roses or unusual plants, you may want to order special varieties now for shipment early next year. If you wait until January, nurseries may be out of rare or popular varieties.

## INDOOR GARDENS

Fall is the time to pot up spring bulbs that you want to force into bloom indoors in winter. Crocuses, daffodils, tulips, and other hardy bulbs can be potted from now until late autumn and placed in cold storage to begin the forcing process. More details on forcing procedures can be found later in this chapter.

In late October or early November you can start planting paperwhite narcissus bulbs at two-week intervals for winter flowers.

If you started new poinsettia plants from cuttings, you can begin to give them long nights now so they will bloom for Christmas.

## LATE AUTUMN

## TEMPERATE CLIMATES

By late autumn, frost has settled over many northern gardens. The clear blue skies and crisp temperatures of October are giving way to the gray, blustery days of November, and winter is on the way. If you live where winters are cold, you must finish cleaning up your garden before the ground freezes and the weather becomes too cold for you to work outdoors.

In established gardens, cut back perennials to 4 or 5 inches. If you have peonies, cut the stems all the way back to the ground. As your chrysanthemums die, cut them back to the

ground as well. Make sure woody perennial vines like wisteria are securely fastened to their supports before winter sets in.

If you grow tropical waterlilies, remove the tubers from their pools or tubs. You can leave hardy waterlilies in place if the water is deep enough that it will not freeze solid during the winter. If the water is likely to freeze solid, remove hardy waterlilies, too, and store them with your tender bulbs over winter.

Shrubs that bloom in late summer and fall, such as abelia, butterfly bush, clethra, and hydrangea, should be pruned in late autumn, several weeks

before the weather turns really cold.

You can continue to plant tulip and lily bulbs until the ground freezes. Gardeners in the mid-Atlantic area, from New Jersey south, can sow sweet peas in pots to be kept in the cold frame over winter and moved to the garden as soon as the soil can be worked next spring.

The last thing you will need to do, after established perennials are cut back and new plantings are in the ground, is to cover the garden with a good layer of mulch. Mulching plants has always seemed to me as if I am tucking a warm, fluffy blanket around them to protect them from winter's cold. But the real purpose of mulch is to keep the ground cold, not warm. Hardy bulbs and perennials go dormant in winter when the soil freezes. The greatest danger winter offers them does not come from frozen soil, but from soil that freezes and then thaws during mild spells. Repeated freezing and thawing causes the ground to buckle and heave, and bulbs and perennial roots can be pushed right out of the soil, where they can be damaged by cold air and frigid, drying winds. The goal of mulching is to keep the soil frozen all winter, so the plants can rest peacefully in their dormancy.

In late fall, you should have available whatever material you plan to use for mulch—shredded leaves, salt hay, compost, or boughs pruned from evergreens are some examples. But wait until the ground freezes before you lay the mulch on the garden. When you do put down the mulch, make it at least 6 inches thick. If you live in the far North, make it a foot thick. Be sure to mulch all your bulbs and perennials, and especially your roses. Azaleas and rhododendrons, if you grow them, should be mulched with an acid material such as pine needles or oak leaves.

When your garden is mulched and ready for winter, it's time to clean and oil your tools and put them away until spring. Now is a good time to sharpen any tools that need it, so they'll be ready to use in spring.

## WARM CLIMATES

Autumn weather is delightful in warm climates, often the best weather of the year. Working in the garden can be a real pleasure during this season. Although warm-climate gardeners don't have to prepare their plants for the extreme conditions northern gardeners face each winter, there are still cleanup chores to finish. Gardens need to be weeded and edged, and in dry climates they need to be mulched, too, to conserve moisture.

Whether or not you grow annuals for winter bloom, in late fall you should continue to pull up summer annuals that have died back. Tender plants such as impatiens and geraniums, which are killed by frost in northern gardens, keep right on growing in warm climates and may look straggly and overgrown by fall. You can remedy the problem by cutting back the plants to shape them and encourage a new flush of flowers or by pulling up the old plants and starting over with cuttings or seedlings.

In established perennial gardens, cut back the plants to 4 to 5 inches if they are dormant. If the tops are still green, leave them in place. After your chrysanthemums finish blooming, cut them back to the ground. This is also a good time to prune magnolias. Do *not*, however, prune azaleas, camellias, rhododendrons, or spiraea, or you will cut off the flower buds.

If you grow lilies, cut off the leaves in late fall and mound a few inches of soil on top of the beds where they are planted to keep mice away from the bulbs during their winter dormancy. If you grow tropical waterlilies, remove them from their pools or tubs and store them in a cool, dry place until spring. Hardy waterlilies can be left in place.

You should also dig and store any summer bulbs still remaining in the garden. If you started biennials or perennials from seed earlier in the season, the seedlings should be ready to transplant to their permanent garden locations. In the lower South and other very mild regions, you can continue to dig and divide perennials.

Crocuses, daffodils, hyacinths, tulips, and other spring bulbs can be planted in the garden now if they have been refrigerated for at least six weeks.

Late autumn is also a good time to start seeds of perennials that bloom in late spring and summer. You can sow delphiniums, gaillardias, larkspurs, poppies, sweet peas, and other flowers outdoors in the garden. You can also start seeds of hardy annuals indoors for planting out later on. Many cool-weather annuals bloom in winter and early spring in warm climates. Some of them, such as bachelor's buttons, larkspurs, and love-in-a-mist, can be sown directly in the garden.

If you live in a dry climate, mulch any new plantings in beds and borders. Mulch your roses, too, if you have not already done so, but wait until winter to prune them.

When most of your autumn chores are complete, you will have some time to clean and check your tools. This is a good time to sharpen any tools that need it.

## INDOOR GARDENS

As autumn draws to a close, you can continue to plant paperwhite narcissus bulbs at two-week intervals to have lots of their fragrant white flowers all winter long.

November is the latest you can pot up hardy bulbs for winter forcing. If you plant them any later, by the time they have gone through the necessary cold storage period they won't bloom much before their normal outdoor blooming time in spring. If you want the bulbs to flower in winter, this is your last chance to plant them.

As your attention shifts from the outdoor garden to the indoor garden in late fall, it's important to watch the houseplants you brought back indoors after their summer vacation outside to make sure they are not carrying any pests with them. As summer-blooming houseplants go into dormancy, cut back on water and stop fertilizing them.

# LIFTING TENDER BULBS

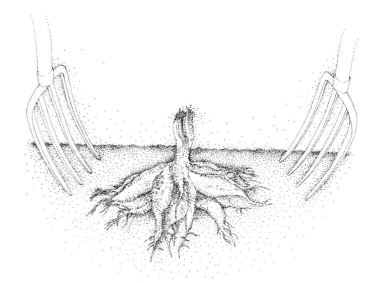

When the first frost strikes, it's time to dig up tender bulbs, corms, and tubers from the outdoor garden and put them in storage for the winter. You can wait to dig most bulbs until the foliage has started to turn brown or has been softened by frost. Exceptions are tuberous begonias and tuberoses, which cannot tolerate even a light frost. Dig them early. Do not delay digging any of the tender bulbs until you get a heavy frost, or the plant crowns or the bulbs themselves may be damaged.

The basic procedure for tuberous begonias and most other tender plants with fleshy top growth is as follows: Begin by loosening the soil around the plant, then carefully lift the entire plant with a spade or digging fork, retaining a good clump of soil around the bulbs. Let the bulbs dry out in a cool, dark, ventilated but frostproof cellar. Remove foliage and stems when they fall off. A few days later, shake off the dry soil and let the bulbs dry out for another day or two. Then pack them in cotton, tissue paper, or dry sand or peat moss. Store them in a dark, dry, airy place where the temperature will not drop below 50°F. Always let your bulbs dry on the surface before you clean and store them, or they may mildew or rot. Sort all the bulbs according to variety or at least by color when you dig them, and label the boxes in which you store them so you will know what you've got at planting time next spring.

Here are some guidelines for storing a number of tender bulbs:

CALLA LILY. Wrap the bulbs in cotton or tissue paper and store them in a dark, dry, cool place.

CANNA. Keep the bulbs moderately cool (55° to 60°F). Place them in shallow boxes and cover them with a thin layer of dry sand or sawdust.

DAHLIA. These are among the last tender bulbs to come indoors, but they, too, must be dug before a severe frost occurs. Do the digging on a frost-free day. You may need a friend with a second spading fork to help you get the large root clumps out of the ground. First cut off the top growth with a sharp knife 3 to 5 inches above the ground. Push the tines of the forks deeply into the soil on opposite sides of the clump, keeping them at least 10 inches away from the stems. Loosen the clump carefully, trying to get beneath it as much as possible. When the clump lifts out, turn it upside down. In an hour or so, remove the soil. Leave the root clumps in the sun for a few more hours to dry the root surfaces. Shorten the stems to 2 to 3 inches with pruning shears. Store the roots upside down in shallow boxes lined with paper. You can store dahlia roots in sand, dry soil, or sawdust to slow the evaporation of moisture. Discard any roots that have become separated from the stem without retaining crowns—they won't grow next spring. Wait until spring to divide the clumps; the roots will store better if left undivided.

FOUR O'CLOCKS (*Mirabilis jalapa*). Pack the roots in dry sand and store

*The best way to lift large clumps of dahlia roots for winter storage is to enlist the aid of a gardening friend who can wield a second spading fork. Drive the forks into the ground on opposite sides of the root clump, and push backward and forward to loosen the soil. Then pull upward simultaneously to lift out the roots. If you have to do all the digging by yourself, loosen the soil on all sides of the plant before you try to lift the roots.*

them at temperatures just above freezing. They can winter over outdoors if they are well protected.

GLADIOLUS. Lift the corms carefully when the thermometer registers above freezing. Turn them upside down in a sunny spot for a few hours, then shake off the soil. Place the corms (with foliage still attached) loosely in shallow boxes so that air can circulate around them. In five or six weeks the soil will have dried out. At that time remove the soil, dead stems, leaves, and roots. Separate any offsets that have formed, and save them to plant out with the larger bulbs in spring. Store the corms in open, shallow boxes or on trays, in a dark, dry, cool but frost-free place.

ISMENE or PERUVIAN DAFFODIL (*Hymenocallis* species). Dig carefully to avoid injuring the thickened, tuberlike roots that have formed below the bulbs during the growing season. It may take four to six weeks after digging for these thick roots to dry enough to be removed without causing the bulb to bleed a great deal. If the bulb does bleed, sprinkle any open wounds with powdered charcoal to prevent decay-forming bacteria from attacking. Store the bulbs in a cool, dry place.

SUMMER HYACINTH (*Galtonia candicans*). Store in dry conditions in a dark, cool place.

TUBEROSE (*Polianthes tuberosa*). Store tuberoses like tuberous begonias, but be aware that these rhizomes must be kept perfectly dry in a cool, dry place.

ZEPHYRANTHES, MONTBRETIA (*Crocosmia* species), OXALIS, and TIGER FLOWER (*Tigrida* species). All these bulbs can be handled like gladiolus. Mice seem to be especially fond of tiger flower bulbs, so wrap the storage box with hardware cloth or wire screening to keep them out.

## HOW TO DIVIDE AND TRANSPLANT PERENNIALS

In the far North where autumn weather is cool and frost comes early, perennials are best divided in early spring. But in most of the rest of the country, transplanting and division can be done in early to mid-fall. Transplanting should be done early enough to allow the plants to send out new feeder roots before the ground freezes in autumn. If you transplant too late, the plants won't have enough time to grow roots, and they will probably die over the winter. The best time to transplant is when the weather is moist and cool. A cloudy day is ideal.

The transplanting process actually begins a few days before the plants are moved. Two or three days before transplanting, thoroughly water the plants to be moved or divided. At this time, cut back the top growth of the plants by about one-third.

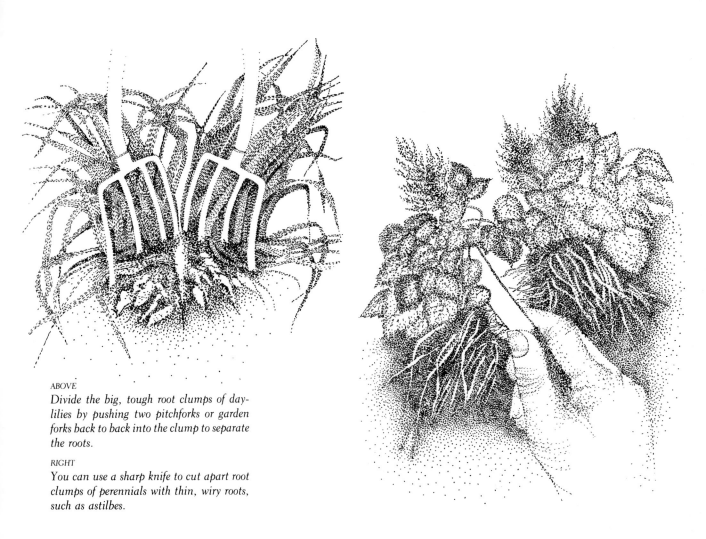

ABOVE
*Divide the big, tough root clumps of daylilies by pushing two pitchforks or garden forks back to back into the clump to separate the roots.*

RIGHT
*You can use a sharp knife to cut apart root clumps of perennials with thin, wiry roots, such as astilbes.*

On moving day, carefully dig around the outside of the clump of plants with a spade or spading fork to loosen the roots. Dig straight down until you are below the main part of the root ball, then angle the spade or fork underneath the plant. Be careful not to injure tuberous root structures and plant crowns (the growth point where stems join roots).

When the plant clump is out of the ground, you can divide it into sections by pulling apart loose clumps, cutting apart a very dense clump with a sharp knife or using two pitchforks to pry apart a large clump (you will need a partner to help you with this last operation). Divide the clump so that each division has one, a few, or several crowns, depending on the type of plant. A good book on growing perennials will give you more information on division and other ways to propagate new plants.

When you are dividing plants, it's a good idea to keep a pail of water handy to soak any divisions that start to dry out before you get them replanted.

Before replanting the newly divided root clumps, look over the roots and prune any broken or straggly ones.

The holes for the transplants should be dug before you dig up the old plants. When you are ready to transplant, add some water to the hole, set in the division, and gently fill in around the plant with good soil and compost. You should plant most root clumps at the same depth they were before or with their crowns even with the soil surface. Two notable exceptions to the rule are irises and peonies, which like to be transplanted with their crowns set a bit lower than they were on the parent plants.

You do not need to fertilize the new transplants, but do give them a good watering. If the weather is dry, continue to water the transplants regularly throughout the dry spell. The divisions need plenty of moisture while they are establishing themselves and producing feeder roots. Keep an eye on them for a few weeks as they settle in.

Finally, label the new transplants both in the garden and on your garden plan, so you will remember next spring what you planted where.

## MOVING HOUSEPLANTS BACK INDOORS

Spending the summer outdoors is beneficial for many houseplants. The increased light, humidity (depending on where you live), and air circulation can give housebound plants renewed vigor. Autumn is the time to bring the plants back indoors. Northern gardeners will start to move the plants back inside in early fall, while in the South and along the West Coast many plants can stay outdoors until later in the season. Here are some tips on how to make the transition easier for your plants.

If your plants have been in a fairly bright location all summer, set them in the shade for several days before you bring them indoors, to accustom them gradually to lower levels of light. To further minimize stress to the plants, make the move indoors on a day when outdoor temperatures are very close to the temperature in your house. If the nighttime temperatures outdoors have been dipping down to 50° or 55°F, you can move your plants to an unheated but protected sun porch or garage (if it has windows) for a few days before taking them into the house. This two-step process will avoid shocking the plants with the difference in temperatures.

Before carrying the plants indoors, inspect each one carefully for signs of disease or insects. If you find any problems, it's best to attend to them right away. If your plants appear to be healthy, it's still a good idea to isolate them from your other houseplants for a week or two after the move, to make sure no pests escaped your notice during the outdoor inspection.

Plants that have grown too big for their pots can be repotted before you bring them indoors. Plants that are not overgrown but have been in the same pot for a year or two will also appreciate a clean pot and fresh soil. Here's how to repot your plants. First, remove each plant from its pot (tap the sides and bottom of the container to loosen the soil ball if necessary—don't just tug on the stem—the soil ball should slide easily out of the pot). Knock off the loose soil and examine the roots for signs of slugs or insect larvae. Some gardeners like to wash all the old soil off the plant's roots at this time, to give them an entirely fresh start. If the plant was rootbound, either get it a bigger pot or prune the roots to keep it in the same-size pot. To prune roots, carefully untangle them if you can, and just cut them back by about one-third, slicing from the sides and bottom of the root ball with a sharp knife. Cut back the top of the plant by the same amount, or the plant will no longer have enough roots to support its top growth.

If you will be reusing the pot, scrub it clean with a brush and soapy water, and soak it for twenty minutes to half an hour in a disinfectant solution of one part liquid chlorine bleach to nine parts water.

Repot the plant in fresh soil mix (see chapter 4 for information on potting mixes) in a clean pot. Wash the plant's leaves (the undersides as well as the tops) with mildly soapy water, and pick off any dead leaves. Some gardeners like to spray their plants with a commercial insecticidal soap as a preventive measure against pests.

## An Autumn Rest for Indoor Plants

Although autumn often brings its share of warm weather, the days are growing noticeably shorter, and the sun's intensity is diminishing as it slips lower in the sky on its journey toward the South Pole. Plants will receive a little less light each day until the December solstice, when the days begin to lengthen again. The shorter days and decreasing light levels in autumn send many spring- and summer-blooming houseplants into a dormant period when they stop actively growing.

In fact, most plants, whether they are growing indoors or out, go dormant at some time during the year. They stop blooming, stop growing, may look a bit faded, and may even lose a few leaves. Annuals die after blooming and setting seed. Bulbs lose their foliage, and some bulbs are lifted from the soil, dried off, and put in storage until new shoots signal the end of dormancy. Herbaceous (nonwoody) perennials growing outdoors in temperate climates die back to the ground in winter. When the dormant rest period is over, plants begin another cycle of growth and show renewed vigor.

The time of year a plant goes dormant is related to its native habitat—the place where it grows in the wild. Many of our garden flowers and houseplants are not American natives and originally came from different parts of the world. Tuberous begonias, for example, come from Central America, just north of the equator, and go dormant in winter the way our native plants do. But cape primroses (*Streptocarpus*) are native to Africa, and in their original species forms they bloom in winter and rest in spring. Some flowering houseplants have been extensively hybridized and bloom off and on practically year-round. Besides *Streptocarpus*, African violets and wax begonias are other good examples of ever-blooming plants. Most houseplants, however, do have definite dormant times.

Some plants' dormant periods can be manipulated to bring the plants into bloom outside their normal season. This process, called "forcing," can reward you with amaryllis blossoms at Christmas and with fragrant narcissus and hyacinths during the bleakest days of January and February.

### HOW TO TREAT PLANTS DURING DORMANCY

Whether plants stayed indoors all summer or spent the season outside, when they become dormant they need less light, water, and food. Northern gardeners don't have to worry about reducing light levels for their dormant houseplants—it will happen naturally as autumn progresses. Gardeners in the South, though, may need to shift plants from one windowsill to another to make sure the light will be sufficiently lessened. South-facing windows get the most light and north windows the least. Eastern exposures are generally brighter than western ones.

No matter where you live, give your plants less water when they are dormant. It's best to water only when the plants start to wilt. This treatment may seem extreme, but it is effective. Another way to tell when it's time to water is to poke a finger a couple of inches into the soil—if the soil is dry that far below the surface, the plant is ready for some moisture. In any case, try not to give your dormant plants more water than they really need. Overwatering, especially during dormancy, is a good way to cause root rot.

Because plants in dormancy are not actively growing, they do not need to be fertilized. In fact, if you do feed them, they could suffer root burn because the soil is dry and their slowed-down metabolic systems cannot absorb as much fertilizer as they can in summer.

When the plants begin to grow again, you can gradually increase the amounts of light, water, and fertilizer.

### WHAT PLANTS NEED TO BLOOM INDOORS

Flowering plants have the same needs indoors as they do in the outdoor garden: moisture, light, food, and air. However, indoors the environment is much more under your control than it is outdoors. The key to success with indoor plants is to choose plants that grow well in the type of environment you have to offer them. For example, without lots of sun and cool temperatures, cacti will not bloom indoors no matter how much fertilizer you give them. On the other hand, African violets are doomed to failure in a cool, dry room. But if the environment in your home is matched to the conditions your plants need to thrive, you will be rewarded with spectacular flowers. Plants suited to their surroundings are almost guaranteed to succeed.

To begin making choices, start with a basic understanding of what indoor flowering plants need to grow well. First, all plants need water. Tropical plants need constant moisture, while others, like succulents and cacti, need long dry periods to stimulate bloom. What no plant likes is too much water—overwatering is the biggest cause of houseplants' untimely demise. It is best to water most plants thoroughly, then let them dry out between waterings. Giving a little bit of water every day or two may result in the surface roots getting waterlogged

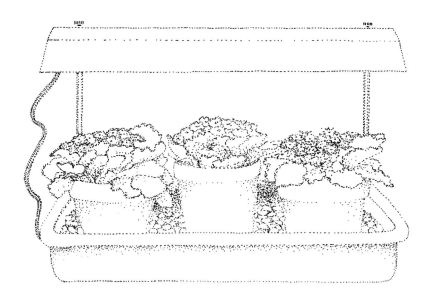

*Fluorescent fixtures are a good way to supplement natural light for flowering houseplants. Compact light garden units like this one can accommodate several plants and supply all the light the plants need to grow and bloom. When the plants are flowering, you can move them to a more prominent place to show them off. If you have a lot of houseplants and not many bright windows, consider installing larger fluorescent fixtures in the basement or a room you don't use often. Full-spectrum daylight tubes, or a combination of cool white and warm white tubes, supply the most balanced light for plants. You don't really need to buy expensive "grow lights."*

and eventually rotting, while deeper roots dry out and cease functioning. Less frequent but thorough watering ensures that *all* the roots receive moisture, and it also flushes excess fertilizer salts from the pot. When you water, continue until you see water accumulating in the saucer beneath the pot. Wait half an hour, then empty any water remaining in the saucer. Letting the pot sit in water for a long time can eventually cause roots to rot.

Most flowering plants like a relative humidity of about 40 to 50 percent. Low humidity can cause buds to dry out or drop off. In fall and winter most of our homes tend to be dry because of central heating. To increase humidity for your plants, mist them regularly and group them on pebble trays. Room humidifiers and containers of water placed on top of nearby radiators also help to boost humidity levels.

Light is another essential for growing plants. Many—but not all—flowering plants do best in a window facing south, especially in winter when the sun is less intense. If you don't have a bright, sunny windowsill, you can supplement the available natural light with fluorescent fixtures placed above the plants. Incandescent lights are helpful, too, but they give off substantial amounts of heat and are costlier to operate than fluorescents.

Because they are growing under higher light levels, flowering houseplants need to be fertilized more often than foliage plants. A balanced, all-purpose plant food is fine most of the year, but it's a good idea to switch to a formulation with more phosphorus and less nitrogen as flowering time approaches. Many good plant foods are on the market, including special formulations for particular types of plants like African violets and orchids. If you are a strictly organic gardener, you can feed your houseplants with fish emulsion, seaweed extract, and bonemeal.

Indoors you need to make sure plants get adequate ventilation, too. They need good air circulation, but you should keep them out of cold drafts. Still air indoors can trap pollutants from building materials and gas used for cooking and heating. This is particularly true in tightly insulated homes. Also, the air in the immediate vicinity of plants tends to lose carbon dioxide (which the plants use for photosynthesis) and hold water vapor. Still, humid air can encourage various plant diseases, so it's important to keep the air moving. A slow fan can do the job nicely.

Woody-stemmed plants may need occasional pruning to produce better flowers and maintain their overall vigor, as well as to keep an attractive shape. Generally speaking, it is best to prune right above a bud or node, where a new shoot can grow from the shortened stem. If you want the plant to grow outward, in a more open form, prune above an outward-facing bud; if you want the plant to grow inward, in a more compact shape, cut above an inward-facing bud. Also prune away any dead or yellowing growth and any water sprouts (fast-growing, weak, tender shoots).

## WHAT TO DO WHEN PLANTS DON'T BLOOM

If your flower plants refuse to flower, here are some questions to ask yourself:

First, is the plant old enough to bloom? Some plants, especially woody ones, have to reach a certain age before they flower. If your reluctant bloomer is a woody-stemmed perennial that's less than a year old, it might not yet be ready to bloom.

Is the plant getting the right amount of light? Many plants need a bright south window in order to bloom indoors. If your plant isn't getting enough light, all the fertilizer in the world won't make it bloom.

Is the plant getting the right duration of light (day length)? Some plants, like Christmas cactus, need short days and long nights in order to set buds. Electric lights burning in the same room with such short-day plants can fool them into thinking the days are long. Conversely, long-day plants can be tricked into blooming if natural light is supplemented with fluorescents for several hours at night to create a longer "day."

Is the temperature too warm or too cool? Many plants need to experience a change of temperature before blooming. Spring bulbs, for example, need a pronounced cold period in order to flower, as do a lot of cacti.

Is the plant getting too much nitrogen and not enough phosphorus? If your plant is producing lots of new leaves but no sign of flower buds during its normal flowering season, you may be giving it too much nitrogen and not enough phosphorus and potassium. If that's the case, a change of fertilizers is in order.

Is the plant getting too much or too little water or humidity? Low humidity and overwatering or underwatering can cause flower buds to fall before they open.

Finally, is the pot too large or too small? Lots of plants bloom best when they're potbound. Examples include amaryllis, clivia, and some African violet relatives. These plants will not bloom if the pot is too big. Other plants won't bloom if their roots are confined in a small pot.

# WINTER PROTECTION FOR ROSES

Where winter temperatures routinely drop below 20°F, roses need protection to avoid damage from the cold. Some types of roses are hardier than others. Many old-fashioned roses such as damask, moss, and gallica types, as well as some of the newer varieties of shrub roses, are very hardy and survive with little or no winter protection in all but the coldest climates. Miniatures and floribundas are somewhat less hardy, and hybrid tea and grandiflora roses are the least hardy of all.

Good growing practices help all roses to withstand cold weather. Tender new growth is most susceptible to winter damage, so be sure to stop fertilizing your roses six to eight weeks before the date you expect the first fall frost in your area. Cut back on watering a bit, too, but don't let the plants dry out. Avoid pruning late in the growing season; pruning encourages new growth, and you don't want your roses to put forth new shoots in fall just in time to suffer winter damage. Roses are best pruned when they are dormant—late autumn is preferable in most parts of the country. Healthy plants will fare better through the winter, too, so keep your roses as free of pest damage as you can during their summer growing season. Healthy leaves ensure that the plant will have stored enough food to get it through the winter.

## PROTECTION METHODS

There are a number of ways to protect roses through the winter. If winter temperatures in your area seldom drop below zero and you have only a few plants, you can simply mound up soil around the base of each one. The soil mound should be 8 to 12 inches high, depending on how far north you live. You can use compost instead of soil if

*To protect individual rosebushes from winter cold, tie the pruned canes loosely together and mound up soil around the base of each plant. In the North, add a layer of loose mulch for extra protection. A simple cylinder of chicken wire or hardware cloth will keep the mulch in place.*

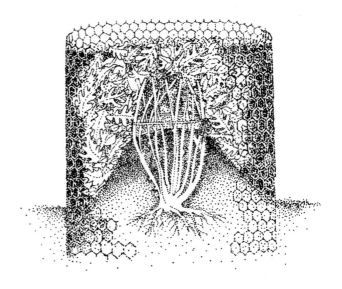

you prefer. And of course, don't take soil from the rose bed to build the mound—bring it in from an empty part of the garden.

In colder areas, the soil mound should be topped with another 8 to 10 inches of loose mulch—leaves, straw, wood chips, evergreen branches, or similar material. You can hold the mulch in place with a cylinder made of hardware cloth or chicken wire. If you live where temperatures dip below −15°F for any length of time, enclose your rosebushes completely by placing caps, cones, baskets, or other covers over them. You can buy specially made Styrofoam cones for this purpose, but make sure you get the kind with hinged or removable lids to allow for ventilation on warm days. Whatever type of cover you use, make sure it is anchored securely so it doesn't blow off in high winds.

The soil mound and mulch protection methods work well for miniatures, hybrid teas, grandifloras, and floribundas—all bush-type roses. When it is time to put the protective devices in place, after you have had some frost but before the ground is frozen solid, prune back the canes to half their length and tie them together with twine. Then make the soil mounds. If you are adding loose mulch on top of the soil, wait until the mounds have frozen before you do so.

## PROTECTING TREE AND CLIMBING ROSES

Climbing roses need a different kind of protection because of their height. The best method is to detach the long canes from their supports, bend them carefully to the ground and peg them down, then cover them completely with soil. When the soil freezes, cover it with a mulch of straw or evergreen boughs. These may sound like drastic

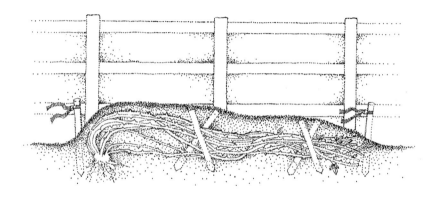

measures, but they will bring your roses through the winter in good shape.

If you have whole beds of roses, protecting each plant individually would be a painstaking, labor-intensive process. It is easier to protect a bed with a portable cold frame that can be simply set in place for winter and removed in spring. The sides of the frame can be made of plywood or scrap lumber, and the top should be hinged or removable to allow for ventilation. Make the lid from a material that lets light through: corrugated translucent Plexiglas is one durable possibility, and old storm windows are another. The cold frame can do double duty as a nursery for other plants in spring when it comes off the rose bed.

*To protect climbing and rambler roses from damage during cold northern winters, remove the canes from their supports, lay them on the ground, and peg them down as shown here. Cover with mulch and/or a soil mound according to the severity of winter weather in your area.*

*If you want to cover a small bed of rosebushes, you can construct a simple rose shelter—a bottomless box with sides of plywood or heavy translucent plastic. Recycle an old storm window for the top. During very cold weather, throw an old blanket over the glass or pile mulch on top. If you leave the glass uncovered, remember to open the top of the shelter slightly on bright, sunny days so the air inside the shelter does not get too warm. Extreme temperature swings could harm the dormant bushes.*

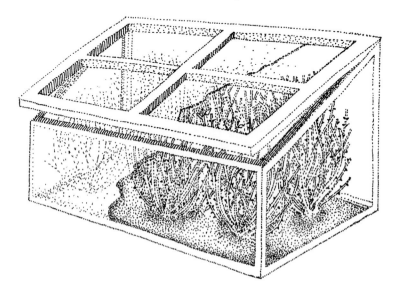

When winter's cold begins to give way to warmer spring weather, you can start removing the loose mulch a little at a time. Leave the soil mound in place until the danger of a hard frost is past. It is best to remove the soil on a cloudy day so that tender new growth is not burned by the sun.

## PREPARING BULBS, CORMS, AND TUBERS FOR WINTER FORCING

Many of your favorite spring-blooming bulbs can be forced into bloom indoors during the bleakest part of winter. The first step toward a winter windowsill full of daffodils, tulips, and other favorites is to purchase the best-quality bulbs you can find. The better the bulb, the more rewarding will be the results. Forcing bulbs is stressful for them, and weak, damaged, or diseased bulbs will bloom poorly or not at all when forced. Buy your bulbs from a reliable company (several are listed in the appendix), and choose carefully. Top-quality exhibition-grade bulbs produce the best flowers.

When you choose bulbs at the garden center or receive them by mail from the nursery, take the time to look them over carefully. The bulbs should be firm, with no soft spots, moldy patches, or nicks. The basal plate (the flat bottom of the bulb from which the roots will grow) should also be firm.

If it is not yet time to plant the bulbs when you get them, you can store them in the refrigerator if you live in a warm climate or in mesh bags or spread out on an open shelf where air can circulate freely around them in cooler climates. Cool, but not freezing cold, temperatures are best for storing bulbs. Never put them in the freezer.

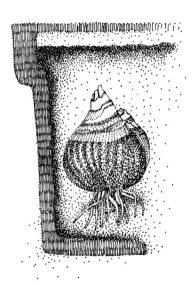

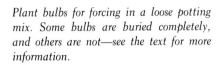

*Plant bulbs for forcing in a loose potting mix. Some bulbs are buried completely, and others are not—see the text for more information.*

To have flowers in winter, you need to begin the process in autumn. In fall, plant the bulbs in pots or deep flats, in good soil. Pots should have drainage holes in the bottom and be 5 to 6 inches in diameter; flats should be 4 to 5 inches deep. A 6-inch pot will hold five to six tulip bulbs, three double-nosed daffodils, or three hyacinths. Use a 5-inch bulb pan (a wide, shallow pot) to force crocuses, irises, squills, or grape hyacinths. Leave about 1½ inches between the bulbs when you plant them. They should be close together but not touching.

If you are reusing old pots, scrub them thoroughly, and soak them in a disinfectant solution of one part liquid chlorine bleach to nine parts water before you plant the bulbs. Soak clay pots in water overnight before planting in them.

No matter what kinds of bulbs you are planting, they will need loose, crumbly soil with good drainage. A potting mix of equal parts of garden loam or potting soil, peat moss, and

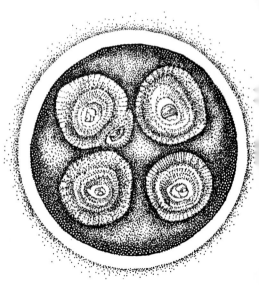

*Set the bulbs close together but not touching. The number of bulbs per pot depends on the kind and size of the bulbs. The five-inch pot shown here can accommodate four tulip bulbs.*

sand is ideal. The bulbs will not need any fertilizer. Most bulbs should be buried only to their tips, with the tips exposed, unless otherwise noted. Allow ½ inch between the soil line and the rim of the pot to allow for watering.

If you want to enjoy continuous bloom over a long period, stagger your plantings. A general rule of thumb is to plant in September for late December or January flowers, October for flowers in February, and November for flowers in March. As you plant, label each pot with the type of bulb, flower color, and date of planting. When the bulbs bloom later on, make a note of the date to help you plan next winter's bulb display.

Water the bulbs thoroughly but gently when the planting is finished. When the bulbs are planted, they need several weeks of darkness and cold storage (at temperatures from about 35° to 48°F) before forcing actually begins, to allow roots to form. Place the potted bulbs in an unheated garage or shed or in an outdoor cold frame, or bury them in the garden and cover them with a layer of straw, sawdust, or wood chips. If you expect temperatures to dip below freezing, insulate the pots. You can also store a pot or two in the refrigerator, if you cover the pots to block out light. If takes an average of eight to twelve weeks for roots to form. During that time keep the soil moist but not wet. Check the pots once a week and water if the soil is dry.

Following are planting instructions for different kinds of bulbs:

• AGAPANTHUS (*Agapanthus africanus*). An exotic plant with the intriguing nickname lily-of-the-Nile, agapanthus is best known as an outdoor summer bloomer, but it can be planted for winter flowers, too. The plant produces clusters of gorgeous blue-violet flowers atop tall, slender stems. There is also a white-flowered form.

Agapanthus blooms best when slightly rootbound, so plant four bulbs in a 12- to 15-inch pot. Set the bulbs so their tops are just below the soil surface. Place the pot in full sun, with daytime temperatures of 68° to 72°F. At night agapanthus needs cool temperatures, 50° to 55°F. Keep the soil evenly moist and feed the plants every month or two with an all-purpose houseplant fertilizer. When the foliage appears, mist it every day.

The plants stay in bloom for as long as two months. When the flowers finish blooming, continue to water and feed the plants regularly until the foliage dies back. When it does, move the pot to a cool room and water only once a month. Do not fertilize. When new growth appears, increase light and warmth and resume the regular schedule of watering and feeding. The plants may last for several years.

• AMARYLLIS (*Hippeastrum* hybrids). These large, trumpet-shaped flowers can be brought into bloom for Christ-mas, in late winter, or in early spring. They are available in shades of red, orange, white, and ivory-striped or blushed with pink. Most amaryllis bulbs are grown in Holland and are precooled before you buy them, so you will not have to give them a cold storage period. Bulb sizes vary; larger bulbs will produce more flowers. For winter flowers, amaryllis bulbs can be potted as soon as you receive them from the mail-order supplier. Just be sure to plant them eight weeks before you want flowers. Plant one bulb in a 5- to 7-inch pot. Allow 1 inch between the top of the soil and the pot rim. Amaryllis grows exceptionally well in a mix of equal parts soil, peat moss, and compost. The upper third of the bulb should be above the soil line when planted.

Because amaryllis does not need a cold period, the forcing process begins at once. Water the bulb well when you first pot it up. Then water sparingly for ten days, by which time root growth should have begun. Use lukewarm water; hot or cold water can shock the bulb. When leaves are growing, water the plant more often and feed it once a month with a diluted, balanced fertilizer. Keep the plant where temperatures are between 60° and 70°F.

• FLORIST'S or POPPY ANEMONE (*Anemone coronaria*). These vivid flowers resemble Oriental poppies, with their dark centers. You can have them in varying shades of red, pink, violet-blue, and cream to white. Good forcing varieties include de Caen (single-flowered) and St. Brigid (double-flowered).

Soak the tubers in lukewarm water before planting to soften them a bit. When they are soft enough that you can dent them with your fingernail, they are ready to plant.

In September or October, plant the tubers in pots of light soil. Water well and move the pots to a moist, cool location where the temperature is about 45° to 50°F. Leave the pots there for six to eight weeks to allow roots to develop. Cover the pots with burlap and keep the soil moist. Then move them to a bright, airy location, also with temperatures around 50°F. Water freely as the plants grow.

• TUBEROUS BEGONIA (*Begonia* × *tuberhybrida*). The showy flowers of tuberous begonias come in a wide range of warm colors, from pastels to brights, along with white and bicolors. Plant five tubers to a 12-inch pot. Set the rounded side of the tuber on the soil, with the concave side facing up. Lightly cover with soil.

Set the pots in a cool place out of direct sun, and water thoroughly. Keep the soil evenly moist. Feed once a month with an all-purpose houseplant fertilizer. When shoots appear, move the pots to a sunny place where daytime temperatures are around 75°F. The plants need a ten-degree drop in temperature at night.

When the plants are finished blooming and the leaves die back, remove the tubers from the pots. Snip off any remaining leaves and let the tubers dry for two weeks. Then store them in dry peat moss in a cool, dark, dry place until planting time next fall.

• CALLA LILY (*Zantedeschia* species and hybrids). These tall, elegant beauties are popular florist flowers and are becoming more popular with home gardeners as well. The best-known species, *Z. aethiopica*, has pure white vaselike flowers (which are actually spathes surrounding the true flowers) and glossy deep green leaves. The cultivar Godfreyana is a more compact plant. There are also yellow-flowered calla lilies: *Z. elliotiana*, called the golden calla, and *Z. pentlandir*, which has variegated foliage and flowers of

*Calla lilies are among the most elegant of flowers. You may think you have to buy them from the florist if you don't live in the tropics. While warm-climate gardeners can indeed grow calla lilies outdoors, gardeners in cooler regions can force the bulbs indoors in winter, when their bold, sleek flowers are a special treat.*

rich golden yellow. Pink-flowered cultivars are available as well.

Plant the rhizomes in September, one to a 6-inch pot, for flowers in December and January. Pot them in a mix of loose, sandy loam and peat moss with a slightly acid pH. Barely cover the top of each rhizome when you plant it, and leave space in the pot to add more soil later on when roots appear on the surface.

Water moderately until the roots are well established. When shoots appear, water thoroughly and often. In fact, calla lilies will thrive if you keep some water in the drainage saucer beneath the pot at all times. Unlike most houseplants, their roots will not rot if kept constantly moist. A greater problem is dryness, which sends the plants into dormancy.

Feed the plants every few weeks with an all-purpose houseplant fertilizer. Keep nighttime temperatures cool—about 55° to 60°F.

• CLIVIA (*Clivia miniata*). Also known as kaffir lily, this species has clusters of bright scarlet-orange flowers with yellow interiors. The flowers resemble lilies or amaryllis and are borne above deep green, straplike leaves. Clivia blooms best when its roots are confined. Plant it in a 6-inch pot with the bulb just barely covered with soil.

Set the pot where it will get direct sun and where daytime temperatures are 68° to 72°F. At night clivias need cool temperatures around 50° to 55°F. Keep the soil slightly moist, but do not overwater or the crown will rot. Feed once a month with an all-purpose houseplant fertilizer.

The plant should bloom in about four weeks. When it has finished flowering, give the plant a rest in a cool, dark place. Cut back on water and withhold fertilizer until new flower stalks appear.

• CROCUS (*Crocus* hybrids). Dutch hybrid crocuses are the easiest kind to force, and they produce the biggest flowers. They come in shades of purple, lavender, golden yellow, and white, as well as white striped with purple.

Plant crocus corms in mid- to late autumn, 1 to 2 inches deep and 1 inch apart. Six corms will fit in a 4-inch pot. The pot should be at least 3½ inches deep to accommodate the roots. Give the potted corms eight weeks of cold storage. Water sparingly until the plants are full grown, then keep the soil moist but not waterlogged.

• DAFFODIL and NARCISSUS (*Narcissus* cultivars). These beloved spring flowers come in a range of sizes and shapes and colors in every imaginable variation of yellow: brilliant lemon yellow, sunny gold, soft, pale yellow, cream, apricot, and bicolored flowers of white or clear yellow with center cups of

orange, rich gold, or salmony pink. There are also double-flowered cultivars in assorted shades. Flowers can be forced for winter or to bloom at Easter time, although for gardeners winter flowers are of most interest.

For winter flowers, pot the bulbs in October in a mix of light soil and peat moss. You can put three bulbs in a 5-inch pot, four or five in a 6-inch pot. Double-nosed bulbs will give you the most flowers. The top of each bulb should be 1 inch below the soil surface. Water thoroughly after planting. Place the pots in cold storage, as described in the beginning of this section, until mid-December.

• FREESIA (*Freesia* × *hybrida*). Spicy-sweet freesias can be forced indoors for cut flowers or potted plants. Extensive breeding has given us hybrids in a luscious array of soft colors: lavender, deep rose, pink, golden yellow, rich orange, creamy pure white.

Plant freesia corms in September or October, six to a 5-inch pot, or in shallow bulb pans or flats. Position the corms 2 inches apart and just below the soil line. Set the pot in a cool (50°F), dark place for six to eight weeks to allow the roots to develop. Keep the soil moist but not soggy; do not overwater. Feed once a month with an all-purpose houseplant fertilizer until buds are set.

When the rooting period is past, move the pots to a bright, warmer (65° to 70°F) location. Make sure the temperature drops at least ten degrees at night. The plants should bloom in three months—midwinter if you planted the corms in September. The weak stems will probably need staking.

When the flowers are over, keep watering and feeding the plants until late spring, then stop. When the foliage dies, store the pots on their side in a dark, dry place until it is time to replant in fall.

• HYACINTH (*Hyacinthus orientalis*). There are three possible blooming seasons for forced hyacinths—Christmas, January-February, and early spring. Each requires a different forcing procedure.

To have hyacinths for Christmas you must use large, specially prepared bulbs. These bulbs are available from growers in September and October and should be planted as soon as you receive them. A 4-inch pot accommodates one of these big bulbs, a 5-inch pot will hold two, and you can put three in a 6-inch pot. Plant the bulbs in light, sandy loam, and make sure the tip of each bulb is ½ inch below the soil surface. Water thoroughly. Store the pots outside in the coldest place you can find and cover them with straw. If you have access to cold storage facilities or a cold cellar, store the bulbs at 45° to 50°F. Around the end of November, move the pots to a warm (70°F), dark place. When the leaves are 8 inches tall, move the plants to a bright location to darken the color of the foliage. Reduce the temperature to 50°F to harden the plants and delay blooming if it looks like the plants will flower before Christmas.

For flowers in January and February you do not need to use prepared bulbs. Pot the bulbs in fall, water them well, and store outside, covered with straw, until mid-December.

Bulbs for early spring bloom should be potted in fall and kept outdoors all winter, covered with straw.

Hyacinths can also be forced in bulb glasses, which are shaped like an hourglass—the bulb rests in the top, supported by the narrow neck of the glass, and the roots grow down through the neck into the larger lower part of the glass. Keep the bottom part of the glass filled with clean water. To give bulbs in glasses a cold period, fill the bottom part with water so it barely touches the bulb's basal plate. Put the glass in a foil-lined insulated bag, tie the top shut, and put the bag in your refrigerator. When the shoot is about 4 inches high, bring the glass into bright, indirect light.

• IRIS (*Iris* species). The small netted irises are the best kind to force. *Iris reticulata* will give you violet-purple flowers, and *I. danfordiae* will give you yellow ones. Plant the rhizomes in mid-fall to have flowers in mid- to late winter. Plant them 2 to 3 inches deep and 3 inches apart, in a light soil mix. Give the potted rhizomes eight weeks of cold storage for roots to develop. When the plants bloom, keep them in a sunny but cool spot.

• IXIA (*Ixia* cultivars). The small corms of ixia, which is sometimes called corn lily, can be planted five or six to a 5-inch pot. Their flowers come in rich shades of yellow, orange, red, and pink, as well as white. They are forced by the same procedure described for freesias. Ixia stems, although slender, are tough and do not usually require staking. The corms can be rested over summer, like freesias, and reused the following season.

• ENCHANTMENT LILY (*Lilium* 'Enchantment'). This outdoor garden favorite, one of the Asiatic hybrids, can be flowered indoors as well. Enchantment is a particularly vigorous lily, which is why it responds to forcing. A single bulb will reward you with ten or even more of the stunning blossoms, which are bright orange with darker spots. The flowers are borne atop 2- to 3-foot stems.

Plant three small bulbs in a 12-inch pot that is twice as tall as the bulbs. Put a 2-inch layer of pebbles in the bottom of the pot before adding the soil—excellent drainage is critical. Plant the bulbs 1 inch deep. Water well and set the pot in a cool (60° to 65°F), dark place—such as a basement—where there is some humidity. Keep the soil evenly moist. From the time shoots emerge, in about three weeks, feed the plants once a month with an all-purpose houseplant fertilizer.

When the shoots appear, move the pot into full sun and keep the soil moist. The plants should bloom in about six weeks. Stake the tall stems to help them support the flowers.

When the last flowers die, cut off the stem right below the lowest blossom. When the leaves die, cut off the stem at ground level. Remove the bulbs from the pot and store them in dry peat moss until planting time next fall.

• LILY-OF-THE-VALLEY (*Convallaria majalis*). Lily-of-the-valley pips are usually shipped from mail-order houses in fall. You can buy them preplanted or plant them yourself. Generally all you need to do is add water and you'll have flowers in two or three weeks. You can plant the pips out in the garden in spring, and they will bloom in successive years.

• PAPERWHITE NARCISSUS (*Narcissus tazetta* 'Paperwhite'). This little narcissus is my favorite flower to force. Its small white blossoms are sweetly fragrant, the bulbs bloom quickly after planting, and the forcing procedure is so simple it's practically foolproof. The flowers grow in clusters around the tops of the foot-high stems. A single bulb, if it is of good quality, will produce several flowering stems.

Two relatives of the paperwhite, the yellow-flowered Soleil d'Or and the Chinese sacred lily (*N. tazetta* var. *orientalis*), can be forced in the same way.

Bulbs of all three narcissus are available in autumn and can be planted anytime after you get them. They need no cold storage period. In fact, they don't even need soil.

You can plant the bulbs in pots of soil or perlite, in bowls of pebbles, or in a bulb glass or other container of water. To plant in soil, perlite, or pebbles, fill the container halfway with the medium of your choice. Set the bulbs on top, about ½ inch apart. Add more of the medium until the bulbs are about one-third covered. Water soil or perlite thoroughly; add water to pebbles until it just touches the bottom of the bulbs. If you are planting in water, fill the glass until the bottom of the bulb is in water but the entire bulb is not submerged.

Some gardeners like to set the containers in a dark place for two or three weeks to let the roots develop, then move the pots into a bright place. I have had good success without a dark period—I put my pots of paperwhites on a bright windowsill until they bloom. The best thing about paperwhites is their speed—they will give you flowers about four weeks after you plant them. They bloom readily anytime from November to April. Bulbs planted in December and January will bloom more quickly than bulbs planted in November. For continuous bloom, start new bulbs every two

weeks. You can save some bulbs to force in late winter and early spring by keeping them cool to prevent sprouting.

After the plants finish blooming, gardeners in the South can plant the bulbs outdoors. Everywhere else they should be discarded, because they cannot survive cold weather.

● RANUNCULUS (*Ranunculus asiaticus*). The flowers of ranunculus, or Persian buttercup, look like big double buttercups in warm shades of yellow, orange, red, and pink. They come in white and bicolors, too. The flowers will last a long time if you maintain cool temperatures when the plants are in bloom.

Soak the tubers before planting to soften them a little. When they are soft enough that you can dent them with a fingernail, they are ready to plant. Follow the forcing procedure described earlier for freesias. Stake the stems to help them support the weight of the heavy flowers.

● SPARAXIS (*Sparaxis tricolor*). The harlequin flower, or wand flower, produces multicolored blossoms in bright shades of purple, rose, red, yellow, or white, with a black band around the

base of the petals and a yellow center. You can force them like freesias. The stems may need staking.

● TULIPS (*Tulipa* hybrids). Hybrid tulips are available for forcing for early, mid- and late-season bloom. Planting pots of each type will give you flowers over a period of several weeks. Tulips can be had in a wide range of warm colors: many shades of red, pink, salmon, orange, yellow, and white are available, along with lavender, purple, and bicolors.

Plant five or six bulbs to a 6-inch pot, with the flat side of the bulb facing toward the outside of the pot. The flowers will turn outward and give the nicest display. Tulips can be forced in any good soil containing plenty of organic matter. Plant the bulbs as soon as they arrive from the nursery, because they bruise easily. Plant the bulbs ½ inch deep. They need twelve weeks of cold storage to form roots.

To bring tulips into bloom, give them good ventilation and plenty of light, but keep them out of direct sun. Keep the soil moist but not soggy.

When you replant the bulbs outdoors, set them a little deeper than they were planted in the pot.

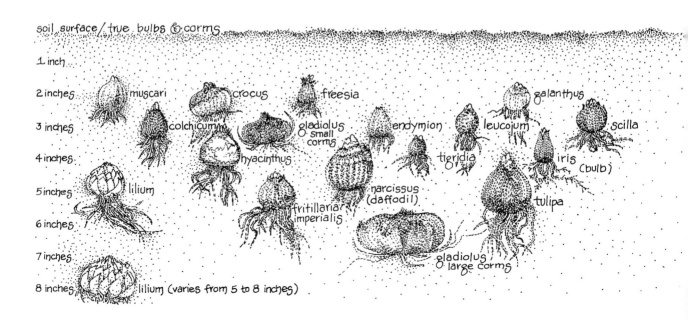

# Planting Spring Bulbs Outdoors

In colder climates, daffodils, tulips, and other hardy spring-blooming bulbs for the outdoor garden should be planted in early to mid-autumn, before the first hard frost in your area. In warm climates, plant later in fall—November or even December where winters are very mild.

Hardy bulbs will thrive in almost any well-drained soil, in full sun or partial shade. To prepare the garden for bulbs, dig out the soil to whatever depth your bulbs need (see the illustration). Loosen the soil and add bonemeal, an all-purpose fertilizer, or a special bulb formula, and plenty of organic matter. If your soil is sandy, dig in some peat moss, leaf mold, or compost. If your soil contains a lot of clay, add sand and peat moss. Then rake the soil surface smooth.

Place the bulbs in the soil where you will plant them, with their pointed end up. For the best display, plant the bulbs in drifts or in clusters of twelve or more. Make sure the bulbs are set firmly in the soil, then cover them with soil, water thoroughly, and mulch the bed with a 2- to 3-inch layer of shredded leaves or other loose mulch.

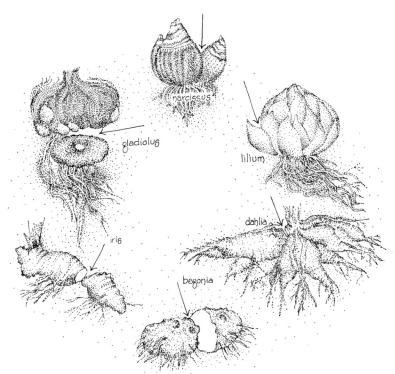

*When bulb plantings become crowded it's time to divide them. There are several ways to divide bulbs and bulblike structures, depending on their type. Bulbs like narcissus form new bulbs from the basal plate that can be gently broken off and planted separately. To divide scaly bulbs like lilies, separate the outer scales (the way you remove a clove of garlic to use in the kitchen) and plant them. The tuberous roots of dahlias can be cut from the crown of the plant and replanted individually or in clumps of two or three. Tubers like those of tuberous begonias can be cut into several pieces. Make sure each piece has at least one "eye," the point from which new shoots will grow. Iris rhizomes, too, can be cut into pieces; again, make sure all the divisions have eyes. Corms, such as gladiolus, form small offsets that can be removed and replanted. In a few years, when the divisions grow to blooming size, you'll have a whole new crop of flowers.*

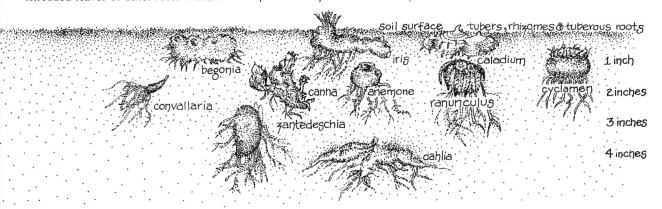

*Average planting depths for bulbs.*

# WINTER

*TEN*

# Winter Flowers

Winter is a time of rest and renewal for gardens and for gardeners. As the year draws to a close, outdoor perennials lie dormant under their blankets of mulch or snow. Last summer's annuals have long since finished their life cycle. In warm regions, new annuals can be grown in winter, but the rest of us will have to wait until next season for them. As the old year wanes, gardeners turn inward, too, and consider the results of the past year's efforts.

But winter is a time of beginnings as well as endings, and even the bleakest of winter days has its joys. Seed and nursery catalogs begin to arrive, and countless hours can be spent lost in their pages and dreaming of spring.

Soon it will be time to start seeds for plants to set out in the garden in spring.

Winter has flowers to offer us, too, even in the North. Outdoors there are flowering shrubs all season in the South (such as camellias, heather, winter jasmine, and winter honeysuckle) and along the West Coast as well (camellias, viburnum, daphne, heaths, and witch hazel). These mild climates also allow winter flowers on primroses, cyclamens, violets, and other cool-weather perennials. In the North late winter brings the earliest bulbs and shrubs. Except in warm climates, the earliest outdoor plants to bloom are usually thought of as early spring flowers. But the flowers that

open in February and March in the North are in bloom several weeks before spring weather arrives, so I consider them late winter flowers. Bulbs that bloom in mid- to late winter, depending on where you live, can be planted in a garden of their own or with early-blooming shrubs.

The early bulbs are a special delight, cheering gardeners' hearts with the sight of flowers blooming outdoors after the long, cold winter. Bulbs should be planted in drifts underneath evergreen or deciduous shrubs, among perennials in beds and borders, in

*OPPOSITE*
*Annuals and forced bulbs fill this conservatory with winter color.*

woodland gardens, or in patches of lawn that can be left unmowed until the bulb foliage dies back in late spring. One caveat is to avoid crocuses in woodland areas—they need lots of sun to put on their best show.

Most of the early bulbs are small and not expensive to buy, so you can plant lots of them. The hours spent planting the bulbs in fall will prove well worthwhile when the flowers burst forth as winter begins to ease its grip.

Indoors in winter, our homes can be full of color and fragrance from the bulbs we started forcing in autumn. Other houseplants, too, bloom in winter. So do plants started from cuttings taken from last summer's outdoor annuals. And winter brings holiday specialties like poinsettias and holly, too.

Anemone blanda *and early tulips bloom in late winter in warmer climates.*

## YEAR-ROUND BLOOMERS

Some houseplants flower off and on all year, and their blossoms are especially welcome in winter, when flower choices are limited for most of us. Consider adding some of these ever-blooming plants to your collection to make sure you'll have plenty of bloom all winter long.

• CHIMENES (*Achimenes* species). Blooms all year under fluorescent lights.

• AFRICAN VIOLET (*Saintpaulia* hybrids). Will bloom under lights or on bright windowsills with as little as two hours of sun a day.

• ALLOPHYTUM (*Allophytum mexicanum*). Blooms best in a light garden.

• ANTHURIUM (*Anthurium scherzeri-anum*). Blooms best in a light garden.

• WAX BEGONIA (*Begonia* × *semperflorens-cultorum*). Blooms with as little as two hours of sun a day.

• CAPE PRIMROSE (*Streptocarpus* hybrids). If grown under full-spectrum fluorescent light, the newer cape primrose hybrids bloom practically year-round.

• CROSSANDRA (*Crossandra infundibuliformis*). Blooms best in a light garden.

• EXACUM (*Exacum affine*). Blooms best under lights.

• GERANIUM, zonal type (*Pelargonium* × *hortorum*). Plants grown from cuttings taken in summer will bloom indoors in winter under lights.

• IMPATIENS (*Impatiens* species and hybrids). Plants grown from cuttings taken in summer will bloom indoors in winter under lights.

• LANTANA (*Lantana* species). Blooms all year in a light garden.

• LOBELIA (*Lobelia erinus*). Blooms all year in a light garden.

• FIRECRACKER VINE (*Manettia inflata*). Blooms off and on all year in a light garden.

• OXALIS (*Oxalis* hybrids). Blooms off and on all year, most heavily in summer and fall.

• PENTAS (*Pentas lanceolata*). Blooms best in a light garden.

• THUNBERGIA (*Thunbergia alata*). Blooms off and on all year.

# Winter Colors

Indoors, a whole palette of colors is available to winter gardeners. Flowering houseplants, forced bulbs and branches, and annuals grown from seeds or cuttings can be chosen and combined in practically any color scheme you like.

Outdoors, the choices are more limited in winter. Most of the winter-blooming shrubs have flowers in yellow or pinkish mauve. They can be beautifully complemented by bulbs that bloom in white (snowdrops, for example) or shades of blue and deep violet (like *Iris reticulata*). One color combination to avoid, though, is a mixture of bright, cool yellow and cool lilac or purple. This color is a classic for crocuses, and it does not harmonize well with many of the early shrubs. Don't plant your lilac crocuses with common forsythia, Korean rhododendron, or witch hazel. There is one forsythia hybrid, however, *F. ×intermedia* 'Spring Glory', whose soft, light yellow flowers mix nicely with lilac crocuses.

Winter's outdoor colors are cool, clear, and clean—mostly cool yellows, blue, violet, and white. You won't find the soft pinks and lavenders of spring, the bright roses, golds, and purples of summer, or the warm bronzes and russets of autumn. Winter flowers, at least to this gardener's eye, match the feeling of the season, with its cold temperatures, clear air, and sense of purity and cleanness.

*Narcissus is easy to force for winter flowers.*

## RED FLOWERS

| | | | |
|---|---|---|---|
| Amaryllis | Cigar plant | Impatiens | Poinsettia |
| Ardisia | Cineraria | Kalanchoe | Poppy anemone |
| Azalea | Cyclamen | Lachenalia | Primrose |
| Begonia | Firecracker vine | Miniature rose | Snapdragon |
| China aster | Flowering maple | Mimulus | Tulip |
| Christmas cactus | Hibiscus | Nasturtium | Winter heath |
| Christmas cherry | Hyacinth | Ornamental pepper | |

## PINK FLOWERS

| | | | |
|---|---|---|---|
| African violet | China aster | Hibiscus | Poinsettia |
| Amaryllis | Christmas cactus | Hyacinth | Primrose |
| Anemone | Cineraria | Impatiens | Streptocarpus |
| Azalea | Clarkia | Miniature rose | Tulip |
| Begonia | Cyclamen | Pentas | Veltheimia |
| Calla lily | Eranthemum | Phalaenopsis | Winter heath |
| Camellia | Freesia | Poet's jasmine | |

## ORANGE FLOWERS

| | | | |
|---|---|---|---|
| Amaryllis | Calendula | Kalanchoe | Snapdragon |
| Calamondin orange | Celosia | Marigold | Thunbergia |
| Calceolaria | Impatiens | Nasturtium | Tulip |

## YELLOW FLOWERS

| | | | |
|---|---|---|---|
| Adonis | Forsythia | Narcissus | Tulip |
| Calceolaria | Freesia | Nasturtium | Winter aconite |
| Calendula | Iris | Paphiopedilum | Winter hazel |
| Calla lily | Lantana | Primrose | Winter jasmine |
| Celosia | Marigold | Snapdragon | Wintersweet |
| Crocus | Mimulus | Thunbergia | Witch hazel |

## BLUE AND VIOLET FLOWERS

| | | | |
|---|---|---|---|
| African violet | Crocus | Grape hyacinth | Streptocarpus |
| Anemone | Eranthemum | Hyacinth | Torenia |
| Browallia | Exacum | Primrose | |
| China aster | Glory-of-the-snow | Scilla | |

## PURPLE FLOWERS

| | | | |
|---|---|---|---|
| African violet | Clarkia | Impatiens | Tulip |
| Anemone | Crocus | Iris | Veltheimia |
| Brunfelsia | Daphne | Mimulus | |
| Bulbocodium | Eranthemum | Pentas | |
| Cineraria | Freesia | Streptocarpus | |

| | | | |
|---|---|---|---|
| Abeliophyllum | Camellia | Hyacinth | Snowdrop |
| African violet | Carissa | Iberis | Spiraea |
| Amaryllis | China aster | Impatiens | Star of Bethlehem |
| Anemone | Christmas cactus | Miniature rose | Streptocarpus |
| Arabian coffee | Christmas rose | Paperwhite narcissus | Thunbergia |
| Arabian jasmine | Cineraria | Phalaenopsis | Tulip |
| Azalea | Crocus | Poinsettia | Viburnum |
| Begonia | Cyclamen | Poppy anemone | Winter heath |
| Calla lily | Freesia | Pussy willow | Winter honeysuckle |

## COMBINING WINTER FLOWERS INDOORS AND OUTDOORS

Here are some plant combinations to experiment with in your winter garden. Most outdoor gardens are based on shrubs and bulbs that bloom in late winter. I have suggested some plant combinations to be used indoors in a variety of color schemes to work with decor, but you can experiment with some of your favorite plants to create a range of effects.

### INDOOR GARDENS

If you started some annuals from seeds or cuttings last summer or fall to have indoor flowers in winter, there are lots of color combinations possible in your indoor garden. Consider, for example, China asters in rosy red and pink, with pink impatiens and purple browallia. Another red-and-pink combination is red hibiscus with pink geraniums, or you might like to display pink camellias with cyclamens in deep rose and soft lavender. Pink geraniums and violet exacums are another unusual—and quite handsome—pair.

African violets in shades of violet, red-violet, pink, and white offer a colorful but simple combination.

*Indoors, magenta bougainvillea and purple streptocarpus make a lovely duo in a cool but sunny spot.*

*Winter Flowers* 175

*Mona Lisa anemones forced for winter bloom.*

Growing cultivars with different flower forms, as well as colors, adds even more variety. You can mix single- and double-flowered types, ruffled flowers, and picotee flowers edged in white, such as the Geneva cultivars. Rosy red, pink, and purple streptocarpus can make their own show in a cool room.

A simple and cheerful reminder of summer is a windowsill full of wax begonias in shades of red, pink, and white. You can add some pink and white geraniums for height, too. A charming multilevel grouping might include cascading pink and cherry red petunias in hanging pots, with impatiens and fairy primroses in shades of pink, freshened with a white-flowered plant or two.

Amaryllis is a classic winter flower. Try it in soft shades of pink and salmon, with the small, fragrant trumpets of freesias in purple and creamy white. Pink and white amaryllis, white cyclamens, and hanging pots of trailing, red-flowered aeschynanthus can fill an entire window.

Tall white calla lilies look lovely behind rose and white cyclamens. For a red-and-white theme, you could try grouping red-berried ardisia with red kalanchoes and white fairy primroses.

An unusual and fiery combination mixes scarlet, red, and orange snapdragons, orange and yellow freesias, and yellow dwarf marigolds. Another hot, summery color combination can be created with yellow and orange calendulas, calceolarias, and marigolds. A cool, sunny window can host pots and hanging baskets of nasturtiums in their assorted shades of mahogany, red, orange, and yellow. Ornamental peppers with red-orange fruits, placed behind a windowbox full of dwarf marigold in bright yellow and orange, might bring back memories of a summer vegetable garden. Red and orange kalanchoes—another favorite

*China asters (Burpee's Pot-'n-Patio) bloom on a windowsill in winter.*

*Marigolds can also be grown indoors from seeds if you give them enough light.*

*Narcissus blooms on a winter windowsill.*

winter houseplant—combine well with orange-and-yellow lantana.

If you are forcing bulbs, try showing off blue, violet, and pink hyacinths with cream-colored daffodils and paperwhite narcissus. For a real taste of spring, group forced daffodils and narcissus in golden yellow, some with orange centers, and crocuses in white, gold, and vibrant purple. A dish garden of blue-violet *Iris reticulata* and dwarf narcissus forced into bloom at the same time can dress up a table or countertop.

If you love fragrant flowers, you'll enjoy a heavenly scented grouping of paperwhite narcissus, lavender, yellow, and white freesias, and sweet olive. Or you can pair sweet olive with the similarly scented jasmine *Jasminum polyanthum*.

For the holidays, red amaryllis makes a fine display with red, pink, and white poinsettias. Or you could combine Christmas cactus in shades of magenta, rose, pink, and white.

For a blue-and-white scheme, the traditional colors of Hanukkah, try blue and white poppy anemones with white China asters, camellias, or chrysanthemums from the florist.

## OUTDOOR GARDENS

A bed of early-blooming species crocuses (such as *C. chrysanthus*) in assorted shades of purple, lavender, golden yellow, and white makes a fine show on its own, especially when the flowers are backed by deep green conifers and other evergreen shrubs. Lavender or yellow crocuses also look lovely in concert with ornamental grasses, which retain their tawny, graceful dry seed plumes all winter. Try fountain grass (*Miscanthus* species) or zebra grass (*Miscanthus sinensis* var. *zebrinus*), for example.

Yellow is a dominant color in late

winter, and there are numerous color schemes you can create with yellow-flowered shrubs and bulbs. A gold-and-white garden can be created by planting snowdrops, winter aconite, and early white crocuses in front of and among dwarf conifers or other evergreens to accentuate the colors. Shrubs such as fragrant witch hazels or winter hazels can be underplanted with snowdrops or early white crocuses.

If you'd like to add blue or purple to a yellow-and-white garden, you could try a combination such as Chinese witch hazel underplanted with snowdrops and blue Siberian squills. Pinkish purple winter daphne, or mezereon, can be underplanted with white snowdrops and early white and yellow species crocuses. Simple bulb gardens can be created with snowdrops, yellow winter aconite, and blue glory-of-the-snow. Or you can substitute purple, white, and yellow crocuses for glory-of-the-snow.

If you prefer yellow-and-blue or yellow-and-purple gardens, you might enjoy an early iris bed of *Iris reticulata* in deep blue and purple with yellow *Iris danfordiae*. Yellow adonis or winter aconite will harmonize nicely with blue Persian or Siberian squills. Glory-of-the-snow can provide a carpet of starlike blue flowers when planted under the branches of yellow forsythias. Evergreen vinca, which begins producing its purple flowers in late winter in warmer climates and early spring farther north, is beautiful when planted around and among yellow and cream-colored daffodils. A pretty blue-and-white duo is pussy willow or abeliophyllum underplanted with blue Siberian squills. An unusual and interesting yellow-and-orange pairing is yellow witch hazel with a coppery-colored forsythia, *F.* × *intermedia* 'Diana'.

In the South and along the West

Coast, gardeners can complement pastel-pink and white camellias with rose or red winter heath or with purple pansies. Another possibility for mild climates or sun-spot gardens in the North is a mixture of pink and white Grecian windflowers (*Anemone blanda*) with *Iris reticulata* and *I. danfordiae* in deep blue, purple, and golden yellow.

## A SUN-SPOT GARDEN TO MAKE SPRING COME EARLY

If you garden in the North and find yourself pining for some color outdoors in the depths of winter, try making a sun-spot garden. The idea is to moderate the environment in a concentrated area by trapping heat from the sun and protecting plants from harsh winter winds. The sheltered environment will allow you to grow winter flowers that aren't normally hardy in your area and bring early bulbs into bloom weeks before their normal flowering time. Your sun-spot garden will behave like gardens one or more climate zones south of where you actually live. You might be rewarded with crocuses in January and daffodils in February. Primroses, pansies, and other cool-weather flowers will bloom early, too.

Creating a sun-spot garden isn't difficult; you won't need any special tools or expensive structures. What you do need is an unobstructed wall that faces south. Locate the sun spot against the south-facing wall of your house where sun exposure is maximum. A small bed will be easiest to protect and to care for. The plants will need protection from cold winds on the east and west sides of the bed. This protection can take the form of a wall, hedge, or

## A COOL PLACE FOR COOL-LOVING HOUSEPLANTS

Forced bulbs, cyclamens, and quite a few other winter houseplants need a cool environment to grow and bloom well. If you don't have a sun porch or other cool but bright place, you can adapt your windowsills to provide the cool place these plants need.

Because it is heavier than warm air, cold air next to windows tends to roll down the wall and spread out over the floor, much the same way cold air outdoors will roll down a slope and collect in a "cold pocket" at the bottom. To trap and hold cold air for those plants that need it, you can

row of evergreen shrubs planted close together. The garden bed should be bordered, at least along the front, with dry pavement that will trap and hold heat from the sun. A brick or stone walkway will provide the necessary heat and radiate it into the air around the plants, keeping the temperature of both soil and air slightly warmer than the air in unprotected parts of your yard. Even without enclosing the sun spot in plastic (which you can do if you want even more warmth), you will have created a warm, sheltered pocket for plants.

A sun-spot garden can give a lift to your winter-weary spirits with its promise of spring.

## WINTER ANNUALS FOR WARM CLIMATES

Gardeners in the South, Southwest, and mild areas along the West Coast enjoy the best bloom from cool-weather annuals outdoors in winter.

The choices are many. Here are some winter flowers to grow in warm climates.

### DEEP SOUTH

| | | | |
|---|---|---|---|
| Baby's breath | Candytuft | Pansy | Statice |
| Bachelor's button | Gaillardia | Petunia | Stocks |
| Browallia | Larkspur | Phlox | Sweet alyssum |
| Calendula | Lupine | Shirley poppy | Sweet pea |
| California poppy | Nicotiana | Snapdragon | Verbena |

### SOUTHERN CALIFORNIA AND THE SOUTHWEST

| | | | |
|---|---|---|---|
| African daisy | Cineraria | Phlox | Scabiosa |
| Blue lace flower | English daisy | Primroses (grown as annuals) | Snapdragon |
| Calendula | Love-in-a-mist |    fairy primrose | Sweet alyssum |
| California poppy | Nemesia |    poison primrose | Sweet pea |
| Candytuft | Pansy |    polyanthus primrose | |

construct a simple three-sided window box that attaches to the inside sill (see the illustration). To make the box useful in other seasons, you might want to hinge the front so that it can swing down to form a shelf for plants in spring and summer. Below is a list of plants that would appreciate the cool environment of the box in winter.

Azalea
Calceolaria
Calendula
Camellia
Christmas cactus
Chrysanthemum
Cineraria
Crocus
Cyclamen
Daffodil and narcissus
Freesia
Hyacinth
Hydrangea
Jasmine
Oxalis
Paperwhite narcissus
Primroses
Miniature roses

Star of Bethlehem
Sweet olive
Tulip

# DECORATING WITH WINTER FLOWERS

Winter is the time when flowers—fresh and dried—are most appreciated. The indoor garden yields potted plants for display, and a light garden can give you some flowers for cutting, too. The holiday season brings classics like poinsettias, which can be combined with evergreen branches and leaves in lovely arrangements, wreaths, and garlands.

Winter flower arrangements call for creativity. You can use outdoor flowers if you have them, forced bulbs and branches, and flowers and leaves from houseplants to get the greatest variety. You can also supplement homegrown flowers with blossoms from the florist.

Poinsettias are probably the favorite Christmas flower, with their colorful bracts in red, pink, white, or white flushed with pink. Traditionally they have not been successful as cut flowers because when their stems are cut they bleed a thick, milky sap (typical of all plants in the genus *Euphorbia*) that prevents the stems from taking up water. But if you place the cut stems in rubbing alcohol for ten minutes after you cut them, the flow of sap will stop. Treated this way, poinsettias will last eight to ten days in the vase. Adding poinsettias to holiday arrangements opens up many new possibilities for colorful seasonal decorations. They work well, for example, with evergreens, boxwood, holly, or dried baby's breath.

## HOW TO DECORATE HOLIDAY WREATHS AND GARLANDS

At Christmas our homes are full of evergreens—garlands, ropes, wreaths, and swags grace our front doors, mantelpieces, tables, and sideboards, festoon stair rails, and surround doorways. When collecting or buying greens to use for decorations, don't just limit yourself to pine. Long-needled pine is lovely, but you can also use fir, balsam, cypress, yew, cedar, and even arborvitae. Or mix in some aromatic boxwood or glossy green bay, magnolia, or camellia leaves.

Wreaths can also be fashioned from

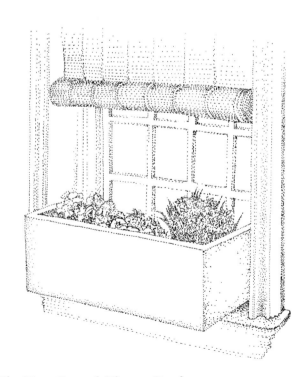

OPPOSITE
*Freesias forced into bloom can perfume an entire room with their sweet scent.*

LEFT
*Many winter-blooming houseplants need cool temperatures to thrive—conditions that are hard to provide in centrally heated homes. A simple three-sided indoor window box traps cool air around the plants while the rest of the room stays warm.*

*When specially treated, poinsettias can be used as cut flowers and combined with seasonal greens for colorful Christmas arrangements.*

# HOW TO MAKE WREATHS AND GARLANDS

To make an evergreen wreath, start with a foam or wire base, which you can find at most craft shops. Lengths of greenery can be attached to wire bases with flexible wire that comes in spools (also available at craft shops) and fastened to foam bases with wire, florist's picks, greening pins, or glue. Overlap the bunches of greens to hide the fasteners and achieve a nice, full look.

To make a garland, use a length of thick rope as a base, or make your own "rope" by twisting together old panty hose or strips of cloth. Attach bunches of evergreens, flowers, and other leaves to the base rope by wrapping spool wire first around each bunch of material, then around the rope. Begin on the outer side of the garland, and point the stem end of each bunch toward the

inside (see illustration). Overlap the bunches and work your way along the length of the rope from the outside toward the inside. When the garland looks well filled and has no empty spaces, it is ready to decorate.

To make a wreath from dried vines, begin by soaking the vines in water for a few hours to make them pliable. Then drain them on towels before you work with them. Start your wreath by forming a length of vine into a circle of whatever size you want. Twist the ends together and fasten them with wire. Weave several more pieces into the circle and tuck in the ends. Then take a long piece of vine and wrap it around the circle in a spiral. Repeat this procedure with a second piece of vine, spiraling it in the opposite direction.

You can decorate your vine wreath with clusters of dried flowers, either fastened to individual picks or glued right onto the vines (a hot glue gun

ivy, dried grapevines, or Virginia creeper vines. You can decorate wreaths, swags, and garlands with holly (besides the familiar green kind, there is also holly with green-and-white variegated leaves), bayberries, mistletoe, and bright orange bittersweet berries. Poinsettias, camellias, amaryllis, and other cut flowers can be cut with short stems and placed in individual plastic water vials (available at most florist shops), which are fastened to the greens and easily camouflaged amid the foliage. You can also decorate wreaths and swags with bunches of dried flowers. Possibilities include small clusters of baby's breath, purple statice, golden yarrow, pink strawflowers, red or pink rosebuds, or magenta globe amaranth. You can also decorate wreaths and garlands with pine cones, nuts (sprayed gold or silver if you like), ornamental peppers, and colorful fruits like apples, kumquats, lemons, and pears.

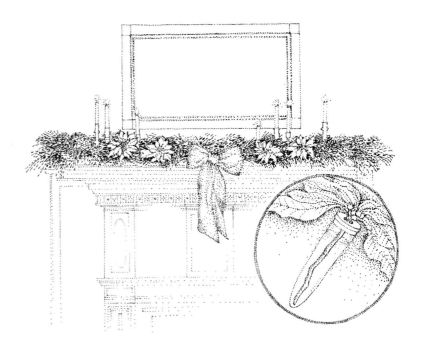

*Evergreen swags and garlands are traditional holiday decorations for mantelpieces and stair rails. To add color, insert fresh flowers in individual vials of water and poke them into the evergreens. The plastic vials are inexpensive, and most florists sell them.*

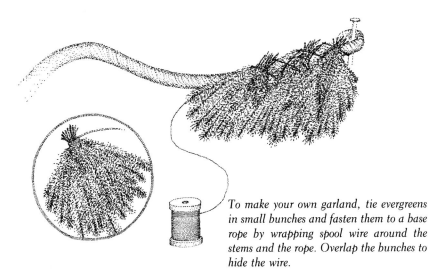

To make your own garland, tie evergreens in small bunches and fasten them to a base rope by wrapping spool wire around the stems and the rope. Overlap the bunches to hide the wire.

works best for this). Finish the wreath with a fabric bow in a harmonious color.

## Bringing Forced Bulbs into Bloom

The bulbs you potted up for forcing in autumn will be ready to bring into bloom at various times during the winter. When bulbs to be forced have been in cold storage for the required length of time, you should bring them from the dark, cold storage place into bright light, but not direct sun. Clean any dirt from the outside of the pot, and cover the top with tissue paper for a few days to make the transition to light gradually.

When the shoots are 2 to 3 inches high and bright green, put the pot on a sunny but cool windowsill. A cool environment is important. If the temperature is too warm, the bulbs may not bloom but will only send up leaves. Give the plants as much light as possible to get the sturdiest growth. Dim light will cause the stems to grow lanky and floppy.

Water your bulbs when the soil (or other potting medium) dries out. You can judge this by the weight of the pot—dry soil is significantly lighter than wet soil. Another way to test for dryness is to tap the outside of the pot: a hollow sound means the soil is dry; a dull sound means it's moist. When it's time to water, use room temperature water; cold water will shock the plants and slow their growth. Unless you plan to discard the bulbs after they bloom, don't stop watering the plants when the flowers fade. Continue watering for a month or two more to let the foliage grow and nourish the bulb. Then gradually taper off watering and let the foliage die back. You can then store the bulbs until it is time to plant them outdoors or begin to force them again, if that is possible (such as for amaryllis).

As the plants grow, turn the pots often so the stems grow straight. Stake plants that need it to keep the stems from bending over. Keep the soil loose and aerated by gently stirring the surface occasionally. Many bulbs need no added fertilizer if they are planted in a good soil mix. Follow the directions in chapter 9 for those that do benefit from feeding.

To get the longest life from the flowers when they do bloom, put them in a cool—but not cold—place at night and keep them away from cold drafts. When the flowers fade, clip them from the plants.

Bulbs forced indoors usually cannot be forced a second time, but they can be planted outdoors if they are hardy in your area. The bulbs should bloom again outdoors the following year, although it may take a couple of years for the bulbs to regain their full vigor.

## Gifts from the Garden

• Flower gardeners are never without homegrown gifts to give friends and family for Christmas and other special occasions. A blooming plant presented in a pretty bowl or basket makes a nice gift, one the recipient can enjoy for a long time to come. The plant can be a winter-flowering houseplant or, for a reminder of summer, an annual flower plant that you started from seed or a cutting last summer or fall.

• If you have flowers in bloom that are suitable for cutting, you can present someone special with a hand-tied bunch of flowers. Cut the flowers right before you are ready to give the gift, and wrap the stems together with florist's wire. Dried flowers can also be presented in a hand-tied bunch, a charming instant arrangement to put in a vase or basket. Another cut flower option is to give someone a small bouquet of winter flowers already arranged in a vase or bowl.

*Pots of forced daffodils and narcissus.*

If you do want to replant forced bulbs outdoors, wait until the foliage has died back. Then take the bulbs out of their pots, brush off the soil, and inspect them for signs of mildew, rot, or disease. When the bulbs are clean and dry, store them in a cool, dry place until planting time in fall.

## More Spring Flowers in Winter— Forcing Branches into Bloom

You can enjoy blossoms from flowering shrubs and trees a month or two ahead of when they will be blooming outdoors, by cutting branches and forcing them into early bloom indoors. Forcing can begin during the bleakest part of winter—January and February—when it seems that spring will never come. Pussy willow (the easiest of all branches to force) and witch hazel can be cut in January in many places. February brings forsythia and cornelian cherry, and in March you can cut branches from flowering crabapple trees.

When deciding which of the shrubs and trees on your property are the best candidates for early forcing, keep in mind that plants that produce flowers before leaves (like forsythia) are easier to force than plants that produce leaves first (such as deutzia and weigela). Consider, too, that the later a plant blooms outdoors, the longer it will take to force. The closer to their natural flowering time branches are cut, the less time it will take to force blooms.

## BRINGING THE BRANCHES INTO BLOOM

Cut the branches you want to force after the buds begin to swell in late winter. Timing is important. If the branches are cut too early, the buds will drop off or shrivel. If you cut them too late, the branches won't bloom any earlier than the plant's normal outdoor flowering time. Watch for that first fattening of buds. It's best to cut the branches on a mild day or during a thaw, around noon. The branches will be filled with sap then and will give you better flowers.

*OPPOSITE*
*Calla lilies make elegant cut flowers and can be forced indoors for winter flowers.*

*A colorful windowsill of forced bulbs goes a long way to counter the drab, gray days of January and February.*

Branches can be cut from spring-flowering trees and shrubs and forced into early bloom indoors. Forsythias are a classic example, but many other kinds of branches can be forced as well.

Cut the branches with a sharp knife or pruning shears. To increase their capacity to absorb water, slit the cut ends and scrape off the outer bark to about 3 inches or split the cut ends with a hammer. Do *not* smash the ends. After cutting, soak the branches—the entire branches, not just the ends—in lukewarm water for twenty-four hours in a warm room where the temperature is 70° to 75°F. Then place the stem ends in a container of cool water in a cool, dim place (a basement or attached garage, perhaps) where the temperature is about 60° to 65°F. It's a good idea to put some filtering charcoal (not barbecue briquettes) in the water to keep it from fouling.

After a few days move the branches to a brighter, warmer spot. Do not put them in a sunny window, though. A north-facing windowsill is a good loca-

OPPOSITE
Forsythia and ranunculus can be forced into bloom indoors weeks before their normal outdoor flowering time.

## How to Make Geraniums Bloom in Winter

Geraniums are among the most popular outdoor container plants in summer, but they're not as widely grown indoors as they used to be. Geraniums can provide plenty of flowers to brighten your home in winter if you grow them especially for this purpose.

A major commercial supplier of geraniums, Fischer Geraniums U.S.A., suggests the following procedure to have geranium flowers indoors in winter:

• The process begins in May, with a compact variety of zonal geranium growing in a 4-inch pot. Repot the plant in a 6-inch pot, and sink the pot into your outdoor garden for the summer, in a place where it will get full sun. When you repot the plant, feed it with an all-purpose houseplant fertilizer.

• In early fall, before the first frost, dig up the pot, check for any signs of pests, and bring the plant indoors, still in its pot. Pinch off all the blossoms and flower buds. Water when the soil dries out, but before the plant wilts. Then feed the plant with a slow-release fertilizer. Although indoor geraniums don't bloom as lavishly as outdoor ones, you will still be rewarded with a winter display of flowers.

• If you like the formal look of topiary, you might like to try training a geranium as a standard (a ball of foliage and flowers atop a long, bare, treelike stem). Start with a cutting taken from a mature plant and rooted in spring. When the new plant is big enough, repot it in a 6-inch pot. Do not pinch the main shoot, as you would if you wanted to keep the plant compact. Instead, tie the main stem to a stake inserted into the soil in the center of the pot. Remove all the side shoots and

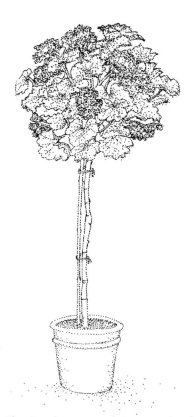

If you've always wanted to try your hand at topiary, you will probably enjoy training a geranium plant as a standard.

flower buds as they appear, but do not pinch off any leaves. When the stem is 30 to 36 inches tall, pinch off the growing tip and allow three to five side branches to develop around the top of the plant. When these side branches are 4 to 6 inches long, pinch their tips so that new branches grow from each stem. Continue this pinching process until your plant has developed a bushy, rounded shape on top of the tall main stem. From this point you can let the flower buds form. Pinch off shoots and leaves only as needed to retain the shape of the plant.

tion. You can add some cut flower conditioner to the water if you like.

Approximately once a week, change the water and cut another inch off the stems. Add fresh charcoal and conditioner whenever you change the water. Once a day, or at least three times a week, mist the branches with lukewarm water to mimic the effect of a gentle, soaking spring rain. Mist thoroughly, until the branches are dripping wet.

As the flowers begin to open, it's time to arrange the branches in the vase in which you want to display them and move them into bright sunshine. The sunlight will intensify the color in mature buds. Flowers allowed to open in the shade will be paler.

If you are forcing the flowers for a special event and you find that they are opening before you want them to, you can slow down the process by moving the branches to a cool, shaded location where the temperature is between 50° and 65°F. If your flowers are opening too slowly, you can speed them up by setting the branches in tepid water (about 110°F) each morning. Let the water cool during the day, and the next morning replace it with fresh water. Misting the branches with warm water will also help to hasten blooming.

*Witch hazel opens its fragrant yellow flowers while winter snow still covers the ground.*

## ELEVEN

# Flowers for Winter Gardens

The flowers you can grow outdoors in winter depend on where you live. Warm-climate gardeners have many more choices than northerners do. But no matter where you live, there are winter flowers you can grow. This chapter contains basic cultural information on a variety of winter plants. For outdoor gardens there are a number of bulbs, along with a shrub or two. For indoor gardens you will find an assortment of houseplants, including some from the Gesneriad family and two orchids that grow and bloom happily on a windowsill.

Other winter specialties, such as bulbs and branches forced into bloom before their normal outdoor season and annuals grown indoors from seeds or cuttings, are not included in this chapter. They are discussed instead in chapters 10 and 12.

### Abutilon / Flowering Maple

The large bell-shaped blossoms of the flowering maples are quite beautiful in pots indoors or, during warm weather, outdoors on patios. They make good cut flowers as well, blooming in a range of shades of red, pink, orange, yellow, and white. Flowering maples were popular in Victorian parlors (they were sometimes called parlor maples), but today there are numerous species and improved hybrids to choose from. Many of today's flowering maples are ever-blooming.

Flowering maples got their common name from the shape of their leaves, which resemble maple leaves to varying degrees. Abutilons are big plants. Give them plenty of pot space, and prune them in spring to keep them bushy. Some of them grow upright, and others are better suited to hanging baskets.

Flowering maples thrive in an all-purpose potting mix of two parts potting soil, one part peat moss, and one part vermiculite. Give them warm daytime temperatures around 70°F, with a ten-degree drop at night. Keep the soil evenly moist, and mist the plants every day to increase humidity levels.

In winter the plants need full sun and a southern exposure. In summer they can be moved to a partly shaded spot outdoors, where they receive four hours of morning sun.

Flowering maples do not need much fertilizer. An occasional dose of a houseplant fertilizer that is low in nitrogen should do the job.

As the plants grow, pinch back the new shoots to encourage a bushy shape. Flowering maples do not go into dormancy but grow year-round. To keep them vigorous, in spring cut back the main stems by half and prune the lateral stems to 3 or 4 inches.

Ever-blooming hybrid cultivars include Apricot Belle (coral pink), Crimson Belle (rich red), Old Rose Belle (deep rose), Satin Pink Belle (pink), Silver Belle (white), Tangerine Belle (orange), and Yellow Belle (yellow). *Abutilon megapotamicum* 'Variegata' has yellow-and-red flowers and

*Flowering Maple.*

foliage mottled with yellow and green. It is a good plant for hanging baskets.

A. *pictum* 'Gold Dust' has bright green maplelike leaves that are mottled with gold. The flowers are orange.

A. *thompsonii* is an upright grower with orange flowers and yellow-and-green variegated foliage.

## Chionodoxa
### Glory-of-the-Snow

These delightful little plants start producing their star-shaped flowers of blue, white, or pink in late winter or early spring, depending upon where you live. They can be used in rock gardens, borders, and beds or naturalized beneath shrubs and trees. The plants will spread from self-sown seeds and through division and will eventually carpet the area with their flowers.

If you live in a cool climate where summers are mild, plant glory-of-the-snow in full sun. If your summers are hot, it is better to pick a site that receives partial shade during late spring and summer. The plants are hardy to about −40°F, and they need some below-freezing temperatures in winter in order to bloom.

Plant the bulbs in autumn, 2 to 3 inches deep and 3 inches apart, in well-drained soil that contains plenty of organic matter. Water regularly during the growing and blooming seasons if rains are sporadic in your area. Taper off watering when the foliage begins to die back.

Glory-of-the-snow multiplies quickly, and bulbs should be dug up, separated, and replanted in early autumn every few years, when the plants noticeably lose vigor and the flower quality and quantity decline.

The most familiar species is *Chionodoxa luciliae*, growing about 6 inches high. Each plant produces about ten bright blue flowers with white centers. Several cultivars are also available:

Alba has larger, pure white flowers; Gigantea has larger violet-blue flowers and larger leaves; Rosea and Pink Giant both have pink flowers.

C. *sardensis* has deep gentian-blue flowers with a tiny white eye. It also reaches a height of about 6 inches.

## Clivia / Kaffir Lily

This beautiful winter-blooming houseplant is closely related to the amaryllis, which it resembles. The plant has long, broad, straplike leaves of deep glossy green. The fragrant trumpet-shaped flowers are orange with yellow centers and come in clusters in the center of the plant. There are several species of kaffir lily, but *Clivia miniata* is the one that blooms in winter.

Clivias grow from bulbs, and their culture is quite similar to that of amaryllis. Plant the bulb in an all-purpose potting mix such as two parts potting soil, one part peat moss, and one part vermiculite. Keep the newly planted bulb in partial shade until the first shoots appear, then move it to a spot on an east-facing windowsill where it will get bright light but no direct sun.

The plants like warm temperatures of 65° to 70°F during the day and five to ten degrees cooler at night. Keep the soil evenly moist as the plants grow. Feed them every two weeks during their growing season with a mild all-purpose fertilizer.

Kaffir lilies bloom best when they are potbound, so repot them only when you find roots pushing through the surface of the soil. This will happen every three to five years.

Cut back the flower stalks when the plants finish blooming. Continue to water and fertilize the plants so the leaves have a chance to nourish the bulbs. The plants rest sometime in late summer or autumn. When they do, move the pot to a cool (45° to 55°F), dark place. Stop fertilizing until new flower stems appear, and water just

*Kaffir lily*, Clivia miniata.

enough to keep the soil from completely drying out.

## Crocus / Early Crocuses

The first crocuses to bloom are the species types, which begin poking their heads above the ground as early as January, depending on where you live. These early-blooming plants with their familiar chalice-shaped flowers will grow cheerfully in pots, beds and borders, and rock gardens and also will grow naturalized in lawns that can be left unmowed until the foliage dies. The flowers come in shades of yellow, white, and purple, and striped and bicolored types are available as well. The slender, grassy leaves are usually striped with white.

The corms of early-blooming crocuses should be planted in early fall, 3 to 4 inches deep and 3 to 4 inches apart, in full sun. You can also plant

*These early crocuses bloom in February in a New York garden.*

them under deciduous trees that will not get their leaves until after the plants finish blooming. In areas where the summer sun is very strong, crocuses will need some filtered shade in summer. Plant the corms in well-drained soil, and water regularly during the growing season if the weather is dry. Taper off watering when the leaves start to die back in summer. Crocuses like a dry dormant period but can tolerate regular rainfall if they are planted in a soil that drains quickly. The corms are hardy to about −40°F, and most types need some below-freezing temperatures in winter. Crocuses spread rapidly and need to be divided every three or four years.

Crocuses can be grown in pots for one season, but they must be planted out in the garden afterward if they are ever to bloom again. To grow them in containers, pot the corms in a mix of equal parts of peat moss, builder's

sand, and organic matter (compost or leaf mold). A small amount of a high-phosphorus fertilizer can be added to the potting mix. A 5-inch pot will hold ten corms.

The angora crocus, *Crocus ancyrensis*, is the earliest crocus to bloom. It grows just 3 inches tall and has orange-yellow flowers.

Scotch crocus, *C. biflorus*, has been grown in gardens since the seventeenth century. It has purplish flowers striped with purple on the outside and yellowish inside. Plants grow 3 inches high.

The snow crocus, *C. chrysanthus*, blooms as the last winter snows are melting. The species form has sweet-scented orange-yellow flowers with black-tipped anthers. It grows 3 inches high.

The early, or Italian, crocus, *C. imperati*, has large flowers of an unusual color on 4-inch plants and blooms at the end of winter. The flowers are buff yellow feathered with red-violet on the outside and violet-rose inside.

*C. korolkowii* opens its golden yellow flowers in late winter. The flowers open into wide stars, and the plants grow just 2½ inches tall. This species is a popular rock garden plant.

Sieber crocus, *C. sieberi*, has lilac-blue flowers with golden throats. It blooms in late winter to early spring in the Northeast as soon as the snow melts.

Cloth-of-gold crocus, *C. susianus*, is a vigorous early bloomer that spreads quickly in the garden. The plants grow 2½ inches high and have brilliant yellow-orange flowers, each petal feathered with bronze down the middle. This crocus blooms in January or February in the West, and in March in the Midwest and East.

*Crocus tomasinianus*, sometimes called tommies, is easy to grow and is tolerant of many kinds of soil. It is similar to the common crocus and naturalizes readily. The plant has lavender-blue flowers and blooms in February or March depending on climate.

## Cyclamen / Persian Violet

This classic winter houseplant has lovely waxy flowers whose curved-back petals give them a form reminiscent of shooting stars. Shooting star is, in fact, another nickname for the plant. Cyclamen flowers come in many lovely shades of pink, rose, magenta, and red, as well as white. Often the color is a deeper shade around the eye, where the flower joins the stem. Cyclamens are becoming increasingly popular winter gift plants, and most florists sell them.

*Cyclamen persicum* is the species from which most of today's indoor cultivars have been bred. The plants grow from tubers and bloom in late autumn and winter. When they stop flowering in spring, move the plants to a cool, dark place and gradually withhold watering to let the leaves die back. Remove all the dead flowers and leaves and allow the tubers to rest over the summer. Keep the soil barely moist; don't let it dry out completely. In late summer when new shoots appear, you can repot the tuber and start watering and fertilizing regularly.

Cyclamens hold up best in cool temperatures of 55° to 60°F, especially when they are in bloom. Give them bright light, but no direct sun, from an eastern exposure. Feed the plants every two weeks with a mild all-purpose fertilizer when they are growing and blooming. Keep the soil evenly moist and set the plants on pebble trays to increase humidity levels.

There is a hardy species of cyclamen, *C. neapolitanum*, that blooms in autumn outdoors. Hardy cyclamen grows best in cool, moist soil and is usually grown in shady rock gardens or

Cyclamen.

woodland plantings. Flowers are lilac-pink. The plants are not always hardy in the North, so mulch them if you live where winters are severe.

## Eranthis / Winter Aconite

The buttercup-yellow flowers of winter aconite (*Eranthis hyemalis*) bloom in late winter along with snowdrops and early crocuses, which make nice companions for them in the garden. The plants form clumps and can be naturalized under trees and shrubs, but

they are also grown in rock gardens and borders. Their sunny flowers are a welcome sight in February, when outdoor color is so hard to find.

Winter aconite will grow everywhere except in very warm climates, and it is not demanding in terms of its care. The plants do fine in any reasonably fertile, well-drained soil. Eranthis grows well in shade, a characteristic that increases its versatility. Even better, the plants can be left undisturbed for years as they spread; in fact, you don't ever have to divide winter aconite

*Winter aconite.*

unless you want to propagate new plants.

Plant the bulbs in late summer or very early autumn, 3 inches deep and about 3 inches apart. The plants grow just a few inches high, and the large flowers have flat, broad petals that are pointed at the tips. The flower stalks arise from a basal mat of finely divided leaves.

## Euphorbia / Poinsettia

The large and amazingly diverse genus *Euphorbia* contains 1,500 species ranging from tender flowering shrubs like the poinsettia to cactuslike succulent plants such as the spring-blooming crown of thorns. Undoubtedly the poinsettia is the best-known member of the clan.

Although we don't think of the poinsettia as a shrub, in its native habitat it is indeed a shrubby perennial. What we recognize as the poinsettia's flower is actually colorful bracts, petallike structures surrounding the true flow-

ers, which are tiny and inconspicuous. The traditional poinsettia color is red, but cultivars are now available in pink, white, and white flushed with pink as well.

Poinsettias bought at Christmastime can be brought into bloom again in subsequent years if you know how to treat them. A good potting medium is made of two parts potting soil, one part milled sphagnum moss, and one part vermiculite. When the plants are growing and blooming, give them warm temperatures of 65° to 70°F during the day, with a ten-degree drop at night. Keep the soil evenly moist but not soggy; do not overwater. A bright southern window covered with sheer curtains that filter the sun is a perfect spot for poinsettias.

The plants go into dormancy when they finish blooming. When their color fades, move them to a cool place with filtered light, stop fertilizing, and water them just enough to keep the soil from completely drying out. When new growth starts in spring, cut back

the stems, repot the plants, and resume regular watering. Feed the plants once a week in summer and fall with a mild houseplant fertilizer. Poinsettias enjoy spending the summer outdoors.

To bring the plants into bloom, you must artificially regulate the day length. Beginning in autumn, give the plants fourteen hours of darkness and ten hours of daylight each day, to simulate the short days and long nights of winter. The plants need two months of this treatment for the bracts to change color.

## Galanthus / Snowdrop

Among the earliest and most welcome heralds of spring in cold climates, snowdrops can be seen blooming in woodlands before the last snow has melted. Several species and varieties are available to gardeners, but all of them have gracefully nodding bell-shaped flowers with six petals; the outer three petals are pure white, the inner three are tipped or flushed with green. Snowdrops can be planted in beds or borders but are best used in rock gardens, under deciduous trees and shrubs, or naturalized in unmowed grassy areas. They bloom at the same time as winter aconite, and the two plants make an attractive combination in the garden.

Snowdrops like lots of sun when they are growing and blooming, but they need to be shaded from the hot summer sun. Under deciduous trees and shrubs is a perfect location for snowdrops—their leaves will provide protection for the plants during the time of year when they need it. Snowdrops are hardy to about −40°F and do need some subfreezing winter temperatures.

Plant the bulbs in autumn, 3 to 4 inches deep and 3 inches apart, in well-drained soil enriched with compost or leaf mold. Snowdrops like heavier soil than most bulbs do, and they also like moisture, so water them when rainfall is sparse. The bulbs do not need to be divided very often. When they do, dig and divide them right after the flowers fade in spring. Transplant the bulbs carefully, and give them plenty of water after you replant them.

Common or garden snowdrop, *Galanthus nivalis*, the most common species, grows 6 to 9 inches tall, with solitary, inch-long white flowers. The flowers hold up well during bad weather, and the plants spread quickly. A double-flowered cultivar, Flore-Pleno, is also available.

The giant snowdrop, *G. elwesii*, is slightly larger, growing to a height of about 12 inches. Its leaves and flowers are bigger than those of the common snowdrop. This species needs less winter cold and is a better choice for gardens in warm climates.

## Hamamelis / Witch Hazel

Although shrubs are not the real focus of this book, there are some that play such valuable roles in the garden that they cannot be left out. One of these is witch hazel, whose fragrant yellow or reddish flowers are so very welcome in late winter.

The shrubs vary in height from 6 to 20 feet, depending upon which species you are growing. The flowers with their narrow, strap-shaped petals look like little bunches of wavy ribbons. Witch hazels are hardy and easy to grow. They tolerate any average garden soil but seem to prefer one that is moist and well drained. You can grow them in either full sun or partial shade.

When the plants open their bright flowers in February, cut a few branches to bring indoors so you can enjoy the pleasant scent as well as the outdoor color.

Probably the best known of the witch hazels is a hybrid, *Hamamelis × intermedia* 'Arnold Promise', which was developed at the Arnold Arboretum in Boston. The plant is a cross between Chinese witch hazel (*H. mollis*) and Japanese witch hazel (*H. japonica*). Arnold Promise has large, bright primrose-yellow flowers 1½ inches across. It can reach 20 feet in height. An added bonus is the bright orange color of the plant's leaves in autumn.

Another hybrid, *H. × intermedia* 'Diana', is much sought after by gardeners because of the unique coppery orange-red color of its flowers. This color is unlike any other seen outdoors at this time of year, and the plant makes an eye-catching addition to late winter gardens. Diana grows 14 to 20 feet tall, and in autumn its foliage turns red and orange.

An even earlier blooming witch hazel is *H. vernalis*, which flowers in January or February in New York City, a bit later farther north, and earlier farther south. The plant grows just 5 or 6 feet tall, making it a good

*Witch hazel.*

choice for small gardens. You can plant individual specimens or line them up to form a hedge. The flowers are soft yellow, with the petals curled and twisted in interesting patterns. This species is an American native and is very easy to grow. It prefers moist, well-drained soil but flourishes in either sun or light shade. It is seldom bothered by pests or diseases.

## *Helleborus* / *Christmas Rose*

This lovely winter-blooming perennial sends out its flowers in early winter in mild climates and late winter in areas where the soil freezes. The plant takes a couple of years to establish itself in the garden, and it is fairly demanding in terms of its environmental conditions, but the rewards are worth the extra effort. The unusual flowers are white and develop a pinkish tint as they mature. Sometimes the flowers are tinged with green as well. They are large—about 2½ inches across—and borne close to the ground.

Christmas roses need a shady spot where the soil is cool, moist but well drained, and rich in organic matter. Dig in lots of compost, well-rotted manure, and leaf mold when you prepare the planting area, and topdress liberally once a year to keep the soil in good condition. The plants spread very slowly, so you will not need to divide or move them. The leaves are evergreen and may dry out in harsh winter winds. If wind is a problem in your garden, you can protect the foliage from the drying effects by spraying them with an antidesiccant.

A closely related species, the Lenten rose (*H. orientalis*), blooms a bit later in colors ranging from cream to the palest purple. These flowers, too, are sometimes tinged with green. Some gardeners think this species is easier to grow than the Christmas rose, but both do well when their needs are met.

## *Hippeastrum* / *Amaryllis*

Although winter is not the only time of year amaryllis bulbs can be brought into bloom, they are most often seen in this season, especially around the holidays. The enormous trumpet-shaped flowers (which can be up to 8 inches across), clustered atop their tall, straight stems, are flashy and hard to miss.

In frost-free areas amaryllis can be planted outdoors, but since most of us grow it as a houseplant, indoor culture is what will be discussed here.

Most mail-order nurseries ship amaryllis bulbs in autumn. If you want to have flowers for Christmas, order your bulbs so you have them by the middle of October. Plant each bulb in an 8-inch pot, in a good all-purpose potting mix, such as two parts potting soil, one part peat moss, and one part vermiculite. Plant the bulb so that the top third of it is above the soil level. Water sparingly until shoots appear, then water regularly to keep the soil evenly moist. The bulb will not need

*Amaryllis.*

any fertilizer to produce its first flowers. Keep the plant in a bright window where it will get some sun, and turn the pot every couple of days so the stem grows straight. The flower stems are very thick and will not need staking. New bulbs usually bloom about six weeks after you start to water them.

Each bulb sends up one, or sometimes two, flower stalks about 2 feet tall, each of which is topped by a cluster of three to six huge, trumpet-shaped flowers. Many hybrid cultivars are available in a range of warm colors, along with white.

The flowers last a long time—a month to six weeks, usually. When they fade, cut off the big stalk and let the leaves grow to nourish the bulb. You can move the plant outdoors for the summer if you like, but in any case you should continue to water it. At the end of summer start cutting back on water to let the foliage die. When it does, remove the dead leaves, stop watering entirely, and set the pot in a cool, dark basement or closet. When new shoots appear in two or three months, move the plant back into the light and resume watering. Feed the plant with a time-release fertilizer, or feed it every two weeks during its growing season with a mild all-purpose plant food.

Amaryllis bulbs usually last for several years. The plants bloom best when they are potbound, so you will only need to repot them every two or three years.

## Jasminum / Jasmine

Outdoor jasmine is usually associated with southern gardens, but the winter jasmine, *Jasminum nudiflorum*, grows as far north as Boston. Better still, it flowers in late winter in the North and practically all winter long farther south. The shrub is quite effective planted in front of a stone wall, along

a bank, or massed into an informal hedge. It has clear yellow, six-petaled flowers.

Winter jasmine sends out its flowers before its leaves. The flowers bloom on wood produced the previous year—a fact to bear in mind when pruning the plant. The shrubs need full sun in order to bloom well, but they are not fussy about soil, growing happily in just about any reasonably fertile, well-drained garden soil.

In addition to winter jasmine, there are several other winter-flowering jasmines that make heavenly scented houseplants. Indoor jasmines need bright light, preferably with direct sun in the morning. A southern or eastern exposure is best for these plants. Pot them in an all-purpose growing medium, such as a mix of two parts potting soil, one part peat moss, and one part vermiculite. Keep the soil moist, and mist the plants once or even twice a day to boost humidity levels. Jasmines like cool temperatures of 50° to 60°F indoors. Feed the plants once a month when they are growing actively, with a mild all-purpose houseplant fertilizer.

The plants are lovely in hanging baskets. Their stems arch over the sides of the pot, and the graceful clouds of sweetly fragrant flowers float airily above the foliage. When the flowers fade, cut back the flowering stems by 2 or 3 inches.

Royal jasmine, *J. nitidum*, bears pure white, star-shaped blossoms on bushy plants with glossy green leaves. It blooms off and on all year.

*J. odoratissimum* is an ingredient in perfume formulas. The compact plants have small yellow flowers and are ever-blooming.

*J. polyanthum*, which is also known as winter jasmine, covers itself with masses of sweetly scented white flowers in winter and spring. The buds are a pretty pastel pink before they open.

## Paphiopedilum
### Lady Slipper Orchid

We tend to think of orchids as delicate, exotic plants that need precise greenhouse conditions in order to bloom. Actually, many orchids are quite durable. If you can give them the environment they need, the plants practically grow themselves and seldom fail to bloom. Lady slippers are among the most widely grown orchids, and many of them are easy to grow and bring into bloom indoors. Many of the hybrids now on the market bloom twice a year, often in winter. The waxy flowers are characterized by their rounded lip, which is called a pouch. The flowers last a very long time on the plant, sometimes two months.

The critical factors for paphiopedilums, as for other orchids, are light, temperature, and humidity. They grow well in a north or east window or under fluorescent lights (where they need twelve hours of light a day). Plants with solid green leaves need temperatures of 60° to 75°F during the day, with a fifteen-degree drop at night. Plants with mottled leaves need to be a bit warmer, 70° to 80°F during the day and fifteen degrees cooler at night. The nighttime drop is crucial, and you may find it easiest to grow the plants in an unused bedroom or a separate plant room where you can regulate the temperature without making your living quarters uncomfortable.

Plant lady slippers in a medium that holds moisture but still drains well, such as osmunda fiber or finely chopped fir bark. It's important to keep the medium evenly moist. Once or twice a month, feed the plants with a mild orchid fertilizer or dilute fish emulsion. To give the plants the 40 to 50 percent humidity they need, keep them on a pebble tray and mist them daily. It is better to mist the plants in

*Many paphiopedilum hybrids bloom in winter. They are among the easiest orchids to grow indoors on windowsills or under lights.*

the morning rather than in the afternoon, for moisture sitting on the leaves at night can cause disease problems. When the first flower bud forms, stake the plant so the slender flower stems will be able to support the weight of the heavy flowers.

Paphiopedilums enjoy spending the summer outdoors in a shady, protected spot. A lath house, if you have one, is ideal.

The plants rest briefly when their new growth has matured. Cut back on watering and stop fertilizing the plants during this time.

There are many hybrid paphiopedilums on the market. They bloom in unusual shades of purple, maroon,

deep red, pink, or white, often striped, streaked, flushed, veined, or mottled on the petals or sepals. Some of the flowers have unusual shades of green and purplish brown in them, too.

### *Phalaenopsis* / *Moth Orchid*

The flowers of moth orchids really do resemble moths, with their broad, flat, widespread petals and sepals. Orchid flowers are highly evolved, and their shapes and color patterns attract pollinators to the plants in nature. One look at a phalaenopsis flower will show you that the target pollinator is a moth. I think the *Phalaenopsis* species are the most beautiful of orchids, and appar-

ently other gardeners do, too, for they are widely grown. The flowers bloom in long, arching sprays, opening in a succession that can continue for an incredible five months.

*Phalaenopsis* likes warm, humid conditions quite similar to those enjoyed by African violets, and some gardeners find that they can grow the two plants together in light gardens.

Most *Phalaenopsis* species bloom in spring, but some hybrids are ever-blooming, and most others bloom anytime during the year, often during the winter.

The plants are epiphytic, meaning that in nature they grow above the ground (often perching in trees) and take moisture and nutrients from the surrounding atmosphere rather than from the soil. What this means for gardeners is that the plants need a looser, coarser potting medium than lady slippers, which are terrestrial plants. You can grow moth orchids in baskets of fir bark mixed with chopped tree fern fiber, or you can attach the plant to a slab of tree fern fiber, not putting it in a pot at all. Give it a bright north or east window where it will not be exposed to direct noontime sun. Or you can give the plant twelve to sixteen hours of fluorescent light a day.

Good air circulation is important for moth orchids, as is moisture. Keep the potting medium evenly moist; if you are growing the plant on a piece of tree fern fiber, mist the roots often. During the day moth orchids need tempera-

A Phalaenopsis *hybrid.*

tures of 70° to 85°F, with a drop to 60° or 65°F at night. Feed the plant with a mild orchid fertilizer or dilute fish emulsion every time you water it, all year-round. Moth orchids, like paphiopedilums, enjoy spending the summer outdoors in a protected place.

The glorious flowers of phalaenopsis can be pure white, shades of pink, or greenish yellow, and a more recent development is a series of hybrids in "desert shades" of apricot, orange, tan, and beige. There are also white flowers with a colored lip, white flowers striped with pink or red, and a host of other spotted, barred, and flushed patterns.

In addition to the hybrids, there is a winter-blooming species suited to indoor culture, *P. amabilis.* It has white flowers with a yellow-and-white lip with red markings. The plant generally starts blooming in fall and continues through winter.

## Primula / *Primrose*

Primroses are favorite spring garden flowers, but some of them bloom indoors in winter, adding their cheerful colors to houseplant displays. All the plants are characterized by flowers growing singly or in clusters on top of tall stems that arise from a basal rosette of slightly fuzzy, oval-shaped leaves. A range of different colors is available.

Grow primroses in a humusy soil mix. A blend of one part potting soil, two parts leaf mold or peat moss, and one part perlite or builder's sand makes a good medium. The plants need cool temperatures: 55° to 60°F during the day, with a ten-degree drop at night. You can grow them in a bright north or east window or under fluorescent lights turned on for twelve to fourteen hours a day. Keep the soil evenly moist, and feed the plants twice a month while they're blooming, with a mild all-purpose fertilizer or dilute fish emulsion or seaweed extract. Prim-

roses will not bloom well if they are potbound, so you will need to repot them after they finish blooming.

Two of the species described below rest in spring after they finish blooming. During this dormant period place them in a cool, partially shady location with good air circulation. Stop fertilizing the plants, and water just enough to keep the soil from drying out. Let the plants rest all summer, and then resume a regular schedule of watering and feeding in the fall.

The fairy primrose, *Primula malacoides,* bears clusters of star-shaped flowers in shades of red, pink, rose, lilac, or white. The plants grow about a foot tall. The flowers are quite pretty, but the plants are difficult to bring into bloom a second time. It's usually best to discard fairy primrose plants after they bloom and buy new plants the following year.

Poison primrose, *P. obconica,* has foot-tall clusters of red, pink, mauve, salmon, or white flowers with a light green eye. The short hairs on the leaves are irritating to the skin, so be careful when handling these plants. Poison primroses can generally be re-bloomed a second year if you treat them as described above.

Chinese primrose, *P. sinensis,* has large single or double flowers in shades of red, rose, pink, purple, and white, with a yellow eye. This species, too, can be brought back into bloom a second time.

## Saintpaulia / *African Violet*

The African violet is the most popular houseplant in America, and with good reason. It adapts well to indoor conditions, blooms year-round, and comes in a staggering array of flower forms, an assortment of pretty colors, and a range of plant sizes, too. Most African violets grow in neat, low rosettes, but there are also trailing and creeping types. The flowers can be single or double, ruffled, fringed, white-edged or bicolored. The color range is limited to purple, pink, and white, but there are so many shades and variations that you won't run out of choices. More than six thousand cultivars are currently registered by the African Violet Society of America, and there are probably several thousand additional varieties on the market.

African violets grow well in a soilless potting mix of equal parts of shredded sphagnum peat moss, perlite, and vermiculite, a medium that holds moisture but drains well. The plants grow well in bright east or west windows or under fluorescent lights kept on for twelve to eighteen hours a day. Place the plants about ten inches below the lights. The plants will tell you if they are getting the right amount of light. If the light is insufficient, the plants will bloom poorly, and the leaves will be dark green in color and ascending toward the light. Variegated leaves may turn solid green. African violets that are getting too much light develop droopy yellow leaves that look burned around the edges. To keep the plants symmetrical, give the pots a quarter turn every couple of days.

African violets like warm temperatures of 65° to 75°F. They like high humidity, too, although they can adapt to the dry atmosphere present in so many homes in winter. Contrary to a common misconception, however, the plants do not need a lot of water. In their natural habitat they grow on rocks. In indoor gardens, overwatering is the most common cause of African violet demise, because the crowns are susceptible to rot. Water the plants only when the soil surface is dry, and avoid getting water on the leaves and crowns. You may find it easier to water the plants from the bottom, by setting the pots in a tray of water. Feed them every week or two with a mild all-purpose fertilizer.

African violets tend to develop long necks below the leaves as they get older, which ruins the look of the plant. To rejuvenate a necky plant, cut through the stem with a sharp knife, about an inch below the bottom leaves. Scrape off the tough outer layer of stem to expose the green tissue below, then place the whole top of the plant in a soilless propagating medium to root. When roots form, pot up the new plant. The topless stem of the original plant can be left in its pot and cut back to 1 inch in length. Give the stub a dose of mild fertilizer, and the plant should begin to send out new leaves in a couple of weeks.

## Schlumbergera
### Christmas Cactus

Christmas cactus (*Schlumbergera bridgesii*) is as easy to grow as its Thanksgiving-flowering relative and requires the same kind of care. Both plants are, in my experience, dependable bloomers, and they grow in the same window in my house. Christmas cactus has a color range very much like that of Thanksgiving cactus—shades of pink, fuchsia, red, rose, and white—but there are more pastel shades among the Christmas cacti.

The plant is distinguished from other members of the genus by the scalloped edges of its flat, segmented stems. The stems grow upright at first, but as they elongate they arch gracefully. The plants grow slowly.

Like the rest of the holiday cacti, the Christmas cactus is an epiphytic plant. It grows best in a light, well-drained potting mix. A blend of one part potting soil, two parts peat moss, and one part perlite or builder's sand suits it well.

The plant thrives in a warm room, with a temperature around 65° to 70°F. Give it an east or west window with bright light. The plants are said to

need long nights and cool temperatures in order to set buds, and to be safe, it is best to give them those conditions. However, mine stays indoors all year and blooms just fine on a natural daylight schedule.

Individual flowers last only a few days, but the plant sets many buds and continues to set more after the first flowers wilt. Keep faded flowers picked off. After the plant finishes blooming it produces new leaves. Throughout this time it appreciates a weekly or biweekly watering and an occasional dose of all-purpose plant fertilizer. Sometime in late spring, growth stops and the plant rests. At this time, water it only when the leaves start to look a little shriveled—every three or four weeks.

In late summer or early autumn, start to water more often and fertilize the plant as it begins to set buds.

## Scilla / Squill

Squills are among the most productive and charming of bulbs. They bloom lavishly and spread quickly, carpeting the ground with their little blue flowers. The most familiar kind, Siberian squill, blooms in early spring in most gardens. But Persian squill blooms in late February, when it adds a dash of cool, clear color to winter gardens.

Because they spread so rapidly, squills are excellent plants to naturalize in lawns, especially beneath the branches of deciduous trees. Their inconspicuous grassy leaves die back before the lawn needs to be mowed in spring. You can also plant scillas in beds and borders and in rock gardens.

Squills are extremely easy to grow. They make themselves at home in any well-drained, loamy soil, especially if it tends to be sandy. An annual top-dressing of compost or leaf mold in fall will ensure that the soil stays rich in organic matter and contains plenty of nourishment for the bulbs. Plant squills in partial shade, about 3 inches

Streptocarpus *hybrids*.

deep and 3 to 4 inches apart, in the fall. They need very little care after planting. You can divide the bulbs every four years or so or just leave them alone to naturalize. In addition to spreading by means of bulblets formed on the bulbs, the plants also self-seed, and the seeds grow into blooming-size bulbs in just a few years.

Persian squill (*Scilla tubergiana*) has only been grown in gardens for about fifty years. It is native to Iran and parts of the Caucasus Mountains. The plants open their drooping flowers, which look somewhat like stars and somewhat like bells, during the second half of February. The flowers are 1 inch across and dangle from 6-inch-high stems. They are pure white with a clear blue stripe down the center of each petal; from a distance the colors blend into a cool ice blue. One plant will send up several flower stems, each of which carries as many as half a dozen flowers. The plants are hardy everywhere.

Siberian squill (*S. sibirica*) blooms a few weeks later, with violet-blue flowers on 6-inch stems.

An even later blooming species, the meadow squill (*S. pratensis*), does not flower until very late in spring. It grows 5 to 10 inches tall and has blossoms of blue-violet.

## Streptocarpus / *Cape Primrose*

This close relative of the African violet is becoming increasingly popular among indoor gardeners. Its tubular flowers bloom in shades of crimson, pink, violet, blue, or white. The newer hybrids flower practically year-round, and they are especially welcome in winter. The flowers are carried above a low rosette of long, broad leaves.

Streptocarpus is easy to grow as long as you can supply its four basic needs: lots of light but no direct sun, cool temperatures, excellent drainage, and plenty of moisture. The plants thrive in the same peat-perlite-vermiculite potting mix that suits African violets. You can grow cape primroses in an east or west window or in a fluorescent light garden with twelve to fourteen hours of light a day.

Group the plants on pebble trays to keep the humidity high. Let the soil dry somewhat between waterings. When the plants are growing actively, feed them with a mild liquid fertilizer every time you water.

Among the available cultivars, those with blue and purple flowers are generally easier to grow than those blooming in red or pink. Look for the Constant Nymph series of hybrids, John Innes hybrids with women's names, Wiesmoor hybrids, and a cultivar named Maasen's White. A recent introduction is the Olympus series of cultivars, which contains flowers in various shades of red, pink, lavender, purple, blue, and white with streaks, veins, and flushes of contrasting colors.

## TWELVE

# Winter Gardening Activities

**W**inter activities are centered around the indoor garden for those of us in temperate climates. While outdoor beds and borders lie frozen and at rest, indoors there are bulbs, houseplants, and annuals to enjoy and also to maintain. In January, though, seed and nursery catalogs arrive, and planning for the next outdoor gardening season begins in earnest. Then in February the earliest bulbs begin to bloom, and the cycle of the gardening year is complete. As winter nears its end, it's time to start sowing seeds indoors for next spring and summer's annuals.

For gardeners in warm climates, the outdoor season never really ends. Winter flowers must be cared for both outdoors and indoors, and outdoor planting begins in February, or even January in some locations.

Here is a rundown of winter gardening activities, followed by some tips on protecting gardens from the adversities of winter and information on caring for plants indoors.

==================== EARLY WINTER ====================

### TEMPERATE CLIMATES

Where winters are cold, most flower-growing activities take place indoors.

Bulbs being forced are in cold storage now, but they do need some attention. Check pots of bulbs you are forcing once a week, to make sure the soil does not dry out. If you are reblooming last year's amaryllis bulbs, remove the top inch of soil from the pot and replace it with compost or fresh soil. If you are adding only new soil, feed the plant with a slow-release houseplant fertilizer.

When Christmas is over, you can help your holiday poinsettias last longer by putting them in a bright window, keeping the soil moist, and lowering the nighttime temperature to about 60°F.

Check your houseplants regularly for signs of pests or disease. If you notice that the foliage of smooth-leaved plants has collected dust, you can clean the leaves by sponging them with soapy water. If you do notice pests, spray the plants with insecticidal soap (Safer's is a good brand) and isolate the affected plants to prevent the problem from spreading.

In the outdoor garden, this is the time to give perennials, roses, and shrubs a final watering before the ground freezes. When the ground has frozen, you can mulch established beds and new fall plantings to prevent soil heaving. The section "Winter Protection for Outdoor Gardens," later in this chapter, will tell you about additional measures you may want to take.

Winter is also a good time to finish revising your garden plans to make changes for next season. Note any alterations you want to make in bed and border layouts, color schemes, and plants. Decide which new plants you want to try, which ones you want to grow again, and which you will discard.

When your plans are complete, you can start making up seed and nursery orders. It's a good idea to order unusual varieties as early as you can, because suppliers may run out of stock.

## WARM CLIMATES

Gardeners in warm climates will have more to do outdoors in winter than gardeners in the North, as well as attending to indoor plants. If you are forcing bulbs, they will now be in a refrigerator or other cold storage area. Check the pots once a week to make sure the soil does not dry out. If you plan to rebloom last year's amaryllis bulbs, this is the time to remove the top inch of soil from each pot and replace it with compost or fresh soil. If you are adding only new soil, feed the plants with a slow-release houseplant fertilizer.

Winter is also a good time to check your houseplants for signs of pests or disease. If smooth-leaved plants are dusty, you can clean the foliage by sponging it with soapy water. If you do notice pests, spray with insecticidal soap and isolate the affected plants to prevent the problem from spreading.

After Christmas you can help holiday poinsettias last longer by putting them in a bright window, keeping the soil moist, and lowering the nighttime temperature to 60°F.

Indoors, you can also sow seeds of pansies, ageratum, candytuft, and lobelia to have seedlings ready to plant outdoors in late winter or early spring. Seeds of cool-weather annuals such as sweet alyssum, forget-me-nots, and sweet peas can be sown outdoors.

Outdoors, it's a good idea to water all your plantings thoroughly before winter really sets in. While you are out in the garden, pull any weeds you find in flower beds and borders.

At the beginning of winter, warm-climate gardeners can feed early-blooming perennials with bonemeal and compost or with an all-purpose fertilizer. You should also fertilize roses that will flower in midwinter.

Winter brings rain in many warm climates. But when the soil in your garden is dry enough to work, you can dig holes for new rosebushes. Put some compost in the bottom of each hole and mix it into the soil.

If a cold spell threatens to freeze your camellias, try covering the buds with plastic bags until the weather moderates. Remove the bags as soon as the weather improves.

It is now time to finish planting out bulbs that have been chilled in your refrigerator for six to eight weeks. You can also set out plants of cool-weather annuals and perennials such as calendulas, delphiniums, larkspurs, poppies, snapdragons, and pansies.

Early winter is also the time to finish revising your garden plans to make changes for next season. Note any alterations you want to make in bed and border layouts, color schemes, and plants. Decide which new plants you want to try, which ones you want to grow again, and which you will discard. When your plans are complete, you can start making up seed and nursery orders. It's a good idea to order unusual varieties as early as you can, because suppliers may run out of stock later on.

## TEMPERATE CLIMATES

As winter progresses, continue to monitor your houseplants for pests, and keep their leaves clean. Be sure to clean both upper and lower leaf surfaces when you wash foliage. To give tropical houseplants a midwinter treat, you can put them in the shower and gently run lukewarm water on them. After five or ten minutes, turn off the water, close the shower curtain, and let the plants bask in the humid atmosphere for an hour or two.

Azaleas and other holiday gift plants need to be kept moist and cool to hold their flowers longer. Azaleas in particular may need to be watered every day if the air in your home is very dry in winter. When poinsettias start to lose their color, you can begin to gradually withhold water to let them go dormant.

Periodically check tender bulbs you are storing over winter to be sure they are not rotting, drying out, or sprouting. If any bulbs are shriveling, mist them lightly. Discard any mildewed, rotting, or damaged bulbs.

In the outdoor garden, check for signs of soil heaving. If you notice any roots or crowns that have become exposed, cover them with soil or compost. If you have not mulched your perennials for winter, you should now mulch any beds where heaving is occurring. If strong winds blow the snow cover off your perennial beds—especially if they are located next to the house where warmth from the house might thaw the ground, you can shovel snow onto the beds to insulate them and keep the soil frozen. After a heavy snowfall, take a broom and carefully sweep the snow from the branches of shrubs to keep them from bending or breaking under the weight.

Gardeners in the North should start slow-growing annuals from seed indoors in January or February to make sure they will bloom by summer. Slow growers include begonias, datura, geraniums, heliotrope, lantana, salpiglossis, salvia, schizanthus, snapdragons, statice, stocks, torenia, and verbena.

In midwinter your seed and plant orders should be completed and mailed.

## WARM CLIMATES

Warm-climate gardeners, too, should continue to monitor houseplants for pests and keep their leaves clean. Be sure to clean both upper and lower leaf surfaces. Azaleas and other holiday gift plants need to be kept moist and cool for the best bloom. Azaleas, in particular, may need to be watered every day if the air in your home is very dry. When poinsettias start to lose their color, begin gradually cutting back on water to let them go dormant.

In the outdoor garden, this is a good time to prune crape myrtle to encourage the growth of new wood, where flowers will form. You can also fertilize azaleas, rhododendrons, camellias, and roses. As winter progresses, start to check your bulb beds for signs of growth. Pull the mulch away from spring bulbs when you see the first shoots. Warm-climate gardeners should sow seeds of pansies, sweet peas, stocks, and other hardy annuals by early January. Late in January you can plant seeds of ageratum, anemones, bachelor's buttons, calendulas, columbines, larkspur, petunias, phlox, poppies, and snapdragons.

In cooler parts of the West, midwinter is a good time to set out calendula, nemesia, pansy, primrose, schizanthus, and sweet william plants. In warmer areas, you can also plant out candytuft, delphiniums, four o'clocks, larkspur, petunias, pinks, poppies, salvia, and snapdragons.

In late January you can begin planting ornamental shrubs. Bare-root and balled and burlapped roses and shrubs are now available from nurseries and garden centers. Buy early to get the best selection. Be sure to plant bare-root roses while the plants are still dormant.

This is a good time to take cuttings from woody perennial vines and shrubs to root for new plants. Cut the bottom at an angle, so you will remember which end goes into the rooting medium.

Finally, finish your seed and plant orders.

### TEMPERATE CLIMATES

If you have forced paperwhite narcissus into bloom indoors, throw out the bulbs when they have finished blooming. Forced crocuses, daffodils, and other hardy bulbs can be saved for planting outdoors. Continue to check your houseplants for pests and diseases, and keep them clean. Periodically check on any tender bulbs you have in winter storage to make sure they are not drying out, rotting, or sprouting.

Outdoors, you can begin to remove winter mulch from beds of crocuses, snowdrops, and other early bulbs when the first shoots appear. Leave mulch in place around daffodils, hyacinths, and tulips. Check your perennial gardens for signs of soil heaving. Press any exposed plant crowns back into the ground, and cover exposed roots with compost or soil. Pile more mulch onto any beds where heaving is occurring.

Late winter is the time to cut branches of forsythias and other early-spring-blooming shrubs and trees to force indoors, when you notice that the buds are swelling.

In February you can sow seeds indoors of annuals and perennials such as begonias, columbines, dahlias, delphiniums, dianthus, geraniums, gaillardia, impatiens, lisianthus, lupines, marigolds, penstemon, petunias, Iceland and Oriental poppies, primroses, rudbeckia, salvia, snapdragons, straw-flowers, and sweet alyssum. Most of these seeds germinate best in warm temperatures of 65° to 75°F. For sturdy, compact plants, give the seedlings plenty of light—a windowsill in full sun or full-spectrum fluorescent lights in a light garden is best.

You can also sow seeds of flowering vines such as cup-and-saucer vine (*Cobaea scandens*) and black-eyed Susan vine (*Thunbergia alata*) to have plants ready to set outdoors when the weather turns warm. If you live in the North, you can start tuberous begonias under lights to have flowers earlier in summer.

### WARM CLIMATES

Keep checking your houseplants in late winter for signs of pests and diseases, and continue to keep their foliage clean. Save the bulbs of paperwhite narcissus to plant outdoors if you live in a frost-free area.

Outdoors, you can start to remove mulches from flower gardens.

It's time to start weeding and fertilizing beds of perennials and biennials. Irises, lilies, and other late bulbs can be topdressed with compost.

This is also a good time to prune perennials that need shaping. Fuchsias, marguerites, and geraniums are three plants that may have become ungainly. It is time, too, to prune rosebushes. After pruning, fertilize them and put down fresh mulch.

In the upper South, you can sow sweet pea seeds outdoors as soon as the soil can be worked. Gardeners in the lower South can set out plants of ageratum, delphinium, dianthus, larkspur, pansies, petunias, phlox, stocks, snapdragons, sweet alyssum, and sweet william around the middle of February or after the last expected hard frost.

It is also time to sow seeds of coreopsis, gloriosa daisies, impatiens, petunias, and sweet alyssum in flats to transplant later. You can sow seeds of California poppies, cosmos, forget-me-nots, and nasturtiums directly into the garden.

If you live in a very mild climate, you can plant gladiolus corms every two weeks during February and March for a succession of flowers later on. You can also plant bulbs, corms, and tubers of hardy amaryllis, tuberous begonia, canna, and dahlia. Fertilize them with compost and bonemeal or bulb fertilizer after planting.

This is the last chance to plant bare-root roses and other ornamental shrubs and vines. Plant on a day when the air temperature is above freezing. Finally, you can now take cuttings from wax begonias, coleus, and impatiens growing indoors to root for planting later on in containers or in outdoor garden beds.

## WINTER PROTECTION FOR OUTDOOR GARDENS

Winter weather in the North puts great stress on plants. Cold temperatures can damage leaves and roots. Snow, if it is the heavy, wet kind, can bend or break tender branches of shrubs and trees. Ice, sleet, and freezing rain can coat branches and even snap them when the coating becomes too thick. Harsh winter winds may dry out leaf tissues and damage them. In cities, temperature swings caused by heat reflecting off nearby buildings and shadows cast by the same buildings can create cold pockets. Chemicals used to melt snow from sidewalks and streets can be very harmful to plants, too.

There are some measures you can

take to protect outdoor gardens from the ravages of winter. First, make sure your perennials and shrubs are well watered when winter's cold sets in. Remember that when the ground is frozen plants cannot get water. Winter rains do no good for plants unless the ground thaws.

Snow insulates plants and is very helpful, but heavy, wet snowfalls can damage shrubs and even break branches. You can wrap shrubs for the winter in burlap or chicken wire to keep the branches upright, but the best approach is to take a broom and gently sweep the snow from the branches and out of the center of the plants.

The best way to prevent problems from ice and sleet is to avoid planting in places where ice is likely to accumulate. One place to keep plants away from is under rain gutters on the edges of buildings; another problem area is near downspouts. In winter, snow and ice melt off the roof on sunny days, and cold water drips from clogged or overflowing gutters. These may actually seem like good places to put plants, because they will get water during the winter. But remember, the water does no good when the soil is frozen, and cold water is not good for plants, anyway. Plants subjected to repeated dripping will eventually be damaged by the cold water; their leaves will turn brown, and delicate branches may die. Also, at night the water freezes again, and the plants may end up with icicles hanging from their branches. It may look picturesque, but the weight of the ice may deform or snap branches.

Cold winter winds can dry plants out very quickly, causing burning or even dying of plant tissue. If your garden site is exposed, you may find it helpful to spray flowering shrubs with an antidesiccant in late fall and again in early spring, when temperatures go above 40°F.

In cities, heat is reflected off concrete and masonry structures—side-walks, brick and stone buildings, roofs, streets—which raises the temperature of plants and soil when the sun is out. When the sun slips behind nearby buildings, the garden is in shadow and the temperature drops off fast. The temperatures themselves are less problematic than the drastic and rapid fluctuations caused by city conditions. The best way to protect ornamental plants is to mulch them and wrap the trunks of shrubs.

Another growing problem in towns and cities is caused by ice-melting chemicals. The rock salt so widely used to melt ice on streets and sidewalks is very harmful to plants when it seeps into the ground around roots. Calcium chloride is less harmful and is a better material to use than rock salt. About the only other thing you can do to protect your plants is give them 6 inches of extra mulch to soak up the salt before it gets into the soil. When winter is over, pick up the mulch and get rid of it; don't throw it on the compost pile.

One other potential problem to keep in mind during winter is traffic over garden beds. Frozen plants can be damaged when people or even pets walk on them. Ground covers are especially prone to this kind of damage. If your kids and pets like to play in the snow near your garden in winter, you might consider fencing off perennial beds and borders and areas carpeted with ground covers.

Indoor plants are not subject to these wintertime difficulties. There is one potential problem to be aware of, however. If the power goes off during a bad storm, sensitive plants will be harmed if your house gets cold. As a safeguard, when the power fails, group together houseplants that need warm temperatures and cover them with heavy-duty plastic. If the house gets really cold, try to put the plants in a room with an auxiliary space heater. Keep the plants covered with the plas-tic, though, because if the heater runs on kerosene, some plants may be sensitive to the fumes.

## MANAGING THE WINTER ENVIRONMENT INDOORS

Central heating changes the indoor environment for plants. Temperatures may vary widely within a room, being hot directly above a radiator, cool next to a window, and cold and drafty near a door. A windowsill can become quite hot on a sunny day and quite cold at night, even when the thermostat in the room records a fairly even temperature. The windowpane—even if you have storm windows—may be cold enough to damage plant leaves that come in contact with the glass. In many rooms, heat sources are located beneath windows, which creates even wilder temperature fluctuations. To avoid shocking houseplants with extreme temperature swings, never put them on windowsills directly above a heat source.

Winter gardeners need to be aware of the indoor environment in order to choose suitable places for plants. Following are some tips.

You can place thermometers on windowsills and other plant-growing places to monitor day- and nighttime temperatures. Then match cool-loving plants to cool places and warmth lovers to warm places (see the table "Temperature Needs of Winter Houseplants").

You should also take steps to increase the humidity level around your plants. Many northern homes in winter have a relative humidity as low as 20 percent (that's drier than a desert). Although that's fine for cacti, most of our favorite houseplants need 40 to 60 percent humidity. Plants growing in too dry air begin to look pale; their leaves curl under and may turn brown at the tips and along the edges. Giving these plants more water will not help.

You need to get water vapor into the air around them.

There are a number of ways to increase humidity indoors. One is to install a permanent humidifier on your furnace. This solution is the most expensive, but you'll only have to do it once. Another option is to get a room-size humidifier. Inexpensive, "low-tech" strategies include grouping plants together on pebble trays (shallow plastic trays of pebbles that are kept filled with water; the pots are set, saucers and all, on top of the pebbles) and misting plants regularly with tepid water. Smooth-leaved plants benefit most from misting. When you mist your plants, be careful not to drench them so that water sits in the leaf axils where it could encourage disease problems. One other way to increase humidity is to set open containers of water around the room and simply let it evaporate. Remember to keep pebble trays, room humidifiers, and containers of water filled at all times.

If the air is so dry that your plants actually wilt, you may be able to save them by enclosing them individually in clear plastic bags. Support the bag with two stakes pushed into the pot. Blow up the bag, place it upside down over the stakes, and fasten it around the bottom of the pot with a rubber band. Move the plant out of direct sun and leave it in the bag until the foliage revives.

## TEMPERATURE NEEDS OF WINTER HOUSEPLANTS

Some flowering plants have a definite need for warm or cool temperatures indoors. Below is a listing of the temperature preferences of various houseplants. Cool temperatures mean approximately 50° to 60°F during the day, with a five-degree drop at night. Warm temperatures are 70° to 80°F during the day, with a ten-degree drop at night.

### PLANTS THAT LIKE IT COOL

| | | | |
|---|---|---|---|
| Ardisia | Cineraria | Jasmine | Streptocarpus |
| Azalea | Cyclamen | Jerusalem cherry | Tulip |
| Calla lily (white varieties) | Freesia | Narcissus | |
| Camellia | Hyacinth | Primrose | |
| Chrysanthemum | Hydrangea | Miniature rose | |

### PLANTS THAT LIKE IT WARM

| | | |
|---|---|---|
| Achimenes | African violet | Crown of thorns |
| Aechmea | Chenille plant | Flame violet |

### PLANTS THAT LIKE IT IN BETWEEN

| | | | |
|---|---|---|---|
| Amaryllis | Christmas cactus | Hibiscus | Wax plant |
| Begonia | Flowering maple | Kalanchoe | |
| Browallia | Fuchsia | Oxalis | |
| Calceolaria | Gardenia | Poinsettia | |

## CARING FOR PLANTS DURING WINTER VACATIONS

If you take a vacation in winter, before you leave you need to make arrangements for your houseplants to survive in your absence. The best solution is to ask a plant-loving friend to stop by every few days and take care of the plants for you. But that's not always possible, and your plants may have to be left on their own while you're gone. With the right preparation, though, your plants should be able to survive two or even three weeks without you.

The basic strategy is to water the plants normally before you leave, then slow down their respiration rates until you come back. One way to do this is to enclose large plants in clear plastic bags. Place three or four stakes in the pot and drape the plastic over them, making sure that the plastic does not touch the foliage. You will be creating, in effect, a miniature greenhouse that will maintain enough humidity around the plant to keep it from wilting. Move the plant away from the window so that it does not receive any direct sunlight, or the air inside the bag will heat up and literally cook the plant.

If you have a number of smaller plants, you can group them together and cover them with an old aquarium. Or you can construct a sort of greenhouse box by making a frame out of wooden lath strips and covering it with plastic. Place the plants on a pebble tray and cover them with the plastic box.

If you are only going to be away for a week, you might try moving your plants into the shower stall in your bathroom. Close the drain and run one-half inch or more of water in the bottom, making the water as deep as possible without flooding the saucers under the pots. Close the shower curtain or door, and leave the ceiling light on until you return home.

It is important not to overcompensate, however. Never overwater plants and then enclose them in plastic. The combination of standing water around roots and lack of ventilation will probably cause root rot. Let the excess water drain from the pots as you normally do before enclosing them in plastic.

Plants that grow well in constantly moist soil can be handled with a system of wicking. One way to do this is to place one end of an old blanket in a bucket of water and the other end in a pebble tray in which your moisture-loving plants are grouped. The blanket will serve as a wick, drawing water from the bucket for the plants. If you use a wicking system, you do not need to enclose the plants in plastic bags.

In addition to moisture and humidity, you need to consider your plants' need for light. Do not leave your plants in the dark while you are gone. If you can leave your curtains or blinds open and the plants are reasonably close to the windows, they should be fine. Just remember to keep them out of direct sun if you have covered them with plastic. You can also set up a timer to turn on the lights in the room for a few hours in the early evening to supplement the available natural light.

When you get back from your trip, inspect all the plants and water those that are dry. Remove the plastic bags gradually, over a few days, to let the plants become reacclimated to the environment in the room.

## How to Buy Healthy Houseplants

The success of your indoor garden of course depends on how well you can meet the environmental needs of the plants in your collection. But it is also important to start out with healthy, vigorous plants. Choosing wisely among the offerings from plant shops, florists, and commercial greenhouses can mean the difference between a windowsill full of flowers and a row of scraggly, anemic-looking plants. Here are some tips on what to look for when buying houseplants.

First, look at the shop itself. Has it been in business for a long time? Is it clean? Consider how the plants are displayed. Are they in conditions that are not stressful? Is there a light source nearby?

Next, take a look at the overall condition of the plants. Are they healthy? Are they clean, well watered, and well cared for?

Are the clerks in the shop knowledgeable and helpful? Do they take the time to answer your questions about the conditions a plant needs in order to do well, and how to care for it?

Be wary of stores that get in truckloads of plants from wholesalers in Florida or the Southwest to sell at bargain prices. Such plants have probably not had time to acclimate to indoor conditions, and chances are they will suffer a serious setback when you move them to your home. If the plants are large, they may not acclimate at all, and no matter how well you care for them, they may die.

Any plant you buy should be healthy and sturdy. Look closely at the leaves: are they a good green color? Leaves that are pale or yellowish, twisted, stunted or distorted, or brown around the edges are evidence of an unhealthy plant.

If the plant looks generally healthy, the next step is to check for signs of diseases or pests. Bring a small magnifying glass with you and inspect carefully any plant you wish to buy. Check the undersides of the leaves and leaf axils in particular. It's a good idea to gently shake the plant—whiteflies, a common indoor plant pest, look like a cloud of white dust when a plant they have infested is shaken. You should examine the soil, too, for evidence of pests.

By all means avoid buying plants that look as if they have been heavily and recently pruned. The store owner may have cut out damaged or diseased growth to conceal a sick plant.

Now that you know what to avoid when buying new plants, here are some things to look for. First, it is better to buy small rather than large plants. They will adapt more readily to a new location. When picking out a plant, look for sturdy, compact, bushy growth. Look also for evidence of healthy new growth. If the plant is flowering, choose a specimen with lots of buds instead of open flowers—it will give you a longer season of bloom after you get it home.

In winter it is best not to buy mature plants that have been enjoying greenhouse conditions. They will be shocked when you take them outdoors and will probably decline in the cooler, dimmer, drier environment in your home. When the weather is cold, wrap new plants carefully in newspaper for the trip home.

When you get your new plant home, inspect it carefully once more. If you find any problems, take it back to the store.

Check the soil mix in which the plant is potted. Wholesalers often ship plants in a "shipping soil," which is usually mostly peat moss (which is lighter than soil and saves on shipping costs). If the soil seems to be mostly peat, you should repot the plant in a good potting mix.

Finally, even though you have inspected the new plant, isolate it from the rest of your houseplants for a couple of weeks to be sure it is not harboring pests or diseases that could spread to the rest of your indoor garden.

Taking the time to choose the healthiest, most vigorous plants from the most reliable suppliers is the best way to get your indoor flower garden off to a beautiful start.

# Appendixes

## Seasonal Blooming Schedules

The following blooming schedules provide a general guide to plants that bloom in each season. Remember that blooming times vary with location, microclimate in the garden, and yearly weather conditions. Although these schedules are geared very loosely to gardens near 40 degrees north latitude, you may find that plants in your garden will bloom a bit earlier or later even if you live in this region.

These lists focus on outdoor plants in spring and summer, with more indoor plants presented in autumn and winter.

For each plant, you will find, in this order, the scientific name, common name, flower color, season of bloom, plant height, and type of plant. The categorization of plant types is rather broad. In particular, I have used the term "bulb" to refer to true bulbs and bulblike structures such as corms, tubers, and tuberous roots.

## SPRING

### Early Spring

**Abeliophyllum**

A. *distichum*, Korean or white forsythia; white, fragrant flowers; early to mid-spring; 5 to 7 feet high; shrub.

**Adonis**

A. *amurensis*, amur adonis; yellow; late winter to mid-spring, depending on location; to 12 inches; perennial.

**Anemone**

A. *pulsatilla*, pasqueflower; lavender to purple, also red-and-white forms; early to mid-spring; 8 to 12 inches; perennial.

A. *magellanica*; white; early spring; 12 inches; perennial.

## Arabis

A. *albida* 'Flore-Pleno', double wall rock cress; double, white; all spring; 10 inches. A single-flowered form is 'Snow Cap.'

A. *caucasica*, wall cress; white; early spring; to 12 inches; perennial.

A. *procurrens*, rock cress; white; early spring; to 12 inches; perennial.

## Aubrieta

A. *deltoidea*, false rock cress; deep rose-pink; early spring; to 6 inches; perennial.

A. *hybrida*, purple rock cress; soft pink to deep purple; prostrate; perennial.

## Aurinia

Aurinia saxatilis (*Alyssum saxatile*), basket-of-gold; yellow; early spring; 12 to 15 inches; perennial.

## Calochortus

C. *albus*, white globe lily; white; early spring; to 2 feet; bulb.

## Chaenomeles

C. *japonica*, dwarf Japanese quince; red; early to mid-spring; 3 feet; shrub.

C. *lagenaria*, Japanese quince; scarlet red; early to mid-spring; 4 to 6 feet; shrub.

## Chionodoxa

C. *luciliae*, glory-of-the-snow; blue with white center; late winter to early spring; 3 to 6 inches; bulb.

C. *sardensis*, glory-of-the-snow; rich blue; 3 to 6 inches; late winter to early spring; bulb.

## Claytonia

C. *virginica*, spring beauty, mayflower; white, sometimes streaked or flushed with pink; early spring; 4 to 6 inches; wildflower. Needs moist woodland soil.

## Clivia

C. *miniata*, kaffir lily; orange-scarlet with yellow center; 1½ to 2 feet; bulb. Blooms outdoors in early spring in mild climates.

## Cornus

C. *mas*, Cornelian cherry; yellow; late winter to early spring; shrub or small tree.

## Crocus

C. *vernus*, common crocus; purple, white striped with purple; early spring; 3 to 4 inches tall; bulb.

Dutch hybrid crocuses; purple, lilac, golden yellow, white, white striped with purple; early spring; 3 to 6 inches; bulb.

## Daphne

D. *mezereum*, February daphne; rosy purple to lilac-purple; late winter to early spring, depending on location; 1½ to 3 feet; shrub.

D. *odora*, winter daphne; rose to rosy purple; late winter to mid-spring; 3 to 5 feet; shrub.

## Erica

E. *carnea*, winter heath, spring heath; pink, white, red-violet; blooms in early spring in the North, winter in the South; to 12 inches; shrub.

## Erythronium

E. *americanum*, yellow adder's tongue; golden yellow; early spring; to 12 inches; bulb.

E. *californicum*, fawn lily; creamy white; early spring; to 12 inches; bulb.

E. *grandiflorum*, avalanche lily; yellow; early spring; 1 to 2 feet; bulb.

E. *montanum*, alpine fawn lily; white with gold center; early spring; to 12 inches; bulb.

E. *revolutum*, coast fawn lily; cream flushed with lavender-pink; early spring; to 16 inches; bulb.

E. *tuolumnense*; buff yellow; early spring; to 12 inches; bulb.

## Forsythia

F. ×*intermedia*, border forsythia; yellow; early spring; 6 to 8 feet; shrub.

F. *ovata*, Korean forsythia; yellow; early spring; 5 feet; shrub.

F. *suspensa*, weeping forsythia; yellow; early spring; to 12 feet; shrub.

## Fritillaria

F. *lanceolata*, checker lily; green mottled with brown; early to mid-spring; to 2 feet; bulb.

F. *meleagris*, guinea-hen flower; white, pink checked with purple; early to mid-spring; 1 to 1½ feet; bulb.

F. *pudica*, yellow fritillary; yellow; early to mid-spring; to 9 inches; bulb.

## Helleborus

H. *orientalis*, Lenten rose; greenish white to rose-purple; early to mid-spring; to 1½ feet; perennial.

## Hepatica

H. *americana*, roundlobe hepatica; white to pale lilac or rose; early spring; 4 to 6 inches; perennial.

## Ipheion

I. *uniflorum*, spring starflower; pale blue; early spring; to 8 inches; bulb.

## Iris

*I. danfordiae*; yellow; late winter to early spring; 4 to 6 inches; bulb.

*I. reticulata*, netted iris; deep violet or blue; late winter to early spring; 4 to 6 inches; bulb.

*I. unguicularis*, Algerian iris; lavender-blue; early spring; 1 to 2 feet; bulb.

## Lachenalia

*L. aloides*, cape cowslip; yellow; early spring; to 12 inches; bulb.

## Leucojum

*L. vernum*, spring snowflake; white; early spring; 12 inches; bulb.

## Lonicera

*L. fragrantissima*, winter honeysuckle; creamy white, fragrant; early spring; 8 to 10 feet; shrub.

## Magnolia

*M. stellata*, star magnolia; white, fragrant; early spring; to 15 feet; shrub.

## Mertensia

*M. virginica*, Virginia bluebells; lavender to blue; early to mid-spring; to 2 feet; perennial.

## Muscari

*M. botryoides*, bluebells, grape hyacinth; blue; early to mid-spring; blue; to 12 inches.

*M. azureum*, grape hyacinth; azure blue; early to mid-spring; to 8 inches; bulb.

*M. armeniacum*, grape hyacinth; deep blue-violet; early to mid-spring; to 12 inches; bulb.

## Myosotis

*M. scorpioides*, true forget-me-not; blue to lavender-blue; early spring to fall; 1 to 1½ feet; perennial.

## Narcissus

N. cultivars, daffodils and narcissus; shades of yellow, apricot, cream, white, bicolors; early to mid-spring; 3 to 16 inches, depending on type; bulb.

*N. cyclamineus*; yellow; early spring; 6 inches; bulb.

## Ornithogalum

*O. umbellatum*, star of Bethlehem; white; early to mid-spring; 6 to 8 inches; bulb.

*O. nutans*, star of Bethlehem; greenish white; early to mid-spring; 8 to 12 inches; bulb.

## Pieris

*P. floribunda*, andromeda; white; early to mid-spring; 3 to 4 feet; shrub.

## Primula

*P. ×polyantha*, polyanthus primrose; red, rose, pink, blue, violet, white, with yellow eye; early spring; 9 inches; perennial.

## Pulmonaria

*P. angustifolia*, blue lungwort; blue-violet; early to late spring; 6 to 12 inches; perennial.

## Puschkinia

*P. libanotica*, blue puschkinia; light blue with darker blue stripes; early to mid-spring; 4 to 6 inches; bulb.

*P. scilloides*, striped squill; white; early to mid-spring; to 6 inches; bulb.

## Ranunculus

*R. asiaticus*, Persian buttercup; red, pink, orange, yellow; early to mid-spring; 6 to 18 inches; bulb.

## Rhododendron

*R. calophytum*, bigleaf rhododendron; white, pink, rose; early to mid-spring; to 36 feet; shrub. Not hardy in the far North.

## Rosmarinus

*R. officinalis*, rosemary; light blue; early to mid-spring; to 6 feet in warm climates; shrub. Not hardy in the far North.

## Salix

*S. discolor*, pussy willow; silvery catkins; early spring; 10 to 20 feet; shrub.

## Scilla

*S. bifolia*, twinleaf squill; blue; early to mid-spring; bulb.

*S. sibirica*, Siberian squill; deep blue; late winter to mid-spring, depending on location; 6 inches; bulb.

## Trillium

*T. erectum*, purple trillium; red-violet; early to mid-spring; 1 to 1½ feet; perennial.

## Tulipa

*T. clusiana*, lady tulip; rose-red and white-striped; early to mid-spring; 8 inches; bulb.

*T. fosteriana*, Fosteriana hybrid tulips; red, scarlet, orange, rose, white; early to mid-spring; 14 to 18 inches; bulb.

*T. kaufmanniana*, waterlily tulips; red, scarlet, salmon, rose, yellow, cream, bicolors; early to mid-spring; 6 to 8 inches; bulb.

## Tussilago

*T. farfara*, coltsfoot; yellow; early spring; 1 to 1½ feet; perennial.

## Veltheimia

*V. viridifolia*, unicorn root; pink; to 2 feet; bulb. Blooms outdoors in early spring in mild climates.

## Vinca

*V. minor*, myrtle, periwinkle; light blue to pale violet; prostrate; early spring to summer; perennial ground cover.

## Zephyranthes

*Z. atamasco*, atamasco lily; white; early spring in warm climates; to 12 inches; tender bulb.

# Mid-Spring

## Actaea

*A. rubra*, red baneberry; white; mid- to late spring; 1½ to 2 feet; perennial.

## Albuca

*A. nelsonii*; white with brownish red stripe; mid- to late spring; to 5 feet; tender bulb.

## Alchemilla

*A. vulgaris* (*A. mollis*), lady's mantle; greenish yellow; mid-spring to early summer; 10 to 15 inches; perennial.

## Allium

*A. neapolitanum*, daffodil garlic; white, fragrant; mid- to late spring; to 1½ feet; bulb. Not hardy in the North.

## Anemone

*A. coronaria*, poppy anemone, florist's anemone; red, pink, blue-violet, white; mid-spring; 1½ feet; bulb. Hardy only in warm climates.

*A. apennina*, Apennine anemone; sky blue; mid-spring; 9 inches; perennial. Not hardy in the North.

## Aquilegia

*A. flabellata* 'Nana Alba', Japanese fan columbine; white; mid- to late spring; 10 to 12 inches; perennial.

## Arabis

*A.* 'Rosabella'; rose-pink; mid- to late spring; 5 inches; perennial.

## Arcotheca

*A. calendula*, cape weed; yellow; mid-spring; to 12 inches; perennial.

## Armeria

*A. maritima*, common thrift; rosy pink; mid-spring to early summer; 6 to 12 inches; perennial.

## Bergenia

*B. cordifolia*, heartleaf bergenia; light pink; mid-spring; 1 to 1½ feet; perennial.

*B.* 'Margery Fish', hybrid bergenia; rose-pink; 1 to 1½ feet; perennial.

## Brunnera

*B. macrophylla*, Siberian bugloss; sky blue; mid-spring to early summer; 1 to 1½ feet; perennial. Sometimes listed as *Anchusa*.

## Caltha

*C. palustris*, marsh marigold; golden yellow; mid-spring; 1 to 2 feet; perennial. Needs wet soil.

## Centaurea

*C. montana*, mountain bluet; blue; mid-spring to early summer; 1½ to 2 feet; perennial. May bloom again in fall.

## Convallaria

*C. majalis*, lily-of-the-valley; white, fragrant; mid- to late spring; 6 to 12 inches; bulb.

## Dicentra

*D. cucullaria*, Dutchman's breeches; white; mid-spring; 10 to 12 inches; perennial.

*D. eximia*, fringed bleeding heart; deep pink to red; mid-spring to mid-summer; 1 to 1½ feet; perennial. Foliage stays attractive all season.

*D. spectabilis*, bleeding heart; pink; mid-spring to early summer; 1 to 2 feet; perennial.

## Diosporum

*D. flavum*, fairy bells; light yellow; mid-spring; 2 to 3 feet; perennial.

*D. sessile*, Japanese fairy bells; white; mid-spring; 1½ to 2 feet; perennial.

## Doronicum

*D. cordatum* (*D. caucasicum*), leopard's bane; yellow; mid-spring; 1 to 2 feet; perennial.

## Draba

*D. densiflora*, rock cress draba; yellow; mid-spring; 2 to 3 inches; perennial.

*D. sibirica*, Siberian draba; yellow; mid-spring; 2 inches; perennial.

## Endymion

*E. hispanicus* (*Scilla campanulata*), Spanish bluebells, wood hyacinth; pastel pink, blue, white; mid- to late spring; to 1½ feet; bulb.

## Epimedium

*E. grandiflorum*, longspur epimedium; dusty rose with white spurs; mid- to late spring; 6 to 12 inches; perennial.

*E.* × *rubrum*, red epimedium; crimson with light pink center; mid-spring; to 12 inches; perennial.

*E.* × *versicolor*, Persian epimedium; pale yellow petals with rose center; mid-spring; to 12 inches; perennial.

*E.* × *warleyense*; pale orange with yellow center; mid-spring; 9 to 12 inches; perennial.

*E. youngianum*, snowy epimedium; white; mid-spring; 8 to 10 inches; perennial.

## Erythronium

*E. dens-canis*, dogtooth violet; rose to purple; mid- to late spring; 6 inches; bulb.

## Euphorbia

*E. characias* 'Wulfenii'; yellow-green; mid-spring; 3 feet; perennial.

*E. cyparissias*, cypress spurge; greenish yellow; mid-spring; 8 to 12 inches; perennial.

*E. epithymoides*, cushion spurge; yellow; mid-spring; to 12 inches; perennial.

*E. myrsinites*, myrtle euphorbia; yellow-green; mid-spring; to 6 inches; perennial.

## Fothergilla

*F. gardenii*, dwarf fothergilla; white; mid- to late spring; 3 feet; shrub. Nice autumn foliage.

*F. major*, large fothergilla; white; mid- to late spring; to 9 feet; shrub. Colorful autumn foliage.

*F. monticola*, Alabama fothergilla;

white; mid-spring; 6 feet; shrub. Colorful autumn foliage.

## Fritillaria

*F. imperialis*, crown imperial; red and yellow; mid-spring; 3 feet; bulb.

## Galium

*G. odoratum* (*Asperula odorata*), sweet woodruff; white; mid- to late spring; to 12 inches; perennial.

## Geranium

*G. dalmaticum*; pink; mid-spring to early summer; 6 inches; perennial.

*G. himalayense*, lilac cranesbill; purple; mid- to late spring; 8 to 15 inches; perennial.

*G. maculatum*; lilac-pink; mid-spring to early summer; 12 to 20 inches; perennial.

## Geum

*G. quellyon* 'Mrs. Bradshaw'; bright red; mid-spring to early summer; to 2 feet; perennial. Sometimes listed as G. *chiloense*.

*G. reptans*; orange-red; mid-spring to early summer; 6 to 8 inches; perennial.

*G.* 'Borisii'; scarlet-orange; mid- to late spring; 8 inches; perennial.

*G.* 'Georgenburg'; yellow-orange; mid- to late spring; 8 inches; perennial.

## Hedyotis

*H. caerulea* (*Houstonia caerulea*), bluets, Quaker ladies; sky blue; mid- to late spring; 4 inches; perennial.

## Hesperocallis

*H. undulata*, desert lily; white, fragrant; mid-spring; to 2½ feet; tender bulb.

## Heucherella

*H. tiarelloides*; pink; mid-spring to early summer; to 1½ feet; perennial.

## Hyacinthus

*H. orientalis* hybrids, garden hyacinth; red, pink, purple, blue, yellow, white; mid-spring; to 15 inches; bulb. Not hardy in the far North.

## Iberis

*I. saxatilis*, rock candytuft; white; mid- to late spring; 6 inches; perennial.

*I. sempervirens*, perennial candytuft; white; mid- to late spring; to 12 inches; perennial.

## Iris

*I. cristata*, crested iris; purple; mid-spring; 4 to 6 inches; perennial (rhizome).

*I. japonica*, fringed iris; lilac; mid-spring; 1½ feet; tender perennial. Grows only in warm climates.

*I. pumila*, dwarf bearded iris; deep violet; mid- to late spring; 4 to 8 inches; perennial.

## Jasminum

*J. nudiflorum*, winter jasmine; yellow; to 15 feet; vine or shrub. Blooms in spring in cooler climates.

## Lathyrus

*L. latifolius*, perennial pea; rose, pink, white; mid-spring; to 10 feet; perennial vine.

## Lilium

*L. longiflorum* var. *eximium*, Easter lily; white, fragrant; mid-spring; tender bulb. Grows outside only in warm climates.

## Lloydia

*L. serotina*; white; mid-spring; 2 to 6 inches; bulb.

## Moraea

*M. ramosissima*; yellow; mid-spring; 2 to 3 feet; tender bulb. Grows outdoors only in warm climates.

## Narcissus

*N.* hybrids, daffodils and narcissus; yellow, cream, white, bicolors; late varieties bloom in mid-spring; to 16 inches; bulb.

## Omphalodes

*O. cappadocia*, navelwort; blue with white center; mid-spring; 6 to 10 inches; perennial. Not hardy in the North.

*O. verna*, creeping forget-me-not; blue; mid-spring; to 8 inches; perennial. Not hardy in the North.

## Paeonia

*P. suffruticosa*, Japanese tree peony; rose-red; mid-spring; 4 to 7 feet; perennial.

*P. tenuifolia*, fernleaf peony; red; mid-spring; to 2 feet; perennial.

## Phlox

*P. divaricata*, wild blue phlox; lavender-blue, also a white form; mid-spring; to 1½ feet; perennial.

*P. stolonifera*, creeping phlox; purple, blue, pink, white; mid- to late spring; 6 to 8 inches; perennial.

*P. subulata*, ground pink; pink, rose, lilac, white; mid-spring; to 6 inches; perennial.

## Pieris

*P. japonica*, Japanese andromeda; white; mid-spring; to 9 feet; shrub.

## Polemonium

*P. caeruleum*, Jacob's ladder; violet-blue; mid-spring; 1½ feet; perennial.

*P. reptans*; creeping polemonium; light blue; mid-spring; 8 to 12 inches; perennial.

## Polygonatum

*P. biflorum*, small Solomon's seal; white, fragrant; mid- to late spring; 2 to 3 feet; perennial.

*P. odoratum*, Solomon's seal; white, fragrant; mid-spring; to 3½ feet; perennial.

## Primula

*P. auricula*, auricula primrose; many colors; mid- to late spring; 8 inches; perennial.

*P. denticulata*, Himalayan primrose; lilac, violet, white; mid- to late spring; to 10 inches; perennial.

*P. × juliana*, juliana hybrid primrose; red, rose, white; mid- to late spring; 5 inches; perennial.

*P. veris*, cowslip; orangy yellow; mid- to late spring; 6 to 8 inches; perennial.

## Pulmonaria

*P. officinalis*, common lungwort; red, turning purple; mid- to late spring; 12 inches; perennial.

*P. saccharata*, Bethlehem sage; reddish violet, blue, white; mid- to late spring; 8 to 14 inches; perennial.

## Pyxidanthera

*P. barbulata*, pyxie moss, flowering moss; white; mid- to late spring; 2 inches; perennial.

## Rhododendron

Kurume hybrid azaleas; carmine, red, rose, salmon, orange-red, red-violet; mid- to late spring; 3 feet; shrub. Not hardy in the North.

*R. mucronulatum*, Korean rhododendron; rosy purple, pink; mid-spring; 6 feet; shrub.

P.J.M. hybrid rhododendrons; lavender-pink; mid-spring; 6 feet; shrub.

*R. yedoense*, Yodogawa azalea; purple; mid- to late spring; 5 feet; shrub.

## Rosa

*R. laevigata*, Cherokee rose; white, fragrant; mid-spring; to 15 feet; climbing shrub. Grown in the South.

## Saxifraga

*S. stolonifera*, strawberry geranium; white; mid-spring; to 2 feet; perennial.

*S. × urbium*, London pride saxifrage; light pink; mid-spring; to 12 inches; perennial.

## Shortia

*S. galacifolia*, oconee bells; white; mid-spring; 8 inches; perennial.

## Smilacina

*S. racemosa*, false Solomon's seal; white; mid- to late spring; to 3 feet; perennial.

## Trillium

*T. grandiflorum*, snow trillium; white; mid- to late spring; 12 to 15 inches; perennial.

## Trollius

*T. europaeus*, common globeflower; golden yellow; mid- to late spring; to 2 feet; perennial.

*T. ledebouri*, ledebour globeflower; orange, yellow; mid- to late spring; 2 to 3 feet; perennial.

## Tulipa

Darwin hybrid tulips; red, rose, pink, yellow; mid-spring; 2 to 2½ feet; bulb.

Double late hybrid tulips; red, carmine, wine red, pink, yellow, white; mid- to late spring; 10 to 20 inches; bulb.

*T. gregii*, Gregii hybrid tulips; red, rose, salmon, pink, bicolors; mid-spring; 12 to 14 inches; bulb.

Lily-flowered hybrid tulips; ruby red, reddish purple, rose, pink, purple, yellow, white; mid- to late spring; 20 to 22 inches; bulb.

Triumph hybrid tulips; red, deep red, scarlet, rose, pink, purple, yellow, white; mid-spring; 1 to 1½ feet; bulb.

## Viburnum

*V. × burkwoodii*, Burkwood viburnum; white, fragrant; mid-spring; 6 feet; shrub. Not hardy in the far North.

*V. carlesii*, Carles viburnum; pinkish white, fragrant; mid-spring; 5 feet; shrub.

*V. farreri (V. fragrans)*, fragrant viburnum; white, fragrant; mid-spring; 9 feet; shrub. Not hardy in the North.

*V. juddii*, Judd viburnum; white, fragrant; mid-spring; 8 feet; shrub.

## Viola

*V. cornuta* cultivars, horned violet, tufted pansy; purple, yellow, apricot; mid-spring to autumn; 5 to 8 inches; perennial. Grow as annual in the far North.

# Late Spring

## Amsonia

*A. tabernaemontana*, blue star; bluish white; late spring; to 2 feet; perennial.

## Anemone

*A. hortensis*, garden anemone; red, violet, purple, white; late spring; 10 inches; perennial.

*A. sylvestris* 'Snowdrop', snowdrop windflower; white with light yellow center; late spring; to 1½ feet; perennial.

## Aquilegia

*A.* 'Biedermeier'; mixed colors: red, pink, blue; late spring; 1½ feet; perennial.

*A. caerulea*, Rocky Mountain columbine; white petals with blue-violet spurs; late spring; 2 feet; perennial.

*A. canadensis*, American columbine; red; late spring; 1 to 2 feet; perennial.

*A chrysantha*; golden yellow; late spring; 2 to 2½ feet; perennial. A hybrid, Silver Queen, has white flowers.

*A.* 'Dragonfly'; cream petals with deep rose-red spurs; late spring; 2 feet; perennial.

*A.* 'Langdon's Rainbow Hybrids'; mixed bright colors; late spring; to 2½ feet; perennial.

*A. longissima* 'Maxistar'; yellow; late spring; 2 to 2½ feet; perennial.

## Arenaria

*A. verna* var. *caespitosa*, Irish moss; white; late spring to mid-summer; to 2 inches; perennial.

## Astrantia

*A.* 'Margery Fish'; shades of pink and white; late spring to midsummer; 2 to 2½ feet; perennial.

## Baptisia

*B. australis*, blue false indigo; violet; late spring; 3 to 4 feet; perennial.

*B. pendula*, white wild indigo; white; late spring; 3 to 4 feet; perennial.

## Campanula

*C. carpatica*, Carpathian harebell; purple; late spring to mid-summer; 6 to 12 inches; perennial.

*C. garganica*; purple; late spring to fall; to 6 inches; perennial.

*C. portenschlagiana*, Dalmatian bellflower; deep purple; late spring to summer; 6 to 8 inches; perennial.

## Centaurea

*C. cyanus*, bachelor's button, cornflower; blue, pink, white; late spring to midsummer; 1 to 2 feet; annual. Often reblooms if cut back after first bloom is over.

*C. moschatus*, sweet sultan; red, pink, purple, yellow, white, fragrant; late spring to midsummer; 1½ to 2 feet; annual.

## Cerastium

*C. tomentosum*, snow-in-summer; white; late spring; to 6 inches; perennial.

## Chrysogonum

*C. virginianum*, golden star; golden yellow; late spring to summer; 4 to 10 inches; perennial.

## Clematis

*C.* 'Duchess of Edinburgh'; white,

double; late spring to early summer and again in early autumn; to 9 feet; perennial vine.

C. *montana* 'Alba'; white; late spring to early summer; to 18 feet; perennial vine. Another cultivar, Tetrarose, has deep pink flowers.

C. 'Nelly Moser'; pink with deep rose stripe down center of each petal; late spring to early summer and again in early autumn; to 12 feet; perennial vine.

Other hybrid clematises bloom in shades of purple and pink.

## Cytisus

C. *decumbens*, prostrate broom; yellow; late spring and early summer; to 8 inches; perennial.

C. 'Lucky'; peach flushed with pink; late spring; to 6 feet; shrub.

C. × *praecox*, cream-yellow; late spring; to 5 feet; shrub.

## Daphne

D. × *burkwoodii* 'Somerset'; white flushed with pink; late spring to early summer; to 3 feet; shrub.

## Dianthus

D. × *allwoodii* hybrids, Allwood's pink; red, rose, pink, white, bicolors, fragrant; late spring to summer; 4 to 12 inches; perennial.

D. *barbatus*, sweet william; red, pink, rosy purple, white, bicolors; late spring to early summer; 1 to 2 feet; biennial.

D. *deltoides*, maiden pink; red, rose-pink, pink; late spring; 4 to 12 inches; perennial.

D. *gratianopolitanus*, cheddar pink; pink, fragrant; late spring; 6 to 8 inches; perennial.

D. *plumarius*, grass pink; light pink with red band around center; late spring to early summer; 9 to 18 inches; perennial.

## Dodecathon

D. *meadia*, common shooting star; white; late spring; 1 to 2 feet; perennial.

## Geranium

G. *endressii* 'A. T. Johnson'; light pink; late spring to midsummer; 1 to 2½ feet; perennial.

G. 'Johnson's Blue', Johnson's blue cranesbill; blue-violet; late spring to early summer; to 12 inches; perennial.

G. *macrorrhizum*, bigroot cranesbill; pink; late spring to early summer; 1 to 1½ feet; perennial.

G. *sanguineum*, bloody cranesbill, blood-red cranesbill; clear pink to violet; late spring to midsummer; 1 to 1½ feet; perennial.

## Hemerocallis

H. *lilioasphodelus* (H. *flava*), lemon daylily; yellow; late spring; to 3 feet; perennial.

## Heuchera

H. *sanguinea*, coral bells; deep red to pink; late spring to midsummer; 1 to 1½ feet; perennial.

## Incarvillea

I. *delavayi*, hardy gloxinia; deep pink with yellow throat; late spring to early summer; 1 to 1½ feet; perennial.

## Iris

Bearded iris hybrids; red, pink, rose, red-violet, purple, violet, blue, yellow, yellow-orange, white, bicolors; late spring; 10 inches to 4 feet; perennial.

Louisiana iris hybrids; blue, red, yellow, white, veined and flushed with yellow; late spring; 3 to 4 feet.

Pacific Coast irises; pale purple, lavender, blue, white, with attractive veining and flushes of deeper blue or violet; late spring; 9 to 18 inches; perennial. Most are difficult to grow in other parts of the country.

I. *pseudacorus*, yellow flag; yellow; late spring to midsummer; to 5 feet; perennial. Needs moist, marshy soil.

I. *tectorum*, roof iris; purple; late spring; 8 to 12 inches; perennial.

## Lathyrus

L. *odoratus*, sweet pea; red, rose, pink, red-violet, violet, blue, yellow, white; late spring to early summer in temperate climates; 2 to 5 feet; annual vine.

## Leucojum

L. *aestivum*, giant snowflake; white; late spring; 1 to 1½ feet; bulb.

## Lilium

L. *amabile*; orange with red spots; late spring; to 3 feet; bulb.

L. *hansonii*, Japanese turk's cap lily; orange with red spots; late spring; 4 to 5 feet; bulb.

L. *martagon*, turk's cap lily; carmine-rose; late spring; 4 to 6 feet; bulb. The variety *album* has white flowers.

L. *pyrenaicum*, yellow turk's cap lily; orange; late spring; 3 to 4 feet; bulb.

## Linaria

L. *genistifolia*, toadflax; lemon yellow; late spring through midsummer; 2½ feet; perennial.

## Lonicera

L. *caprifolium*, common honeysuckle; creamy white, fragrant; late spring to early summer; to 20 feet; perennial vine.

L. *flava*, yellow honeysuckle; orange-yellow, fragrant; late spring to early summer; to 10 feet; perennial vine.

*L. korolkowi;* pale rose; late spring to early summer; 8 to 12 feet; shrub.

*L. maacki;* white, turning yellow; late spring to early summer; 10 to 15 feet; shrub.

*L. sempervirens,* trumpet honeysuckle; late spring to late summer; perennial vine.

*L. tartarica,* tartarian honeysuckle; white, pink; late spring to early summer; 8 to 10 feet; shrub.

## Lychnis

*L. viscaria,* German catch-fly; rosered; late spring to early summer; 1 to 1½ feet; perennial.

## Lysimachia

*L. punctata,* yellow loosestrife; yellow; late spring to early summer; 2 to 3 feet; perennial.

## Meconopsis

*M. cambrica,* Welsh poppy; bright yellow; late spring to early summer; to 2 feet; perennial.

## Myosotis

*M. sylvatica,* annual forget-me-not; blue; late spring to midsummer; 6 to 9 inches; annual.

## Nemesia

*N. strumosa* var. *suttoni;* purple, yellow, white; late spring to midsummer; 8 to 18 inches; annual.

## Nigella

*N. damascena,* love-in-a-mist; blue, white; late spring to late summer; 12 to 15 inches; annual.

## Paeonia

*P. lactiflora,* Chinese peony; crimson, red, pink, white; late spring; 2 to 3 feet; perennial.

*P. officinalis* cultivars, common peony; red, rose-red, rose, pink, white; late spring; to 3 feet; perennial.

## Papaver

*P. nudicaule,* Iceland poppy; red, orange, salmon, yellow, cream, white; late spring to early summer; 1 to 3 feet; perennial. Often grown as an annual.

*P. orientale,* Oriental poppy; red, orange, salmon, with dark center; late spring to early summer; 1 to 4 feet; perennial.

## Philadelphus

*P. coronarius,* common mock orange; creamy white, fragrant; late spring; to 10 feet; shrub.

## Physalis

*P. alkekengi,* Chinese lantern; orange; late spring; to 2 feet; perennial.

## Potentilla

*P.* ×*tonguei,* staghorn cinquefoil; yellow with reddish center; late spring to early summer; 8 to 12 inches; perennial.

## Primula

*P. japonica,* Japanese primrose; rose, purple, white; late spring; 1 to 2 feet; perennial.

*P. sieboldii,* Japanese star primrose; rose, magenta, lavender, periwinkle; late spring; to 1 foot; perennial.

## Ranunculus

*R. repens* var. *pleniflorus,* creeping buttercup; yellow, double; late spring to early summer; 1 to 2 feet; perennial.

## Rhododendron

*R. carolinianum,* Carolina rhododendron; rosy purple; late spring; 6 feet; shrub.

*R. catawbiense* hybrids, catawba rhododendron; red, pink, rose, fuchsia, magenta, lilac, purple, violet, white; late spring; 6 feet or more; shrub.

*R. fortunei* hybrids, fortune rhododendron; carmine, red, rosy lilac, blush pink, pink, mauve, rose, fragrant; late spring; 12 feet; shrub. Not hardy in the far North.

*R.* ×*gandavense* hybrids, Ghent azaleas; carmine, scarlet, red-orange, pink, orange, yellow-orange, bronze, yellow, white; late spring; 6 to 10 feet; shrub.

Indian hybrid azaleas; red, rose, pink, salmon, white; late spring; shrub. Grown outdoors in the South; indoors in the North.

*R. kiusianum* hybrids, Kyushu azaleas; lilac-purple, pink, white; late spring; 3 to 6 feet; shrub.

Knap Hill and Exbury hybrid azaleas; red, red-orange, rose-pink, pink, orange, apricot, orange-yellow, yellow, white; late spring; 7 feet; shrub.

*R.* ×*kosterianum* hybrids, mollis hybrid azaleas; shades of red, rose, pink, ivory, white; late spring; 5 feet; shrub.

*R. obtusum* hybrids, Hiryu azaleas; includes Kaempferi hybrids; red, red-violet, magenta, rose, pink; late spring; 3 feet; shrub. Not hardy in the far North.

*R.* ×*rutherfordianum;* red, rose; red-violet; purple; white; 6 feet; shrub. Not hardy in the North.

*R. vaseyi,* pinkshell azalea; light rose; late spring; 6 to 9 feet; shrub. Very hardy.

*R. yunnanense,* Yunnan rhododendron; lavender, pink, white; late spring; 10 feet; shrub. Not hardy in the North.

## Saponaria

*S. ocymoides*, rock soapwort; pink, red, white; late spring to early summer; 6 to 12 inches; perennial.

## Stylophorum

*S. diphyllum*, celandine poppy; yellow; late spring; to 1½ feet; perennial.

## Syringa

*S. vulgaris*, common lilac; purple, lilac, white, fragrant; late spring; to 20 feet; shrub.

## Thalictrum

*T. aquilegifolium*, columbine meadowrue; deep purple; lavender, light pink, orange, white; late spring to early summer; 2 to 3 feet; perennial.

## Thermopsis

*T. caroliniana*, Carolina thermopsis, false lupine; yellow; late spring to early summer; 3 to 4 feet; perennial.

## Tradescantia

*T.* ×*andersoniana*, common spiderwort; pink with rose-red center; late spring to early summer; 2 to 2½ feet; perennial.

*T. hirsuticaulis*; purple; late spring to early summer; to 12 inches; perennial.

## Tulipa

Fringed hybrid tulips; red, violet, yellow, white with fringed petals; late spring; 18 to 20 inches; bulb.

Parrot hybrid tulips; red, rose, pink, salmon, purple, yellow, white, often flamed or striped with contrasting color, and with fringed petals; late spring; 20 inches; bulb.

Single late hybrid tulips (cottage and old Darwin hybrids); shades of red, rose, pink, purple, violet, yellow, white; late spring; 1½ to 2 feet; bulb.

Viridiflora hybrid tulips; rose, pink, yellow, white with green stripes or markings; late spring; 16 to 18 inches; bulb.

## Uvularia

*U. grandiflora*, big merrybells; dark yellow; late spring; to 2½ feet; perennial.

## Valeriana

*V. officinalis*, common valerian; pink, lavender, white; late spring to early summer; 2 to 4 feet; perennial.

## Veronica

*V. latifolium* 'Crater Lake Blue'; deep violet; late spring to midsummer; 1 to 1½ feet; perennial.

## Viola

*V. odorata*, sweet violet; shades of purple, white veined with purple, fragrant; late spring; 6 to 8 inches; perennial.

## Weigela

*W. florida*; rose-pink, pink, white; late spring to early summer; 8 to 10 feet; shrub.

*W. japonica*; white turning to red; late spring to early summer; 8 to 10 feet; shrub.

## Wisteria

*W. floribunda*, Japanese wisteria; purple, white, fragrant; late spring to early summer; perennial vine.

*W. sinensis*, Chinese wisteria; purple, mauve, white, fragrant; late spring to early summer; perennial vine.

## Zantedeschia

*Z. aethiopica*, calla lily; white; late spring to early summer outdoors; 1 to 3 feet; tender bulb.

# Spring-Blooming Houseplants

## Abutilon

*A. megapotamicum* 'Variegata', variegated flowering maple; lemon yellow with red calyxes, variegated leaves; late spring to mid-autumn. Trailing variety.

## Acacia

*A. armata*, kangaroo thorn; bright yellow; early to mid-spring; shrub. Needs moderate light.

## Bougainvillea

*B.* hybrids, paper flower; brilliant red, crimson, magenta, rose, pink, salmon, orange, purple, white; blooms indoors in spring, outdoors in warm climates in spring and summer; tender perennial vine. Needs greenhouse or very sunny window, warm and somewhat dry, to bloom indoors.

LEFT
Aurinia saxatilis, *basket-of-gold.*

BELOW
*Pink astilbe.*

OPPOSITE
A *garden of annuals.*

### Catharanthus

*C. roseus*, Madagascar periwinkle; rose, pink, white; spring to fall. Can be summered outdoors to provide cut flowers; buds will continue to open in vase.

### Clerodendrum

*C. thomsoniae*, bleeding heart vine; red flowers with white sepals; spring and summer, may bloom again in fall; vine. Especially nice when trained around a window.

### Clivia

*C. miniata*, kaffir lily; scarlet with yellow interior; spring; 2 feet; bulb.

### Episcia

*E. cupreata*, flame violet; red; spring into summer; 12 inches, often semi-trailing; gesneriad.

### Euphorbia

*E. milii* var. *splendens*, crown-of-thorns; salmon pink, red, yellow; spring; to 3 feet; spiny shrub.

### Fuchsia

*F. hybrids*; shades and combinations of red, rose, pink, purple, white; spring

and summer. Grow in hanging baskets.

### Gardenia

*G. jasminoides*, cape jasmine; creamy white, very fragrant; may bloom from late winter into summer, depending on conditions; 2 to 4 feet; shrub.

### Hibiscus

*H. rosa-sinensis*, rose mallow; red, pink, orange, yellow, white; spring and summer; 3 to 4 feet; shrub.

### Ixora

*I. coccinea*, flame of the woods; rose to red, star-shaped; spring and summer; to 4 feet; shrub.

### Jacaranda

*J. acutifolia*; silky blue-violet flower panicles; spring and summer; tree. Will lose some leaves before flowering.

### Justicia

*J. brandegeana*, shrimp plant; bronze, pink, yellow-green bracts; spring through summer; to 3 feet; shrub. Needs bright light.

### Lachenalia

*L. hybrids*, cape cowslip; yellow or white, usually tinged with red; bloom in early spring if planted in late summer; to 12 inches; bulb.

### Ledebouria

*L. socialis* (*Scilla violacea*), squill; greenish white; spring; 6 inches; bulb. Blooms same season if planted in early spring.

### Manettia

*M. inflata*, firecracker vine; red tipped with yellow; spring and/or fall; trailing vine.

### Pelargonium

*P. ×domesticum*, Martha Washington geranium, regal geranium; red, rose, pink, white; spring and summer; 1½ feet.

*P. peltatum*, ivy-leaved geranium; pink, white; spring and summer; trailing.

### Rhipsalidopsis

*R. gaertneri*, Easter cactus; red, rose, pink, salmon, white; spring; 12 inches; cactus.

# SUMMER

## Early Summer

### Achillea

*A. filipendulina*, fern leaf yarrow; yellow; early to midsummer; 3 feet; perennial.

*A. filipendulina* 'Coronation Gold'; large yellow flower heads; early to midsummer; 2 to 2½ feet; perennial.

*A.* 'Gold Plate'; large yellow; early to midsummer; 4 feet; perennial.

*A. taygetea*; golden yellow; all summer; 1½ feet; perennial.

*A. taygetea* 'Moonshine'; pale yellow; early summer to early fall; 1½ feet; perennial.

*A. millefolium*, milfoil; pink to red; all summer; 1½ to 2 feet; perennial.

*A. ptarmica* 'The Pearl'; round white flowers; early summer to early fall; 3 to 4 feet; perennial.

## Ageratum

A. *houstonianum*, flossflower; blue, white, all summer; 14 inches; annual.

## Allium

A. *giganteum* 'Moly', giant garlic; rosy purple; early summer; 3 to 4 feet; hardy bulb.

## Amorpha

A. *fruticosa*, false indigo; blue-violet; early summer; 15 feet; shrub.

## Anthemis

A. *tinctoria*, golden marguerite; golden yellow; all summer; to 3 feet; perennial.

## Anthericum

A. *liliago*, St. Bernard's lily; white; early to midsummer; to 3 feet; perennial.

## Antirrhinum

A. *majus*, snapdragon; crimson, scarlet, rose, pink, orange, yellow, white; early summer to midsummer; 8 inches to 3 feet; annual. Blooms in winter in mild climates.

## Armeria

A. *maritima* and cultivars, thrift, sea pink; purple, pink, white; early to midsummer; 5 to 10 inches; perennial.

## Artemisia

A. *ludoviciana* var. *albula*, silver king; white foliage; all season, 2 to 3 feet; perennial.

A. *schmidtiana* 'Silver Mound'; silvery white leaves; all summer; 4 to 6 inches; perennial.

A. *stelleriana*, dusty miller, beach wormwood; white leaves; early to midsummer; 1½ to 2 feet; perennial.

## Aruncus

A. *sylvester*, goatsbeard; white; early to midsummer; 5 feet; perennial.

## Astilbe

A. × *arendsii* cultivars, astilbe, false spiraea; white, pink, rose, red; early to midsummer; 2 to 3 feet; perennial.

## Baptisia

B. *australis*, blue false indigo; blue; early summer; 3 to 5 feet; perennial.

## Bougainvillea

B. hybrids, paper flower; brilliant red, crimson, magenta, rose, pink, salmon, orange, purple, yellow, white; all summer; to 60 feet; tender perennial vine. Grown outdoors in warm climates.

## Calendula

C. *officinalis*, pot marigold; orange, yellow, gold, cream; early summer to fall; 1 to 2 feet; annual.

## Campanula

C. *carpatica*, Carpathian harebell; blue, white; early to midsummer; 8 inches; perennial.

C. *glomerata*, clustered bellflower; violet; early to midsummer; 1 to 1½ feet; perennial.

C. *latifolia*, blue-violet; early to midsummer; 2 to 4 feet; perennial.

C. *persicifolia*, peach bells; blue, white, pink; early to midsummer; 2 to 2½ feet; perennial.

## Centaurea

C. *dealbata*; inner flowers on head are red, outer ones white or pink; early to midsummer; 1½ to 2 feet; perennial.

C. *macrocephala*, globe centaurea; yellow; early to midsummer; 2 to 3 feet; perennial.

C. *montana*, mountain bluet; violet; early to midsummer; 1½ to 2 feet; perennial.

## Chrysanthemum

C. *coccineum* cultivars, pyrethrum, painted daisy; red, pink, lilac, white; early to midsummer; 2 to 2½ feet; perennial.

C. *maximum* cultivars, Shasta daisy; white, single or double; early summer to early fall; 1 to 2 feet; treat as biennial.

## Clematis

C. *integrifolia* 'Coerulea', blue solitary clematis; porcelain blue; early summer to mid-autumn; 2½ feet; perennial vine.

C. *recta* 'Grandiflora', ground clematis; white, fragrant; early to late summer; 2 to 5 feet; perennial vine.

## Cleome

C. *spinosa*, spider flower; rose, pink, light purple, white; early summer to fall; to 4 feet; annual.

## Coreopsis

C. *auriculata* 'Nana', dwarf-eared coreopsis; orange-yellow; early to midsummer; 8 inches; perennial.

C. *lanceolata*; yellow; early to late summer; to 3 feet; perennial.

## Delphinium

D. *ajacis*, annual or rocket larkspur;

pink, lavender, purple, blue, white; early to late summer; 1½ to 5 feet; annual.

## Dictamnus

D. *albus*, gas plant, fraxinella; white; early summer; 2 to 3 feet; perennial.

## Digitalis

D. *purpurea*, foxglove; purple-spotted, white, pink, lavender; 2 to 4 feet; early to midsummer; biennial.

## Eremurus

E. *stenophyllus*, foxtail lily, desert candle; orange-gold; early summer; 2 to 5 feet; perennial.

## Erigeron

E. *speciosus*, Oregon fleabane; deep violet-blue; early to midsummer; 1½ to 2½ feet; perennial.

## Erodium

E. *chamaedryoides*; white veined with pink; early to midsummer; 4 inches; perennial.

## Filipendulina

F. *hexapetala*, dropwort; white; early summer; 2 to 3 feet; perennial.

F. *rubra*, queen-of-the-prairie; magenta; early to midsummer; 4 to 7 feet; perennial.

F. *ulmaria*, queen-of-the-meadow; white; early to midsummer; 3 to 5 feet; perennial.

## Gaillardia

G. *grandiflora*, blanket flower; yellow flushed with red in center; all summer; 2 to 3 feet; perennial.

## Galega

G. *officinalis*, goat's rue; pink, lavender, white; all summer; 2 to 3 feet; perennial.

## Geranium

G. *cinereum* cultivars; lilac to bright magenta; all summer; 6 inches; perennial.

G. *ibericum*, Iberian cranesbill; violet-blue; early to midsummer; 10 to 20 inches; perennial.

G. *psilostemon*, Armenian cranesbill; magenta to rose; early summer; to 2 feet; perennial.

## Gypsophila

G. *repens*, creeping baby's breath; white, pink; early summer; 6 to 8 inches; perennial.

## Hemerocallis

H. hybrids, daylily; red, scarlet, orange, gold, yellow, apricot, cream, other warm shades; early to late summer; 1 to 3 feet; perennial.

## Hesperis

H. *matronalis*, dame's rocket; purple, lilac-purple, mauve; early to midsummer; 2 to 3 feet; perennial.

## Iberis

I. *umbellata*, annual candytuft, globe candytuft; pink, lavender, white; early summer to early fall; 8 to 15 inches; annual. Often self-sows.

## Inula

I. *ensifolia*, swordleaf inula; yellow; early to midsummer; to 12 inches; perennial.

## Iris

I. *kaempferi*, Japanese iris; purple, blue-violet, red-violet; early to midsummer; 3 to 4 feet; perennial.

I. *sibirica*, Siberian iris; deep purple; early summer; 2 to 4 feet; perennial.

## Kniphofia

K. *uvaria*, red hot poker; scarlet, red, orange, yellow; early summer to fall; 2 to 6 feet; perennial.

## Lavandula

L. *officinalis*, L. *angustifolia*, lavender; lavender to purple; early to midsummer; 1 to 3 feet; perennial.

## Lilium

L. *canadense*, meadow lily; yellow, yellow-orange, red with dark spots; early summer; to 5 feet; bulb.

L. *candidum*, Madonna lily; white, fragrant; early to midsummer; 3½ feet; bulb.

L. *concolor*, star lily; bright red; early summer; 3 to 4 feet; bulb.

L. *hansoni*, Japanese turk's cap lily; orange-yellow, fragrant; early summer; 4 to 5 feet; bulb.

L. Mid-Century Hybrids; red, crimson, scarlet, orange, gold, yellow; early to midsummer; 3 feet; bulb.

L. *pumilum*, coral lily; coral-red; early summer; 2 feet; bulb.

L. *regale*, regal lily; white with yellow throat, fragrant; early to midsummer; 4 to 6 feet; bulb.

## Linum

L. *flavum*, golden flax; gold; early summer; 1 to 2 feet; perennial.

L. *perenne* and cultivars, blue flax, perennial flax; blue, white; all summer; 1 to 2 feet; perennial.

### Lisianthus

*L. russelianus* (*Eustoma grandiflorum*), prairie gentian; pink, blue, white; all summer; 2 to 3 feet; treat as annual.

### Lonicera

*L. henryi*, honeysuckle; red-violet; all summer; perennial vine.

### Lupinus

*L. polyphyllus* cultivars, perennial lupine; yellow, white, blue; early summer; 2 to 5 feet; perennial.

*L. 'Russell Hybrid'*, Russell lupine; red, rose, pink, yellow, lavender, purple, blue, white; early summer; 2 to 3 feet; perennial.

### Lychnis

*L. chalcedonica*, Maltese cross; scarlet; early to midsummer; 1½ to 2½ feet; perennial.

*L. coronaria*, rose campion; magenta-pink; early summer; 1½ to 3 feet; perennial.

*L. viscaria*, German catch-fly; magenta, early summer; 1 to 1½ feet; perennial.

### Lysimachia

*L. clethroides*, gooseneck loosestrife; white; early to midsummer; 2 to 3 feet; perennial.

### Malva

*M. alcea*, hollyhock mallow; lavender-pink; early to midsummer; 2 to 4 feet; perennial.

### Oenothera

*O. fruticosa*, evening primrose; bright yellow; early to late summer; 1½ to 2 feet; perennial.

*O. missouriensis*, Missouri primrose; yellow; early to midsummer; 3 to 6 inches; perennial.

*O. speciosa*, showy primrose; pale pink; early summer; 6 to 18 inches; perennial.

*O. tetragona*, sundrops; golden yellow; early to midsummer; to 1½ feet; perennial.

### Opuntia

*O. compressa*, prickly pear cactus; yellow; early to midsummer; 6 to 12 inches; perennial.

### Petunia

*P. hybrida*, petunia; all colors plus bicolors; early summer into fall; 1 to 2 feet; annual.

### Potentilla

*P. fruticosa*, shrubby cinquefoil; yellow; early to late summer; 2 to 4 feet; shrub.

*P. nepalensis*, Nepal cinquefoil; rose; early to late summer; 2 feet; shrub.

### Rhododendron

*R. arborescens*, sweet azalea; white, fragrant; early summer; to 9 feet; shrub.

*R. calendulaceum*, flame azalea; yellow, orange, red-orange; early summer; 9 feet; shrub.

*R. decorum*, sweetshell azalea; white to pink, fragrant; early summer; 18 feet; shrub.

*R. macrophullum*, California rhododendron; pale rose to purple; early summer; 9 feet; shrub. Not hardy in the North.

*R. viscosum*, swamp azalea; white, fragrant; early to midsummer; 9 feet or more; shrub. Very hardy.

### Rosa

Floribunda roses; many shades of red, rose, pink, yellow, white, fragrant; all summer; 2 to 3 feet; bush form.

Grandiflora roses; shades of red, rose, pink, orange, yellow, white, fragrant; all summer; 5 to 6 feet; bush form.

Hybrid tea roses; shades of red, rose, pink, orange, yellow, white, fragrant; all summer; 3 feet or more; bush form.

Miniature roses; shades of red, rose, pink, orange, yellow, white; all summer; 1 to 2 feet; bush form.

Climbing roses; bloom off and on all summer; red, pink, yellow, white, fragrant; 10 feet.

Rambler roses; early summer, may bloom again in early fall; red, rose, pink, yellow, white; 10 feet.

Shrub roses; some types bloom once in early summer, others bloom continuously all summer; shades of rose, pink, yellow, white, fragrant; 4 to 12 feet.

### Scabiosa

*S. causasia* and cultivars, pincushion flower; red, rose-pink, salmon, lavender, blue, white; early summer to early fall; 1½ to 3 feet; annual.

### Sidalcea

*S. malviflora* cultivars, checkerbloom, prairie mallow; pink, white, purplish; early to midsummer; 1½ to 3½ feet; perennial.

### Stachys

*S. byzantina*, lamb's ears; grown for its silvery leaves; all summer; to 1½ feet; perennial.

### Tagetes

*T. erecta*, *T. patula*, *T.* hybrids, marigolds; yellow, gold, orange, rust, cream; early summer into fall; 7 to 36 inches; annual.

### Tradescantia

T. *virginiana*; pink, blue; early summer; 2 to 2½ feet; perennial.

### Tropaeolum

T. *majus*, nasturtium; yellow, orange, crimson, mahogany, pink, cream; all summer; 1 to 3 feet; annual.

### Verbascum

V. cultivars, mullein; white, yellow; early to midsummer; 3 to 5 feet; perennial.

### Verbena

V. *hortensis*, garden verbena; red, pink, yellow, white, fragrant; early to late summer; to 12 inches; tender perennial.

V. *peruviana*; red, early to midsummer; 3 to 4 inches; perennial.

V. *rigida*, vervain; pinkish purple; early to midsummer; 1 to 2 feet; perennial.

### Veronica

V. *incana*, woolly speedwell; violet-blue; early to midsummer; 8 inches; perennial.

V. *latifolia* (V. *teucrium*), germander speedwell, rock speedwell; blue-violet, white; early to midsummer; 1 to 1½ feet; perennial.

V. *spicata*, spike speedwell; violet-blue, white, pink; early to late summer; 15 inches to 2 feet; perennial.

### Zinnia

Z. *elegans* cultivars, zinnia; all colors except blue; all summer; 8 inches to 3 feet; annual.

---

# Midsummer

### Abelia

A. species; white, pink; midsummer; 3 to 6 feet; shrub. Not hardy in the North.

### Acanthus

A. *mollis*, bear's breech; white, lilac, rose; midsummer to late summer; 1½ feet; perennial.

A. *spinosus*, spiny bear's breech; pale purple; midsummer to late summer; 3 to 4 feet; perennial.

### Achillea

A. *tomentosa*, woolly yarrow; yellow; midsummer to late summer; 10 inches; perennial.

### Adenophora

A. *confusa* (A. *farreri*), Farrer's ladybell; violet; midsummer to late summer; 3 feet; perennial.

### Agapanthus

A. *africanus*, African lily, lily of the Nile; blue, violet, white; midsummer; 1½ to 3½ feet; tender bulb.

A. *orientalis*; blue; midsummer; 2 to 3 feet; tender bulb.

### Allium

A. *stellatum*, prairie onion; rosy pink; midsummer to autumn; 1½ feet; bulb.

A. *pulchellum*; pinkish purple; midsummer; 1½ to 2 feet; bulb.

A. *senescens*; pink; midsummer; to 2 feet; hardy bulb.

### Althaea

A. *rosea* cultivars; pink, rose, red, maroon, violet, yellow, copper, cream; midsummer to late summer; 2 to 6 feet; biennial but often self-sows.

### Anaphalis

A. *margaritacea*, pearly everlasting; white; midsummer to late summer; to 20 inches; perennial.

### Asclepias

A. *tuberosa*, butterfly weed; orange; midsummer to late summer; 1½ to 2 feet; perennial.

### Aster

A. *amellus*, Italian aster; purple; midsummer to late summer; 1½ feet; perennial.

### Belamcanda

B. *chinensis*, blackberry lily; orange; midsummer to late summer; 3 to 3½ feet; perennial.

### Callistephus

C. *chinensis*, China aster; white, pink, rose, scarlet, blue, yellow; midsummer to frost; 9 to 24 inches; annual.

### Campanula

C. *lactiflora*, milky bellflower; blue, white; midsummer to early fall; 3 to 5 feet; perennial.

*C. medium*, Canterbury bells; blue; midsummer; 2 to 4 feet; treat as annual.

**Campsis**

*C. radicans*, trumpet vine; orange-red; midsummer to late summer; to 30 feet; perennial vine.

**Cassia**

*C. marilandica*, wild senna; yellow; midsummer; 3 to 5 feet; perennial.

**Celosia**

*C. cristata*, crested cockscomb; yellow, orange, bright red, magenta; midsummer to frost; 10 to 24 inches; annual.

*C. plumosa*, plumed celosia; deep red, gold, bronze, orange-apricot, yellow, cream; midsummer to frost; 8 to 20 inches; annual.

**Centaurea**

*C. americana*, basket flower; rose, pink; midsummer; 4 to 6 feet; annual.

*C. dealbata* 'Sternbergii', Persian centaurea; bright purple with white center; midsummer to late summer; 2 feet; perennial.

**Chelone**

*C. glabra*, turtlehead; pinkish to white; midsummer to fall; 2½ to 3 feet; perennial.

**Chrysanthemum**

*C. parthenium*, feverfew; white with yellow center; midsummer; 2 to 3½ feet; perennial.

**Cimicifuga**

*C. racemosa*, black cohosh; white; midsummer; 4 to 5 feet; perennial.

**Clematis**

*C. jackmanii*, violet-purple; midsummer; to 12 feet; perennial vine.

*C. viticella*, small white flowers; midsummer to fall; to 25 feet; perennial vine.

**Coreopsis**

*C. verticillata*, thread-leaf coreopsis; bright yellow; midsummer to early autumn; 2 to 3 feet; perennial.

*C. verticillata* 'Moonbeam', soft yellow; midsummer to early autumn; 1½ to 2 feet; perennial.

**Dahlia**

*D.* hybrids; shades of red, pink, orange, yellow, purple, white, bicolors; bloom from midsummer well into autumn; 1 to 6 feet; tender bulb.

**Delphinium**

*D. elatum* hybrids; purple, violet, blue, lavender, pink, white; midsummer; to 6 feet; perennial.

**Dianthus**

*D. caryophyllus*, carnation; pink, red, white; midsummer to early fall; treat as annual.

**Echinacea**

*E. purpurea*, purple coneflower; purple; midsummer to late summer; perennial.

**Echinops**

*E. ritro*, small globe thistle; blue; midsummer to late summer; 3 to 4 feet; perennial.

*E.* 'Taplow Blue', globe thistle; steel blue; midsummer to early fall; 3 to 4 feet; perennial.

**Erigeron**

*E. aurantiacus*, double orange daisy; bright orange; midsummer to late summer; to 10 inches; perennial.

*E.* hybrids, fleabane; pink, lilac, lavender, violet-blue; midsummer to late summer; 1 to 2 feet; perennial. May bloom all year in warm West Coast climates.

**Eryngium**

*E. alpinum*; soft blue; midsummer; 2½ feet; perennial.

*E. amethystinum*, amethyst sea holly; steel gray to amethyst; mid- to late summer; 2 feet; perennial.

*E. giganteum*; silvery gray, tinged with blue or violet; midsummer; 2 to 3 feet; perennial.

**Euphorbia**

*E. corollata*, flowering spurge; white; mid- to late summer; 1 to 3 feet; perennial.

**Fuchsia**

*F.* hybrids; shades of red, rose, pink, purple, white; all summer; trailing or upright to 20 feet; tender shrub. Grown outdoors in warm climates; elsewhere used as summer bedding or hanging basket plants. See also "Summer-Blooming Houseplants."

**Gentiana**

*G. asclepiadea*, willow gentian; deep blue; midsummer to late summer; 2 feet; perennial.

**Gladiolus**

*G.* hybrids; many shades of red, rose, pink, salmon, orange, yellow, lavender, purple, and white; bloom from midsummer until frost, depending on planting date and variety; 2 to 5 feet; tender bulb.

*G. tristis*; yellowish white, sometimes with purple streaks, fragrant at night; midsummer; 2 to 3 feet; tender bulb.

## Gypsophila

*G. elegans*, annual baby's breath; white; mid- to late summer; 10 to 18 inches; annual.

*G. paniculata*, baby's breath; white, pink; mid- to late summer; 1½ to 2½ feet; perennial. Bristol Fairy is a double-flowered variety.

## Helianthus

*H. annuus*, common sunflower; yellow with brownish center; midsummer to early fall; to 12 feet; annual.

*H. decapetalus*, river sunflower; yellow; midsummer to early fall; to 5 feet; perennial.

## Heliopsis

*H. helianthoides*, false sunflower; yellow; midsummer to early fall; 3 to 5 feet; perennial. Cultivars include Gold Greenheart (bright yellow) and Incomparabilis (yellow).

*H. scabra*, orange sunflower; orange-yellow; midsummer to early fall; 3 to 5 feet; perennial.

## Hemerocallis

*H. fulva*, tawny daylily; orange; midsummer; 4 feet; perennial.

Hybrid daylilies are in peak bloom in midsummer.

## Hosta

*H. fortunei*; lavender; mid- to late summer; 1½ to 2½ feet; perennial. Cultivars include Albomarginata (light green leaves edged in white), Albopicta (light green leaves), and Honeybells (grass-green leaves).

*H. sieboldiana*; lilac; midsummer; 2 to 4 feet; perennial. Cultivars include Elegans (blue-green leaves) and Frances Williams (deep green leaves edged in gold).

*H. undulata* 'Erromena'; pale lavender; mid- to late summer; 2½ to 3½ feet; perennial. Bright green leaves.

*H. ventricosa*; purple; mid- to late summer; 3 feet; perennial. Has larger, showier flowers than most hostas.

## Hydrangea

*H. macrophylla* (*H. hortensia*); pink, blue; midsummer; to 12 feet; shrub. Not hardy in the far North, this is the hydrangea sold by florists.

*H. paniculata* var. *grandiflora*, peegee hydrangea; white, changing to pink or purple; midsummer; 8 to 25 feet; shrub.

*H. quercifolia*, oak-leaved hydrangea; white; midsummer; to 6 feet; shrub.

*H. serrata*, tea-of-heaven; blue, white; midsummer; 3 to 5 feet; shrub.

## Hypericum

*H. kalmianum*, St. John's wort; yellow; mid- to late summer; 2 to 3 feet; perennial.

*H. patulum* var. *henryi*, St. John's wort; yellow; midsummer to early fall; 2 to 3 feet; shrub.

*H. prolificum*, bush broom; yellow; midsummer to early fall; 4 to 5 feet; shrub.

## Lamium

*L. maculatum*, spotted dead nettle; red-violet, white; midsummer; to 1½ feet; perennial. Cultivars include Beacon Silver (silvery leaves, pink flowers), Aureum (yellowish leaves), and White Nancy (white flowers).

## Liatris

*L. punctata*; rose-purple; mid- to late summer; 12 to 20 inches; perennial.

*L. pycnostachya*, Kansas gayfeather; rose-purple; mid- to late summer; 3 to 6 feet; perennial.

*L. scariosa*, gayfeather; bluish purple, white; mid- to late summer; 3 to 5 feet; perennial. Not hardy north of Pennsylvania.

*L. spicata*, gayfeather; rosy purple, white; midsummer to early fall; 4 to 6 feet; perennial.

## Lilium

*L. auratum*; white banded with gold; midsummer; 3½ to 5 feet; bulb.

*L. canadense*, meadow lily; red, orange-yellow; midsummer; bulb.

*L. chalcedonicum*, scarlet turk's cap lily; scarlet; midsummer; 3 to 4 feet; bulb.

*L. pardalinum*, leopard lily; orange with purple spots; midsummer; 5 to 7 feet; bulb.

*L. sargentiae*; white with yellow throat; midsummer; 4 to 6 feet; bulb.

There are also many hybrid lilies flowering in midsummer. See chapter 5 for more information.

## Limonium

*L. latifolium*, sea lavender, statice; lavender-blue; mid- to late summer; 2 to 2½ feet; perennial.

*L. sinuatum*, statice; violet, lavender, rose, yellow, white; midsummer to early fall; 1½ to 2½ feet; treat as annual. This is the type grown for the florist trade.

## Lobelia

*L. cardinalis*, cardinal flower; red; midsummer to early fall; 2 to 4 feet; perennial.

## Lonicera

*L. heckrotti*, honeysuckle; purplish outside, yellow inside; midsummer; shrub.

*L. japonica*, Japanese honeysuckle; white fading to yellow, fragrant; midsummer; 20 to 30 feet; perennial vine.

## Lythrum

*L. salicaria*, purple loosestrife; purple; mid- to late summer; 2 to 3½ feet; perennial. The cultivar Morden's Pink has pink flowers.

## Macleya

*M. cordata*, plume poppy; cream to white; mid- to late summer; to 7 feet; perennial.

## Malva

*M. moschata*, musk mallow; pink, white; mid- to late summer; 1 to 3 feet; perennial.

## Monarda

*M. didyma*, beebalm, bergamot; scarlet; mid- to late summer; 2 to 3 feet; perennial. Cultivars include Cambridge Scarlet (bright red) and Croftway Pink (soft pink).

## Nymphaea

*N.* hybrids; waterlilies; red, rose, pink, purple, yellow, white; all summer. Both hardy and tropical waterlilies bloom in summer. Many cultivars are available.

## Penstemon

*P. barbatus*, beard tongue; red; midsummer; 2 to 4 feet; perennial.

## Phlox

*P. drummondii*, annual phlox; rose, pink, lavender, purple, white; mid- to late summer; to 1½ feet; annual.

*P. paniculata*, garden phlox; rose, pink, salmon, lavender, purple, white; mid- to late summer; 3 to 4 feet; perennial.

## Physostegia

*P. virginiana*, false dragonhead; lavender, pink; midsummer to early fall; 2 to 4 feet; perennial.

## Platycodon

*P. grandiflorum*, balloon flower; purple, white; mid- to late summer; 1½ to 3 feet; perennial.

## Rosa

Bush roses—floribundas, grandifloras, hybrid teas, and miniatures—are still in bloom in midsummer.

## Rudbeckia

*R. fulgida* 'Goldsturm', black-eyed Susan; golden yellow with dark center; midsummer to frost; 2 feet; perennial.

## Salvia

*S. farinacea*, mealycup sage; blue; early summer to early fall; 1½ to 3 feet; tender perennial. Cultivars include Blue Bedder and Victoria. Grow as annual except in warm climates.

*S. praetensis*, meadow clary; lavender-blue; mid- to late summer; to 3 feet; perennial.

*S. splendens* cultivars, scarlet sage; brilliant scarlet; midsummer to fall; 1 to 3 feet; treat as annual. A purple cultivar is also available.

*S. superba*, violet sage; purple, deep violet; mid- to late summer; 1½ to 3 feet; perennial. Cultivars include East Friesland (purple) and Mainacht (blue-violet).

## Sanguisorba

*S. obtusa*, Japanese burnet; pink; midsummer; 3 feet; perennial.

## Saponaria

*S. officinalis*, bouncing bet; white to pink; midsummer; 1 to 3 feet; perennial.

## Sedum

*S. spurium*; pale pink; midsummer; to 6 inches; perennial.

## Stachys

*S. grandiflora*, big betony; violet; midsummer; 1½ to 3 feet; perennial. Sometimes sold as *Betonica grandiflora*.

## Stokesia

*S. laevis* cultivars, Stokes' aster; blue, pink, white; midsummer; 1 to 2 feet; perennial.

## Tritonia

*T. crocosmaeflora*, blazing star, montbretia; orange-red; mid- to late summer; tender bulb. Grow like gladiolus.

## Tunica

*T. saxifraga*, saxifrage pink, tunic flower; pink, lilac; midsummer to frost; to 10 inches; perennial.

## Veronica

*V. incana*; blue; midsummer; 1 to 1½ feet; perennial.

*V. longifolia* cultivars; blue, white,

rose-pink; midsummer; 2 feet; perennial.

V. *spicata*, spike speedwell; blue; midsummer; 1½ to 2 feet; perennial.

### Yucca

Y. *filamentosa*, Adam's needle; creamy white; midsummer; 5 to 6 feet; perennial.

## Late Summer

### Aconitum

A. × *bicolor*, hybrid monkshood; blue tinged with white; late summer; 3 to 4 feet; perennial.

A. *carmichaelii*, azure monkshood; violet-blue; late summer to fall; 2½ to 3½ feet; perennial.

A. *napellus*, common monkshood; blue-violet to purple; late summer to fall; to 4 feet; perennial.

### Artemisia

A. *abrotanum*, southernwood, old man; yellow; late summer; 2 feet; perennial.

A *absinthium*, absinthe; white, yellow; late summer; 2 feet; perennial.

A *lactiflora*, white mugwort; white; late summer to early fall; 4 to 6 feet; perennial.

### Buddleia

B. *davidii*, butterfly bush; lilac, mauve, rose-purple; late summer to early fall; 4 to 10 feet; shrub.

### Chelone

C. *lyonii*, pink turtlehead; deep rose; late summer to early fall; 2½ to 3 feet; perennial.

### Chrysanthemum

C. × *morifolium* hybrids; crimson, red, scarlet, orange, rust, bronze, yellow, pink, purple, white; 1 to 3 feet; perennial. Hybrid chrysanthemums

begin blooming in late summer but reach their peak in early autumn.

### Clematis

C. *heracleifolia* var. *davidiana*, blue tube clematis; deep blue, fragrant; late summer; 2 to 3 feet; shrub.

C. *texensis*, scarlet clematis; scarlet, rose-pink; late summer; 4 to 6 feet; perennial vine.

### Clethra

C. *alnifolia*, sweet pepper bush, summer sweet; white, fragrant; late summer to mid-autumn; 3 to 9 feet; shrub.

### Coreopsis

C. *rosea*, pink tickseed; rose-pink, late summer to early fall; 2 feet; perennial.

### Eryngium

E. *bourgatii*, Mediterranean sea holly; steel blue; late summer; 1½ feet; perennial.

### Gentiana

G. *septemfida*; deep blue; late summer to early fall; 9 to 15 inches; perennial.

G. *sino-ornata*; violet-blue; late summer; 6 to 8 inches; perennial.

### Helenium

H. *autumnale*, yellow star; yellow, orange, mahogany; late summer to early fall; 4 to 6 feet; perennial.

### Hibiscus

H. *moscheutos* hybrids, hardy hibiscus, rose mallow; red, pink, white; late summer to early fall; 3 to 7 feet; shrub.

H. *syriacus*, rose-of-sharon; red, pink, magenta, white; late summer; 5 to 15 feet; shrub.

### Hosta

H. *lancifolia*; lavender; late summer to early fall; 2 feet; perennial.

H. *undulata*; lilac; late summer; 1½ feet; perennial. A popular cultivar is Albo-marginata or Medio-picta, which has green and white variegated foliage.

### Hyssopus

H. *officinalis*, hyssop; blue; late summer; 1 to 1½ feet; perennial.

### Lagerstroemia

L. *indica*, crape myrtle; red, pink, white; late summer; 5 to 25 feet; shrub. Some varieties bloom earlier in summer.

### Ligularia

L. *dentata*, ragwort; orange; late summer; 3 to 4 feet; perennial.

### Lilium

*L. formosanum*; white, fragrant; late summer; 1½ feet; bulb. The late-blooming form of this lily flowers in late summer.

*L. henryi*; orange with brown spots; late summer; 7 feet; bulb.

*L. speciosum*, Japanese lily; white or pinkish with red spots; late summer; 3 to 5 feet; bulb.

*L. tigrinum*, tiger lily; orange with purple spots; late summer to early fall; 4 to 5 feet; bulb.

Many hybrid lilies bloom in late summer. See chapter 5 for more information.

### Limonium

*L. latifolium*, statice, sea lavender; blue-violet, white; late summer to early fall; 1 to 2 feet; perennial.

### Lobelia

*L. siphilitica*, blue lobelia, great lobelia; deep blue to blue-violet; late summer to early fall; 3 feet; perennial.

### Polygonum

*P. aubertii*, silver lace vine; white, fragrant; late summer to early fall; to 25 feet; perennial vine.

### Rudbeckia

*R. hirta* hybrids, black-eyed Susan; yellow, red-brown, late summer to early fall; 1 to 3 feet; annual or biennial.

*R. laciniata* var. *hortensis*, golden glow; yellow; late summer; 8 to 12 inches; perennial.

### Salvia

*S. patens*, blue sage; blue; late summer; 1½ to 2½ feet; perennial.

*S. pitcheri* (*S. azurea* var. *grandiflora*), azure sage; light blue; late summer to early fall; 4 to 5 feet; perennial. Not hardy in the North.

### Sanguisorba

*S. canadensis*, great burnet; creamy white; late summer to fall; 3 to 6 feet; perennial.

### Sedum

*S. maximum* cultivars; pink; late summer to fall; 1 to 2 feet; perennial.

*S.* 'Autumn Joy'; rosy pink changing to salmony bronze; late summer to early fall; perennial.

### Thalictrum

*T. rochebrunianum*, lavender mist meadowrue; purple, lavender, lavender-pink; late summer; 3 to 5 feet; perennial.

### Zauschneria

*Z. californica*, California fuchsia; scarlet; late summer to early fall; 8 to 15 inches; perennial.

## *Summer-Blooming Houseplants*

### Achimenes

A. hybrids, magic flower, monkey-faced pansy; red, rose, pink, lavender, purple, yellow, white; all summer; 10 to 30 inches, upright or trailing; gesneriad. Trailing forms are pretty in hanging baskets, indoors or outdoors.

### Agapanthus

See listing under "Midsummer." Can be grown indoors or outdoors.

### Aphelandra

*A. squarrosa*, zebra plant; yellow, orange; summer; 1 foot. Flower spikes last up to six weeks.

### Campanula

*C. isophylla*, bellflower; violet-blue, white; summer; trailing. Good hanging basket plant.

### Crossandra

*C. infundibuliformis*, firecracker flower; salmon-pink to orange; all summer; 1 to 2 feet; tender shrub.

### Fuchsia

*F.* hybrids; shades of red, rose, pink, purple, white; all summer; trailing; tender shrub. Need bright light and cool temperatures indoors. Also grown outdoors; see "Midsummer" for information.

### Gloriosa

*G. rothschildiana*, glory lily; red and yellow; late summer; to 4 feet; tender bulb. Flowers resemble reflexed lilies.

### Hoya

*H. bella*, miniature wax plant; white with pink center, fragrant; all summer into fall; 1 to 2 feet; shrub. Grow in hanging basket.

*H. carnosa*, honey plant, wax plant; red, pink, white, fragrant; all summer; perennial vine.

### Ixora

*I. coccinea*, flame of the woods,

ABOVE
*An autumn border of chrysanthemums.*


RIGHT
Aster × frikarti, *Wonder of Staffa.*


OPPOSITE
*The winter garden before the earliest bulbs have come up.*

jungle geranium; salmony red; summer into fall; to 4 feet; shrub.

*I. javanica*, flame of the woods; red-orange; summer into fall; 3 to 4 feet; shrub.

### Jasminum

*J. officinale*, common jasmine; white, fragrant; summer into fall; shrub.

### Kohleria

*K. amabilis*, tree gloxinia; rose spotted and banded with red-violet; summer into fall; 2 feet; gesneriad.

*K. bogotensis*, tree gloxinia; yellow with red spots; summer into fall; to 2 feet; gesneriad.

*K. eriantha*, tree gloxinia; orange-red with yellow spots; summer into fall; to 4 feet; gesneriad.

*K. hirsuta*, tree gloxinia; orange-red; summer into fall; to 3 feet; gloxinia.

*K. lindeniana*, tree gloxinia; white marked with purple and flushed with yellow; summer to fall; 1 foot; gesneriad.

### Lantana

*L. camara*, yellow sage; yellow, orange-yellow changing to red or white, fragrant; summer; to 4 feet; shrub.

*L. montevidensis*, weeping lantana; rose-pink with yellow center, lavender, white, fragrant; summer; trailing, to 3 feet long; perennial.

### Pachystachys

*P. lutea*, lollipop plant; yellow and white; all summer; to 1½ feet; shrub.

### Passiflora

*P.* ×*alatocaerulea*, passionflower; purple and white; late summer to early fall; to 20 feet; perennial vine.

*P. caerulea*, blue passionflower; combination of white, purple, and blue in each flower; late summer to early fall; to 20 feet; perennial vine.

*P. vitifolia*, crimson passionflower; bright red; summer; to 20 feet; perennial vine.

### Sinningia

*S. speciosa* hybrids, florists' gloxinia; red, violet, white; summer; 1 foot; tuberous gesneriad.

# AUTUMN

## Outdoors

### Abelia

*A. chinensis*; white; early autumn; 3 to 5 feet; shrub. Not reliably hardy north of Philadelphia but can survive with winter protection.

### Aconitum

*A. carmichaelii*, azure monkshood; dark blue; early to mid-autumn; 3 to 4 feet; perennial.

### Allium

*A. tuberosum*, garlic chives; white; early autumn; 15 to 20 inches; perennial.

### Anemone

*A.* ×*hybrida* (*A. japonica*), Japanese anemone; crimson, rose-red, rose-pink, pink, white; early autumn; 2 to 2½ feet; perennial.

### Artemisia

*A. lactiflora*, white mugwort; clusters of tiny cream-colored flowers; early autumn; to 5 feet; perennial.

*A. ludoviciana*, Silver King artemisia; clusters of tiny grayish white flowers; early autumn; to 3 feet; perennial. Artemisias are most valuable for their foliage, but they do produce flowers as well.

### Arum

*A. italicum*, Italian arum; produces spikes of bright red berries in autumn; 1 to 1½ feet; perennial.

### Aster

*A. acris*; mauve-blue; early autumn; 2 to 3 feet; perennial.

*A. ericoides*; tiny white flower heads; early autumn; 3 to 5 feet; perennial.

*A.* ×*frikartii*, lavender-blue, fragrant; early autumn; 2 to 3 feet; perennial. The best variety is Wonder of Staffa.

*A. novae-angliae*, New England aster, Michaelmas daisy; red, rose, pink, lilac; early autumn; 3 to 5 feet; perennial.

A. *novi-belgii*, Michaelmas daisy, New York aster; red, rose, pink, lilac, blue, purple, white; early autumn; 1 to 1½ feet; perennial.

## Boltonia

B. *asteroides*; white; early to mid-autumn; 3 to 4 feet; perennial.

## Calluna

C. *vulgaris*, heather; red, rosy pink, white; early autumn; to 1½ feet; shrub. Blooms from midsummer to mid-fall, depending on location and variety.

## Camellia

C. *japonica*, camellia; red, rose, pink, white; late autumn and winter; to 25 feet outdoors; shrub. A highlight of fall and winter gardens in the South; in the North an indoor and greenhouse plant.

## Caryopteris

C. *incana*, blue spiraea, blue mist; bluish purple flower clusters; early to mid-autumn; 2 to 5 feet; shrub.

## Ceratostigma

C. *plumbaginoides*, plumbago, leadwort; deep gentian blue; early autumn; 6 to 10 inches; perennial.

C. *willmottianum*, hardy plumbago; blue; autumn; shrub. This species is grown mostly along the West Coast.

## Chrysanthemum

C. × *morifolium* hybrids; garden or hardy chrysanthemum; red, rose, pink, salmon, orange, terra-cotta, rust, yellow, gold, bronze, lilac, purple, white; early to mid-autumn; perennial. Single or daisy mums grow 12 to 20 inches high; decorative mums grow 1½ to 3 feet high; cushion mums grow 10 to 20 inches high; pompon mums grow 1½ to 2 feet high; football mums grow about 3 feet high; and spider mums grow 1½ to 2 feet high. See chapter 8 for more information.

C. *nipponicum*, Nippon chrysanthemum; white with yellow center; early autumn; 1½ to 2 feet; perennial.

## Cimicifuga

C. *simplex*, Kamchatka snakeroot; white; early autumn; 3 to 4 feet; perennial.

## Clematis

C. *paniculata*, Japanese clematis; white, fragrant; early to mid-autumn; 20 to 30 feet; perennial vine.

## Colchicum

C. *autumnale*, autumn crocus, meadow saffron; rosy purple, lilac, white; early autumn; 4 to 6 inches; bulb.

C. *bornmuelleri*, autumn crocus; pale pink deepening as flowers age, fragrant; early to late autumn; 6 inches; bulb.

C. *speciosum*, autumn crocus; raspberry red; early to mid-autumn; 5 inches; bulb.

C. 'Waterlily'; rich rosy lavender, double; early to mid-autumn; 6 inches; bulb.

## Crocus

C. *goulimyi*, autumn crocus; pale to deep purple; early autumn; 4 inches; bulb.

C. *kotschyanus*, autumn crocus; pale lilac-blue; early to mid-autumn; 4 inches; bulb.

C. *laevigatus*, autumn crocus; rose-lilac, fragrant; late autumn to early winter; 3 inches; bulb. Flowers smell like freesias.

C. *medius*, autumn crocus; deep lavender-purple; mid-autumn; 4 inches; bulb.

C. *pulchellus*, autumn crocus; lilac or lavender with faint blue stripes and yellow throat, fragrant; early to mid-autumn; 4 inches; bulb.

C. *sativus*, saffron crocus; white, lilac; mid-autumn; 4 inches; bulb.

C. *speciosus*, autumn crocus; bluish purple, lilac, white; early to mid-autumn; 4 inches; bulb.

## Cyclamen

C. *neapolitanum*, hardy cyclamen; rosy pink; early autumn; 8 to 10 inches; perennial.

## Elaeagnus

E. *pungens*; white, fragrant; early to mid-autumn in the North, mid- to late autumn in the South; 10 to 15 feet; shrub.

## Elsholtzia

E. *stauntonii*; pinkish lavender, fragrant; early to mid-autumn; 2 to 4 feet; shrub.

## Eupatorium

E. *coelestinum*, hardy ageratum, mist flower; light blue to violet-blue; early autumn; to 2 feet; perennial.

E. *purpureum*, joe-pye weed; pinkish purple; early autumn; to 7 feet; perennial.

## Gentiana

G. *endrewsi*, bottle gentian; purplish blue; early to mid-autumn; 1 to 1½ feet; perennial.

## Helenium

H. *hoopsei*, sneezeweed; yellow; mid-autumn; 2 to 3 feet; perennial.

### Lespedeza

*L. thunbergi*, bush cover; rosy purple; mid-autumn; 3 to 6 feet; perennial.

### Leucojum

*L. autumnale*, autumn snowflake; white tinged with red; early to mid-autumn; 7 to 9 inches; bulb.

### Lilium

*L. speciosum* 'Uchida'; deep rose-crimson marked with white; early autumn; 3 to 4 feet; bulb.

*L. tigrinum*, tiger lily; orange with purple spots; reaches its peak in early autumn; 4 feet; bulb.

### Lycoris

*L. radiata*, spider lily; pink to bright crimson; early autumn; 1 to 1½ feet; bulb. Hardy from Virginia south.

*L. squamigera*, magic lily; lilac-pink, fragrant; early autumn; 2 to 3 feet; bulb.

### Nerine

*N. bowdenii*, nerine lily; pink; early autumn; 12 inches; bulb. Grow outdoors in warm climates, indoors in a cool greenhouse in the North.

### Osmanthus

*O. fortunei*, sweet olive; white, fragrant; early autumn; to 25 feet; shrub.

### Oxalis

*O. bowiei*; rosy purple; early autumn; 8 to 10 inches; tender bulb. Grow like gladiolus.

### Polianthes

*P. tuberosa*, tuberose; white, fragrant; blooms in autumn in the South; 1 to 2½ feet; tender bulb. Grow indoors in the North.

### Polygonum

*P. aubertii*, silver lace vine; white, fragrant; late summer to mid-autumn; to 25 feet; perennial vine.

### Prunus

*P. subhirtella* var. *autumnalis*; pink, semidouble; blooms in either spring or fall; 6 to 12 feet; shrub.

### Salvia

*S. pitcheri* (*S. azurea*), azure sage; blue; late summer to early autumn; 3½ feet; perennial.

### Schizostylis

*S. coccinea*, crimson flag, kaffir lily; scarlet, pink; early to mid-autumn; tender bulb. Grown outdoors in the South, indoors in the North.

### Sedum

*S. sieboldii*; pink; early to mid-autumn; 1 foot; perennial. Hardy, but blooms best in areas where autumn weather is mild.

### Sternbergia

*S. lutea*, winter daffodil, lily of the field; rich golden yellow; mid-autumn; 8 to 12 inches; bulb.

### Tricyrtis

*T. hirta*, toad lily; white spotted with purple outside, blackish inside; autumn; 2 to 3 feet; tender bulb. Take indoors and store over winter in the North.

### Urginea

*U. maritima*, sea onion, sea squill; whitish; autumn; to 1½ feet; bulb. Not hardy in the far North.

*V. noveboracensis*, ironweed; dark purple; early autumn; 3 to 7 feet; perennial. Best in the wild garden.

### Yucca

*Y. gloriosa*, Spanish dagger; creamy white, sometimes tinged with red; early autumn; 2½ feet; shrub. Grows outdoors only in warm climates.

## Autumn-Blooming Houseplants

### Exacum

*E. affine*, Arabian violet; lavender-blue, fragrant; autumn; 8 inches; perennial. Difficult to rebloom; treat as annual and discard after flowering.

### Haemaria

*H. discolor*, jewel orchid; white to pink, fragrant; autumn to early spring; orchid. Has beautiful dark green leaves veined with red and white.

### Laelia

*L. autumnalis*; rosy purple with white or purple lip, fragrant; late autumn to early winter; orchid.

*L. pumila*; rosy purple with deep mauve lip; autumn; orchid.

### Myrtus

M. *communis*, Greek myrtle; white to pink; autumn; to 3 feet; shrub. Foliage is aromatic.

### Oxalis

O. species, shamrock plant; pink, rose, lilac, white; bloom off and on all year but most heavily in autumn; to 12 inches; bulb.

### Paphiopedilum

P. *insigne*, ladyslipper orchid; green sepals with brown spots and green veins, pale yellow petals with brown veins, yellow-green pouch; autumn to spring; orchid.

### Pentas

P. *lanceolata*, Egyptian star cluster; pink, lilac, purple, white; autumn and late winter; 1 to 2 feet; perennial.

### Phalaenopsis

P. *amabilis*, moth orchid; white with white-and-yellow lip marked with red; autumn through winter; orchid.

### Rivina

R. *humilis*, rouge plant; small white flowers are followed by sprays of red berries in fall; to 2 feet; perennial.

### Ruellia

R. *makoyana*, trailing velvet plant, monkey plant; rose; autumn and winter; to 2 feet; shrub.

### Schlumbergera

S. *truncata* hybrids, Thanksgiving cactus; red, rose, pink, white; mid- to late autumn; branches to 3 feet long; cactus.

### Veltheimia

V. *viridifolia*, forest lily, unicorn root; pink, purplish, yellowish with yellow-green spots; late autumn; 1½ feet; tender bulb. Plant in late summer for fall bloom.

# WINTER

## Outdoors

### Abeliophyllum

A. *distichum*, white, 2 to 3 feet; shrub; late winter in the South, spring in the North.

### Adonis

A. *amurensis*, amur adonis; yellow; late winter to mid-spring, depending on location; to 12 inches; perennial.

### Anemone

A. *blanda*, Grecian windflower; white, pink, lavender, blue; blooms in late winter in many areas, early spring in the North; 6 inches; bulb.

### Bulbocodium

B. *vernum*, spring meadow saffron; pinkish purple; late winter to very early spring; 3 inches; bulb.

### Camellia

C. *japonica* and hybrids; white, pink, rose, red, crimson; late autumn to midwinter in the South; to 30 feet; shrub.

### Chimonanthes

C. *praecox*, wintersweet; pale cream to yellow, fragrant; late winter; 8 to 10 feet; shrub. Not hardy in the North, but in a sheltered spot may survive as far north as New York City. Flowers are valued more for their fragrance than their looks.

### Chionodoxa

C. *luciliae*, glory-of-the-snow; blue with white center; late winter to early spring; 3 inches; bulb.
C. *sardensis*; blue; 3 inches; late winter to early spring; bulb.

### Corylopsis

C. *spicata*, winter hazel; yellow, fragrant; late winter; to 6 feet; shrub.

### Crocus

C. *ancyrensis*, angora crocus; orange-yellow; mid- to late winter; 3 to 4 inches; bulb.
C. *biflorus*, Scotch crocus; white or lilac-blue, striped or flushed with purple; late winter to early spring; 3 to 4 inches; bulb.
C. *imperati*; buff or yellowish outside, purple inside; late winter; 3 to 6 inches; bulb.
C. *susianus*, cloth-of-gold; orange-yellow; late winter to early spring; 3 to 4 inches; bulb.
C. *tomasinianus*, tommies; pale lavender; late winter; 3 to 4 inches; bulb.

### Daphne

*D. mezereum*, mezereon; lilac-purple to pinkish purple, fragrant; late winter to early spring; 1½ to 3 feet; shrub.

*D. odora*, winter daphne; pinkish purple, fragrant; late winter to early spring; 3 to 5 feet; shrub. Needs protected site where temperatures do not fall below 0°F.

### Eranthis

*E. hyemalis*, winter aconite; golden yellow; late winter to early spring; 3 to 8 inches; bulb.

### Erica

*E. carnea*, winter heath; red, rose, or white; midwinter to early spring; 1 foot; shrub. Not hardy in the North without protection.

### Galanthus

*G. elwesii*, giant snowdrop; white with green spots at tip and base of petals; late winter to early spring; 10 to 15 inches; bulb.

*G. nivalis*, snowdrop; white with green spots at tip and base of petals; late winter to early spring; 6 to 10 inches; bulb.

### Hamamelis

*H. × intermedia*, witch hazel, hybrid between Chinese and Japanese species; yellow, fragrant; mid- to late winter; to 20 feet; shrub. The cultivar Arnold Promise has clear yellow flowers; Diana has coppery orange-red flowers.

### Helleborus

*H. niger*, Christmas rose; greenish white or pinkish; early to late winter; to 12 inches; perennial. Long-lasting in garden; cut flowers last up to 3 weeks.

*H. foetidus*, stinking hellebore; green edged with maroon; late winter to early spring; 1 to 1½ feet; perennial.

### Iberis

*I. sempervirens*, perennial candytuft; white; blooms in late winter in the South; to 6 inches; perennial.

### Iris

*I. reticulata*, netted iris; violet-purple, fragrant; late winter to early spring; 6 to 12 inches. Can also be forced indoors.

*I. unguicularis*, Algerian iris; violet; midwinter, sometimes autumn. Grows on West Coast and in South as far north as Virginia; 15 inches to 2 feet; perennial.

*I. danfordiae*, yellow; late winter to early spring; 4 inches; perennial.

Dutch iris hybrids bloom in winter in the deep South and along the West Coast if planted in fall.

### Jasminum

*J. nudiflorum*, winter jasmine; yellow, fragrant; all winter in protected places, though flower buds may freeze in the North; to 10 feet; shrub.

### Lonicera

*L. fragrantissima*, winter honeysuckle; creamy white, fragrant; blooms in winter in the South; 8 to 10 feet; shrub. Not hardy in the North.

### Narcissus

*N.* 'February Gold'; yellow; late winter in the South; to 12 inches; bulb.

*N.* 'February Silver'; white with pale yellow cup; late winter in the South; to 12 inches; bulb.

*N.* 'Paperwhite'; white, fragrant; outdoors in winter in the South; to 1½ feet; tender bulb.

### Primula

*P. veris* var. *elatior*, polyanthus primrose; red, rose, pink, yellow, blue, white with yellow center; winter in the South and on the West Coast, spring in the North; 6 to 8 inches high; perennial.

*P. vulgaris*, common primrose, English primrose; yellow; late winter to spring, depending on location; 6 inches; perennial.

### Salix

*S. discolor*, pussy willow; grayish white catkins in late winter; can be forced indoors in midwinter; 10 to 18 feet; shrub.

### Scilla

*S. tubergeniana*, Persian squill; blue-white; late winter to early spring; 4 to 5 inches; bulb.

### Spiraea

*S. thunbergi*, winter jasmine; white; late winter in the South, spring in the North; 3 to 5 feet; shrub.

### Viburnum

*V. fragrans*; white, fragrant; winter in the South and on the West Coast, spring in the North; 5 to 9 feet; shrub.

Hardy annuals can also be grown for winter flowers in warm climates.

### Abutilon

A. species, flowering maple; soft orangy red; bloom in winter in cool rooms; 2 to 3 feet; shrub.

### Anemone

A. *coronaria*, poppy anemone; red, blue, white with dark center; mid- to late winter when forced; 6 to 18 inches high; bulb.

### Antirrhinum

A. *majus*, snapdragon; red, crimson, scarlet, orange, yellow, white; blooms in winter from seed sown in summer; 7 to 24 inches high; annual.

### Ardisia

A. *crenata*, coralberry; red berries last all winter; 1 foot; shrub.

### Aster

A. *chinensis*, China aster; scarlet, rose, pink, blue, white; compact varieties such as Pot n' Patio bloom indoors in winter from seed sown in summer; annual.

### Begonia

B. × *semperflorens-cultorum*, wax begonia; red, scarlet, salmon, rose, pink, white; blooms indoors in winter from seed sown in late summer or from cuttings taken in fall from outdoor plants; 6 to 12 inches high; annual. Try compact varieties such as the Cocktail series, Linda, Scarletta, Thousand Wonders Red, and Thousand Wonders White.

### Browallia

B. *speciosa*, sapphire flower; violet; blooms in late winter from seed sown in midsummer; 2 feet; tender perennial.

### Brunfelsia

B. *pauciflora*, yesterday, today, and tomorrow; purple with white centers; midwinter until summer; 2 to 3 feet; shrub.

### Calceolaria

C. *multiflora*, pocketbook plant; yellow, orange, bronze, spotted with purple or bronze; late winter to early spring in bright, cool window; 1 to 2 feet; annual.

### Calendula

C. *officinalis*, pot marigold; yellow, orange; mid- to late winter from seed sown in summer; 2 feet; annual. Needs a cool room.

### Camellia

C. *japonica* and hybrids; pink, rose, red, white; late winter indoors in the North in cool room; shrub.

### Capsicum

C. *annuum*, ornamental pepper; red fruits in winter; 1 foot; treat as annual.

### Carissa

C. *grandiflora*, natal plum; white, fragrant; winter indoors in cool room; shrub. Can be grown outdoors in warm climates, where it may reach 15 feet in height.

### Celosia

C. *plumosa*, plume celosia; orange, apricot, gold, bronze; blooms indoors in winter from seed started in summer; 1 to 2 feet; annual.

### Chrysanthemum

C. × *morifolium*, florist's or garden chrysanthemum; red, crimson, orange, yellow, bronze, apricot, pink, mauve, purple, white, cream; 1 to 2 feet; can be forced with some difficulty for winter bloom indoors; perennial.

### Citrofortunella

C. *mitis*, calamondin orange; orange fruits in winter; 2 to 15 feet; shrub.

### Clarkia

C. *elegans*; rose, purple, pink; 1½ to 3 feet; blooms indoors in winter from seed sown in summer; annual.

### Coffea

C. *arabica*, Arabian coffee plant; white, fragrant; blooms indoors in winter; 4 to 6 feet; shrub. Needs at least three hours of sun a day.

### Convallaria

C. *majalis*, lily-of-the-valley; white, fragrant; 5 to 8 inches; mid- to late winter when forced indoors; bulb.

### Crocus

Dutch hybrid crocuses; lavender, purple, gold, white, cream, bicolors; 4 to 6 inches high; bloom in mid- to late winter when forced indoors; bulb.

## Cuphea

*C. ignea* (*C. platycentra*), cigar plant; red with black tips; can be grown for winter bloom indoors; 8 to 10 inches; tender perennial. Can also be grown as summer bedding plant outdoors.

## Cyclamen

*C. persicum* (*C. indicum*), Persian violet; red, rose, pink, purple, white; 8 inches; all winter in a cool room; tender bulb.

## Dendrobium

*D. crepidatum*; white with lavender-and-yellow markings; late winter to early spring; orchid.

## Eranthemum

*E. pulchellum*, blue sage; rose, purple, blue; late winter to early spring; 2 to 4 feet; shrub.

## Euphorbia

*E. fulgens*, scarlet plume; scarlet; 2 to 4 feet; winter; shrub.

*E. pulcherrima*, poinsettia; red, pink, white; 2 to 3 feet; early to midwinter; shrub.

## Exacum

*E. affine*, Arabian violet; blue, fragrant; 8 to 10 inches; blooms in winter from seed started in summer; treat as annual.

## Forsythia

*F.* species and cultivars; yellow; branches cut from outdoor shrubs can be forced into bloom indoors in late winter.

## Freesia

*F.* hybrids; rose, pink, lavender, purple, yellow, white, fragrant; can be forced indoors for winter bloom; 1 foot; tender bulb.

## Heliotropum

*H. arborescens*, heliotrope; greenish, fragrant; blooms in winter from seed sown in summer; treat as annual.

## Hibiscus

*H. rosa-sinensis*, rose of China; various shades of red and pink; can bloom in late winter through spring indoors; 3 to 4 feet; shrub. Needs lots of light, water, and fertilizer.

## Hippeastrum

*H.* hybrids, amaryllis; red, pink, orange, salmon, white, striped; early to midwinter when forced; 2 feet; tender bulb.

## Hyacinthus

*H. orientalis*, hyacinth; red, rose, pink, violet, blue, white, fragrant; midwinter when forced; 1 foot; bulb.

## Impatiens

*I.* hybrids; red, rose, salmon, pink, orange, purple, white, bicolors; bloom in winter from seed sown in summer; 6 to 12 inches high; treat as annual. Try compact varieties such as the Accent or Super Elfin series.

## Jasminum

*J. polyanthum*, poet's jasmine; rosy pink outside, white inside; fragrant; winter to early spring; perennial.

*J. sambac*, Arabian jasmine; white, fragrant; winter; shrub. Needs at least three hours of sun a day.

## Kalanchoe

*K. blossfeldiana*; red, orange; 1 foot; early winter to early spring; succulent.

## Lachenalia

*L. aloides*, cape cowslip; red and yellow; 1 foot; late winter to early spring; bulb.

## Lantana

*L. camara*, yellow sage; orange-yellow changing to red or white; cultivars available in red, yellow, lilac, blue, white; 1 to 4 feet; blooms in winter from seed sown in summer; perennial.

## Manettia

*M. inflata*, firecracker vine; red with yellow tips; midwinter to spring; perennial vine. Likes a warm room.

## Mimulus

*M.* hybrids, monkey flower; yellow, rose-red, rose-purple; blooms in winter from seed sown in summer; to 2 feet; annual.

## Muscari

*M. armeniacum*, grape hyacinth; blue to violet; can be forced indoors for winter bloom; 8 to 12 inches; bulb.

## Narcissus

*N.* hybrids, daffodils and narcissus; yellow, cream, white, bicolors; mid- to late winter when forced; 1 to 1½ feet; bulb.

*N. tazetta* 'Paper-White', paper-white narcissus; white, fragrant; 1½ feet; early to late winter when forced; bulb.

*N.* 'Soleil d'Or', yellow, fragrant; 6 to 10 inches; early to late winter when forced; bulb.

## Ornithogalum

*O.* species, star of Bethlehem; white, fragrant; blooms in winter indoors; 1 to 1½ feet; bulb.

## Osmanthus

*O. fragrans*, sweet olive; white, fragrant; early to late winter in bright light; 3 to 6 feet indoors; shrub.

## Paphiopedilum

*P. insigne*, lady slipper orchid; yellow and green with brown spots; winter; orchid.

*P. villosum*; yellow-brown and white; winter; orchid.

Some *Paphiopedilum* hybrids also bloom in winter with as little as two hours of sun a day.

## Pelargonium

*P.* × *hortorum*, zonal geranium; red, pink, salmon, magenta, white; blooms in winter from seed started in summer or cuttings taken from outdoor plants in early fall; 2 to 3 feet; grow as annual. Try varieties like Cherry Border, the Deacon hybrids, Earliana, Rose Diamond, Showgirl, and the Sprinter series.

*P.* species, scented geraniums; pink, white, with fragrant foliage; often bloom in winter; 6 to 12 inches; perennial. Need full sun—six hours a day or more.

## Pentas

*P. lanceolata*, Egyptian star cluster; pink, lilac, purple, white; late winter; 1 to 2 feet; shrub.

## Phalaenopsis

*P. amabilis*, moth orchid; white and yellow with red markings; all winter;

orchid. Needs at least three hours of sun a day.

Some *Phalaenopsis* hybrids are also winter bloomers.

## Primula

*P. malacoides*, fairy primrose; red, pink, mauve, lilac, white; 1 to 2 feet; winter to spring; grow as annual.

*P. sinensis*, Chinese primrose; red, pink, purple, white with yellow eye; 1 foot; winter to spring. Needs a bright window or a cool spot under fluorescent lights.

## Punica

*P. granatum* 'Nana', dwarf pomegranate; orange flowers followed by reddish fruit in winter; to 3 feet; shrub. Needs three to five hours of sun a day.

## Rhododendron

*R.* hybrids, azalea; red, rose, pink, white; late winter in a cool room; shrub. Difficult to rebloom indoors; discard after flowering.

## Rosa

*R.* hybrids, miniature roses; red, pink, white; bloom indoors six to eight weeks after beginning to grow following a dormant period; 1 to 2 feet; shrub. Need full sun—six or more hours a day.

## Saintpaulia

*S.* hybrids, African violet; purple, violet, pink, rose, white, lavender, bicolors; 6 inches; gesneriad. Will bloom off and on all year with as little as two hours of sun a day.

## Salpiglossis

*S. sinuata*, painted tongue, velvet flower; red, crimson, rose, pink, gold,

blue; blooms in winter from seed sown in summer; 2½ feet; annual. Needs bright window or a cool spot under fluorescent lights.

## Schlumbergera

*S. bridgesii*, Christmas cactus; red, rose, pink, salmon, white; 12 inches; early to midwinter; cactus.

## Senecio

*S.* × *hybridus*, cineraria; red, rose, pink, purple, white; late winter; to 2 feet. Needs bright, cool window. Discard after blooming.

## Solanum

*S. pseudocapsicum* 'Nanum', Christmas cherry, Jerusalem cherry; scarlet fruits; early to midwinter; 10 to 12 inches; biennial.

## Streptocarpus

*S.* hybrids, cape primrose; purple, violet, rose, pink, white; 6 inches; gesneriad. Needs three to five hours of sun a day in a cool room.

## Tagetes

*T. patulum* hybrids, French marigolds; yellow, orange, cream, bicolors; bloom in winter from seed sown in summer; 6 to 10 inches; annual. Try dwarf varieties such as Cheerful, Happy Days, Naughty Marietta, Pigmy, Pretty Joy, and Queen Sophia.

## Thunbergia

*T. alata*, black-eyed Susan vine, clock vine; yellow, orange, or white with black center; blooms in winter from seed sown in summer; 2 to 4 feet long; treat as annual.

### Torenia

*T. fournieri,* wishbone flower; blue-violet; blooms in winter from seed sown in summer; 8 inches; annual.

### Tropaeolum

*T.* species; nasturtium; mahogany, red, orange, yellow, white; blooms in winter from seed sown in summer or cuttings taken in early fall; 6 to 24 inches; annual.

### Tulipa

*T.* hybrids, tulips; red, scarlet, salmon, pink, orange, yellow, purple, white, bicolors; mid- to late winter when forced; 1 to 2 feet; bulb.

### Veltheimia

*V. viridifolia,* forest lily; pink, purple; early winter; 1½ to 2 feet; bulb.

### Zantedeschia

*Z. aethiopica,* calla lily; white; winter when forced; bulb.

# Seed and Plant Sources

Many of the seed and nursery companies listed here sell vegetables, herbs, fruit trees and plants, and other ornamentals as well as flowers. Sources of houseplants as well as outdoor plants are included. Some of the catalogs are free, and others are available for a small fee. Write for further information.

There are many other specialty suppliers across the country, in addition to the companies listed here. An excellent reference for sources of seeds and plants is *Gardening by Mail 2*, by Barbara J. Barton, published by Tusker Press.

## Seed Companies

Abundant Life Seed Foundation
P.O. Box 772
Port Townsend, WA 98368

*Garden flowers and wildflowers, plants native to the Northwest.*

W. Atlee Burpee Co.
300 Park Ave.
Warminster, PA 18974

*Annuals, a growing selection of perennials, roses, bulbs, some houseplants. One of America's most venerable seed companies.*

Comstock, Ferre, & Co.
P.O. Box 125
Wethersfield, CT 06109

*Traditional garden flowers, along with some newer hybrids.*

The Country Garden
Route 2, Box 455A
Crivitz, WI 54114

*Annual and perennial seeds, plants, and bulbs for cutting gardens.*

DeGiorgi Company, Inc.
P.O. Box 413
Council Bluffs, IA 51502

*Annuals and perennials.*

Henry Field Seed and Nursery Co.
407 Sycamore Street
Shenandoah, IA 51602

*Annual and perennial seeds, perennial plants, roses.*

The Fragrant Path
P.O. Box 328
Ft. Calhoun, NE 68023

*Specializes in scented plants of all sorts, also traditional garden flowers.*

Joseph Harris Company, Inc.
3670 Buffalo Road
Rochester, NY 14624

*Garden annuals and perennials.*

J. L. Hudson, Seedsman
P.O. Box 1058
Redwood City, CA 94064

*Seeds of many rare and unusual flowers.*

Ed Hume Seeds, Inc.
P.O. Box 1450
Kent, WA 98032

*Garden flowers and bulbs suited to the Northwest.*

Johnny's Selected Seeds
P.O. Box 2580
Albion, ME 04910

*Carries seed for garden annuals.*

J. W. Jung Seed Co.
335 S. High Street
Randolph, WI 53957

*Flower seeds, perennial plants, roses, ornamental vines and shrubs.*

Earl May Seed & Nursery Co.
Shenandoah, IA 51603

*Flower seeds, perennial plants, bulbs, ornamental shrubs.*

Nichols Garden Nursery, Inc.
1190 N. Pacific Highway
Albany, OR 97321

*Annuals and perennials, many suited to the Northwest.*

L. L. Olds Seed Co.
P.O. Box 7790
Madison, WI 53707

*Flower seeds, bulbs, roses.*

Geo. W. Park Seed Company, Inc.
P.O. Box 31
Greenwood, SC 29847

*Annuals, perennials, ornamental shrubs and vines.*

Plants of the Southwest
1812 Second Street
Santa Fe, NM 87501

*Wildflowers, shrubs, cacti and succulents for dry Southwestern gardens.*

Seeds Blum
Idaho City Stage
Boise, ID 83706

*Garden flowers, including seed collections for fragrance gardens, cutting gardens, and cottage gardens.*

Shepherd's Garden Seeds
7389 W. Zayante Road
Felton, CA 95018

*Specializes in European vegetables but also sells everlasting flowers.*

R. H. Shumway, Seedsman
P.O. Box 1
Rockford, IL 61101

*Carries an assortment of flower seeds.*

Thompson & Morgan
P.O. Box 1308
Jackson, NJ 08527

*The U.S. branch of a well-known British company. Large selection of annuals, perennials, and houseplants.*

Abbey Gardens
4620 Carpenteria Avenue
Carpenteria, CA 93013

*Cacti and succulents.*

Barnee's Garden
Route 10, Box 2010
Nacoydoches, TX 75961

*Daylilies and irises.*

Bernardo Beach Native Plant Farm
Star Route 7, Box 145
Veguita, NM 87062

*Perennials, vines, shrubs, wildflowers, and cacti for Southwestern gardens.*

Blackthorne Gardens
48 Quincy Street
Holbrook, MA 02343

*Lilies, alliums, and other bulbs; clematis, hostas, wildflowers.*

Bluestone Perennials
7211 Middle Ridge Road
Madison, OH 44057

*Many hardy perennials; lots of chrysanthemums.*

Bradshaw Gardens
1060 S. Chase Street
Lakewood, CO 80226

*Begonias, geraniums, passionflowers, and other flowering houseplants.*

Breck's
6523 N. Galena Road
Peoria, IL 61601

*Daffodils, narcissus, tulips, and other Dutch bulbs; tuberous begonias, dahlias, daylilies, gladiolus, lilies, and other summer bulbs.*

Lee Bristol Nursery
R.R. 1, Box 148
Gaylordsville, CT 06755

*Wide assortment of daylilies.*

Buell's Greenhouse, Inc.
P.O. Box 218
Eastford, CT 06242

*African violets and other gesneriads.*

California Epi Center
P.O. Box 1431
Vista, CA 92083

*Flowering cacti, especially epiphyllums and holiday cacti.*

Carroll Gardens
P.O. Box 310
Westminster, MD 21157

*Perennials, roses, ornamental shrubs.*

Clifford's Perennial and Vine
Route 2, Box 320
East Troy, WI 53120

*Daylilies, irises, peonies, and other perennials; azaleas and other flowering shrubs; ornamental vines.*

Dogwood Hills Nursery
Route 3, Box 181
Franklinton, LA 70438

*Azaleas, camellias, hydrangeas, jasmines, and other flowering shrubs.*

Dutch Gardens, Inc.
P.O. Box 588
Farmingdale, NJ 07727

*Dutch bulbs, cannas, dahlias, gladiolus, lilies, amaryllis, and other bulbs.*

Fischer Greenhouses
Oak Avenue
Linwood, NJ 08221

*African violets and other gesneriads.*

Fleming's Flower Fields
P.O. Box 4617
Lincoln, NE 68504

*Many kinds of chrysanthemums and other perennials.*

Garden Place
P.O. Box 388
Mentor, OH 44061

*Good selection of perennials.*

Gladside Gardens
61 Main Street
Northfield, MA 01360

*Cannas, gladiolus, and other tender bulbs, garden perennials.*

Holbrook Farm & Nursery
Route 2, Box 223
Fletcher, NC 28732

*Large selection of perennials, hardy bulbs, wildflowers, and ornamental shrubs.*

Jackson & Perkins Co.
P.O. Box 1028
Medford, OR 97501

*Roses, hardy bulbs, some houseplants.*

Jones & Scully, Inc.
18955 SW 168th Street
Miami, FL 33187

*One of the country's best-known orchid nurseries.*

Kartuz Greenhouses
1408 Sunset Drive
Vista, CA 92083

*Begonias, gesneriads, and other flowering plants to grow outdoors in warm climates and indoors elsewhere.*

King's Mums
P.O. Box 368
Clements, CA 95227

*Large selection of chrysanthemums.*

Klehm Nursery
Route 5, 197 Penny Road
South Barrington, IL 60010

*Daylilies, hostas, irises, peonies, and tree peonies.*

Lauray of Salisbury
Undermountain Road
Salisbury, CT 06068

*Begonias, gesneriads, orchids, cacti and succulents.*

Logee's Greenhouses
55 North Street
Danielson, CT 06239

*Begonias, gesneriads, jasmines, passionflowers, and many other flowering plants for indoors or outdoors in warm climates.*

Louisiana Nursery
Route 7, Box 43
Opelousas, LA 70570

*Lilies, waterlilies, daylilies, irises, hostas, cacti and succulents, ornamental shrubs.*

Lyndon Lyon Greenhouses, Inc.
14 Mutchler Street
Dolgeville, NY 13329

*African violets and other gesneriads, miniature roses.*

McClure & Zimmerman
1422 W. Thorndale
Chicago, IL 60660

*Wide variety of bulbs, both hardy and tender, including common and hard-to-find types. Daffodils, crocuses, colchicums, winter aconite, magic lilies, tulips, irises, freesias, ranunculus, and many more.*

Milaeger's Gardens
4838 Douglas Avenue
Racine, WI 53402

*Good selection of perennials and special collections for butterfly, cutting, fragrance, and other gardens.*

Nor'East Miniature Roses
58 Hammond Street
Rowley, MA 01969

*Many miniature roses.*

Orchids by Hauserman, Inc.
2N 134 Addison Road
Villa Park, IL 60181

*One of the largest orchid nurseries in the United States.*

Rex Bulb Farms
P.O. Box 774
Port Townsend, WA 98368

*Specializes in lilies and offers a wide selection.*

Roses of Yesterday and Today
802 Brown's Valley Road
Watsonville, CA 95076

*Heritage roses and modern hybrids.*

John Scheepers, Inc.
63 Wall Street
New York, NY 10005

*Large selection of spring and summer bulbs.*

Spring Hill Nurseries Co.
6523 N. Galena Road
Peoria, IL 61632

*Perennials, roses, ornamental shrubs, bulbs, some houseplants.*

Thon's Garden Mums
4811 Oak Street
Crystal Lake, IL 60014

*Large selection of many kinds of chrysanthemums.*

Van Bourgondien Bros.
245 Farmingdale Road, Route 109
Babylon, NY 11702

*Hardy bulbs, summer bulbs, perennials, ornamental shrubs, houseplants.*

Andre Viette Farm & Nursery
Route 1, Box 16
Fisherville, VA 22939

*Daylilies, hostas, irises, and other perennials.*

Wayside Gardens
Hodges, SC 29695

*Perennials, roses, ornamental shrubs, wildflowers.*

White Flower Farm
Litchfield, CT 06759

*Chrysanthemums, dahlias, lilies, many perennials, rock garden plants, ornamental shrubs.*

Gilbert H. Wild & Son
1112 Joplin Street
Sarcoxie, MO 64862

*Daylilies, irises, and peonies.*

# SUBJECT INDEX

Page numbers in *italics* refer to illustrations.

247

# INDEX OF PLANT NAMES

Page numbers in *italics* refer to illustrations.